D1231378

DUTCH ANABAPTISM

DUTCH ANABAPTISM

ORIGIN, SPREAD, LIFE AND THOUGHT

(1450 - 1600)

by

CORNELIUS KRAHN

MARTINUS NIJHOFF — THE HAGUE — 1968

PRINTED IN THE NETHERLANDS

To Hilda
Marianne, Karla, Cornelia

CONTENTS

ABBREVIATIONS

Amstel	*Jaarboek van het Genootschap Amstelodamum*
AfR	*Archiv für Reformationsgeschichte*
BMHG	*Bijdragen en Mededeelingen van het Hist. Genootschap te Utrecht*
BRN	*Bibliotheca Reformatoria Neerlandica*
CW	*Complete Writings* by Menno Simons
DB	*Doopsgezinde Bijdragen*
Elsass	*Elsass,* I. Teil und II. Teil (*Quellen zur Geschichte der Täufer,* VII)
JGKAE	*Jahrbuch der Gesellschaft für bildende Kunst und vaterländische Altertümer zu Emden*
LCC	*Library of Christian Classics*
LFR	*Linker Flügel der Reformation* (H. Fast)
ME	*Mennonite Encyclopedia*
ML	*Mennonite Life*
MQR	*Mennonite Quarterly Review*
MSB	*Bibliography of Menno Simons* (Irvin B. Horst)
NAK	*Nederlandsch Archief voor Kerkgeschiedenis*
Opera	*Opera omnia theologica* ... van Menno Symons (1681)
QGT	*Quellen zur Geschichte der Täufer*
VfR	*Verein für Reformationgeschichte*
WZ	*Westfälische Zeitschrift für vaterländische Geschichte und Altertumskunde*

PREFACE

This book features Anabaptism of the Low Countries from its earliest traceable beginnings to the end of the sixteenth century. The major part of the book is devoted to the hundred years preceding the death of Menno Simons in 1561, after whom the Anabaptists received the name, Mennonites. A decade later the Netherlands gained independence and the Anabaptists were granted relative freedom. Prior to this Dutch Anabaptist refugee settlements and churches had been established along the North Sea and the Baltic Coast from Emden and Hamburg-Altona up to the mouth of the Vistula River.

The roots of Dutch Anabaptism, similar to those of the Dutch Reformed Church, can be found in the native soil and were nourished and stimulated from near and far. The emerging humanistically-influenced Sacramentarian movement of the Low Countries modified and spiritualized the meaning of the remaining two sacraments, baptism and the Lord's supper. Dutch mysticism, the Brethren of Common Life, Erasmian humanism, the chambers of rhetoric, and the ties with Wittenberg (Luther, Karlstadt, Müntzer), Cologne (Westerburg), Münster (B. Rothmann), Strassburg (Bucer, Capito), Zürich (Zwingli), and Emden led to the introduction of Anabaptism in the Low Countries by Melchior Hofmann, coming from Strassburg in 1530.

After the first decisive and troubled years, such men as Menno Simons and Dirk Philips came into leadership and consolidated the movement. Many suffered persecution and death up to the 1570's, when the Netherlands gained independence. During the following decades the persecuted Anabaptists, who had contributed to a radical reformation in the Netherlands, had to work out a relationship with the emerging Reformed Church on a local and national level. They did this in discussions and disputations, and literary dialogues.

Throughout the featuring of these events, the basic Anabaptist views, such as the effort to establish a truly Christian fellowship or church inspired by an eschatological hope and the practice of Christian discipleship, were constantly kept in mind.

Special appreciation is expressed to those who inspired and helped with the writing and shaping of this book based on numerous sources listed in the 25-page footnotes. Mention should also be made that this research was made possible through a leave from Bethel College (1963-64), a Social Science Research Council Fellowship and grants from the American Philosophical Society (1963-64 and 1966). Among the libraries and archives most extensively used were the Bethel College Historical Library and Archives (which has most of the books and archival materials used), the Archives and Library of the Mennonite Church of Amsterdam and the University Library of Amsterdam. The Free Lutheran Theological Seminary Library of Oberusel, Germany, was also a help.

Berneil Mueller deserves special mention for styling the manuscript, and Irvin B. Horst (Amsterdam) for checking the manuscript in regard to factual information. Recognition is also due to the late N. van der Zijpp (Rotterdam) and J. P. Jacobszoon (Haarlem), who read parts of the manuscript. Special appreciation is due to H. W. Meihuizen (The Hague), who kindly read the page proofs of the book and made many helpful suggestions. Many others gave invaluable service imperative for the production of the book.

The Footnotes starting on page 263 present a record of all sources used, while the Selected Bibliography at the end points out only a few of the major books and sources. The detailed Index should prove helpful to locate the desired information more easily. Many of the quotations in the text are translations by the author from Dutch and German books and other sources.

Cornelius Krahn

Bethel College
North Newton, Kansas
Christmas, 1967

I

THE LOW COUNTRIES DURING
THE MIDDLE AGES

The Low Countries of the Middle Ages and of the days of the Reformation comprise, roughly speaking, the present-day Netherlands and
Belgium. However, the treatment of our subject matter will take us
into the adjacent German Lower Rhine area, Westphalia, Oldenburg,
East Friesland, and even Schleswig-Holstein and more distant areas
into which the upheaval of the sixteenth-century scattered religious
refugees. The Low Countries constitute the north-western corner of
the vast plain which extends from the North Sea over Germany,
Poland, and European Russia to the Ural Mountains.[1]

The Rhine, Schelde, and Meuse rivers have deposited their silt
among the sea-created dunes that lie around the mouths of these
rivers. The struggle with the sea, its sand, and its salt has molded the
character of the countries' population, and the population in turn has
given shape to the land. As the saying goes: "God created the world,
but the Dutch created the Netherlands."

1. The Geographic and Ethnic Background

The skills and the character of the nation developed as the population won the land from the grasp of the sea. This struggle imbued
the inhabitants with qualities noticeable to this day, not only among
those who have remained in their native land, but also among those
who, through the centuries, have pioneered in adjacent and faraway
lands, whether in the Hanseatic cities or in the Americas, in Africa
or the Far East.

If the inhabitants of Western Europe count every inch of land,
the people of the Low Countries count that inch twice. There was,
and is, no waste land. Through the means of native skill which is
today linked with modern techniques, the Dutch have not only been
able to keep the invading waters out of the country, but have also

added many an inch of land in a bloodless conquest of the sea. As a result of industry, the Low Countries have become the vegetable and flower garden of more than Western Europe. Without the vegetables of The Netherlands, the diet of western Europe would be different. Once the tulip bulbs took root in the sandy soil, they prospered and conquered the world market.

Like many other parts of Europe, the Low Countries were once occupied by the Romans, who have given us the first information about the countries' early history. At the time the first messengers spread the Gospel of Christ in Palestine, the Romans were colonizing the Low Countries. The population then consisted of remnants of the earlier Celtic and the later Germanic races.[2] The southern Low Countries were occupied primarily by the Franks, while in the western parts the Saxons, and in the northern parts the Frisians, predominated. The southern region became a part of the French-speaking population, while in the northern areas a great variety of dialects of Germanic or Celtic background were preserved. A substratum of the Celtic population has been preserved to this day in Zeeland and Belgium.[3] In addition to the information left by Roman historians, excavations are producing significant information about the early inhabitants and their culture and history. Although the early anthropological and cultural history presents a very interesting quilt, we cannot deal with this matter except in very general terms.

After the withdrawal of the Roman legions, Christianity was introduced during the seventh century under Frankish rule. Best known are the missionaries Willibrord and Boniface. The latter died at the hands of some heathen Frisians near Dokkum in 754. Around 800 the territory under consideration was divided into the archbishopric of Reims which included the bishoprics of Tournai (Doornik), Artois (Atrecht), etc., and the archbishopric of Cologne, with the bishoprics Utrecht, Liege (Luik), Münster, etc. This division remained more or less unchanged until 1559.[4]

2. The Political Constellations

During the feudal period of the Middle Ages, a number of earldoms and duchies were formed which remained to predestine the fate of the Low Countries. A relative independence gave the Low Countries an opportunity to develop their own culture and follow their own political course. Persons like Jan van Ruysbroeck (1296-1381) and Geert Groote (1340-1384) contributed greatly to the development of an independent cultural life. In spite of this independence, Flanders was, to some extent, under the influence of France, while the northern parts of the Low Countries were influenced by the German Hanseatic cities.

The earldom of Flanders played a significant role in the early history of the Low Countries. Brugge and Gent became the leading centers of early industry and culture. Several cities in Flanders had a thriving cloth industry. In the fifteenth century, however, England contributed to the decline of this industry because she began to process her own wool. When Flanders suffered this setback, the duchy of Brabant, east of Flanders, grew in prominence. Brabant was able to develop a prosperous textile industry that included the weaving of linen and carpets. The cities of Brussels and Mechelen became important governmental centers. The port of Antwerp, the most significant in Europe around 1500,[5] contributed to that city's prosperity, while Louvain grew in fame due to its university.

In the northern Netherlands, east of Utrecht, most of the cities belonged to the Hanseatic League. Among them were Deventer, Groningen, Kampen, Zwolle, and Arnhem.[6] Although the city of Amsterdam, located on the Amstel River, had a late start, it gradually developed strong shipping and fishing industries. It became the connecting link between the Baltic cities and the cities of Flanders.[7] Other cities in the "provinces" of Zeeland and Holland developed seafaring industries until the ships and merchants of the Low Countries could be found on the Rhine River and on the seas in the ports between Lisbon and the mouth of the Vistula River.

Around 1400 the feudal splits, not treated here, subsided. Since most of the ruling houses had died out, foreign rulers tried to establish themselves. The Frenchman, Philip the Good, succeeded in uniting most of the principalities of the Netherlands, (parts of Holland, Zeeland, Flanders, Brabant, Luxemburg, Lorraine, etc.) giving the various rulers and cities a limited independence. His son, Charles the Bold, overreached himself in his ambitious plan to enlarge his territory and to establish a kingdom. He lost his life in a battle and was succeeded by his daughter, Maria of Burgundy, who married Maximilian of Austria and thus fatefully paved the future of the Netherlands.

Maximilian ruled Burgundy for his son, Philip the Fair, from 1482 to 1494. He succeeded in establishing peace by force within the country and made peace with France. When he was chosen emperor of the German Reich in 1494, Philip succeeded him as ruler of Burgundy. Unlike his father, Philip was accepted by the population as one of them since he had been raised in the country. During his reign he took into consideration the old privileges and gave the "provinces" more autonomy.[8]

Internal and external peace marked the reign of Philip the Fair. He married Joanna, the daughter of Ferdinand of Aragon and Isabella of Castile. This union not only linked Burgundy to the Spanish monarchy, but also constituted "the bridge over which the house of Habsburg passes to almost universal monarchy."[9] Their son Charles, born at Gent in 1500, not only inherited Burgundy, Spain, and the Habsburg monarchy, but also became the ruler of these vast territories during the decisive years of the Reformation. When Charles became emperor in 1519 his aunt Margaret of Austria (Savoy) became the ruler of the Netherlands (1519-1530), a position she had previously held under Maximilian.

Maximilian had already made Burgundy a district of his empire and had added the eastern part of the Netherlands to the Westphalian district of the empire. It was the plan of Charles V to combine all of the Netherlands into one district. At the Reichstag of Augsburg in 1548, he declared that the Netherlands from Artois to Groningen were to constitute the Burgundian district of the empire. Some independence in legal and financial matters and protection through the empire were promised.[10]

An outstanding opponent of the plan of Charles V was Charles van Gelder (Gelderland). He had ambitious plans of his own. Not only did he maintain his independence, but he also played the role of the "big brother" in his neighborhood.

When Friesland was weakened because of the fight of all against all, the city of Groningen took advantage of the situation and added one Frisian city after the other to its territory. When Maximilian made Albert of Saxony imperial lord over Friesland, both the Frisians and the Groningers called on Charles van Gelder for help. He succeeded in breaking the Saxon dictatorship, but then his turn came. Charles V forced him out of Friesland, and in 1524 the Frisians had to acknowledge Charles V as "lord of Friesland."[11]

Throughout this struggle the bishopric of Utrecht played a significant role. When bishop Philip of Burgundy died in 1524, Henry of Bavaria was elected bishop of Utrecht. He was expected to be neutral in the struggle between Charles V and Charles van Gelder. When the latter entered the country, the bishop turned his secular authority over to the emperor, whose course of action has been noted. Charles van Gelder had to release the present provinces of Groningen and Drente to Charles V. Furthermore, he had to agree that after his death Gelderland would be turned over to the emperor. Thus the emperor added to his domain the provinces of Friesland, Groningen, Drente, Overijssel, Utrecht, and Gelderland, making most of present-day Belgium and the Netherlands subject to him.[12]

From the time of Philip the Fair (1494-1506), the central government of the Netherlands constituted a compromise between the emperor and the states general. The chancellor of Burgundy was responsible for the execution of the practical work of the government during the absence of the emperor. The high court (Hoge Raad) of Mechelen constituted the court of justice.

In 1531 Charles V replaced the office of the chancelor with that of a governorship (landvoogdij). The big council (Grote Raad) he subdivided into the council of state (general government) and the secret council (legal matters). The states general consisted of the representatives of the districts which Charles V inherited. These representatives were called into session when the emperor needed money, which was rather often.

After Charles V had established the Burgundian district in 1548, he came to the Netherlands and announced at the states general assembly that Philip his son would succeed him as ruler of the Netherlands. When Philip arrived he proved to be a disappointment for his subjects. Surrounded by Spanish noblemen he spoke only Spanish. This was a bad omen.

When in 1555 he took over the rule as Philip II, he was determined to destroy the last resemblance of Dutch autonomy and to crush all efforts of those in favor of a reformation of the church. When religious reform and Dutch independence became the motto of the oppressed nation, he sent Alva to the Netherlands to crush all resistance through the arm of the inquisition.[13]

3. The Cultural Life

During the Burgundian and early Habsburg eras, the Low Countries

experienced a foretaste of the Golden Age which followed the establishment of the independence of the Netherlands. Flanders and Brabant, famous for their industry, nourished the early cultural life. The
first Flemish school of art had its centers in Gent and Brugge and
later in Louvain, Brussels, and Antwerp. This art was primarily of
a religious nature and was introduced in the form of miniature por-
trayals used in prayer and devotional books. Hubert and Jan van
Eyck, the fathers of the Flemish school of art, introduced the three-
panel painting used mostly for altars. One of their famous works
of art was The Adoration of the Lamb (Gent, 1426). Gent, Brugge,
Brussels, and Louvain attracted artists from far and near. Hans Mem-
ling was one of those from a distance. The cities of other regions
began to flourish as art centers. For example, Jan van Scorel did most
of his work in Utrecht and Lucas van Leiden in his home town, Leiden.

The painter of the common life of Brabant, Pieter Breughel (1520?-
1569), brought the Flemish school of art to a climax and close. After
him Italian influences became predominant.[14]

Remnants of early Romanesque architecture which took its inspiration from the cathedral of the German Rhine area, can be found
in the eastern part of the Low Countries. However, the Gothic style
that developed under the French influence in Brabant, Flanders, Zeeland, and Holland was predominant. Outstanding examples of church
architecture of that time can be found in Mechelen, Louvain, Antwerp,
and Breda. The family Kelderman of Mechelen produced many famous architects. Noteworthy city halls built at that time are those of
Brussels, Gouda, Gent, and Middelburg. Other traces of the influence
of the architectural style of that period can be found in many of the
Hanseatic cities from Antwerp to the east along the coast of the North
and Baltic seas.

Most of the large Gothic churches of the Low Countries were built
during the fifteenth century.[15] Among them are Sint Bavo of Haarlem,
the old and new churches of Amsterdam, Sint Laurens of Rotterdam,
and Sint Martini in Groningen. Most of the best known towers were
built between 1450 and 1550.[16] For the construction of the early
churches, stone was imported. Gradually brick became the most common medium in the construction of the churches and public buildings.
This building material gave the Dutch Gothic architecture its unique
character.[17]

Jan Romein states that Flanders and Brabant developed the richest
Gothic style. This style became later a "formless beauty" which did

not create space but filled all space. It had achieved "a perfect and playful technical mastery." "There has never been art that has striven more for perfection than Gothic, nor has there ever been one that ended thus in beauty." [18] Comparing the developments of the Gothic of the southern and the northern parts of the Low Countries, Romein makes some interesting observations about the differences. In comparison to the development of the Gothic of the south, he describes that of the north as follows: "Sturdy and as if with difficulties rising out of the ground, threatening and untransparent stand the towers of Dordrecht, Rotterdam, or Ransdorp – above the level ground as monuments of brick symbolizing the spirit which was not open to the playful piety of the late Gothic period of the south." [19]

The literary productions of this period do not compare favorably with the other forms of art. The Low Countries did not develop a Minnesong tradition or a significant literature centering around the chivalry of the Middle Ages, although some works were imported and imitated by clerks of the emerging middle class. Such a writer was Jacob van Maerlant. A number of satirical pieces were written. Aernout-Willem, author of Reynard the Fox, ridiculed not only the popular narrative tale of the period of chivalry, but also the feudal system of the day. [20] The special role which the religious or devotional literature played during this period will be presented later.

A very significant form of the fine arts was constituted by the chambers of rhetoric (rederijkerskamers) which originated in Flanders and Brabant and spread into the northern parts of the Low Countries. The chambers of rhetoric promoted the fine arts on a more popular level and therefore reached the common people more readily than other media of communication. They encouraged the writing and presentation of plays of a religious or secular nature. They helped in the observations of the festive celebrations of the church and offered criticism of existing conditions within the church. [21] A more detailed presentation will follow in connection with the treatment of the rise of the Sacramentarian movement.

Although the Netherlands lacked a Minnesong tradition, folk songs were popular, and their tunes played a significant role in the spread of the Reformation movement in the Netherlands. [21] The hymn tunes of the Sacramentarians, the Anabaptists, and later of the Reformed, shared the characteristics of the Dutch folk tunes which influenced the early hymnbooks. [22]

During the Middle Ages many of the larger churches had good

choirs. These choirs were often polyphonic and consisted of either
volunteers or professional paid singers. Some groups performed for
a number of churches and even in foreign countries. Because of this
publicity, certain choir directors became famous all over Europe. The
choirs were usually sponsored by large and wealthy churches, cities,
or noblemen.[23]

At the turn of the century the Netherlands produced some outstanding composers who influenced western European music. The best
known were Jan Okeghem (1430-1495) and Jacob Obrecht (1450-
1505). Adding to the Netherlands' musical fame was the production
of music books at Mechelen and Antwerp.[24]

4.   The Religious Life

The questions pertaining to the religious life of the late Middle
Ages have been dealt with by many scholars and laymen of both religious and secular backgrounds. Various schools of thought have developed, particularly in connection with the origin of the Protestant
movement in the Low Countries. A key question has been asked: Was
this movement primarily influenced by outside forces, or did it origi-
nate in the native soil? There is a general agreement that the various
Protestant denominations of the Low Countries had their roots, to a
large extent, in their own land.

Hand in hand with this emphasis goes the tendency to portray
the decay of the church of the Middle Ages in dark colors and to
present, by contrast, the Dutch Reformation in bright tones. The
corruption of the clergy, the monks, and the nuns, and the superstition
of the people are featured as a background. The revolutionary reformation is seen as ushering in a new era as does the sunny spring day
after a severe cold winter. The primary sources show that the decay
of the era had to lead to a reformation of the church, a reformation
which found its origin in Dutch mysticism and biblical humanism.

Some Catholic scholars of our day are challenging these traditional
Protestant views.[25] Their sources are the same, and there is little quarrel about the sources' authenticity. It is a matter of approach and interpretation. These scholars are inclined to spread the darkness of the
Middle Ages over a longer period of time. Furthermore, they state
that the religious life of the fifteenth century was possibly on a higher
level than at any previous time. The church was still in the process
of "Christianizing" the population. The Catholic scholars point out

that this Christianization of the Low Countries gradually produced, with certain ups and downs, a higher Christian and cultural level. What is sometimes described as a decline was really an uphill development.

As far as the value of the statements made by the great critics of the church is concerned, L. J. Rogier has the following to say: "... it is inspiring to listen to the great critics of every age, but we should also be aware of their overstatements." He concludes by asking whether "there has ever been a theologian who spoke of his time as one that was pious and pleasing unto God." [26] In addition, Catholic scholars object particularly to the common practice of claiming all great critics of prevailing conditions as forerunners of the Reformation. It is pointed out that these forerunners such as Geert Groote, Thomas a Kempis, the Brethren of the Common Life, Johannes Brugman, and Erasmus remained in the Catholic Church in leading positions.

For this reason it is maintained that it is inconsistent for the various denominations to lay claim on certain favorites who supposedly paved the way for their groups' origin and development. Certainly not all critical attitudes and reformation efforts within the Catholic Church throughout the ages led to a break with the church. Most of the movements which led to the founding of new monastic organizations can be compared with the efforts of the forerunners of the Reformation. The church always checked all volcanic eruptions and made use of their creative power for its own purpose. The great question is why the church failed, at the time that is called the Reformation, to control this power.

Another point not to be overlooked is the fact that unsatisfactory religious and moral conditions do not necessarily lead to prophetic criticism and an ultimate reformation. A criticism that is merely negative and is not supported by a strong positive faith will ultimately disperse like a stream in the desert. But in this case, the various reformation leaders furnished the needed positive element although they differed greatly depending on their personalities and the localities in which they worked.

In our presentation of the various factors which led to the break with the old church and which brought forth the various new movements, it will be our aim to take into consideration the questions raised and the information presented by the various schools of thought.

For the modern reader it is possibly not inappropriate to point out that if Paul had appeared during the Middle Ages at various places of worship, be it in Rome, Flanders, or in a remote Frisian village, he would likely have said the same thing that he told his more sophisticated contemporaries of Athens when he said: "Men of Athens I see that in everything that concern religion you are uncommonly scrupulous" (Acts 17:22, NEB). The day of the secularization of all life was still far away, and the practice of superstition in various forms was strong. The line between a truly Christian faith and superstition was rather thin and at times the two were even intermingled. "Only the society in which the whole is penetrated by the religious element and which considers faith as something that is taken for granted knows all these excesses of degeneration" says J. Huizinga, the author of *The Waning of the Middle Ages*.[27]

In setting out to describe the religious life of the common people, L. J. Rogier states that they have no history because the account of their "faith and prayers, their stumbling and rising goes with them to the grave; there remains no trace of them on earth." [28] The religious life of the Catholic during the Middle Ages was an inherited part of life as were property and folkways. In fact, it was more of the nature of a folkway than a personal and fully integrated faith. It was understood that each person was baptized, married, and buried in the context of the church and that during one's lifetime one had certain relationships to the church. But the common person often grasped and practiced very little of the full meaning and implications of the Christian faith. The festivals of the church had become popular folk festivals. The church aided in sanctifying superficially all aspects of the home life and the social activities of the community.

There was not much understanding of the deeper meaning of the worship service. The churches furnished the framework for miracle-performing images and relics. Throughout the day candles were lit and flowers put up while multitudes of women and children came to kneel and kiss objects of adoration in moved piety. For most of the worshippers, the adored relics were more important than the deeper meaning of the mass.[29] A sentimental literature added to these conditions. Numerous were the legends about the miraculous intervention of Mary when she helped her servants in need or aided the innocent and pure. Stories were told of how Jesus revealed to his faithful unknown details about his childhood and life.[30]

The church frequently offered too much food for popular imagination and consequently did not succeed in keeping "that imagination

within the limits of a healthy and vigorous piety." The presence of a
visible image of an abstract thought or personage often sufficed to
establish truth or fact. All conceptions expressed in paintings, statues,
and images became matters "of faith in a most direct manner; they
passed straight from the state of images to that of convictions." The
church furnished the simple mind with an abundance of pictorial and
speculative fancy and thus gave cause for a deviation from the pure
doctrine. The church was very much concerned about the "danger"
of giving the scriptures into the hands of the simple believer, fearing
that he might give them a wrong interpretation. The same church that
was so scrupulous in dogmatic matters was lenient and indulgent
towards those who rendered more homage to images than was proper.[31]

In his chapter "The Vision of Death," J. Huizinga points out the
significance, during the Middle Ages, of the very primitive image of
death which was continually impressed on all minds. Popular were the
woodcuts that portrayed the theme of the death dance and helped to
spread the fear of death.[32] Both woodcuts and sermons stressed the
brevity of all earthly glory and life. A scholar who asked God that a
man would show him the way of truth was sent to church where he
found a man in rags. The poor man proved to be of great humility
and showed the seeker the way of truth through his example.

When the reform movements attacked the practices of superstition,
many of these latter evaporated. "Piety had depleted itself in the image,
legend, the office" and the "cult of the saints was no longer rooted
in the domain of the unimaginable." However, the practice of witch-
craft and the exercise of other forms of demonology continued their
popularity into the Protestant era.[33]

5. Faith, Life and Leaders

The seven sacraments which developed through the centuries had
become the most significant means through which the church administered the grace of God to the needs of men. Outstanding among
them were those two first in use in the church and considered most
significant in the life of each Christian: baptism and the Lord's supper
(eucharist). They were the main and absolutely necessary means of
salvation.

Baptism was administered once and constituted the regeneration
of the individual in the removal of the original sin and the becoming
of the child of God. The eucharist was a partaking of the flesh and

blood of Christ for the removal of the committed sins and was to be observed at least four times annually, preceded by the confession of sins. Many, however, came to communion only once a year, namely at Easter time.[34]

The meaning and significance of the sacraments were the primary issues which caused the ultimate reformation of the Netherlands. Consequently we will deal frequently with the question of what the sacraments meant to the believers at the various stages of their religious life. The turn of the century and the beginning of the Reformation will be the setting for this observation. First the Catholic doctrine pertaining to the eucharist was challenged and altered and then the meaning of baptism was questioned.

During the Middle Ages the eucharist was often considered more of a miracle-performing source than a means of spiritual nourishment of the soul. A host of legends developed around the ever-present Lord in the consecrated sacrament. The real spiritual meaning of communion was overshadowed by the common belief that the host in the hands of a priest performed miracles. And the servants of the church were not yet ready nor able to disperse such notions.

Not only were the blind, the crippled, and those endangered by the Moslem helped miraculously through the consecrated host, but also a lamb pursued by a wolf could be saved with its powers.[35] An anonymous priest even put the host on the tongue of a sick cow in order to effect its cure. Numerous were the legends of how the host turned into a child, or how it bled. It was believed that one could not get certain sicknesses on a day that one had heard mass or that one did not grow older during the time spent in attending mass.[36]

Outstanding among the legends pertaining to the eucharist is the Miracle of Amsterdam. It was said to have occurred in 1345 and increased the fame and development of the city. When a sick person partook of the eucharist, he vomited out the host which was thrown into a fire but remained unconsumed. The *Heilige Stede* erected on the Rokin of Amsterdam to house and honor the miracle-performing host became an object of pilgrimages of the faithful.[37]

Rogier points out, however, that the piety of the common people had a dualistic character. In addition to the cult of miracles, there was present a simple faith which spoke of the eucharist as the Christian's nourishment and the sinner's protection. In support of this view, he refers to the devotional literature of that time.[38] Furthermore, it must be pointed out that Dutch mysticism stressed and practiced a spiritual communion with Christ without regularly partaking in the visible elements of the eucharist. The Brethren of the Common Life, Wessel Gansfort, and particularly Thomas a Kempis, whose expressions are found in the *Imitatio Christi,* kept alive the tradition of a more spiritually conceived communication with God than that popularly practiced.[39]

After having dealt with the spiritual flock, it is well to turn to its shepherds. If the flock was not always properly cared for, was this perhaps due to a lack of a sufficient number of shepherds? We would answer to the contrary. Inadequate guidance was more likely due to the fact that the spiritual level, the concepts, and the ideals of the shepherds were much the same as those of the flock for which they cared. Fortunately there were exceptions.

Most of what constitutes the present-day Netherlands was, at that time, a part of the bishopric of Utrecht. According to available statistics some 600, 000 persons were spiritually cared for in this bishopric. This was also the number of Catholic parishioners of this diocese in 1950. Around 1500 some five thousand priests took care of these 600,000 people. In 1950 only eight hundred priests were in charge of the same number of parishioners, while the others took care of other functions in connection with the worship, the activities, and the administration of the church. Shortcomings of the church cannot be blamed on a lack of priests. In fact, this "large number of priests is one of the peculiarities which explains many of the sixteenth century symptoms." [40]

It was common that a pastor of a parish did not reside in the parish, but had a substitute (vice-pastor or vice-*curatus*) take care of the work for which he was hired. For example, in 1517 in 137 parishes in the province of Holland eighty-seven clergymen had the title pastor and fifty-seven vice-pastor.[41] This is an example of the relationship of the regular pastors and those substituting for a pastor. The income of the substitutes was, as a rule, so meager that they had to find some other source of support. Most of the remuneration for their work was kept by the priest in *absentia.* Some of these vice-pastors raised cattle, farmed, or were in business. Many were innkeepers, because, as priests, they were taxfree. They were known not to baptize children or listen to confessions without pay. They are credited to have inspired the saying that "the goodness of God and the avarice of the priests are both without end." [42] Undesirable as the conditions may have been, these vice-pastors or hirelings are probably blamed for more than their share of the wrong.

The church did not concern herself directly with the education of the clergy, but examined candidates who wanted to become priests. The universities made provision for the training of priests, but such training was not required of candidates to the priesthood. Each prospective priest obtained his training where he found it suitable or was able to pay for it. Almost every village had an elementary school, and most of the cities had some kind of a secondary school, some of which were church schools. Thus a child could attend a writing school from the age of seven to nine years and a secondary school from nine to fifteen years of age. After this followed the fine arts course at the university from sixteen to nineteen and the theological studies from nineteen to twenty-five or longer. A candidate for the priesthood could also study under a priest or carry on an independent study.[43]

It is estimated that about one fifth of the clergy of the Netherlands at the beginning of the sixteenth century had attended a university for two or three years, possibly at Louvain, Cologne, or Paris. But very few obtained a full theological training for the priesthood. Some pursued only a fine arts course at the university without specializing in theology and nonetheless became priests. Others studied law. Most of the priests had no more education than that offered by a secondary school of that day. Some had only an elementary training.[44]

The examination which was required in order to qualify for the priesthood took place under the chairmanship of the professor of a chapter school. The standards were not high either scholastically or as far as the character of the candidate was concerned. Some had acquired some technical knowledge as altar boys or custodians of a church but had no knowledge of Latin. Others had graduated from the chapter schools of Deventer and Zwolle and had thus acquired a fairly good training. These latter usually became priests in cities.[45]

The number of books at the disposal of the clergy was small in number. The minimum was a service book pertaining to the sacraments, a prayer book, a collection of sermons, and a collection of legends about the saints. A notable library of the time belonged to the archbishop of Utrecht. He had 180 books of which nearly one third were of a religious nature.[46]

In addition to the educational aspect of the clergy, its total cultural, moral, and economic status is significant in any attempt to evaluate the life of the church of that time. Among the sources commonly used for this purpose are the various church visitation reports.[47] Although some scholars question some aspects of their validity, they contain, as compared with other sources, the most valid information available.[48]

One of the most conspicuous and embarrassing problems was the matter of the celibacy of the clergy. This practice had been obligatory in the Roman Catholic Church since the eleventh and twelfth centuries, but it was not fully enforced in the Low Countries, particularly in Friesland. When attempts of enforcement were made, they were simply ignored by many of the priests.[49] Rogier estimates that of the 350 priests of Friesland around 1580, about sixty percent lived in concubinage or in a common law marriage.[50] Although common law marriages of priests were more prevalent in Friesland than in the other parts of the Low Countries, the situation was basically the same throughout the region. Erasmus, Rudolf Agricola, and Lambertus Hortensius of Utrecht were all sons of priests. Cornelis Adriaansz, an opponent of the Anabaptists, was the son of the priest Adriaan Corneliszoon; the Anabaptists Obbe and Dirk Philips were also sons of a priest. Among noblemen conditions were even worse. Philip of Burgundy, Bishop of Utrecht, was an illegitimate son of Philip the Good. Rogier uses Philip of Burgundy and Frederik Schenk van Toutenburg, archdeacon of Utrecht, as examples of how even such high offices of the church were used to take advantage of illicit and indiscriminate sex relationships. He labels this practice as fornication in contrast to the practice of a priest who lived in a common law marriage which the community considered a legal marriage.

The sexual irregularities of the clergy led to incongruous situations. On the day that the unmarried pastor Hendrik Huysman became the abbot of the convent of Selwerd, he also received the news of the birth of his son, Rudolf Agricola. "Thus I have become father twice today," he exclaimed unconcernedly when the news reached him.[51]

The well-known Catholic writer and priest Lambertus Hortensius, mentioned previously, made this somber report about the clergy of Utrecht: "The council and the people at last have complained publicly that they are being pressed by payments. The clergy has an abundance of money and wealth and bathes in luxury, pleasure and sensuality; the naked and poor artisans are starving while the clergy possesses everything."[52] This may be more of an outburst of disgust than an objective description of conditions; nevertheless it describes the situation as a contemporary saw it.

Post summarizes his findings regarding the clergy by stating that there were "certainly many violations of the celibate and that many priests and their housekeepers lived as man and wife. Generally this was tolerated by the members of the church as well as by the ecclesiastical and secular authorities and patrons." The law against the practice remained in force, but the violators were hardly ever punished except in cases of adultery.[53]

6. *Asceticism and Monasticism*

Asceticism and monasticism were integral parts of the missionary outreach of the church in the early Middle Ages when Christianity spread from the south to the north into the Germanic countries in the making. The ascetic movements created not only missionary and cultural outposts, but also provided severe critics of the institutionalized church. However, this criticism served as a leaven of the church which was in need of forgotten ideals. The ascetic and monastic movements did not break with the church, but they, too, became institutionalized. Revivals of the early ascetic and monastic ideals eventually led to the founding of new orders.

The influence of monasticism in spreading the gospel of Christ and the ideals of Christianity, the movement's work in the settlement of nomadic tribes in Western Europe, and its role in the development of the tribes' culture – all are outstanding. Ascetic and monastic ideals also played a significant role in the early history of the Low Countries. The work of Willibrord and Boniface has been mentioned. Even though there was an inflation of the monastic ideals, and the popularity of the orders as welfare institutions increased, the ideals of asceticism and a sense of mission were kept alive. Ultimately this spirit contributed both to the origin of the reformation movement in the Netherlands and to the rejuvenation of the Catholic Church.

The popularity of the monastery and the covenant as places for young people to enter their gates and bid the world farewell can hardly be comprehended in our day and age. The Bishopric of Utrecht had 477 monastic institutions in 1517, of which 193 were for men and 284 for women. The total number of monks was 3,100; there were 10,000 nuns. In addition to this the bishopric had some 5,000 priests as has been noted earlier. The total population of the bishopric was about two million.[54] One can justly raise the question: What made monastic life and the calling of the clergy so attractive to the young people of the Middle Ages?

First of all, this popularity should be an evidence that the monastic institution was still an integral part of the church and the Christian life of that time. Asceticism and the mortification of the flesh were meaningful in some way. That this was still one of the most promising roads to heaven which the church had to offer could be posed as one answer. But there are more reasons.

Although the regulations required certain ages for entry into the orders, they were often not strictly observed. Between 1403 and 1463, of the eighty-three girls who entered the St. Agnes convent, twenty-eight were between seven and fifteen years of age, thirty-six between fifteen and twenty, and twelve between twenty and twenty-five. Boys often entered a little later. The monastic vows were usually taken two years after the entry.[55]

It is evident that entry into such an institution for a lifetime at such an early age must have been determined under the influence of the parents, relatives, and guardians. Parents with a large number of children often sent some to a monastic institution. Members of the upper classes quite frequently disposed of their bastard children in this manner. That priests followed the same practice has been previously illustrated. In cases like these there was little religious or ascetic motivation on the part of the entrant. Such conditions and practices helped to establish the ill repute of the monastic institutions. Naturally the monastic order began to lose its popularity. Many who had involuntarily joined the orders escaped. Some of the monastic institutions founded for children of the nobility were ultimately secularized so that their children would not be bound by a vow and yet they would receive the material benefits of the institution. These latter turned into endowed welfare institutions.[56]

Within the monastic orders, there were other unsatisfactory conditions. During the sixteenth century one fifth of the land of Friesland and Groningen belonged to monastic organizations.[57] The abbots of these land-holding monasteries represented a powerful force in the economic life of the country. The land was seldom rented out to the surrounding peasants, but was farmed by the monasteries. However, even the large number of occupants was not sufficient to take care of the work, and consequently semi-monastic laborers, called *conversen,* helped the monks and nuns in their work. These laborers constituted a significant element in the accumulation of wealth by the monasteries and in the lowering of the spiritual and moral level of asceticism. The role and fame of the *conversen* can be compared with the same aspect of the assistant priest, the vicar-*curatus,* who supposedly brought the clergy and church into disrepute. The real blame in both cases should be laid to the system which was created and administered or tolerated by the leaders of the church and the monastic institutions.

The abbots of the monasteries tried to get as many *conversen* as they could in order to till the soil, develop industries, and increase the prestige of the orders. Cheap labor, and originally also tax exemption, made it possible to increase the land holdings. Past were the days when the truly ascetic pioneers established centers of Christian civilization, drained swamps, built dams, tilled the soil of the desert, and introduced a higher culture to a barbarian population. Past were the days when this was done for a great cause, be it to save one's soul or that of others or to improve the life of others on earth. Monasticism at this stage was knowingly or unknowingly engaged in an economic battle with the society which had produced it and which it now exploited. The peasants hated this institution because it took the land from them, the middle class hated it because the monasteries constituted a threat to the industries of the towns and cities, and the nobility hated the growing power and prestige of the prosperous institution, especially since the cause and fame of the upper class were on the decline. The abbots were often stronger than the occupants of castles, and the two engaged in frequent quarrels and regular warfare.[58]

With the coming of a new era, there developed a new attitude concerning the special economic privileges which the monasteries had enjoyed. Changes came about through the pressures of the guilds and all those who objected to the competition of the monasteries. This economic battle began during the 15th century and continued and increased during the 16th century. Laws were passed prohibiting the purchase of additional land, the establishment of new industries, and even the acceptance of gifts. Not only local authorities, but also Philip the Good, the bishop of Utrecht, and Charles V passed restrictions and taxed the property.[59] The taxations and the changed atmosphere brought about by the Renaissance and the approaching Reformation introduced a test which the medieval institution did not withstand because its occupants had lost the enthusiasm and idealism it would have taken to weather the onslaught.

But let us probe further into the cause of the monasteries' decline in idealism and popularity. It is significant to note that the interest in the priesthood did not suffer as that in monasticism did. The prerequisites for becoming a priest were always on a more sound and more mature basis thans those for taking the monastic vows. Furthermore, the new era that began with the 16th century merely transformed the priesthood while it severely damaged the attractiveness of the life in the monasteries. Luther's word about the freedom of a Christian was heard and read in the Netherlands. Now many parents were not so eager to place their children into a life of seclusion and circumscription. The children who were put into the monastery or convent could escape more easily as the popularity of the institution decreased.

As with the priesthood, moral conditions certainly had something to do with monastic difficulty. There is something to be said in favor of the observation by Catholic authors that the moral conditions in the monasteries were not necessarily worse at the beginning of the 16th century than they had been previously. But this observation is not very convincing. Some of the greatest criticisms of the conditions in the monasteries came from persons who knew them out of personal experience. Among them were Geert Groote, Erasmus, and Gnapheus. In an attempt to remedy the situation, the *observantie* movement at the turn of the century aimed to introduce a more faithful and rigid observation of the monastic rules which were neglected in many monasteries. This renewed effort, which concentrated in the fraternity houses of the Brethren of the Common Life, was later channeled into two reformation forces, one of which became effective in the old church and the other which created a new stream culminating in the Sacramentarian and resulting movements.

Monasticism did not see the handwriting on the wall announcing its coming doom. In a comparatively short time, this old institution which had contributed so much to the development of the country, the establishment of a Christian culture, and the church itself was gone. By 1570 most of the fifteen or more orders formerly represented in the Netherlands had been swept away by the Reformation movement.[60] Only in the Catholic Counter-Reformation did the best efforts of monasticism survive.[61]

7. The Administration of the Church

Up to the year 1559, the Netherlands were divided into the following bishoprics: Utrecht, Luik (Liege), Kamerijk (Cambrai), Doornik (Tournai), Atrecht (Artois), and Terwaan, with minor parts belonging to the bishoprics of Cologne, Münster, and Osnabrück. These bishoprics were parts of the archbishoprics of Reims and Cologne. In 1559

Philip II divided the Netherlands into the archbishoprics of Utrecht, Mechelen, and Kamerijk (Cambrai) thus freeing them from "foreign" jurisdiction.[62]

In most of the bishoprics, the bishop was both the secular and spiritual ruler. The sees of the bishoprics were usually occupied by persons of noble rank with the necessary political qualifications and experiences. As with the priesthood, the spiritual and theological qualifications were usually not seriously taken into consideration. During the crucial period from 1496 to 1529, the bishopric of Utrecht was occupied by the following: Frederik of Baden (1496-1517), Philip of Burgundy (1517-1524), Henry of Bavaria (1524-1529). Their official dealings and personal life do not reveal that they were particularly well qualified to be bishops of the church. Their moral character and spiritual leadership were not beyond reproach.

The bishop observed the practice of calling a synod at the beginning of his reign. At this time he confirmed the rules and laws of his predecessor. New regulations could be introduced and passed. Other business was taken care of. The bishops delegated church matters to two vicar-generals. One was in charge of the general spiritual matters and the other of ordinations and consecrations.[63]

When Charles V took over the functions of the secular office from Henry of Bavaria, Henry was left with only the functions of the spiritual responsibilities which, however, he left in the hands of the vicar-generals. Stripping the office of the bishop of Utrecht of all secular power and prestige and a lack of the spiritual qualifications on the part of the noblemen, made the position undesirable for their sons. Frederik Schenck van Toutenburg was appointed by the king[64] as the first archbishop of Utrecht in 1560.

Dark as the Middle Ages were in the Low Countries, as elsewhere, this darkness was never without a ray of light and hope. Even at this time there was a religious sincerity and a searching for light which soon burst forth to meet the dawn of a new day.

II

THE DAWN OF A NEW DAY

The church had become institutionalized during the Middle Ages, and its theology had become scholastic and sterile. A practical and devout piety, however, was found side by side with the corrupt practices of the church. This inner piety, which was known as Christian mysticism, and which was the background of various reformation movements of the late Middle Ages, was God- and Christ-centered. It shared with the later Pietism the emphasis on the personal element in the experience of salvation and in the devotion to Christ. This contemplative, personal and mystic piety was fostered in many of the monastic orders and found expression in such classic devotional books as the *Imitatio Christi* and *Theologia Deutsch*. Great Christian mystics of this period were Meister Eckhart, Johann Tauler, Heinrich Suso, Jan van Ruysbroeck, Geert Groote, and Thomas à Kempis. To list them in one sentence should not mislead one to assume that all belonged to the same school of mysticism. There were considerable differences among them, but they had enough in common to be grouped together, particularly by virtue of the fact that all influenced the early reformation movements. Luther felt the influence of mysticism. He discovered and published the *Theologia Deutsch,* and although he soon turned away from the views expressed in this classic of mysticism, some of his early co-workers, among them Andreas Karlstadt and Thomas Müntzer, continued in the tradition of mysticism. Mysticism, like the monastic orders which fostered it, was characterized by an ecumenical or international spirit and spread rapidly.[1]

A. THE SOIL AND THE SEED

In the Low Countries this mysticism was strongly represented. It might well be said that it furnished the soil in which a new seed was planted. The *Imitatio Christi,* ascribed commonly to Thomas à Kempis,

became the classic of Dutch mysticism and, next to the Bible, one of
the most printed books. Albert Hyma states that the *Imitation of
Christ* "may be called the Gospel of the *Devotio Moderna,* that great
religious and educational revival which originated in the Low Countries and spread far beyond the boundaries of its native soil." [2]

1. The 'Devotio Moderna'

The *Devotio Moderna* was the old way of salvation with a "new"
approach. This new approach was first advanced by Jan van Ruysbroeck, who, in 1344 at the age of 50, joined the Augustinian order.
In a Franciscan manner, he was desirous to offer his soul to God and
to practice humility. His mystical views were expressed in many books.
Ruysbroeck had some communication with Johann Tauler and Heinrich Suso,[3] but his most important contact was with his outstanding
pupil, Geert Groote, who embodied Ruysbroeck's views in the fellowship of the Brethren of the Common Life. In this form contemplative
and speculative mysticism became more practical. The Brethren of the
Common Life lived in community houses. They were not bound by
a vow, but practiced obedience, celibacy, and poverty. Their contributions ranged from the copying of books to the development of a strong
educational program. Among Groote's young scribes and pupils, Flo-
rens Radewijns was outstanding. He continued the work after Groote's
death in 1384. The movement started in Deventer, Zwolle and Win-
desheim and spread over the Netherlands and into the neighboring
countries, establishing monasteries. The Brethren of the Common Life
became a strong spiritual force and greatly influenced the church,
other monastic orders, and the communities in which the movement
was established.[4]

The *Imitatio Christi* originated in the atmosphere of the Brethren
and expresses well the spirit and the challenge of the movement.
Geert Groote was an outstanding preacher of repentance and a critic
of existing conditions in the church and in the monasteries.[5] After an
attempt was made to silence him in 1383, he continued to teach, to
write, and to foster the *ynnich leven* (inner or spiritual life).[6] This
"new devotion" was coupled with the mystically experienced and
applied "imitation of Christ."

Thomas à Kempis was born a few years before Geert Groote died.
This "greatest son" of Groote lived for seventy years in the monastery
at Agnietenberg near Zwolle, where he wrote a number of books

including the biography of Groote. He is usually credited with writing the *Imitatio Christi* of which more than 2000 editions have appeared and which consequently has exerted an unusual influence not only prior to and during the Reformation, but also continuing throughout the centuries up to the present time. Its fame has spread to all countries and all denominations.[7]

The question as to what extent the Brethren of the Common Life and the *Devotio Moderna* actually contributed to the Reformation of the Low Countries receives no answer. Most writers of Protestant and humanist background answer this question positively. The many writings of J. Lindeboom are an example.[8] W. J. Kühler saw a great similarity in the views of the Brethren of the Common Life and the Anabaptists. N. van der Zijpp corrects and supplements Kühler's claim by stating that the *Devotio Moderna* prepared the soil for the seed of a later period.[9]

The modern reader of the *Imitation of Christ* immediately becomes aware of the fact that he is placed into the Middle Ages. The frame of mind, the terminology, and the theology are those of that day. The *Imitation* is Christ-centered, with a strong emphasis on spiritual communion. Tending toward moralism and perfectionism, the writing admonishes the believer to avail himself of the visible sacrament, for "it is exceedingly hurtful to defer the Communion long." If, however, "a man sometime abstain out of humility, or by reason of some sound cause, he is to be commended for his reverence." Such abstention is permissible because "any devout man is able every day and every hour to draw near to Christ in spiritual communication for his soul's health and without hindrance." [10] In the *Imitation of Christ,* the criticism of the institutionalized church was still very mild.

Reading the *Imitatio* today, one can ask whether such a work could have sufficiently inspired the determination necessary to start reformatory movements. This classic of devotional literature, the *Imitatio,* and the atmosphere and spirit in which it was born, the *Devotio Moderna,* obviously contained more explosive elements for the people of that day. How else could they have furnished the potential and inspiration for a reformation that went far beyond the pale of the *Imitatio*? The inspiring force of the *Imitatio* must be kept in mind when the Sacramentarian, the Anabaptist, and later the Reformed movements come into being.

2. *From Mysticism to Humanism*

The tradition of the Brethren of the Common Life was carried on by a number of outstanding men of whom Johannes Pupper van Goch and Wessel Gansfort should be mentioned. They studied together in Cologne and became friends. Johannes Pupper van Goch was in touch with the Brethren early and became rector of the Augustinian convent at Mechelen. Among his unpublished writings, the most timely was *De libertate christiana,* which he wrote shortly before he died in 1475. It was published at the beginning of the Reformation and exerted a considerable influence.[11]

Gansfort visited Thomas à Kempis at Agnietenberg, received his training in the school of the Brethren of the Common Life and spent considerable time at the universities of Cologne, Paris, and Heidelberg. After teaching at Heidelberg, he returned to Groningen.[12]

Gansfort was the type of person who was claimed as the forerunner of many and various groups. One extreme position presents the following view: "It is indeed very doubtful whether Luther was a greater theologian than Gansfort. He may not even have had so much influence as the latter..." [13] Hyma is of the opinion that Gansfort had a very strong influence on Luther and that he had come to a very similar conviction long before Luther. On the other hand, claims are being made that Gansfort remained "Catholic in the basic doctrines: he believes in transubstantiation, accepts tradition next to the Bible as a basic source, recognizes the merit of good works, believes in purgatory, recommends the prayer for the dead and is for the adoration of the saints." [14]

Considering his life, it is not surprising that such a diversity of views can be expressed about Gansfort. He became a *magister contradictionis.* While teaching at the University of Heidelberg, he became involved in the controversy between the nominalists representing the *via antiqua* and the realists of the *via moderna* from which struggle he evolved as a representative of the latter.[15]

Gansfort was a radical and independent thinker within the Catholic tradition. He intended to remain a good son of his church as did his friends, Rudolf Agricola and Erasmus. And yet, as a fearless independent seeker, who placed the Bible foremost, he helped to usher in a new era. Gansfort's *Farrago* appeared in 1521 in Zwolle, in 1522 in Wittenberg, and in 1523 in Basel. Luther was so impressed by his writings that he said, "If I had read his works earlier my enemies might think that Luther had absorbed everything from Wessel: his spirit is so in accord with mine." [16]

M. van Rhijn has demonstrated how large a circle of friends Gansfort had.[17] Among those influenced by him directly or indirectly were Goswinus van Halen, Albertus Hardenberg who wrote his biography, Johannes van Amsterdam, Jacobus Hoeck, Cornelis Hoen, and Hinne Rode. The latter two were instrumental in making his writings public. Luther's positive reaction to Gansfort's written works has been mentioned. When, however, on the basis of Gansfort's *De sacramento eucharistiae,* Cornelis Hoen developed some independent thoughts about the eucharist and Hinne Rode presented these views to Luther, Luther rejected them. The influence of these views in the Low Countries and in Switzerland will be dealt with later.

Wessel Gansfort's influence was strong among those who remained in the church and was still noticeable among some who left the church at the beginning of the Reformation. Above all, he was the link between the mystic tradition of the Brethren of the Common Life and the Christian Humanism of which Rudolf Agricola and Erasmus, especially, were representatives.

It is well to take note of the warning by M. van Rhijn that Gansfort's thinking in regard to the eucharist differed considerably from that of those who followed him.[18] That the thought patterns of the pupils of Gansfort led off in different directions can be inferred from a letter which Gansfort wrote to Johannes van Amsterdam: "... I therefore beg you that you do not give up the struggle for truth at Agnietenberg and that you do not rest until you have, either as victor or defeated, conquered the truth which illuminates all darkness." [19]

3. Desiderius Erasmus

Although Desiderius Erasmus has been acclaimed the father of even more movements than Gansfort, it is not an overstatement to say that he was the greatest among the Christian humanists and contributed more toward preparing the way for a reformation of the church than any other person. After Luther's reformation was underway Erasmus turned away from what he had helped to usher in, but he continued to influence the reformation of the Catholic Church whose faithful servant he intended to remain. First Erasmus was admired by all because of his learning and because of his efforts to improve the church. This admiration later turned to mistrust and he was even hated because he deliberately refused to take sides. His decision not to join the Reformation nor to oppose it made him walk a lonely path. He thought this was the only sound approach to his desire to reform the internal aspects of the church of the ages. His "ecumenical" attempt to preserve the unity of Christianity when it was breaking up was neither appreciated nor understood.

He desired to be "a citizen of the world, common to all, or rather, a stranger to all" and considered it "vain ... glorification ... when a city or nation boasts of producing a man who has become great through his own exertions and not by the help of his fatherland." [20] To this, a Dutch scholar, resenting the claim which Dutch Protestantism has made regarding Erasmus' influence in the Netherlands, adds: "If we contain the cosmopolitan Erasmus within the narrow confines of our country and attempt to make the movement of which he became the center, one-sidedly Netherlandish, ... what right do we have to exclude from it the Italian Christian humanists and the friend of Erasmus, Thomas More?" [21] It is not only the Netherlands, both Catholic and Protestant populations, that can lay a claim to Erasmus, but all the countries that are a part of or have been exposed to Western civilization. As he was an ecumenical world citizen, so is his heritage. His memory is rightly being honored in Louvain where he started his career, in the Cathedral of Canterbury among the great of England, and in the *Grosse Kirche* of Basel where he was buried. [22]

It is not on national grounds that Erasmus of Rotterdam can be claimed by the Low Countries. That would not only violate historical facts, but also be contrary to the spirit of Erasmus. The claim on Erasmus must be based on the fact that many of his native countrymen voluntarily exposed themselves to his influence even though he had become a world citizen and had chosen to live abroad most of his life. This claim on Erasmus is made more valid by the fact that his heritage has remained alive to this day in the land of his birth.

Erasmus tried to erase some of the memories of his early experiences in his home country. There was the fact that he and his brother, as sons of a priest, did not have a normal home. Furthermore, their father and mother died when they were young. After having attended monastic schools, they were persuaded by their guardians to enter the monastery. When Erasmus finally received permission to leave the monastery and had an opportunity to develop his great talents in centers of culture like Louvain, Paris, and Basel, he came to his own. But he continued to see "everything, having had this dark period in his life, in the most gloomy colors – except himself." [23] The shadow of this experience remained with him throughout his entire life. He even tried to obscure the fact that he was the son of a priest. He continued to direct his "strongest barrages against monasticism and celibacy." [24]

Erasmus started out as a man of the *bonae litterae* in the wake of the Renaissance. With the greatest zeal he devoted himself to studies of the literature of antiquity. There were many others doing the same. It was possibly because of his training in the schools of the Brethren of the Common Life that he did not pursue the study and publication of classical literature as an end in itself. His interest also embraced Christian antiquity. "The two major influences of classical and Christian antiquity together with a basic view of their relation to each other were operative in Erasmus' early period as they were throughout his career." [25]

Erasmus is remembered for his *Novum Testamentum* (1516), his *Annotationes,* and his biblical studies which were of great influence in the Low Countries. An outstanding and influential contribution was his *Enchiridion Militis Christiani* which he wrote to be used as a "handsome weapon of a Christian knight" (1503). At the beginning of the Reformation it became "one of the most popular books in Europe and exercised a strong influence upon Zwingli, Bucer, the Spiritualists and Anabaptists..." Erasmus wrote to his friend Colet that he had written the book "only for the purpose of correcting the common error of those who make religion consist of ceremonies... while they are singularly careless of things that belong to piety." [26] Erasmus' books were widely published, translated, and circulated in the Netherlands. [27] They could be found even in remote Frisian villages. [28] A number of devotional writings were produced under the influence of Erasmus. Among them should be mentioned *Troost ende Spiegel der siecken* by Willem Gnapheus.

Erasmus called for a return to the Scriptures. From Paul and Peter one was to learn what faith and charity were; such learning would be more profitable than if one "had walked to Rome ten times." When he quoted Paul who taught true Christianity – "Stand fast therefore in the liberty wherewith Christ hath made us free, and be not entangled again with the yoke of bondage" [29] – it sounded like the trumpet of John the Baptist preparing the way for the blast which was to follow from Wittenberg.

One could ask what direction the reformation effort of Erasmus would have taken if the energy exerted by him and his friends would have broken through the boundaries and overstepped the sanction of the church as happened in the case of Luther and the other reformers. But such a question is superfluous since Erasmus spent as much time and energy on keeping the efforts of his reform work within the church as he did to stimulate this reformation on the basis of the Scriptures and the *bonae litterae*. He "spiritualized" and revitalized within the church concepts, doctrines, and traditions which were either dormant or misunderstood. His rebellion took an overt form only when he stimulated some to leave the church and start a variety of movements ranging all the way from Luther to the most radical reformers.

The fame and friendships of the great Rotterdamer spread into both high and low places. His books were found in the parsonages of priests, in the homes of humanistic educators, in monasteries, and in government circles. Maria of Hungary, who became the governess of the Low Countries in 1531, was an admirer of Erasmus. In 1532 Erasmus dedicated his *De vidua christiana* to her.[30] Erasmus received an unusual request from Johann III of Cleves-Mark, who wanted the great humanist to help with the preparation of a new church constitution. K. von Hersebach was sent to Freiburg to consult with Erasmus about this.[31]

In Amsterdam there was a group of friends of Erasmus. The feeling of dedication and admiration between teacher and students was reciprocal. Among these friends were Nicolaas Cannius who had been Erasmus' secretary, Alardus van Amsterdam, the priest-humanist, and Johannes Sartorius, the humanist educator. Sartorius prepared a Dutch edition of Erasmus' *Adagia,* while Alardus spent the major part of his life in preparing the writings of Rudolf Agricola for print. Other members of the group were associated with the humanistic schools. Erasmus had words of praise for the school books written by the humanist educator, Cornelis Crocus. Among the humanistic men of art were Jan van Scorel and Jacob Cornelisz van Oostsanen. Other educators were Alexander Hegius, the teacher of Erasmus, and Johannes Murmellius of Alkmaar. These educators, in many instances, expressed themselves by writing and directing dramatic presentations. The founders and teachers of the humanistic schools of Amsterdam and Alkmaar spread and promoted Christian humanism in the Netherlands.

Just as with the founders of Christian humanism, so also among the followers of Erasmus came the hour of decision as to whether they were to remain faithful to their church or accept the "new" message which was spreading. Some, like Alardus, became strong opponents

of the approaching Sacramentarian movement while others, like Sartorius and his friend Wouter Deelen, accepted the ideas of the movement and suffered persecution from the hands of their former friends.[33]
The dividing line was drawn right through the ranks of the Christian
humanists, the followers of the *Devotio Moderna,* and those practicing
the *Imitatio Christi.*

4. *The Role of Drama*

In its outreach the church has always used, for means of communication, the spoken and the printed word supported by works of art.
Artistic representations were made use of particularly during the
Middle Ages. During the Reformation the emphasis was placed on the
spoken and printed word while works of art were widely discouraged
because of the misuse of images and other media of the fine arts. With
the invention of movable type, the printed word became a very strong
and significant medium of communication.

Music, too, became a valuable tool, particularly in worship services
where musical instruments and choirs were used. The latter have been
mentioned briefly. But mention should be made of another medium
which, at times, became very popular in the work of the church and
in civic life. Drama and rituals are very likely as old as any form of
religion. For centuries the church had used drama successfully in
promoting the truths presented in sermon and ritual. At times this
practice became a problem child of the church. The incidental or pe-
ripheral in the presentation became so popular that the drama gradually distorted the truth which it was to portray. Heretical ideas
crept in. On the other hand dramatic forms could be used to present
shortcomings of the church and its clergy.

In the Low Countries the presentation of plays became very popular
in Flanders during the Middle Ages. Antwerp had an annual *Landju-
weel* at which occasion visiting chambers of rhetoric (*rederijkerskamers*)
would compete for prizes. The earliest version of the play *Everyman*
is supposed to have received the first prize at such an occasion.[34] Morality plays were given throughout the Middle Ages based mostly on
biblical subjects. They greatly influenced the religious thinking of that
time. Some Latin plays, written by Roman writers or contemporary
playwrights, were presented by the humanistic schools during the Renaissance.[35]

As early as 1408 the chambers of rhetoric had their problems with the censors. In that year an edict was published in Doornik (Tournai) forbidding the "enactment of the mystery of the holy sacrament and other matters touching our faith." [36] Most likely this edict had nothing to do with the later Sacramentarian pronouncement that denied the actual presence of Christ in the eucharist. The church probably wanted to prevent possibilities of making light of something that constituted the heart of the faith.

In his plays written during the Reformation, Cornelis Everaert van Brugge criticized the social and economic conditions of his day. [37] On February 4, 1528, it was stated that the *rederijkers* of Holland and Friesland were giving daily plays whereby they "scandalized" or misled people in their religious lives. [38] In 1539 the chambers of rhetoric were competing for prizes at Gent with dramas that answered the question. "What is, in dying, man's greatest consolation?" The results revealed the religious situation of that time as well as the significance of the dramatic clubs in the coming and spreading of the Reformation in the Low Countries. The church, the sacraments, or any other means of the church were not hailed as the final alleviation; the ultimate consolation was shown to be the mercy of God through Christ alone. [39]

Other playwrights in the chambers of rhetoric deserve to be mentioned. An outstanding and active participant in both the writing and production of plays was Willem Gnapheus, treated elsewhere. Of the later Anabaptists who started as members of the chambers of rhetoric, the following can be named: David Joris, Jan van Leiden, and Leenaert Bouwens. The father of David Joris is said to have played the role of David for the chambers of rhetoric and thus gave this name to his son. David Joris used the stage to promote his religious ideas as did others. [40]

Thus the former morality and mystery plays became a channel of severe criticism of existing conditions; the plays also functioned as a positive witness of the Reformation. It is not surprising that edicts were issued forbidding the presentation of plays that had not been licensed or religious plays in general and that authorities resorted to the publication of indexes of forbidden plays. [41]

B. IN THE EMBRACE OF A WORLD REVOLUTION
(1517-1530)

The stage was set in the Low Countries for a great presentation! The Netherlands were experiencing prosperity and a developing culture. A revived interest in a deeper understanding and practice of the Christian faith was spreading by means of a Christian humanism rooted in the *Devotio Moderna* of the Brethren of the Common Life. In the midst of this dynamic age people began to read and hear of the otherwise unknown town named Wittenberg and the previously unknown Augustinian monk named Martin Luther.

It is understandable that the news about Luther's message was not always clearly comprehended when it reached the Low Countries through merchants and sailors via the routes of the Hanseatic League. Even the monastic orders and the academic channels of that day could not give reliable information. Luther himself did not yet have clear concepts about much of his new-found faith and its consequences. Thus if the original sound of the "Wittenberg Nightingale" was not clear, how much less was this the case with the echo of his message in a faraway country.

One thing, however, did become clearly fixed. The heresy or glad tidings, call it what you will, came from a *Luyter,* and it became known as *Luytery.* Under this name much went on record when the church and government authorities became alarmed about the unfolding drama on the stage of the Lowlands. The most careful examination of the records from the days of the great upheaval will not answer the question fully as to who of these *Luyterans* were labeled thus justly and who received the tag as a matter of convenience. Modern research in the Low Countries indicates that the attachment of *Luytery* or any other name to a person of that day does not necessarily imply a full-fledged follower of the person named. But neither the investigating authorities nor those under investigation understood this or wanted to understand it. Needless to say, the reformers had not reached a clear and mature stage at the beginning of the Reformation. To expect from those on trial or from those of the inquisition machinery clear concepts associated with later denominational or confessional lines would be asking too much.

In a time of revolutionary change and suspicion, labels are distributed freely and in a streamlined fashion. Labeling is not an invention of modern dictatorship, but is as old as society itself. Even in a democracy or bureaucracy political and social labeling seems unavoidable. It makes all machinery, be it social, political, or religious, seem to function so much more smoothly.

1. Channels of Communication

There was an immediate response to the message from Wittenberg both by those who looked for an improvement of the religious life and practices and by those in authority who were concerned about this response. Corrections are needed on this point, for modern scholarship dealing with the roots of the Dutch Reformation and its early development seems not to have fully recovered from the views which tradition has shaped, namely that in the Low Countries "Lutheranism was little known during the first half of the sixteenth century."[42] Evidence to be presented later will show that Lutheranism was well-known at this time in the Low Countries. However, from the examination of resources on this subject, it is clear that this region was not predestined to become Lutheran. For various reasons successive waves of religious influences followed which overshadowed the original impact which *sola fideism* had made.

The gateways through which news spread in those days were the cities of trade, of shipping, and of fairs, such as Antwerp, Deventer, Groningen, and Emden. The university and ecclesiastical centers of Louvain, Cologne, Utrecht, and Münster were significant as information and clearing centers. Other channels of communication with Wittenberg were the monastic orders, particularly the Augustinians and the Brethren of the Common Life.[43] The country was susceptible to the new thoughts from Wittenberg because of the reformatory tendencies inspired by the *Devotio Moderna* and Christian humanism. Furthermore, these tendencies were moderately tolerated under such rulers as Johann III of Cleves-Mark or outrightly promoted by Edzard I and his successors in East Friesland.[44]

Antwerp was one of the first and chief centers for spreading the influence of the Reformation in the Low Countries. Writings of Luther reached Antwerp by 1518, and some were reprinted as early as 1520. Of the 129 editions of Luther's writings published in the Low Countries from 1520 to 1541, at least 85 were published in Antwerp.[45] In addition, many other writings of reformers appeared in that city.

Many and various were the people who helped to promote the teachings of Luther. Even Erasmus helped in the promotion of the books by Luther. Merchants from Augsburg and Nürnberg, who hosted Albrecht Dürer during a visit in Antwerp (1520-1521), spread Luther's fame. The prior of the Augustinian monastery, Jacobus

Praepositus, had graduated at Wittenberg with a *lic. theol.* defending a thesis dealing with "Spirit and Letter." After his return to the Netherlands, he started his evangelical preaching in Antwerp. He continued his reformation efforts in Bremen. His successor in the Augustinian monastery of Antwerp, Hendrik van Zutfen, who had lived with Luther in the same monastery at Wittenberg, continued the reformation in Antwerp, but had to flee and became a martyr at Bremen in 1522. The Augustinian monastery of Antwerp was destroyed, and two of its monks, Hendrik Vos and Johannes van Essen, were burned at the stake. Luther composed a memorial to them in his well-known hymn, "Ein neuwes Lied wir heben an." By this time, other Augustinian monasteries of the Low Countries found themselves under the influence of their Wittenberg brethren.[46]

On November 19, 1519, the University of Louvain condemned the writings of Luther; this condemnation was repeated in February, 1520.[47] Among the many printers who risked their lives in publishing or printing prohibited books were Jan Seversz of Leiden and Jacob van Liesveldt of Antwerp. The latter lost his life because he featured the devil in monk's habit.[48] Books were confiscated, burned publicly, and placed on the index of forbidden volumes.[49] Nevertheless, some found their way into the Low Countries, even into remote villages. Menno Simons was a priest in the little Frisian village of Pingjum when he started reading the Bible and writings by Luther and other reformers in 1526. Books by *Martinus Luyter* and his *adherenten* were confiscated the following year in the parsonage at Witmarsum.[50]

Hanseatic cities such as Deventer, Amsterdam, Antwerp served as channels for the flow of books into the Low Countries. East Friesland, a refuge for the persecuted Evangelicals from the various Dutch provinces, also served as a gateway for books and ideas to penetrate the Low Countries. From the Dutch province of Friesland numerous young men went to Wittenberg to study under Luther and his coworkers.[51] Upon their return they spread the views and books which they had acquired.

Peasants were easily won to these views. Some claimed that Luther proved his views clearly through the gospels and writings of Paul.[52] The peasants were critical of their priests who were trading churches and spiritual estates for the sake of material gain. Thus the evangelical movement contributed to the decrease of interest in the institutions of the church including the monasteries. Boxhorn reported in 1524 that many monks and nuns were leaving the orders in Holland, Zeeland, and Flanders.[53]

2. From Antwerp to Wassenberg

Turning now to the southeastern part of the Low Countries, this account will deal with the bishopric of Liege (Luik); it will then proceed to the archbishopric of Cologne, the bishopric of Münster, and East Friesland. Luik is a part of Belgium today, and the other areas mentioned belong to Germany. The continuity that they possess for the purposes of this discussion lies in the fact that they constitute an integral part of the territory in which the development and spread of the evangelical and Sacramentarian movement took place.

The bishopric of Luik covered the territory surrounding the city of Luik (Liege) in present day Belgium. From here we proceed via Aachen to Cologne, following the Rhine River north to the Dutch border near Cleve, and then we return south along the border between the Netherlands, Belgium, and Germany and back to Liege.

From 1505 until 1538 the bishopric of Luik was ruled by the spiritual and secular bishop Erardus van der Marck. He was opposed to any evangelical changes and functioned somewhat as a "general inquisitor" of the Netherlands. He helped Nuncio Aleander enforce the papal bull against Luther, boasting that he had read none of his books, and spoke against him at the Reichstag in Worms in 1521. Nevertheless, some priests who had studied in Germany and some merchants became messengers of Lutheran ideas. Gateways for the transmission of such ideas were Cleve, Jülich, Aachen, and Antwerp.[54]

More freedom for the spread of evangelical ideas was found in the northern part of the bishopric in the United Duchy of Cleve under the secular rule of Johann III. Johann III attempted a moderate reformation of the church by preparing a new church constitution. That he sought Erasmus' aid in this matter has already been indicated. His daughter married a son of Frederick the Wise, the Saxon, sponsor of Luther. Luther's books were officially forbidden but due to the favorable atmosphere, found entry into this region.[55]

Of great significance in the spread of the Reformation was a little place between Aachen and Roermond called Wassenberg. An active group of evangelical priests, whose influence reached far beyond their immediate environment, became known as Wassenberg *predikanten*. Not only was the development of the evangelical cause in Cologne influenced by them, but also the evangelical and Anabaptist movement in the city of Münster. The main sponsor and protector of the Wassenberg *predikanten* was Werner von Palant, bailiff of Wassenberg,

whose castle was a haven for persecuted evangelicals. Among those
with whom he associated and whom he protected were Johannes Campanus, Johannes Kloprys, Dionysius Vinne, Hendrik Slachtscaep, Hendric Rol, and Theodorus Fabricius. Some had studied in Cologne, some
in Wittenberg, and all were won for an evangelical cause similar to the
Sacramentarian movement of the Low Countries. This Sacramentarian
movement will be taken up in the next chapter. Unfortunately, von
Palant was discharged in 1534 because Johann III could not tolerate
a bailiff who did "not believe in infant baptism or in the bodily presence of Christ in the eucharist." [56]

The Wassenberg *Predikanten* were closely related spiritually to
the Sacramentarian movement of the Low Countries and to some cur-
rents of the religious atmosphere of Cologne. Andreas Bodenstein von
Karlstadt's spiritualism was spreading in this area. Cologne was a
gateway through which his views penetrated the Low Countries.

3. Cologne and Münster

The Wassenberg *predikanten* were closely related spiritually to
Lower Rhine and some parts of the present day Netherlands. The
bishoprics of Liege (Luik), Utrecht, Münster, etc. were subject to the
archbishopric of Cologne at least nominally. During the crucial years
of the Reformation the see of the archbishopric was occupied by
Herman von Wied (1517-1546). He was first interested in a gradual
and humanistically orientated reformation of the church. Soon, however, he came to the point of lining up more fully with the Reformation. As a result he was forced to give up his position in 1546.

Cologne was shaken by intellectual and spiritual disagreements. In
their sharp and satirical *Epistulae obscurorum virorum*, the humanists
accused the Dominicans of Cologne of extreme ignorance. The university, formerly attended by students from the Low Countries, lost
much of its enrollment because it blocked humanistic influences and
adhered to scholasticism. Nevertheless, Cologne had been a harbor of
"sectarian" views and could not be bypassed in days when the world
was aflame with new ideas. [57]

Among the outstanding evangelical pioneers was the martyr, Adolf
Clarenbach, who with Peter Fliesteden was burned at the stake in
Cologne on September 28, 1529. He had studied in Cologne, taught
at various places, and was a friend of the Wassenberger, Johann Kloprys. Clarenbach and Fliesteden were accused of "heretical Lutheran

teachings" which included the refusal to swear oaths, the opposition
to all ceremonies in worship, and the symbolic interpretation of the
eucharist and baptism. Clarenbach's and Fliesteden's views were much
the same as those held by Werner von Palant and the Sacramentarian
Wassenberg *predikanten*.[58]

Others who supported a reformation were Theodorus Fabricius and
particularly Gerhard Westerburg who was of patrician background
and a native of Cologne. Westerburg had studied at Cologne and
Bologna and had associated with Luther, Andreas Karlstadt, and Nicolaus Storch in Wittenberg (1522). He married a sister of Karlstadt
and became an ardent promoter of his brother-in-law's views. He even
supported Karlstadt in his publication efforts. One of the notable
events of Westerburg's reformation career was his publication of a
popularized sermon of Karlstadt entitled *Vom Fegefeuer* (purgatory),
which he dedicated to the magistrate of Cologne. A number of German editions appeared, and 3000 copies of a Latin edition were sent
to the Low Countries for distribution.

In 1524, accompanied by two other followers of Karlstadt, Nicolaus
Symmen and Martin Reinhard, Westerburg returned to Cologne "in
order to save the divine word and to fortify the truth." After a time
they went to Jena. In 1526 Westerburg appeared in Zürich and Basel
armed with manuscripts written by Karlstadt dealing with the Lord's
supper. The Swiss Anabaptists-to-be helped him with the printing and
distribution of these. Back in Cologne Westerburg continued to testify
through the spoken and printed word and witnessed the martyrdom of
Clarenbach and Fliesteden. He and his brother Arnold later became
Anabaptists and promoted this group in Cologne.[59]

These "Lutheran heresies," as the records call them, were views of
the emerging Sacramentarian movement. Clarenbach and the Wassenberg *predikanten* were typical representatives of this movement. Westerburg, a promoter of these views, was, in addition, very strongly
influenced by Karlstadt.

The vibrations of the Peasants' Revolt (1524-25) which took place
in Central and South Germany added to the disturbances of the religious Reformation. The effects were felt in numerous northern cities
including Cologne and Münster. The economic advantages of the religious orders were the envy of all. Furthermore, the guilds were dissatisfied with the patrician city government. In thirty-six articles,
proposals were made to remedy the situation in Münster. Improvement
of the conditions in the church was included. But Franz von Waldeck,

who was the bishop and secular ruler of Münster in Westphalia, prevented the acceptance of these articles.[60]

The humanistic influences continued to be significant. C. A. Cornelius has furnished some excellent information about the humanistic tradition of Münster and its background in the Deventer school of the Brethren of the Common Life. Rudolf van Langen of Münster, who had received his education in Deventer, was instrumental in establishing a school which found great support in the leading citizens of Münster and which became the model for many other schools. Among those going forth from this school were the humanists Hermann von dem Busch, Theodorus Fabricius, and Johannes Murmellius. The first two joined the Reformation leaders, and Murmellius trained humanists in the school of Alkmaar in the Netherlands. Other humanists trained in the school of Münster who were active in reformation efforts were Johann Glandorp, Adolf Clarenbach, Gerhard Schliepstein, and Bernhard Rothmann. The Münster school also produced some humanists who remained faithful to their church.[61]

Another split among the humanistic reformers occurred when, under the leadership of Rothmann and others, the foundation was laid for the radical Anabaptist kingdom by the introduction of adult baptism and other "heretical" practices. The relationship of these developments to the Netherlands will be treated later.

4. East Friesland

Generally speaking, the reformation movement got a foothold in the northwest German cities of Hamburg, Lübeck, Oldenburg, and Emden by or soon after 1520. Many and various were the channels and motives of the movement of change. The church and secular authorities had to decide whether a reformation was desirable. If the decision was affirmative, to what extent was the church to be changed? Needless to say, some bishops and rulers wavered because of a lack of conviction, and neither group was above following a wait-and-see policy in order to make the greatest possible political or economic gain. Political unions and the prospect of confiscating property of churches and monasteries for the needy treasuries helped in some instances to determine the course which was ultimately followed. Luther's course was most popular in the north. And Lutheranism won the race in most of the bishoprics, cities, and territories where the Reformation was introduced mostly on the basis of *cujus regio ejus religio* (whose territory, his religion).

Many voices, in addition to those coming from Wittenberg, pleaded for a hearing. In many respects, a more radical program was offered from Zürich by Zwingli, while from Strassburg originated a moderate and a more tolerant way through its spokesmen, Bucer and Capito. Soon there was also to come from this city the radical prophetic voice of Melchior Hofmann, a disappointed follower of Luther. He and Andreas Bodenstein von Karlstadt, another disillusioned co-worker of the Wittenberg reformer, were to meet in East Friesland to find a fertile soil for their seed. Of all the Hanseatic cities with which the cities of the Low Countries had economic, cultural, and spiritual ties, Emden was predestined to become one of the most important in the crucial years of the Reformation of the Low Countries.

East Friesland was racially, linguistically, and geographically, because of its location on the North Sea, more closely related to the Dutch provinces of Groningen and West Friesland than to its neighbors to the south with whom it had loose political ties. Because of the close contacts of East Friesland with Groningen and the Low Countries in general, the influence of the mystic piety of the Brethren of the Common Life, particularly as expressed in the thoughts of Wessel Gansfort, was strong. Among those who worked to make the influence of Humanism strong in East Friesland were two brothers of Rudolf Agricola, Johannes and Heinrich, and his friends Hicco von Dornum and Jacobus Canter, both of Emden. Kochs states that "the thoughts of the Brethren, of Gansfort, and of the humanism of the Netherlands merged in a stream which flooded East Friesland at the beginning of the 16th century." By 1522 the number of students from this area attending various universities had reached a peak of 220. Among the universities, Rostock was the most popular. Rostock also had a school of the Brethren of the Common Life. There were none of these schools in East Friesland, but the region was strongly influenced by the Dutch schools. "The spokesmen of the Reformation (in East Friesland) were with few exceptions from the Low Countries," says Kochs.[62]

Most important in the early development of the Reformation in East Friesland was Ulrich van Dornum, a friend, co-worker, and advisor of Edzard I and his son Enno I. *Junker* Ulrich resided at the castle of Oldersum, which became the refuge of a great variety of evangelicals. Among those who found shelter and protection here were Karlstadt, Melchior Rinck, Melchior Hofmann, and Menno Simons. Ulrich read writings of Luther and other reformers and was in touch with Wittenberg, the Strassburg reformers, and possibly with

THE DAWN OF A NEW DAY

Sebastian Franck. Evidence for this last association is found in Franck's letter to the "Oldersum church." This church was made evangelical through the efforts of Ulrich and his co-worker *Junker* Hicco Houwerda of Uphusen.[63]

In 1526, Ulrich von Dornum sponsored a religious discussion between Catholics and evangelicals. The heated discussion took place in the church at Oldersum. The Jacobite monk Laurens Laurensen came from Groningen for this purpose; Georgius Aportanus was the spokesman for the evangelicals. At the end of the meeting, late in the afternoon, Ulrich invited all for a meal. Apparently some sense of humor remained, for Aportanus quoted scriptures to support the view that one should not be "unequally yoked" while eating with the "unbelievers." Others joked saying, "Let us knock on some caps and see whether there are monks under them." Both groups claimed the victory of the debate. During the same year Ulrich published a report which appeared in Wittenberg.[64]

Another discussion of this nature was precipitated when the Dominican Heinrich Rese of Norden posted twenty-two theses on the doors of the churches and announced that he would defend these evangelical statements publicly on New Year's Day. The discussion was chaired by two representatives of Edzard I. Rese presented his statements against many practices and beliefs on the church including the eucharist, confessions, the saints, and vows; the abbot Gerhard Schnell, of the Liebfrauen monastery, responded. Many monks followed the example of Rese, who renounced his Catholic faith in connection with this discussion. He became the first evangelical minister at Norden.[65]

The Sacramentarian movement, which originated in the Low Countries and which was inspired and supported by the spiritualist reformer, Karlstadt, and the Zwinglian movement of Zürich, was, by now, developing definite characteristics in East Friesland. Hinne Rode, one of the leaders of the Dutch Sacramentarian movement, had been in Wittenberg (1521) and also in Zürich and Strassburg (1524) presenting Cornelis Hoen's views pertaining to the eucharist. Rode came to East Friesland in 1525.[66] When he became the minister in Norden, Lubbert Cansen, an evangelical refugee, arrived from Münster. Under the leadership of another representative of the Low Countries, views pertaining to the symbolic meaning of the sacraments had been shaped by 1526. Georgius Aportanus stated in a writing that circumcision, baptism, and the Lord's supper, like the signs and seals of the Old Testament do not constitute an actual "divine cleansing," but are only definite and sure symbols and signs of this cleansing. In 1527, Rese presented the same views in a hymn consisting of 16 verses in which he emphasized the faith of the Christian and the symbolic meaning of the eucharist.[67]

Following their statements in writing and song, Aportanus and Rese introduced a new form of communion service. They placed, in the center of the church, a long table around which the members of the congregation were seated. They used both bread and wine. It was ordinary bread broken and put into the hands of the partakers.[68] This was likely the first occasion where the Sacramentarian views of the Low Countries were put into practice.

In 1528, these and other views were presented in a confession of faith. It began with the assertion that "God's own inner work" is useful and necessary "for justification and salvation" and ended by stating that "baptism and the Lord's supper, with all other works" should remain where they belong, namely as an outward visible service of the congregation. "They cannot and should not stand for Christ, the only mediator between God and us." [69] No wonder Capito could write a jubilant letter to Zwingli in 1526 reporting that Hinne Rode had gone to East Friesland and that "the truth about the eucharist is known everywhere in Friesland." [70] Sacramentarianism had been firmly established in East Friesland. When Karlstadt and Melchior Hofmann arrived soon afterwards, they found a fertile soil for their message.

But before that phase is taken up, it is necessary to return to the Low Countries proper, and to summarize the impact the continental Reformation made on the Netherlands. Following that, the development of the Sacramentarian movement, which is the uniquely Dutch form of the Reformation, will be presented.

5. The Range of the Reformation

The opponents of the Reformation usually blamed Luther for all religious, social, and even political changes which took place during the 16th century. Quite often there was no distinction made between the teachings of Luther, Karlstadt, Zwingli, Oecolampad, and the more radical reformers. The Lutherans, the Sacramentarians, and the Anabaptists were similarly abominable.[71] Luther's personal and theological development was influenced by these accusations. The directions into which some of his prodigal children went pained and grieved him.[72] In fact, he did not recognize them as his sons and would not have been pleased with the application of Goethe's words from "The Pupil in Magic".

> Great is my dismay!
> Spirits raised by me
> Vainly would I lay! [73]

In Luther's immediate vicinity in Saxony, Andreas Karlstadt and Thomas Müntzer were the leading spirits, the latter being connected with the Peasant's War. In the more distant Zürich, there was Zwingli whom Luther usually named in the same breath as the Anabaptists. Bullinger came to the defense of Zwingli, when he was blamed for this extreme radicalism, claiming that Anabaptism had its origin among Luther's followers, Karlstadt and Müntzer.[74] Luther most generously considered all those who did not agree with him simply as *Schwärmer*, which is possibly best rendered as "spiritualizing fanatics."

Luther and *die Schwärmer* are to this day, consciously or subconsciously, contrasted as day and night, light and darkness, or God and the devil. All enlightenment, secularization, and scholarship have not yet fully established a more objective evaluation of the total range of the reformation efforts. Even doctoral dissertations, supposedly the crown of scholarship, perpetuate a biased tradition.[75] It is true that men like Ludwig Keller, C. A. Cornelius, Walther Köhler, Roland H. Bainton, George H. Williams, and many others [76] have contributed greatly to a fairer distribution of light and darkness within the total range of the Reformation, including in it the "classic" or "territorial" efforts as well as the "left wing" or the radical reformers. Many other scholars and ecumenically inclined Christians are embarrassed in our day about the bias of the reformers, particularly of Luther, and try to correct and balance the total picture.

If a clear and objective view of the total range of the reformation efforts and forces can, even in our day, not always be taken for granted, how much less was this the case when it seemed that a world order was collapsing? Our records speaking of "Luther" and "Lutheran heresy" may give Luther too much credit or blame. Some of this same credit or blame is surely due to some of his opponents. And one must remember that opponents of reformation efforts would tend to blame Luther, Karlstadt, Zwingli, and Oecolampad or the Lutherans, Sacramentarians, and Anabaptists for the same causes and effects.[77]

That Luther's influence in the Netherlands must still get the first place seems evident. Erasmus wrote to Pirkheimer on August 28, 1525, stating that "the largest part of the people of Holland, Zeeland and Flanders know the teachings of Luther." [78] This statement may have expressed more fear of what would happen than a description of the actual status at that time. Nevertheless, the University of Louvain had already studied and condemned his books by November 7, 1519. [79] Public burning of his books took place at Louvain (1519), Antwerp (1521, 1522), Gent, Utrecht, and Amersfoort (1521). [80] The well-known bibliographer, M. E. Kronenberg, has convincingly demonstrated that as far as literary output is concerned, Luther's books must have been most popular in the Low Countries during the years from 1520 until 1541. Of the total of 129 editions of Luther's writings published in the Low Countries during this time, the first 74 items were books and pamphlets in the Latin, Dutch, Danish, French, and Spanish languages. The numbers from 75 to 91 consisted of writings and letters of Luther added to writings by other authors, while the numbers from 92 to 129 were Bible editions or parts of the Bible. Most popular places of publication were Antwerp, Leiden, Deventer, and Amsterdam. Challenged by a statement that "Lutheranism was little known during the first half of the 16the century" in the Netherlands, M. E. Kronenberg presented these facts and concluded with the remark "that the size of the list will prevent future statements that Lutheranism was little known during the first half of the 16th century" in the Low Countries. [81] W. J. Kühler stated fittingly that Luther, in the fullness of time, aroused the spiritual resources in the Low Countries, established the Bible as an authority, and furnished the heroic example for others. [82]

It is regrettable that a similar study has not yet been made regarding the influence of other reformers during the first years of the Reformation. We know that Westerburg sent three thousand copies of the pamphlet dealing with the "Purgatory" to the Netherlands. [83] Thomas Müntzer's writings were also read in the Low Countries. [84] A report about the Leipzig Disputation between Eck and Karlstadt was made available through Jan Seversz in Leiden. A recent study of the relationship of Bucer to the Netherlands makes it clear that he exercised considerable influence on the early developments. His two trips to the Netherlands in 1521 and 1522 were likely not as significant as his later writings which reached the Netherlands. Hinne Rode's visit to Strassburg in 1524 about which Bucer reported in detail was also important. Through his contact with Dutch refugees in Strassburg, Rode influenced developments in the Netherlands. [85]

It has become apparent that, through the gateways of Cologne and East Friesland, Karlstadt had a considerable influence. K. Vos raised the question whether it was not possibly Karlstadt instead of Zwingli who should get the credit for having influenced Dutch Sacramentarian views. He has presented a number of reasons which need serious consideration. Vos also points out that numerous early Dutch writings show influence by Karlstadt. The books by Karlstadt must have been widely read, and were forbidden as early as 1526.[86] In a list of forbidden books compiled by the University of Louvain in 1550, all books by Karlstadt were forbidden to be read. Christiaan Sepp stated that it was hard to determine to what an extent Zwingli's writings spread during the first years of the Reformation. By 1550 they were on the list of the forbidden books.[88]

News of the Reformation spread by various means of communication. The writings of the reformers were highly significant; personal contacts were also numerous. Communications between monastic organizations and the attendance of the Dutch students at the University of Wittenberg cannot be underestimated. Contact through the shipping industry and through the business channels of the Hanseatic League helped to publicize the upheaval. Of particular importance was the harbor of Antwerp. East Friesland's influence increased as time went on.

As has already been pointed out, the influences from abroad, wherever they came from, were in no way merely echoed or duplicated in thought patterns and practices. The Low Countries produced their own Reformation which in the earliest stage is commonly known as the Sacramentarian movement. The origine of this movement has already been presented in part, and its development is to be dealt with in the next chapter.

III

THE EVANGELICAL SACRAMENTARIAN
REFORMATION

The term "Sacramentarian" originated in the Low Countries in connection with the Reformation efforts and was used by the opponents of the movement. The Amsterdam humanists used the appellations *Sacramentisten* and *Sacramentariers* in their writings against the movement as early as 1535.[1] It is likely that the designation originated before that time. The uninformed could assume that a Sacramentarian emphasized the significance of the sacraments more than this was traditionally done. The opposite is true. The Sacramentarians challenged the traditional sacramental character of the ordinances, particularly that of the eucharist to which they gave a symbolic interpretation.

This spiritualizing tendency was hardly ever limited to one of the sacraments, but by necessity had a bearing on the others. Furthermore, the "sacramentarian" or spiritualizing forces were not limited to select groups, but were at work in the total range of the Reformation. The differences in expression consisted in the degree to which the interpretation was applied in the realms of doctrines and liturgy and the tradition in general. The relaxation of views pertaining to the sacraments had an effect on other doctrines and concepts. It is, however, more appropriate to reverse the order and to state that the return to the Scriptures and a more evangelical Christianity had an effect on the view of the sacraments. In this context, the terms "evangelical" and "Sacramentarian" will be used interchangeably to describe the resulting viewpoints.[2] A brief summary of the doctrinal and historical development of the eucharist is in place.

A. FROM SACRAMENT TO SYMBOL

1. *The Catholic Tradition*

The early Christians honored the death of Christ by partaking of the blessed bread and wine within the regular evening meal eaten as a congregational fellowship meal. The sacramental part was gradually separated from the fellowship meal until it became an integral part of the Sunday morning worship. The emphasis now was one of thanksgiving for the blessed bread and wine and their significance. Thus the Lord's supper had become a eucharist, or thanksgiving. Another step in the development was the increased emphasis on the sacrifice of the Lord as not only commemorated, but gradually also repeated as a "true sacrifice" made effective through a fixed ritual in the hands of the priest presenting it on the altar and to the partakers. The parallel emphases on the uniqueness of Christ on the cross, on one hand, and the bloodless repetition of his sacrifice on the altar in the hands of the priest, on the other hand, resulted in controversies which aimed to explain this conflict. The presence and sacrifice of the Lord were explained as being either real or spiritual or symbolic. Gradually the doctrine of the actual sacrifice and real presence of the Lord in the bread and wine on the altar was accepted, and the aspects of the eucharist (thanksgiving) and the fellowship, which were so strong among the early Christians, were overshadowed or disappeared.[3]

The Fourth Lateran Council of 1215 stated, "There is one general church of the believers, outside of which no one can be saved, in which he, the same priest, Jesus Christ, is the sacrifice whose body and blood are truly present in the bread and wine in the sacrament of the altar ... after the bread has been transformed into the body and the wine into the blood through divine power."[4] The same Council made it compulsory that each Christian had to partake in the communion at least once a year. The Council of Constance made it a fixed doctrine in 1415 that laymen were not to partake of the wine.[5]

In spite of the official doctrine of transubstantiation, deviating interpretations of the meaning of the eucharist survived in some form, be it in mysticism or in such groups as the Waldenses. The Hussites represented the best known protest movement against the withholding of the wine from the laymen.[6]

The peculiar characteristic of the sacrament during the Middle Ages was that it was considered to be effective *ex opere operato,* that is, that the outward administration of the sacrament by the priest produced the intended results. This applied in the case of all sacraments. In the case of the bread and wine this meant that they were transformed into the actual body and blood of Christ but that they retained their former qualities.[7]

As the guardian of the eternal truth and the custodian of the saving

grace of God, the church thought it to be her duty to cleanse the body
of Christ of any malignant growth that might endanger its life. As a
precaution, the church of the Middle Ages, through the agency of
scholasticism, developed all aspects of salvation to minute details; the
seven sacraments became the welldefined major channels of God's grace.
Baptism became an absolute need for every infant since it constituted
the sacrament of regeneration and the washing away of original sin.
The eucharist was the spiritual medicine which removed the stain of
personally committed sin;[8] it was to be partaken of as often as possible, but at least once a year. These two sacraments were fountains of
blessing for many and stumbling blocks for others. The abuse of them
and the other sacraments by the institutionalized church and the gulli-
bility of the superstitious masses helped to make the Reformation, at
some places, erupt like a volcano. A thorough examination of the theology, practices, and tradition of the church on the basis of the Scriptures drastically altered the doctrine pertaining to the sacraments. Only
two of the sacraments or ordinances survived the revolutionary changes
of the Reformation, and even they were modified and stripped of
their meaning depending on the spiritualizing tendencies of the reformers. These two were baptism, administered in the West by sprinkling
and in the East by immersion, and the eucharist which constituted a
central part of the worship in both the West and the East.

Although Luther had at first been the most radical and boldest of
the revolutionaries, after the unintended break with Rome he became
the most conservative of the reformers on the continent in regard to
the break with tradition and the spiritualizing of the sacraments.
Others went far beyond his intentions. Whatever the degree of radicalism was, for the Catholic Church all were inspired by the same
revolutionary spirit which originated with Luther. A severance from
the church, "outside of which no one can be saved," by altering or
disregarding the church and its sacraments was unpardonable. To
abstain from the means of salvation entrusted to the one and only
church could not be tolerated nor could the modification of the sacraments. This does not mean that the church did not distinguish between
the milder and the more radical breaks. But basically they were all
traced to Wittenberg.

The sacramental character of the Lord's supper which had emerged
from a fellowship meal had been challenged before at various stages
of its development. It was different now. The church had now sanctioned the ritual and it had become one of the most significant of the

seven sacraments. The Lord's supper was repeated in every worship service and emphasized as being the main channel of man's salvation. To deny the actual presence of the Lord in the bread and wine, the transubstantiation, was equal to denouncing Christ himself and his church. The Council of Trent (1545-1563), in dealing with the Reformation challenge pertaining to the eucharist, decreed that Christ himself had given the church this sacrament and it was therefore "most certainly a completely unworthy and impious behavior when certain quarrelsome and pernicious people change [the words "this is my body"] to fictitious phrases originating in their imagination through which they deny the reality of Christ's body and blood contrary to the unanimous consensus of the church." [9] This was a mild statement compared with the decrees issued by church and state and the inquisition machinery that was set up to cleanse the church from this "heresy."

In our day when we are accustomed to hearing and seeing the major events of history on a global scale, we are inclined to underestimate the speed with which news that shook the world was broadcasted in the Middle Ages. Furthermore, we can hardly comprehend why such news would upset the world of that day. Obviously we have lost the sense of the message's vitality and significance at that time. To deny the actual and bodily presence of the Lord in the eucharist in that day could possibly be compared with a present day report that some of our towns had been invaded by living beings from another planet.

After having done away with five of the sacraments and after spiritualizing the meaning of the eucharist, there was only one more step left. That was to challenge the sacramental character of baptism. This step was first taken by Karlstadt in 1523 when he and his co-workers postponed or discontinued the baptism of infants. For the faithful and responsible Catholic this was incredible and shocking news and obviously those who were afflicted by these heretical views had to be dealt with in a most radical manner. And yet this situation had not come about suddenly for those who were or could have been informed. The road to this development had been prepared by men who meant and wished to be faithful sons of the church, particularly the representatives of Christian humanism.

2. Christian Humanism

The church had built up a sacerdotal system whereby it was believed that the clergy was endowed with special divine power to mediate between God and man. The main media through which the priest performed this service lay in the sacraments functioning *ex opere operato*. However, in the same manner that these doctrines and practices had gradually been built up and accepted, they were gradually altered through the new views and theological developments of the representatives of mysticism and Christian humanism. The desire for the miraculous and spectacular which helped to create this system made room for the desire of a more personal relationship to God through Christ and the "priesthood of all believers." The mystics, who in their daily contemplation communed with Christ spiritually, furnished the background for the modification of the sacerdotal and sacramental system of the church and the inception of the spiritualized views of the Sacramentarians.

The readers of the *Imitatio Christi* and those practicing the *Devotio Moderna* could easily develop independent views along these lines. Such an outstanding independent seeker and thinker was Wessel Gansfort, who had been trained in the school of the Brethren of the Common Life at Deventer. J. Lindeboom refers to him as the "oldest representative of biblical humanism in the Netherlands." [10] Gansfort was well acquainted with the writings of the early church fathers and the theologians of the Middle Ages. As a pupil of Geert Groote and Thomas à Kempis, and as student, teacher, and visitor at places like Cologne, Paris, Heidelberg, Rome, Florence, and Venice, he had done more than rub shoulders with the scholars and theologians of his day. He himself was a great theologian, but he took neither the vows of monasticism nor of the priesthood, likely out of a deep desire to safeguard his theological independence. Early in his career he exchanged the *via antiqua* of scholasticism for the *via moderna* of nominalism. Upon returning to the Netherlands he associated at Zwolle, Groningen, Aduart, and St. Agnietenberg with men like Rudolph Agricola, Alexander Hegius, Rudolph van Langen, and Hendrik van Rees, the abbot of the Cistercian monastery at Aduard.

Like the mystics Gansfort believed that man has a divine spark used by God to lead him on to a closer union with Christ. Showing himself to be in agreement with the *Imitation of Christ,* he emphasized the significance of regularly partaking in the eucharist, but also made provision for the spiritual communion. The *Imitation* stated: "For any devout man is able every day and every hour to draw near to Christ in spiritual communion to his soul's health and without hindrance" and "he communicateth mystically and is invisibly refreshed, as often as he devoutly calleth to mind the mystery of Christ's incarnation and passion, and is inflamed with the love of him." [11] This is what Gansfort was in harmony with when he explained the words of Christ, "Except ye eat the flesh of the Son of man and drink his blood...," as meaning that "we are to understand that it is an inward eating and drinking, that is, of the inner man..." He continued by saying, "He who thus eats already has the benefit of outward sacramental eating, just as Paul, the first hermit, and very many after him had it even without the outward sacramental eating." [12]

However, it must be pointed out that Gansfort did not deny the bodily presence of Christ in the eucharist. He stated, "I do not say that it is possible for every Christian, who so desires, to have Christ present in the eucharist, since this is given to the priests only. But I do say that Jesus Christ is present for him who contemplates over his name, and this not only in his divinity but also in his flesh and blood and his total humanity." [13] Thus Gansfort believed in the actual bodily presence of Christ in the eucharist, but also allowed for the mystical communion with him outside of the sacramental system. The most important writing of Gansfort as far as the eucharist is concerned was his book *De sacramento eucharistiae*.

M. van Rhijn has raised and studied most thoroughly the question regarding the influences which Gansfort underwent in the formation of his views along this line. He comes to the conclusion that neither the Waldensians nor the humanists could have exerted a great influence on him, but considers the possibility that Rupert van Deutz of Cologne, from whose writings Gansfort is known to have copied some notes regarding the eucharist, could have influenced him. He considers it likely that Gansfort was influenced by Johannes Tauler and Peter Dieburg. Tauler enumerated the possibilities of communicating with the Lord through sacraments. His fourth type of communication was spiritual, "without the sacrament, taken by good, pure and clean hearts, who desire the sacrament... This a good person can take a hundred times a day, wherever he is, well or sick." Tauler was inclined to place this spiritual communion above the sacramental one. [14]

Dieburg related that during a papal interdict, the Brethren of the Common Life near Hildesheim were deprived of the use of the sacra-

ments. Thus they developed a spiritual reliance on Christ that was
stronger than before. Being himself one of the Hildesheim group,
Dieburg consequently stressed the spiritual communion with Christ
without the sacramental means. Whether Gansfort was strongly influenced by Dieburg's report or not is possibly not so important as
the fact that spiritualizing tendencies were widespread at that time.
The questions and doubts about transubstantiation that had prevailed
for a long time had come to be public knowledge.[15]

It can be said that Gansfort aims to retain the traditional Catholic
concept of the eucharist including the doctrine of transubstantiation
but emphasizes in addition to it the experience of the presence of
Christ by the true believer independently of the sacrament of the
altar. With Tauler he considered the spiritual communion with Christ
on a higher level.[16]

The influence which Gansfort exerted on the rising Sacramentarian
movement was of great significance. Since his writings appeared in the
Latin language, he reached the humanists first of all, and they in turn
transmitted the message to the common people through the Latin
schools and the priests who were able to read his writings.[17] Gansfort's
interpretations of the eucharist were seized upon by Cornelis Hoen
and his followers. Stimulated by Gansfort's writings Hoen developed
his own thoughts about the eucharist which affected the reformation
efforts not only of the Netherlands, but also of Switzerland, Strassburg, and other places. But before this subject is explored, it is necessary to present the influence of the humanists along these lines, particularly that of Erasmus.

Erasmus did not meet Gansfort personally, but knew him through
his writings where he found that Gansfort had much in common with
Luther. Erasmus was also well acquainted with some friends of Gansfort, through whose contact he was stimulated in his work and thinking.[18] The severe criticism that Erasmus aired against the church's and
monasteries' abuse and misuse of doctrine and ceremony was stimulated, in part, by Gansfort, the *magister contradictionis*. Erasmus
singled out for rebuke many of the practices of the church, such as
the calling on saints, the adoration of Mary, the reliance on superstitions, and the sale of indulgences or other means to extract money. He
went so far as to say that the soldier and the monk "differ merely in
the nature of the means they use in order to bring in booty." [19]

Erasmus was also indebted to Gansfort for interpretations of purgatory and the eucharist. In his explanations of the Lord's supper,

Erasmus attempted to incorporate both orthodox and new views. He emphasized that the elements of the sacrament were symbols or signs of the death of Christ, but he carefully avoided denying the actual and bodily presence of the Lord[20] although he spoke of it as an "incomprehensible mystery" to him, "good for the theologians to argue about."[21] Erasmus used the terms "sign" and "symbol" with a very definite mysterious or sacramental connotation whereby the object of the symbol was very realistically involved. Köhler compares this relationship with the hat in the hall which is a sign that the lord of the house is at home.[22]

Erasmus continued to believe in the efficacy of the priest in administering divine grace, but he modified the traditional views of the eucharist by emphasizing strongly the commemorative and ethical element of the Lord's supper. Through the eucharist God "binds men to each other and makes them cleave in harmony to God."[23] To Noel Beda, a defender of the orthodox view, he said, "In my opinion Paul meant the same as we do, that the Lord's body is distributed as a sign of inexplicable unity between the head and the limbs, and between the limbs themselves by the breaking of the bread in which the Lord's body is hidden."[24] The eucharist is partaken of "so that the same love, with which Christ gave himself for his people, would unite us, who often partake of the same bread and of the same wine."

It is apparent that Erasmus spiritualized the meaning of the eucharist. Echoing Christ's words as found in the Gospel of John, he stated that "my flesh is of no avail, it is the spirit that creates life." He himself did not partake of the visible elements of the eucharist for long periods of time.[25] Gottfried G. Krodel has recently done extensive research regarding the concepts held by Erasmus pertaining to the eucharist. He comes to the conclusion that Erasmus cannot be classified as a symbolist, but that he represented the nonscholastic tradition of the piety of the laity.[26]

Erasmus attempted to coordinate two other aspects of his religious life – his intellectual powers and his obedience. His position is illustrated by the following incident. When Oecolampadius published a treatise in 1525 on the Lord's supper, some of his humanist and Lutheran friends were alarmed about the influences of Hoen, Karlstadt, and Zwingli noticeable in his symbolic interpretation and urged him to return to more orthodox views. The reaction of Erasmus was: "Oecolampadius' opinion would not displease me, if the consensus of the church were not opposed to it.... I do not know what the authority of the church means to others, but it means so much to me that I could agree with Arians and Pelagius, if the church sanctioned what they taught." [27] This explains why Erasmus, the Christian humanist, who spiritualized concepts and traditions of the Catholic Church and who strongly influenced the Sacramentarian views of the Netherlands and other countries, sacrificied his own views when they threatened the unity of the church. He persisted in this stand even after it was apparent that the church's unity could not be maintained nor restored. The eucharist continued to mean for him "a visible sign of a sacred object, which stands in a mysterious relationship to the object itself." [28] Erasmus' spiritualizing tendencies affecting the doctrines, ceremonies, and sacraments were the greatest stimuli which the wide range of reformatory forces received.

The influence of Erasmus on the Sacramentarian movement was in no way restricted to the Low Countries. Some of the most lively and heated discussions pertaining to the sacraments, and particularly to the eucharist, took place in Wittenberg, Zürich, Strassburg, and Marburg. The Sacramentarian movement in the Netherlands was influenced by these discussions and in turn had a bearing on them. For this reason a brief presentation of some aspects of the issues and contacts will be presented here before the developments in the Netherlands will be taken up. [29]

3.   Wittenberg and Zürich

Luther had broken the fetters of a church in bondage. Never again would a religious institution have such a grip on the souls or its members as had been the case during the Middle Ages. What the mystics for centuries had meditated over and whispered to fellow brethren in monastic cells, namely that each soul can have direct access to the throne of grace without the mediation of a church, was now preached from pulpits, at city squares and street corners, and could be read in the language of the people in many books and pamphlets. "Man is saved by faith alone" and not through the corrupted media of the church. The slogan On Christian Liberty was good news for those burdened with the yoke of the church and society. That the most precious and most lasting gift of God came to man without prerequisites on his part was the most revolutionary proclamation since Augustine. The forceful and consistent hammering of this message shook the foundation of the church more than any deviating teaching ever had.

Princes and priests, bishops and burgers, peasants and beggars accepted the message. Monastic mystics and learned humanists saw their dreams come true.

It was not surprising that such a variety of followers and enthusiasts was a cause for concern to some. The Christian humanist Erasmus spoke for many others, and not without justification nor entirely without sarcasm, when he said that the tree planted through reformation efforts was not bearing the fruit that could be expected. A "faith without works is dead," they said repeating the words of James. Some of Luther's immediate co-workers raised similar questions. They were afraid that the *sola fide* theology and practices would prevent a really penetrating reformation and a thorough cleansing of church and society. Being of this persuasion, Karlstadt and Thomas Müntzer emphasized the mystic tradition of self-denial and Christian discipleship *(Gelassenheit)*. Going beyond Erasmus and Luther, they found in both traditions, particularly in Luther's *sola fide,* the dynamite which continued to revolutionize the church. Although Luther had spoken clearly about the only source of salvation, he had been hesitant in removing the road blocks of tradition. He had given preaching and teaching a prominent place, but had left the sacraments and the ceremonies without basic alteration.

While Luther was translating the New Testament at the Wartburg in 1521, Karlstadt and his co-workers began to change and simplify the worship service at Wittenberg. Karlstadt observed communion without a robe and let the communicants take bread and wine into their own hands. He did away with the elevation of the host, advocated the elimination of the images and the organ, and introduced a simpler German liturgy. Expelled from Wittenberg after Luther's return, he put his views into practice in Orlamünde and even advocated the postponement of the baptism of infants until they would understand what was involved. In his writing *Vom Priestertum und Opfer Christi,* published in 1523, Karlstadt eliminated the concept of transubstantiation. A number of other writings followed. Gerhard Westerburg and others spread his tracts and views in the Lower Rhine area, including the Netherlands, in Switzerland, and in Strassburg.

Upon instigation by Luther, Karlstadt was expelled from Saxony in September, 1524. He went to Switzerland where he published a number of tracts (1524) dealing with the Lord's supper. They were promoted by Gerhard Westerburg and the Swiss Anabaptists-to-be. At the same time Luther wrote a booklet against all spiritualizing efforts of Karlstadt and his co-workers entitled *Wider die himmlischen Propheten*, which Karlstadt answered in *Anzeig etlicher Hauptartikel christlicher Lehre* (1525). Karlstadt now helped with the Reformation effort in Denmark, East Friesland and Schleswig Holstein. He spent the last years of his life in Switzerland as minister in Zürich (1530-1534) and as professor in Basel (1535-1541).[30] Here, in the former city of Erasmus, whom he admired and who had influenced him,[31] he died during a pestilence.

Karlstadt must have been in contact with the many students coming to Wittenberg from the Netherlands during the decisive days of the Reformation, including Hinne Rode, who brought Gansfort's writings and Hoen's Sacramentarian *Epistula christiana* along. According to Hardenberg, Karlstadt asked Luther, in the presence of Hinne Rode, to accept Hoen's view pertaining to the eucharist. Luther declined. Barge has asked whether Karlstadt might have been influenced by Hoen's *Epistula,* but gives little weight to this theory, since the arguments against the real presence are not the same.[32]

All reformers agreed that the concept of the sacrifice in the eucharist had to be removed. Such unanimity did not exist regarding the actual presence of the Lord in the bread and wine. Through Erasmus the emphasis on the symbol or sign was strengthened which, however, did not automatically indicate a purely symbolic interpretation of the eucharist. Luther spoke of symbols and signs, but they were signs filled with power. "In the case of Luther the spiritual and the physical factors are becoming more and more interwoven, the seal becomes the document and the power is in it, with it and under it."[33] All symbolic interpretations of the eucharist appeared to him as *Schwärmerei,* and thus Karlstadt, Zwingli, and the Anabaptists were lumped together under this label of extreme heresy.

Zwingli kept the spiritual and the physical factors apart. At first influenced by Luther, he later gave precedence to the views of Erasmus which is shown in his tendency to spiritualize while stating his views in orthodox terms. The true Christian could get along without the crutches of the cult and the ceremonies. The validity of the eucharist was made dependent on faith. Only believers could truly partake of the communion. Karlstadt and Hoen were the next to contribute to the development of Zwingli's views. Zwingli received Karlstadt's tracts dealing with the Lord's supper before he received the *Epistula* from Hoen. After having received one of Karlstadt's booklets which presented the tropological view of the eucharist, he stated that he liked many of the views expressed by Karlstadt, but found others unacceptable. When Zwingli read Hoen's *Epistula* after perusing Karlstadt's treatise in 1524, he boldly replaced the word *est* (is) in the words of the installation of the Lord's supper with *significat* (signifies), following Hoen. Zwingli joined with Karlstadt and Hoen in rejecting the last resemblance of a corporal presence of the Lord. Hoen compared the eucharist with the ring which a bridegroom gives to the bride, being a sign and a promise. In this ensuing struggle with the *Schwärmer*, Luther withdrew more and more to the position of the actual presence although in a somewhat modified form. Of Erasmus' *Stufenschichtung* (layers) the emphasis on faith, the real presence in a mystical form, and the stress of ethical commitment – the first and the last remained and the mystical element had been removed. Instead the Lord's supper had again become a fellowship meal in memory of the death of Christ.[34]

The foregoing account indicates that the influences of Karlstadt and Hoen were, for Zwingli, the most decisive and lasting. After the contact with Hoen's letter, Zwingli turned away from Erasmus and against Luther. The "Zwinglian" concept of the eucharist, inspired by many and molded by the one whose name it bears, became not only the accepted view of the Reformed churches, but also more or less that of most radical reformers including the Anabaptists. The latter were still on Zwingli's side in the midst of the struggle for a new concept of the church when the new view of the eucharist emerged in contact with Karlstadt and Hoen.[35]

In Switzerland the Anabaptists-to-be promoted Karlstadt's and Müntzer's views regarding the Lord's supper and in the Netherlands they emerged out of the Sacramentarian movement as congregations first observing this form of the Lord's supper. Allowance must be made for the fact that this happened previously in some Sacramentarian fellowships similarly to the more official practice established in East Friesland as early as 1527. Here a regular loaf of wheat bread was broken into pieces and given into the hands of the members of the congregation seated around a simple wooden table in the church.[36] The emerging Anabaptist movement had an active part in the struggle for the Sacramentarian or symbolic or Zwinglian view of the Lord's supper both in the Netherlands as well as in Switzerland. The Anabaptists continued to share in this view of the Lord's supper.

A combination of Zwingli's precise formulation plus his reputation as an outstanding reformer resulted in the acceptance of his view by a large part of Protestantism. And yet it must be remembered that neither Zwingli nor Hoen were the inventors of the views shaping the symbolic interpretation of the eucharist. Similar views, and particularly doubts about the transubstantiation, were common and were by no means limited to the Low Countries during the Middle Ages and the days of the Reformation. The symbolic interpretation was but an echo of the original concept attached to the Lord's supper, which had become overshadowed in an age and tradition of sacerdotalism and theological speculation supported by the hunger of the masses for miracles and magic.[37]

B. THE EVANGELICAL MOVEMENT

The impact of the Reformation movement during the first years has been related. The faith, the witness, the persecution, and the courage of those influenced by the evangelical movement is to be presented on the following pages. Emphasis will be placed on the unique characteristics of the evangelical movement of the Low Countries.

1. Faith and Witness

Among those traditionally named as the first evangelical leaders are the Dominican monk, Wouter, and Gellius Faber. The latter is supposed to have been an evangelical preacher before Martin Luther, but this notion is based on unreliable sources. Faber did not leave the priesthood of the Catholic Church before the year 1536. No evangelical preacher could have occupied the pulpit and performed the duties of a priest for that length of time in any of the parishes of the Low Countries without being apprehended.[38]

Wouter had won a number of outstanding followers in Delft by 1520. Among them were Cornelis Hoen, who has been referred to as the Sacramentarian leader, Frederik Hondebeeke, Willem Gnapheus, Johannes Sartorius, all three humanists and educators, Jan de Bakker (Pistorius), a martyr, and David Joris, one of the first Anabaptists.[39]

About Wouter and Sartorius conflicting reports prevail. They have been presented both as early Sacramentarian leaders and also as humanists teaching Hebrew, Greek, and Latin in Amsterdam where they promoted the evangelical cause. Most scholars attribute diverse characteristics as belonging to only one Wouter or one Sartorius. A study by J. F. M. Sterck has made it clear that there was, in addition to the "Lutheran" Wouter, a humanist teacher of Amsterdam named Wouter Deelen. The former has already been referred to as a Dominican monk and leader of the Delft group. He was influenced by Luther and witnessed for the gospel with such a zeal that he was given the nickname "Lutheran monk." He was a bold preacher of the "Lutheran" gospel that salvation is obtained free through Christ and not through certificates of indulgences and other "works." Under persecution he fled to Strassburg where he remained until his death.

Wouter Deelen played a significant role as humanist educator and writer and promoter of the evangelical cause. While in Amsterdam he associated with Johannes Sartorius, who also taught in that city. In the course of his religious career, Wouter Deelen was accused of Anabaptist leanings.[40]

The statements made by the first martyrs of the evangelical faith at Brussels in 1523 serve to illustrate the issues with which many of the aforenamed leaders concerned themselves. These martyrs confessed their faith under sixty-two articles. They stated that "if the sinner trusts that his sins are forgiven, they will be forgiven" and that "every Christian, who has humbled himself has been freed of punishment and guilt without certificates of indulgences." It is evident that we encounter the influences of Luther here. But when the witnesses stated that "the body of Christ is not being sacrificed but partaken in his memory," they expressed a view which was not Luther's but which was rapidly spreading in the Netherlands.[41]

Although the sale of indulgences did not play so significant a role in the Low Countries as in Central Germany, there were strong protests expressed. In addition to the above statement, the confession of Wouter, the "Lutheran monk," should be mentioned. "If forgiveness of sin can be purchased for money, how would God, the Lord of heaven and earth, have sent his only begotten son in the flesh in order to atone for our sins through his blood and his death on the cross?" he asked while preaching in Delft. Such views led him to discontinue the wearing of his monk's habit and to preach the gospel as an independent evangelist.[42]

The attack on the sale of indulgences came from many sources. "How many," exclaims a writer, "will the devil drag to hell because they depended on the certificates of indulgences instead of on the Scriptures?" This observation was made after relating the story of a monk who, with a certificate of indulgences in his hands, died and was taken to hell. He appeared to his fellow monk complaining about the circumstances. "How did it happen?" asked his compassionate friend. "Was there anything wrong with the certificate?" "The certificate was all right, but the seal of Christ was missing on it," he replied.[43]

That the common people began to criticize and attack such practices as the sale of indulgences, the adoration of saints, and the implied validity of the sacraments was the result of the penetrating influences of Luther, Erasmus, Wessel Gansfort and other reformers. Gansfort had severly criticized many of the abuses as had Erasmus and the circle of his humanist friends in the Netherlands.[44]

At this point a note of caution is in order. In presenting the development of the evangelical movement, one must beware of leaving the impression that negative forces were predominantly at work, disrupting in a revolutionary manner a more or less well-functioning system through which the individual soul received its spiritual nourishment. The criticism exerted and the changes ushered in were based on and motivated by a very positive concern originating in the reading of the newly-discovered Scriptures. They had opened the realm and availability of the grace of God through Christ to every one, and each one in this emerging fellowship of believers had direct access to the throne of God. Thus each believer could be his own and everybody else's priest in this fellowship of the priesthood of all believers. It was not necessary to have a priesthood especially set aside, nor was the church the sole distributor of the grace of God. On this basis the means of the distribution of the grace of God by the Catholic Church was questioned and attacked. The new fellowship found it sufficient to have the Scriptures and Christ in their midst in order to find forgiveness of sin, full salvation, and the challenge to follow Christ in their daily walk.

It is in this context that the focus on the eucharist as a distinguishing mark of the Sacramentarian movement must be seen. And it is for this reason appropriate to speak of the evangelical Sacramentarian movement. From the new experience and emerging concepts of the gospel, new light was shed on the total sacerdotal and sacramental system of the church, including the seven sacraments offered as channels of salvation. Many of the practices, ceremonies, and even sacraments were declared not only not helpful but even harmful, while others were altered. Five of the sacraments were soon eliminated while the meaning of baptism and the eucharist were changed. The focus was first placed on the eucharist and soon after ushering in the Anabaptist movement, on baptism.

As has already been related, an outstanding representative of the Sacramentarian views pertaining to the eucharist was Cornelis-Hoen, lawyer at the Court of Holland at the Hague, who was won for the evangelical cause by the converted Dominican monk, Wouter. Stimulated through his encounter with Wouter and the evangelical circle of Delft, he continued his search for truth in the writings of Luther, Erasmus, and Wessel Gansfort. It was Gansfort's *De sacramento eucharistiae* which led Hoen to formulate his own views pertaining to the Lord's supper in his *Epistula christiana admodum*. When Luther received the manuscript of this *Epistula* at Wittenberg in 1521, he rejected it. It was accepted by Oecolampadius in Basel, Zwingli in Zürich, and Capito in Strassburg in 1523-1524. Zwingli found in it "a pearl of great value" and published it in 1525. Interestingly enough, it was not published in the Low Countries before 1917.[45]

In view of the fact that the *Epistula christiana admodum* was not published in the Netherlands and that Hoen died in 1523, soon after he formulated his views, the influence which he exerted must have come primarily through a short period of association with others of a similar mind and possibly through the distribution of handwritten copies and the publication of this tract in Switzerland. Soon the memory of Hoen was overshadowed by Zwingli, the promoter of Sacramentarianism in Switzerland. Even in the Low Countries the Sacramentarian views became known as "Zwinglian."

Regardless of how strongly or how little the *Epistula* of Hoen influenced the Sacramentarian development in the Low Countries, its content is significant as one of the few documents of that time expressing the Sacramentarian views pertaining to the eucharist. Hoen's views went far beyond those of Gansfort and Erasmus. Faith became most important and the mystical implications of the actual corporal presence were completely removed. Well known is the parable of the symbol of the ring which the bridegroom gives to his bride as the token of an assurance of his love for her. This was Christ's intention in the Lord's supper. The "pearl of great value" which Zwingli found in this letter was the interpretation that when Christ said, "this *is* my body," he meant to say that it signified his body. Hoen went on to point out that if we insist on a literal meaning of Christ's word "this *is* my body" then we must be consistent and interpret literally all other cases, such as Christ's saying "I am the true vine" or Paul's saying "the rock was Christ."[46]

Hoen's formulation of the symbolic view of the Lord's supper was one of the bold steps which created doubt and agony for many, as will be seen, and which offered the joyous solution of problems which they had in regard to the doctrine of transubstantiation. It is, however, entirely possible that an even greater influence was exerted by the book of Johannes Sartorius (Jan Snijder) entitled *De sacra eucharistia* published in 1525. Knappert has referred to this book without stating what his sources are, where it appeared, and whether copies are extant. L. J. Rogier states that Sartorius "wrote Latin school books and spread theological tracts including subjects over justification by faith, good works, the Bible and the eucharist." [47] Kölker, in presenting the views of Alardus van Amsterdam and Cornelis Crocus, the humanistic opponents of Johannes Sartorius and Wouter Deelen, scarcely touches upon the views of the latter and their writings and does not name Sartorius' eucharist writing at all. Although J. F. M. Sterck does not mention it either, and although he avoids theological questions, he does present information that is more specific. H. F. Wijnman's contribution, too, is of a detailed nature. [48]

Johannes Sartorius (Jan Snijder), who wrote his Sacramentarian and theological treatises under the name Joannes Torsarius Aquilovicanus, was born around 1500 in Amsterdam. He was destined to belong to an outstanding circle of humanists in Amsterdam, some of whom were educators and priests. Among this group was Wouter Deelen, a fellow educator of Sartorius. A reciprocal feeling of admiration existed between Erasmus and this group. Sartorius edited Erasmus' *Adagia,* adding a Dutch translation to the three thousand sayings. But there was not complete unity within the group of humanists. Alardus van Amsterdam and Cornelis Crocus were suspicious of Sartorius' and Deelen's dual activities as writers of textbooks and as promoters of the evangelical cause. After the publication of his book dealing with the Lord's supper (1525), Sartorius "was brought to repentance through incarceration," but continued his evangelical efforts throughout his life. Some loyalty to Sartorius is indicated in Gnapheus' dedication of his comedy *Acolastus* to Sartorius in 1529. [49]

Wouter and Sartorius belonged to the strongest promoters of an evangelical Sacramentarianism and Alardus and Crocus were the guardians of traditional orthodoxy with an Erasmian touch. Alardus had met the challenge of the Sacramentarian movement already in 1523 when he published his *Ritus edendi paschalis Agni* in which he used orthodox arguments, compared the Sacramentarians with the plagues of Egypt, and issued a call to make use of the miracle-performing

Heilige Stede of Amsterdam so that the *Lutherianen-Luciferianen,* pigs and frogs might be dispersed. Woodcuts were used in this crusade. An interesting one by Jacob Cornelisz van Oostsanen portrayed the event which inspired the establishment of the *Heilige Stede* and increased the fame of Amsterdam. A woman is shown picking out of the flames the unconsumed host which had been vomited by her sick husband; angels kneel before the host in prayer. Sterck assumes that this woodcut, made in 1518, was used to counteract the Sacramentarian movement before its appearance in the book. Alardus gives support to this assumption when he complains in his book of 1523 that for four years human feelings had disappeared and there was no respect for the Apostolic tradition, ceremonies of the church, and the pronouncements of the fathers. He was making full use of his pulpit to counteract the Sacramentarian movement.[50]

Beginning in 1529, Sartorius apparently occupied himself as a private educator in Amsterdam. In this year Alardus requested that Crocus, acting as rector of one of the two Latin schools in Amsterdam, do something to stop the sectarian activities of his friend Sartorius. Accusations against Sartorius, which were not voiced until several years later, indicated that he instilled his pupils with unorthodox views. He charged the priests and monks with misleading the world; he disregarded the sacrament; and he said that he "wanted to go to the *Heilige Stede* to hear the dog bark, when the monk Cornelis of Naerden was to preach there." Crocus followed through with the request of Alardus and in 1531 published the *Epistula Croci ad Joaennem Sartorium* in which he begged his "beloved brother" to give up his *sola fide* views so that he would not become guilty of the disruption in the church. Crocus treated his colleague gently, trying to win him back to the "true" church. He pleaded that Sartorius leave those who tore the seamless garment of Christ, an act which not even the soldiers under the cross dared to do. The letter breathes the concern and spirit of Erasmus and is far from the vehement attacks of Alardus, who was a friend of Erasmus and a lifelong editor of the writings of Agricola. Some evidence shows that an answer by Sartorius must have appeared in Basel.[51]

In 1533, Wouter Deelen became the "first professor of Hebrew of Amsterdam." He would not have received this call or kept his position if he had not been strongly supported by some ruling fathers of Amsterdam. His inaugural address, given in this same year, was attended by leading educators and citizens, including Crocus.

Wouter gave daily lectures in Greek and Hebrew in the room of the chambers of rhetoric in the center of the city at the Dam. (It has been reported that Sartorius lectured in this same place, an assumption that Wijnman questions.)[52] After Wouter's inauguration lecture, Crocus had expressed his displeasure with his colleague since he had expressed himself very favorably about Luther. It was too much for Crocus when, with his pupils, he attended a public lecture of Wouter in which the latter spoke about the bread of Moses, the bread of God, and the bread of life (John 6:32-35), thereby expressing Sacramentarian views.

Efforts were made to rid Amsterdam of both Sartorius and Wouter. Then an event took place which speeded up the process. During the night of May 10, 1535, some radical Anabaptists occupied the city hall but were defeated. As a result, the reluctant authorities were forced to be more vigilant regarding all "sectarian" efforts. To top it off Wouter was accused of Anabaptist leanings. Not only must he have had contacts with the Anabaptists but also with Pieter van Montfoort of the Court of Brussels, who negotiated with the Anabaptists during the siege of Münster in order to gain some advantages from this disaster. After having triumphed over these accusations, possibly because of help from protectors, Wouter was again accused of heresies. Following his exile on January 2, 1536, Wouter became the librarian of Henry VIII and was an active member of the Dutch refugee church of London. He was able to spend some time in Emden, editing, translating, and publishing books. He died in London in 1563.[53]

After being forbidden to teach and refusing to obey the order, Sartorius was exiled on December 9, 1535. He went to Noordwijk near Leiden where he taught and was influential among the Sacramentarians of Leiden and Haarlem. Ultimately he went to Basel where he died in 1557. Sartorius published several textbooks and theological books in addition to the writing on the eucharist. He contributed a commentary on the prophets. His last book was published in Basel in 1561 and was entitled *Adagiorum Chiliades tres*.[54]

This brief summary of the activities of four Christian humanists who worked together and took different stands in their attitude toward the Reformation is selective, but characteristic for a large section of the Low Countries and could be duplicated. In Amsterdam the circle of the humanists included others such as Nicolaas Cannius who had been the secretary of Erasmus, and Pompejus Occo, who combined banking with the promotion of humanism and the collection of rare books. Another similar circle was in Alkmaar with its Latin school under the leadership of Joannes Murmellius and attended by such humanists as the famous artist, Jan van Scorel, and Alardus van Amsterdam.[55]

In summary it can be said that the circle of humanists in Amsterdam illustrates how humanists everywhere were in favor of a reformation of the church and an improvement of the cultural level. They had to decide whether their objectives could best be accomplished by joining the evangelical Reformation or by continuing to try to effect the change from within the church. The priest, Alardus, and the educator, Crocus, fortified their efforts within the church and defended their views and the church against all attempts which would lead to a break. They named in one breath Luther, Oecolampadius, Karlstadt, and Lutherans, Sacramentarians, and Anabaptists, accusing them of *sola fideism,* sacramentarian views, and the neglect of good works and the tradition of the church. Wouter and Sartorius on the other hand were strong representatives of the evangelical Sacramentarianism which was spreading rapidly during the second decade of the sixteenth century. They knew how to defend their newly won evangelical faith and did so even if they had to go into an exile instigated by their former friends and co-humanists. Their writings and influence deserve a more complete presentation than can be given here.

Of the original Delft fellowship of Sacramentarians gathered together by Wouter, the "Lutheran monk," few survived the first years of the movement. Wouter fled to Strassburg during the early years, Hoen died in 1523, Hondebeeke went into exile in 1525 and Hinne Rode in 1526. David Joris' subsequent activities will be treated later, but brief mention should be made here of Jan Janszoon de Bakker (Joannes Pistorius) and Willem Gnapheus. After his studies in Cologne, Gnapheus became rector of the Latin school at the Hague in 1520. Because of his "Lutheran" heresy he was imprisoned with Hoen. After his release he continued to write against the unsatisfactory conditions in the monasteries and sent in a petition in behalf of Jan de Bakker (Pistorius), who was imprisoned in the Hague in 1525. Again imprisoned, Gnapheus kept a record of the faith and martyrdom of Jan de Bakker which he later used in a biography. Following his second release in 1530, he fled because of renewed persecution. After having taught in Elbing, he went to Königsberg and taught until he was accused of being an Anabaptist. He now became a tutor of the sons of Countess Anna of East Friesland and became burgomaster at

Norden. He made an outstanding contribution as an educator-writer of plays and devotional books. In the latter he revealed the influence of Erasmus by stressing the shortcomings of the Catholic Church and by emphasizing the faith which finds expression in Christian love. In regard to the eucharist he shared Hoen's views. Before he fled from the Hague he had written the much-read devotional book *Een troost ende spiegel der siecken* which was not published until 1531.[56]

Jan Janszoon de Bakker (Pistorius) was born in 1499. Following his training in the school of Hinne Rode and at Louvain, he became a priest in 1522. Upon being accused of heresy, he became a traveling evangelist. When he was apprehended in 1525, he confessed that he recognized the Scriptures alone as final authority and that he believed in the priesthood of all believers. His defense of his marriage as a priest was particularly objectionable to his enemies. He was condemned to be burned at the stake as a *ketter ende heretyck*. At the occasion when he was deprived of his priesthood a monk enumerated his heretical views: The pope can neither bind nor loose; meat can be eaten on Friday; it is permissible for priests to marry; every one who has the holy spirit can administer the eucharist. Jan audibly denied some portions of the statement. When he was led to be burned at the stake on September 15, 1525, he passed by those imprisoned with him for the sake of their faith. He said to them, "I precede you," to which they replied, "We will follow you" and began to sing the *Te Deum laudamus.*[57]

2. *The Literary Stimulation*

Humanism, the schools of the Brethren of the Common Life, and now particularly the Evangelical movement influenced the reading and the production of religious literature in general and Reformation pamphlets and books in particular. The layman's discovery of the Bible was most significant. The book of books gave him the sure foundation for his faith. Although the Bible had appeared before in the Dutch language, it was during the first years of the Reformation that it, particularly the New Testament, became a popular book. The Gospel of Matthew appeared in 1522. In Antwerp during the same year, the four gospels were published by Jacob van Liesveldt while Hans van Roermonde printed the entire New Testament.[58]

Between 1522 and 1530 two complete Bibles, four editions (either portion or complete) of the Old Testament, and twenty-four editions (either portions or complete) of the New Testament were published. Many translations were based on that of Luther. Others followed the Vulgate so that complications with the censors would be avoided. The Latin New Testament edited by Erasmus was translated, and his preface, in which he admonished the reader not only to read the holy gospel of Jesus Christ but also to live it, was added to some.[59] These Bibles and New Testaments were read not only privately in homes but also in groups and fellowships which became the nucleus of the Reformation movement or of Sacramentarian influences. The discovery of the word of life and the study of the Scriptures made out of simple and uneducated laymen Bible students eager to share their source of information and Christian experience with others. Their sense of mission and the boldness of their witness grew.

This courage was also found among some of the printers and publishers who challenged the inquisitors. Hans van Roermonde published the 1526 New Testament in which the beast in Revelation has the crown of the pope on his head, and the well-known publisher Jacob van Liesveldt died the death of a martyr because he had featured the devil referred to in Matthew 4:3 with a monk's habit. For this reason, "annotations, commentaries and prefaces" were strictly forbidden.[60]

Hymns played a significant role in the spread of the evangelical faith. Some mocked the ceremonies or pointed out the general shortcomings of the church in ballad-like narratives. The rhymes were often written to be used with common folk tunes thus insuring their popularity. The beast in Revelation, the anti-Christ, or the whore of Babel were among the names freely used to describe conditions in the church.

> Ghij weet wel (hoep ick) wie ick meyne
> Die ick Syon of Babel naem..." [61]

Everybody knew whom the author had in mind, including the representatives of the church and the inquisitors.

But the critical aspect of the Sacramentarian movement was undergirded by a strong and positive faith which, too, found its expression in hymns. Some of these hymns may have been inspired by a sermon or were themselves sermons in rhyme. Others reflected the faith, courage, and martyrdom of the believers. Imprisoned and locked up in a tower the witness nevertheless saw the light rise and heard truth speak to him.

> In doots ghewelt lach ik gheuaen,
> Versoncken in Godes tooren,
> Van verre sach ick een licht opgaen
> De Waerheyt liet haer hooren...[62]

The well-known early martyr Weynken Claes (Wendelmoet Claesdochter), who was burnt at the stake in November, 1527, was memo-
rialized in a song that told of her faith, trial, courage, and suffering.
Gladly she gave an account of her faith, taking the occasion to witness
for her Lord. When sentenced to die, she willingly gave her life into
the hands of the Lord.

> De buel trat aen om worgen:
> Doen sloot sy haer oogen fijn,
> Hebbende int hert verborghen
> Een trooster, niet om sorgen,
> Verlangende thuys te zijn.[63]

David Joris, who joined the Sacramentarians in Delft under the
"Lutheran monk" Wouter and who later became an Anabaptist, published a hymnbook in 1531 which contained eight of his own hymns.
Joris had been a member of the chambers of rhetoric and was representative of the artists making use of their talents for the cause of
Sacramentarianism. His hymns were devotional, calling sinners to repentance and encouraging the believers to remain steadfast even in
persecution.[64]

The metrical Psalms were popular in the Netherlands long before
the Reformation. These Psalms or *Souterliedekens* were never placed
on the index of forbidden books, but they became so popular among
the Sacramentarians that they came into discredit in the Catholic
Church and those singing them were suspected of heresy. Nevertheless,
the singing of these Psalms attracted many to the forbidden Sacramentarian meetings. Folk melodies were frequently used to sing them. A
tolerable coupling was *Genadige Heere mijn toeverlaet* (Ps. 69) with
the folk tune *Doen Hanselijn over der heyden reedt*. Later, the Reformed Church retained the metrical Psalms in the worship but
cleansed them of the secular melodies. The Anabaptists never made
much use of either version of the Psalms.[65]

Among the devotional and Reformation books which influenced
the Sacramentarian movement, *De libertate christiana*, written by
Johann Pupper van Goch around 1472 and published by Cornelis
Grapheus in 1521, and *Summa der godliker scrifturen...* by Hendrik

van Bommel, which appeared in 1524, should be mentioned. "The foundation of Christianity is faith," said the latter. It proclaimed that baptism without faith was of no avail and that the water used in baptism was a sign of the grace of God which saves man.[66] This book used Sacramentarian terms to minimize the significance of the ceremonies and sacraments.

In 1520 Niclaes Peeters wrote *Hier beghinnen de Sermonen...*, which was followed by *Christelike Sermonen*. He stated that "Christ alone can cleanse us, if we believe in him and if we believe that his purity and unreproachable life is ours given to us as our own through his undeserved mercy."[67] He suggested a symbolic interpretation of the eucharist, emphasizing strongly that it is to remind us of the forgiveness of sins which we have in Christ. It was Peeters' view that Christ issued his salvation without consideration of the works of the saved. But those who were saved would naturally serve the Lord out of an inner compulsion.[68] Peeters criticized the Catholic practice of withholding from the laymen the communion wine, a custom he found unscriptural.[69]

Reference has been made to the chambers of rhetoric in connection with their influence on the development of the religious and cultural life of the Low Countries. J. te Winkel states that the chambers had their origin in the religious life and that they never denied their religious character, not even in the days when they were extremely critical of the church.[70]

Part of this criticism was couched in the language of drama. In 1528, when "scandalous" plays were given in various cities of Holland and Friesland, one of the plays given by one of the two chambers of Amsterdam was found so offensive that nine members were ordered to make a pilgrimage to Rome.[71] In this play dealing with the "sick city" of Amsterdam, "scriptural preaching" was ordered to leave the city. "Hypocrisy" and "tyranny" caused so much trouble that the "sick city" was near death. When the "true physician" was found at last, he diagnosed the cause of the sickness as being the rule of "false religion and tyranny," and that health would be restored as soon as the "good ministers" were permitted to return to the city.[72]

In spite of the fact that plays criticizing the church and the clergy were forbidden, they were presented constantly. Some stated that certificates of indulgence were good for rich people but not for poor sinners. Or that the priests were asking for so much money for their service while Christ gives each one his kingdom free of charge.[73]

But not all chambers of rhetoric nor all writers of plays promoted the criticism of the old and the acceptance of the new. Anna Bijns of Antwerp published a volume of plays in 1528 in which she "refuted all errors and great abuses which originated with the cursed Lutheran sect which is not only justly condemned by all doctors and universities but also by the imperial majesty." She saw herself as a great defender of the true church since "pope, cardinals and bishops seemed to be asleep." She was also very critical of the church she defended and charged that the "bishoprics were ruled by children," that not all clergymen were saints, and that the scholars paid more attention to "imagination, poetry, and philosophy" than to religion and "treated the heretics too sweetly." But there was nothing worse than the "pope of Wittenberg" and the preaching against "good works" which was inspired by sensuality. The fruit revealed the nature of the tree.[74]

3. Spread and Growth

The rapid spread of the evangelical movement and the resistance against the church authorities frequently aroused the concern of the spiritual and secular rulers who enacted drastic measures in an attempt to stop the movement. Conversely, the resulting and severe persecution of the dissenters strengthened their zeal and their missionary efforts. The fellowships and congregations in exile resulted in the establishment of the Anabaptist and Reformed churches in the Low Countries.

The evangelical movement spread through the personal witness of those touched by the message and by means of the printed word. In large cities with their international contacts through their business and shipping enterprises, in university centers, and in monastic organizations, the oral and the written witness was especially effective and produced immediate results. But even remote villages were reached sooner or later. This is illustrated in the experience of Menno Simons who had been ordained as a priest in 1524 and who then began serving in that capacity in Pingjum, Friesland. During the same year he stated that whenever he "handled the bread and wine in the Mass," it would occur to him "that they were not the flesh and blood of the Lord." First he "thought the devil was suggesting" this in order to separate him from his faith. He confessed it often and brooded over the matter; still he could not rid himself of these thoughts. The "whisperings of the devil" that tempted him to doubt the doctrine of transubstantiation were very likely simply prompted by the views spread by the Sacramentarian movement.

When Menno finally dared to examine the New Testament, which he had never touched before, he discovered that he had been deceived. His troubled conscience "was quickly relieved, even without any instruction." However, he admitted that Luther, to whose writings he now turned, helped him to grasp the concept that "human injunctions cannot bind into eternal death." [75] It is likely that Menno read Luther's *Von menschen leren tzu meyden* which was published in 1522 and which must have become popular in the Netherlands since a Dutch edition appeared by 1534. [76] At any rate, Luther and the Sacramentarian movement had, by 1526, helped Menno to accept the authority of the Scriptures and to place them above tradition.

Menno Simons recorded that he now studied the Scriptures daily, increasing his knowledge until he was considered to be an "evangelical preacher" and a "fine man" who "preached the word of God." Now, without conjecture, we know that he had access to books by *Martinus Luyter* and his *adherenten*, for the pastor and his assistant at Witmarsum, the neighboring village in which Menno was born, had these books which were confiscated by the authorities of Leeuwarden. [77]

By 1526 other "evangelical" or "Lutheran" Sacramentarian priests were preaching the gospel from their pulpits, the strength of their message depending on insights, courage, and the local situation. In February, 1529, the stadholder of Friesland reported that "secret Lutheranism" had increased considerably during the last year. [78] Some priests responded in the manner of Menno Simons. Faber, a priest at Jelsum near Leeuwarden, to whom Menno later wrote about this early development, left his parish at the same time with Menno in 1536. [79] Although Friesland was officially subject to the bishop of Utrecht, it, in reality, enjoyed great freedom. Usually the parishes could choose their pastors. The spiritual commissioners representing the bishop were concerned primarily with financial matters. Thus Friesland was quite independent from the bishopric of Utrecht at the time of the Reformation. Such independence was not the result of disinterest on the part of the authorities in Utrecht and Rome, but could be traced back to the Frisian's tradition and jealously safeguarded love of freedom. [80]

In 1524 Petrus van Thabor described the effects of Luther's Reformation; among other countries he included Friesland. He reported that many sympathized with Luther "because he proves his views so clearly through the Gospel and the Epistles of Paul ... so that many learned join him." Thabor stated that since Luther strongly opposed the church authorities, the pope, and the bishops and attacked particularly the sale of indulgences and the monastic establishments, many were leaving the monasteries. However, this desertion of the orders was not so common in Friesland.[81] Thabor added that two Friesland monks had gone to Wittenberg in 1524. J. G. de Hoop Scheffer supplements this information by naming sixteen who went from Friesland to Wittenberg to study under Karlstadt, Luther, and Melanchthon between 1522 and 1532.[82]

In the neighboring Groningen, the link between the two Frieslands which was at this time subject to Charles van Gelder, the spirit and tradition of Wessel Gansfort and the Brethren of the Common Life was still kept alive. Here Goswinus van Halen and Willem Frederiks led in a gradual reformation. They were supported by the humanists and opposed by the Dominicans under the leadership of Laurens Laurensen. Laurensen will be recognized as a spokesman at the religious discussion sponsored by Ulrich von Dornum at Oldersum, East Friesland in 1526. A similar debate took place at the Dominican monastery at Groningen. One side emphasized the oppression of heresy and the authority of the pope and the church, while the other stressed the independence of the bishops who were to be directed only by their spiritual characters, and the authority of the Scriptures. Some attempts were made to halt these reformation activities, but the area may have escaped undue severity because Laurensen, even though he became the inquisitor for the bishoprics of Utrecht and Münster did not exert his power here. The foundation for a reformation of the church was laid in Groningen by Willem Frederiks and his co-workers. Although under severe pressure the Sacramentarian movement continued in the city of Groningen and the *Ommelanden* (environs).[83]

Charles van Gelder had lost Overijssel in 1522 and Friesland in 1523, but he retained control over Gelderland and Drenthe. Gelderland's school of the Brethren at Doesburg with its sponsor, Joannes van Heussen, was the center of the promotion of reform and Christian humanism. In Harderwijk the writings of Luther were read and praised.[84] But Charles van Gelder was a staunch promoter of Catholic orthodoxy, being under the impression that the disfavor of God came over a ruling house which introduced changes in the religious heritage. He issued an edict on April 17, 1529, against all "Lutheran heresy."

Prior to this date, the evangelical Reformation had been furthered in Gelderland and other places by Gerard Geldenhauer, a significant humanist leader and the secretary of Philips of Burgundy, the bishop of Utrecht. After the death of the latter in 1524 Geldenhauer introduced considerable changes at Tiel where he served as pastor. He was in touch with the leading representatives of the evangelical movement of the Low Countries in Deventer, where he had attended the school of the Brethren, in Louvain, where he studied and associated with Erasmus, and also in Wittenberg, where he spent considerable time with Luther, Melanchthon, and Karlstadt in 1525. After his return to Tiel he instituted even more changes in the direction of the Reformation movement. However, he found that he had to cope with the problem of interpreting the differences among the three Wittenbergers; in addition he had the domestic problem of introducing the desired changes successfully. His efforts were short-lived; he seemed to find no place in the Low Countries where he could realize his ideal. He followed the route Wouter, the "Lutheran monk," had taken and went to Strassburg, continuing his influence from abroad and concluding his life work as professor of theology at the University of Marburg. But his efforts in Gelderland were not in vain. Others continued his work to the best of their abilities.[85]

Utrecht, an ancient city and bishopric with secular and spiritual authority, constituted a center of contradicting views and compromises. The two bishops during the crucial years (1517-1529), Philips of Burgundy and Henry of Bavaria, were not particularly qualified to furnish religious leadership.[86] That Philips of Burgundy had some interest in humanism and moderate changes may be deduced from the fact that he had Gerard Geldenhauer as a secretary. In spite of the fact that here in the spiritual metropolis the edict of Charles V had been made public in 1521, Hinne Rode managed to remain the rector of the Latin Hieronymus school until 1522 at which time he had to leave the city since he was a "Lutheran." Wouter, the "Lutheran monk," had been exiled from Utrecht in 1520. Among those severely criticizing the conditions of the church and the monastic organizations were Herman Gerrits, who preached Sacramentarian views in the Jacobs church, and Willem Dirks. The former fled and the latter became the first martyr of the North Netherlands when he was burned at the stake after the death penalty had been pronounced under the chairmanship of the papal inquisitor Jakob van Hoochstraten. He was pronounced guilty of depending on "grace alone" and, as a Sacramentarian, denouncing the validity of the ceremonies and the aid of saints.[87]

At this point brief mention should be made that the Sacramentarian movement of Amsterdam was not restricted to humanistic educators, such as Johannes Sartorius and Wouter Deelen, discussed previously. Even before the efforts of these two leaders became public, there were reports about "secret meetings of men and women in private homes." These fellowship groups not only helped to spread the Sacramentarian movement, but they were the nucleus of the Anabaptist movement, soon to emerge from the Sacramentarian fellowship, as well as of the later Reformed churches.

Even priests attended the gatherings and very likely made use of them to spread their deviating views in small circles. In 1524 six priests were named as promoters of the Sacramentarian movement by means of the small fellowship groups. Among these was Claes van der Elst who had been a student of Luther at Wittenberg. In this same year two women were punished for having housed such secret meetings. However, the secret associates found a protector in the sheriff, Jan Hubrechtsz, who associated with them.[88] In addition, the government representatives, all of whom were burgomasters of Amsterdam during this crucial period, were Cornelis Benninck, Pieter Colijn, and Allart Boelensz, sympathizers and promoters of the evangelical Sacramentarian views.[89] This situation explains how Sartorius and Wouter Deelen could enjoy freedom in the same Amsterdam in which Alardus and Crocus defended their faith with such zeal. However, the boldness of some of the Sacramentarian Anabaptists, who aimed to take over the rule of the city similarly to the "kingdom" at Münster, ended the period of moderate freedom very abruptly. So widespread was the Sacramentarian movement that a chronicler of 1525 reported that "in some cities the holy sacrament, the holy ointment and the ceremonies of the holy church were very dishonestly neglected" and in "some cities the priests were driven away." It must be taken into consideration that this statement was made by someone who saw the world doomed and was thus inclined to make overstatements.[90]

Fellowship groups also met north of Amsterdam, in the towns and villages along the Zaan River up to Alkmaar and Hoorn. In Hoorn the vice-*curatus,* Jan Cornelisz Winter, was apprehended and later beheaded in Utrecht on June 24, 1533.[91] In Limmen near Alkmaar twenty persons from Amsterdam, Alkmaar, and Krommenie met on June 24, 1533, to listen to a preacher from Amsterdam. Some of these participants later became identified with the Anabaptists.[92] Monnikendam, which became known as *Luiterschendam,* was the home of

Weynken Claesdochter (Wendelmoet), whose martyrdom has been related. She definitely objected to infant baptism as early as 1527.[93] Haarlem had "various meetings and secret preaching and discussions during the evenings and other times which were attended by many people." Jan Matthijs of Haarlem, the well-known Münsterite Anabaptist, was tortured in 1528 because he had blasphemed against the sacrament of the altar.[94]

Various means were used by the Sacramentarians to draw attention, to disturb, or to convey a message. They posted announcements on the door of the church, or, as happened in Leiden, they threw them into the pulpit while the priest was speaking. Even "marches" took place as well as "large meetings of many diverse people, men, and women" where the Scriptures were interpreted.[95]

Delft, like Amsterdam, was a center from which the evangelical movement spread into other cities and towns, including Rotterdam. Delft has been referred to as the meeting place of the first evangelicals led by Wouter, the "Lutheran monk." Another leader in this area was David Joris who was tortured on July 30, 1528, and exiled for three years. Joris' efforts won numerous followers, including Jan Volkertsz Trijpmaker, the first Anabaptist of the territory now comprising the Netherlands.[96]

The present-day province of Zeeland was influenced by the exiled King of Denmark, Christian II, who stayed at Middelburg from 1523 until 1525 where he had contact with the population. Among those who were strongly influenced and who consequently spread the evangelical message were the priest Adrianus Cordatus and the Augustinian Frans van Iperen. In Vere, which was also under the influence of the Lutheran court of Christian II, meetings took place attended by up to forty or fifty people.[97]

Throughout the second decade of the century of the Reformation, Flanders, and Brabant and Maestricht continued to play a very significant role, especially because of their printing presses and other channels of communication. Their influence continued in spite of very strong opposition from the government, church, and university centers of Mechelen, Brussels, and Louvain.

Antwerp, Brugge, and Gent remained centers of Lutheran and Sacramentarian activities. The seed sown at Antwerp by Jacob Praepositus and by Cornelis Grapheus was bearing fruit. Hendrik Vos and Johannes van Essen gave impetus to the movement by giving their lives for their newly won faith. All scholars agree that the printing press of Antwerp played a very significant role in the total Reformation effort of the Low Countries. But this has been demonstrated most strikingly and convincingly only in the present age with M. E. Kronenberg's report that, of the 129 editions of Luther's writings published in the Netherlands from 1520 to 1540, more than ninety had appeared first in Antwerp. If this is indicative of the total output of the Reformation literature, the impact of the printing press of Antwerp must have been most significant. Of the twenty-one publishers and printers, the following printed seven or more items: Jan van Ghelen, Mich. Hillen van Hoochstraten, Joh. Hoochstraten, Mart. de Keyser, and Jacob van Liesveldt. The largest number of writings appeared during the years 1520-1521, 1530-1531, and 1540. Of the thirty-eight editions of the Luther Bible, which were either complete or extracted, twenty-four appeared in Antwerp. Seven were printed by Jacob van Liesveldt who ultimately paid with his life.[98] Next to the Bible and devotional books by Luther, publications dealing with his "revolutionary" Christian ideas seem to have been most popular during the first years that the echo from Wittenberg reached the Low Countries. *Tractatus de libertate christiana,* published by Mich. Hillen van Hoochstraten, appeared in Antwerp three times in 1520-1521 (Nrs. 5, 6, 8), once in Zwolle (Nr. 7), once in a Dutch translation (Nr. 61), and once in a French translation (Nr. 91). *De Captivitate Babylonica ecclesiae* was published during the first years in Latin as well as in a Dutch translation (Nrs. 2, 30).[99]

Lutheranism probably had a better chance of putting its roots into the soil of Flanders, side by side with Sacramentarianism, than it did in the North. Radical reformers flourished for some time in Flanders.[100] In Brussels fellowships grew into small congregations which met in homes. By 1524, Kortrijk had cells of Lutheran fellowships. Brugge established a Lutheran congregation in 1527.[101] But retaliation and punishment accompanied the growth of the movement. On July 25, 1521, in the presence of Emperor Charles V, the king of Denmark, government representatives, and a large crowd of people, the burning of a large quantity of Luther's writings took place in Gent and similarly in Antwerp. In 1526, three distributors of Luther's books were banned for fifty years. During the year of 1527 alone, some sixty persons were apprehended. In this same year Hector van Drommele became the first martyr of Brugge. Numerous other persons died martyrs' deaths including William Tyndale, the well-known translator of the English Bible.[102]

In this connection it should be stated that a final history of the early evangelical movement of the Southern Netherlands has not been written. It is possible that the early movement had a little more of a Lutheran tint than was the case in the Northern Netherlands, but to present it as a thoroughly Lutheran movement would not be entirely accurate. That Sacramentarian notions were also found in the South is apparent in the case of the martyrs Hendrik Vos, Johannes van Essen, and others.[103] The Anabaptism of the South and North of the Low Countries was rooted deeply in the soil of the Sacramentarian movement. If the soil of the Southern Netherlands would have been considerably different, it would be difficult to explain the similarity between the Anabaptism of the South and North of the Low Countries.

The basic elements of the early evangelical movement of the Low Countries were derived from the Scriptures which were discovered locally through Christian humanism influenced by the Brethren and stimulated and challenged internationally by the Lutheran movement and its related channels. It was, however, a more radical reformation in its break with tradition, its spiritualizing of the meaning of the sacraments, and its emphasis on the ethical.

The beginning and spread of the evangelical Sacramentarian movement in the Low Countries has been presented. What remains to be covered is the opposition of the total movement encountered by the church and the local secular and imperial authorities. This will be done in a selective way up to the beginning of the Anabaptist movement in 1530.

4. Inquisition by Church and State

The church had always had the problem of dealing with delinquent members, dissenters, and heretics. What originally had been a concern of the brotherhood became a matter dealt with by a legal machinery for the enforcement of which the state lent a hand. Heretics were exiled or put to death. In extreme cases wars were waged against them as was the case with the Albigenses and the Waldenses. During the Middle Ages a special department, the inquisition, was created by the pope to deal with heresy.

During the Reformation there were four legal authorities to deal with matters of heresy: the bishop, the pope, the emperor, and the local courts. Of the first two, the papal authority was stronger during the Middle Ages. But the third, the imperial inquisition, took over the initiative under Charles V during his attempt to cope with the schism created through the Reformation.[104] His use of the local courts in the Low Countries really constituted a compromise on his part. Similarly, at times he gave the pope the satisfaction of making it appear as if he were still the head of the church in matters of disciplinary questions.

During the papal inquisition the Dominicans were usually in charge, as they were in the Low Countries during the beginning of the 16th century. The inquisition machinery and the laws in accordance with which it operated had been worked out in great detail during centuries of combating heresies in old and new forms. What constituted a heresy? Once it had been detected, what was the proper procedure in dealing with it? Methods of trial, torture to extract confessions, information about other heretics, codes of penalties applied for offences, death penalties, burial, and many other questions had to be worked out in detail. Prerequisites for the functionaries, their relationship to each other and to their duties had to be decided.[105]

In the development of the administration of the persecution of the heretics of the evangelicals, the ambitions and policies of Emperor Charles V were decisive. His determination to fortify and strengthen his political power by preventing the split within the Catholic Church played a significant role. When it became apparent that this was impossible since kings and dukes were taking the side of Luther and were banding themselves together in an effort to protect and promote the Reformation, his chief concern became to check the spread of the disruptive influences within and beyond his empire. Burgundy had been linked to the Habsburg monarchy at the time of his birth. When Charles became emperor in 1519 in the midst of the religious struggle, his aunt Margaret of Austria (Savoy) became the ruler of Burgundy (1519-1530). It became his plan to absorb as much of the Low Countries as possible into a unified district of the monarchy in order that he might strengthen his European position. If he failed to achieve his goal to prevent the religious disruption in central Europe, perhaps he could establish a stronghold in the Low Countries. These considerations made him change the pattern of the inquisition tactics of the past centuries. His own supervision of the inquisition, instead of the pope's, was to serve his political ambitions.

When Luther nailed his ninety-five theses to the door of the church at Wittenberg, the signal for a reformation of the church was given.

But during Luther's stand at the Reichstag of Worms, the signal for the division of the church was given. Charles V issued the Edict of Worms, May 26, 1521, through which Luther and those adhering to his views, as well as his books, were condemned. Hieronymus Aleander was the right hand of Charles V in executing the edict he had written.[106] It was at this point that Charles V decided to strengthen his own position by appointing, on April 23, 1523, Frans van der Hulst, a layman and member of the council of Brabant, general inquisitor of the Netherlands, to supplement the existing inquisition offices of the pope, the bishops, and the local courts. Hulst received assistance in the person of Joost Laurens, member of the great council of Mechelen, and in some professors of the University of Louvain. The Edict of Worms was at once enforced in the Low Countries and resulted in the first casualties of persecution and some strong opposition to the new arm of inquisition.[107]

Considering Frans van der Hulst unfit for his office, Margaret of Austria, the regent of the Low Countries, deprived him of his office and suggested three candidates from whom the pope was to choose one. Oliver Buedens, Nicolaas Houzeau, and Nicolaas Coppin were appointed general inquisitors, and numerous provincial inquisitors functioned as assistants to them. Erardus van der Marck, bishop of Luik, was named, but not accepted, as general inquisitor. The model of the Spanish inquisition was followed: The candidates for the office of the general inquisitor were presented to the pope for approval, but the secular high court of Mechelen, subject to the regent and the emperor, made the decision in each case of heresy presented. The pope appointed the general inquisitor, but the numerous assistants in the provinces were appointed by the emperor, who gave them legal instructions to be carried out. Gradually the emperor extended his jurisdiction beyond the territory inherited by him to the northern provinces, but this development belongs to a later period.[108]

The opposition which Frans van der Hulst had faced, and which caused his replacement, had come from the local courts which were accustomed to taking care of all legal matters. The edicts dealing with heresy were now imperial edicts, and all matters pertaining to heresy were consequently dealt with by the imperial courts. This was considered an infringement on the rights and freedom of the provinces and led to a compromise solution of cooperation between local and imperial courts.[109]

The Edict of Worms, enforced in the Low Countries in 1522, declared it illegal to sell, buy, or read the books of Luther. As a result the printing, sale, and reading of the Reformation books went down after 1522 as indicated in the report about the book market of Antwerp. Books by Luther were publicly burned at many places in the presence of large crowds and dignitaries of secular and spiritual status. Indexes of forbidden books were issued from time to time, constantly adding new names to the list of writers and books. Details concerning the censorship of books were prescribed. Particularly dangerous were considered the commentaries to the epistles and gospels, be they from the pulpit, in public, or in print. All foreign books had to be approved by the provincial council.[110]

An Edict of July 17, 1526, repeated many of the forbidden items and added that it was illegal to discuss heresies from the pulpit. No doubt this practice had aroused the curiosity of the listeners and produced unintended results. The purely technical application of the law pertaining to illegal books was handled by local courts. Punishment usually consisted of exile and confiscation of property. The Edict of October 14, 1529, made provision for the death penalty in cases of possession of heretical books and took such matters out of the hands of the local courts, transferring them to a newly created Commissariate Concerning Lutheran Heresy, which was modified again in 1531. In reality, the local courts handled cases of heresy, including capital punishment, throughout the first years. As a rule, they were assisted by theologically trained priests or monks.[111]

The locally exiled Sacramentarians became the messengers in other areas unless they chose to remain underground. Many went abroad to places like Emden, London, Strassburg, Basel, and neighboring places where they fellowshipped with like-minded converts and became the nucleus of congregations. Those found guilty of grave heresy and unable to escape were usually burned at the stake on market squares as a spectacle for many. (The aspects of trial, imprisonment, torture, and the death penalty will be dealt with later). Castles now serving as museums had prisons in those days. Those at Antwerp, Brussels, and The Hague, contain in vivid and real form the record of man's attempt to eradicate faith, convictions, and ideas of dissenters considered dangerous to society and church.

Even more complicated were the legal procedures in the area of the Free Imperial City of Cologne which was the see of the archbishop, who administered a secular and ecclesiastical court. Rivalry and feuds about the authority in daily matters between the Free City and the archbishop took place in the combat of heresy. The edicts of the emperor were announced and enforced. Test cases were the trials of Adolf Clarenbach, P. Fliesteden, and Johann Kloprys. They were apprehended by the ecclesiastical inquisition arm of the bishop. Claiming the right to a preliminary examination of Clarenbach, the court of the Free City of Cologne held him in custody. After long feuds between the two authorities, they agreed that Clarenbach be burned at the stake with Fliesteden.[112]

By 1530 the evangelical movement had spread into a number of cities in Westphalia. Münster was also undergoing a change on the social and religious level as has been pointed out before. The opposition of the bishop Franz von Waldeck was not very strong. By 1532 the city became evangelical in spite of the bishop's threat that he would enforce the imperial edicts. The efforts of Charles V were ignored.[113] Influenced by humanism and the *Devotio Moderna* of the Low Countries, including the Sacramentarian preaching of Bernhard Rothmann and the Wassenberg *predikanten,* Münster had developed a brand of evangelicalism of its own. The introduction of a radical Anabaptism changed the situation completely not only for Münster and Westphalia but also for other parts of Europe and particularly for the peaceful Anabaptists. They were all treated alike – as criminals and heretics.

Different was the situation in East Friesland where Edzard II ruled. Freer from the enclave of the empire of Charles V and under the strong influence of various Reformation efforts ranging all the way from Luther to Karlstadt and from Melchior Hofmann to the Sacramentarian movement of the Low Countries, no imperial edict or mandate of foreign origin was enforced here during Edzard's reign. This was indeed the haven of the exiles and the launching base for spiritual conquests of the movements soon to be known in this area and the Low Countries as Anabaptist and the Reformed Church. Melchior Hofmann was the father of Northern Anabaptism which started in Emden, East Friesland.

IV

MELCHIOR HOFMANN: A PROPHETIC LAYMAN

The early evangelical or Sacramentarian movement took root deeply in the soil of the Low Countries which had been well prepared by the Brethren of the Common Life and Erasmian humanism. Stimulated by influences from Wittenberg, the evangelical movement went beyond Luther in the break with Rome, partly through the influence of men like Karlstadt. However, because the influence of the Strassburg and Swiss reformers was not so strong during the first decade of the Reformation, and because of the prominence of Luther, all inquisition efforts, even in the Low Countries, seemed to concentrate on Martin Luther during the first years. He was given the credit, or the blame, for whatever transpired here and there. Luther was hated and despised by the Catholics, admired and worshiped by his followers, and scorned and mistrusted by the radical reformers and the disappointed humanists. Among the many who were disillusioned about Luther, one was predestined to play a significant role in the further development of the Sacramentarian movement. This was the furrier Melchior Hofmann who had become an ardent follower of Luther and a zealous evangelist. Dissatisfied, however, he turned against Luther in a manner similar to Karlstadt. For both, Luther did not go far enough in his return to the Scriptures and in his break with tradition.

There were some differences between the two. Karlstadt was an intellectual and theologian who, in a Tolstoyan manner aimed to identify himself with the peasants and laymen while Hofmann had these (for Karlstadt desirable) prerequisites by birth and background. To some extent they were the cause of his problems and disillusionment, as will be seen later. Although Karlstadt advocated the postponement of the baptism of children, for which belief his wife and child were expelled from the Wittenberg territory, he did not initiate believers' baptism nor did he join the Anabaptists of Strassburg, Zürich, and Basel when he resided next to them. Preparing the soil

for a more radical reformation, Karlstadt and Hofmann labored together in East Friesland, but it was Hofmann alone who, five years
after the beginning of Anabaptism in Switzerland, carried through
Karlstadt's principles and the spiritualization of all sacraments in the
North. He joined the Anabaptists in the capital of the Reformation
refugees and the radical Strassburg reformers and hastened to carry
this message to Emden in 1530. In a radical application of these
views to the concept of baptism, he initiated a movement in the North
which swiftly spread through all the centers of the Sacramentarian
fellowships from Emden to Antwerp. Now he accepted the distinguishing mark of the "consistent" Sacramentarians, that of believers' baptism, which gave him the name "Anabaptist" on the official records.

To remove five of the sacraments and alter two substantially would
have been enough to increase the persecution and to stigmatize the
movement. In this area such steps were more drastic than labelling
the movement "Lutheran." The geographical distance from the Wittenberg reformer was too great and furthermore, Luther did not recognize these as his legitimate children. In addition Hofmann emphasized the commonly accepted eschatological expectations. These views
were soon perverted by some of his followers and got out of control.
After his imprisonment in Strassburg, there occurred some disastrous
developments in Münster, Amsterdam, Bolsward, and other places.
Radical attempts to establish the "kingdom of God" by force gave
the Sacramentarian Anabaptist movement a stigma and a loss in popularity from which it never recuperated. The authorities opposing any
form of reformation took full advantage of the situation in order to
stamp out heresy by force. Force met force – one was victorious and the
other was defeated. The authorities received the halo of righteousness
and the radical reformers the stigma of heresy. In order to understand
the background of this development, it will be necessary to present
some highlights from the spiritual pilgrimage of Hofmann.

A. FROM WITTENBERG TO STRASSBURG

1. Luther's Messenger

Melchior Hofmann was born at Schwäbisch Hall in South Germany where he learned the trade of a furrier. About his education and
early contacts with the Lutheran message little is known, but it is
accurately reported that he discovered the gospel with the help of

Luther. Whether his trade or the desire to preach his new-found gospel carried him to Wolmar in Livonia is not known, but in 1523 he was to be found preaching in that city. There he "suffered persecution" and was expelled by the Teutonic Order ruling the country.[1] He continued his evangelical mission in Dorpat where he also suffered persecution not only from the opposing Catholics but because he was a "simple person and a stranger," even from those who claimed to be evangelical. When social unrest, dissatisfaction with the bishop, and the evangelical preaching against the misuse of images led to an iconoclastic outburst of the populace, Hofmann's social status came to his aid. Only his popularity among the common people prevented his arrest. Still dissatisfied, however, the theologically trained clergy requested from the layman, Hofmann, a statement of approval by Luther. Hofmann went to Wittenberg and returned proudly with the desired document in his hands. Luther admonished the Livonians to a peace and a tolerance that would allow for differences in Christian practices. Not only had Luther and Bugenhagen listened with interest to Hofmann's report about the spread of the gospel in the Baltic and written letters to the churches of Livonia expressing their confidence in Hofmann, but they also included his writing in the collection of their letters which was published in 1525. This first writing of Hofmann is a valuable source of information about his early thinking.

Late in 1525 Hofmann returned to Livonia, but the problems he confronted were not all removed by the letters written by the highest authorities of the Reformation. The differences in background, training, and personality between Hofmann and the other Lutheran pastors presented too great a gap to bridge. Not only did Hofmann not use enough tact in dealing with the others, but he also antagonized them with an increasing emphasis on the second coming of the Lord. Furthermore, the tendency to spiritualize the sacraments and the ceremonies displeased his Lutheran colleagues. Sylvester Tegtmeyer, in particular, turned into a temperamental opponent of Hofmann. In the fall of 1525 Hofmann left for Reval, also in Livonia, where his troubles started all over again. Tolerated as a "servant of the sick" he found some work but was suspected of heresy. When he had to leave Livonia, he was disgusted with the conditions because the "second devil was worse than the first," but his faith in Luther was not yet shaken.

2. Under Kings and Dukes

Early in 1526 Hofmann became the minister of a German Lutheran church at Stockholm and wrote his exposition of the twelfth
chapter of Daniel and his *Formaninghe*, the latter in response to Tegtmeyer's writing. Basically Hofmann was still adhering to Luther's doctrinal views regarding justification and even predestination. In addition he presented such terms of mysticism as the *vergötterte Mensch*
and *Gelassenheit*. The latter could indicate the influence of Karlstadt.
In regard to the Lord's supper he also combined early views of Luther
with those of Karlstadt. "Whoever does not have faith should not
approach this sign and should beware of it like death." The ministers
were to be regarded as the shepherds of the flock and not the lords.
Each member was to contribute his share to the kingdom of God.

The uncertainty of the outcome of the Reformation efforts did not
make the presence of the fiery preacher of repentance desirable. Hofmann moved again and went to Lübeck where he arrived in 1527
with wife and son.[2] Here his stay was brief. Since the city had not
yet introduced the Reformation officially, the imperial edicts were
being enforced. "The regents of Lübeck were after his neck, blood,
body and life but God helped the furrier." In Schleswig Holstein, at
that time a part of Denmark, he found a field of labor, for just prior
to his arrival an edict of tolerance had been issued.

But once more, he longed to go to Wittenberg, this time possibly
not so much so that he could learn, but with the intention of presenting a prophetic message. In May, 1527, he proceeded to Wittenberg,
stopping at Magdeburg to see Nicolas Amsdorf who not only showed
no interest in his newly acquired insights, but treated him roughly and
sent him away. Amsdorf's farewell was a three-page warning against
the "false prophet, liar, and devil." From this "inflated spirit," Hofmann now went to Luther. His reception in Wittenberg was not much
better. When he tried to impress the reformers with his symbolic scriptural interpretation, the "little worm was considered a big sinner and
dreamer, and he was mistreated, blasphemed, and despised!" Nevertheless in his response to the brochure by Amsdorf he treated him
"with all love."[3]

After Hofmann's return to Schleswig Holstein, he made a favorable impression on King Frederick I who granted him permission to
preach in the whole country and assigned him to the *Nicolaikirche* at
Kiel. Emphasizing the need to make use of all of the Scriptures, he

still gave obvious preference to an allegorical interpretation and the eschatological writings. Little inclined to do the daily tasks of a pastor in quietness, Hofmann freely attacked conditions and persons in the pose of an Old Testament prophet. This shortened his stay at Kiel. Wilhelm Pravest, with whom Hofmann shared the work, speeded up his downfall. He wrote Luther inquiring about the soundness of Hofmann's doctrines to which Luther now gave a negative answer. Pravest, whose teaching had a strong Catholic leaning, misused the information from Luther. Luther had only cautioned the disregard of ceremonies, but Pravest used Luther's admonition to stop the reformation efforts in Kiel. As soon as Luther heard about it, Pravest's turn came and he retired hastily to a monastery.

What brought the *Königlicher Würden gesetzter Prediger zu Kiel im Lande Holstein,* the title proudly displayed on each title of Hofmann's booklets and pamphlets, into disfavor and led to the final break with Hofmann's Lutheran sponsors in Wittenberg and Schleswig Holstein was not only his eschatological views, his allegorical interpretation of the Scriptures, his sharp criticism as a preacher of repentance, and his inconsiderate rash actions, but above all his unorthodox view on the Lord's supper. This became apparent after the publication of his booklet entitled *Inhalt und bekenntnisse vom Sacrament und testamente des leibes und blutes Jesu Christi* (1528). Although no copy has been preserved to inform us about the content, the storm that spontaneously resulted is sufficient evidence that this was the crucial matter. That Hofmann requested help from Karlstadt to defend his views at the ensuing Flensburg disputation dealing with the Lord's supper also indicates that he had moved closer to the symbolic interpretation.[4] When Christian, Frederick's son and ruler of Schleswig Holstein and the sponsor of the disputation, requested permission from Luther for Amsdorf to defend the Lutheran cause, he appointed Bugenhagen, who was in Hamburg instead. Such a move indicates that all considered it a major issue. Karlstadt followed the invitation of Hofmann to help him, but received no permission to be present.

The day before the disputation Hofmann submitted a book by Luther, dealing with the eucharist to Duke Christian in which he found his own views "clearly and brightly written that the bread of the Lord is partaken in as a seal and sign." These were his last efforts to prove his true and genuine Lutheran views. That very evening Christian invited him to go over some of the points to be discussed and gave him a fair warning about the possible outcome of the disputation. Hofmann's response was: "If there will be just and fair judgment, nothing evil can happen to me, and if God should permit that force is used against me, then you can take from me the garment of flesh but on the day of judgment Christ will give me a new garment." When Christian asked "Melchior, if you dare to speak like this to me, how do you speak to the people?" he responded, "If all emperors, kings, princes, popes, bishops, and cardinals should be together in one place, truth shall and must, nevertheless, be confessed to the glory of God; may my Lord and God grant me this." [5] Although he had gained neither the confidence of Luther nor of the Lutherans, he still seemed to have the courage of the former.

The following day, April 8, 1529, the disputation took place in a monastery at Flensburg. King Frederick may have been in the area at that time but likely did not attend the meeting. Hofmann was met on his way to the monastery by Duke Christian and Bugenhagen, the latter making insinuating remarks about Hofmann's companions and his deviating view regarding the Lord's supper. Bugenhagen chaired the meeting. The hall was filled by some four hundred theologians, noblemen, citizens, as well as followers of Hofmann. Many had to stay outside.

After the opening by Bugenhagen, Hofmann was asked why he had used such harsh words as *Seelmörder* in regard to the ministers, to which his answer was that they were claiming to present Christ in a piece of bread. He stated that Christ had given the sacrament and the promise, the seal to be received with the mouth and the promise with the heart. After this his opponent Hermanus Tast presented in detail the Lutheran view of the transubstantiation and the actual presence of the Lord in the eucharist. A long discussion followed in which Johannes Campanus, Jacob Hegge, and Jacobus van Dantzig participated on Hofmann's side. The following day all four were informed that they had to leave Holstein. Hofmann complained later that he had been expelled with wife and child, his house plundered, and an estate of 100 guilders in books and printing equipment taken. Since he was no more under the protection of the king, he barely escaped, but God "saved him from the hands of the murderers and tyrants." [6] Luther, Amsdorf, and Bugenhagen had contributed to the fact that a zealous layman-preacher was not only lost for their cause, but also expelled from a country where a king had granted him asylum.

Barge assumes that Karlstadt, although not permitted to be present at the disputation at Flensburg, was in Kiel at that time and that he and Hofmann left Holstein together. Karlstadt blamed Bugenhagen for his expulsion while the latter asserted that it was merely an answer to his prayer: "Expel, O Lord, those who have offended Thee." In any event, Hofmann and Karlstadt were drawn together as expellees for the same cause, and Karlstadt probably helped Hofmann with his report about the Flensburg disputation.[7] It is likely that the two had met before in Wittenberg in 1527 and that they were acquainted with each other's writings. Now they went together to East Friesland, the haven of Sacramentarian refugees. Karlstadt found many open doors and preached from many pulpits; some places, however, were closed to him. He wrote from here to Philip of Hesse and offered to attend the approaching Marburg discussion dealing with such crucial questions as the divisive eucharist. If Luther would approve of it, it would be all right with him, was Philip's response. Karlstadt knew that seeking Luther's approval was futile, for Luther was trying hard to get him out of East Friesland and to win it to his side.[8]

The two refugees had arrived in East Friesland late in April or early in May, 1529. They were guests of Ulrich von Dornum at Oldersum, where von Dornum often sheltered religious refugees in his castle. Hofmann worked on his *Dialogus*, a report about the Flensburg disputation. There were some indications that he appeared in public as Karlstadt did and exerted some influence, but for some reason he hastened to Strassburg, possibly to have some books printed. He arrived there before June 30. The following year two books appeared, one of them dedicated to Ulrich von Dornum, his host and protector.[9] In any event, the reason for his departure was not lack of hospitality in East Friesland.

Karlstadt enjoyed the hospitality of various leading and ruling families. According to a report he even started farming.[10] But his stay was also not long enough to reap what he sowed on the Frisian fields or in their hearts. Because the new policy of Count Enno I favored a stronger Lutheran emphasis, Karlstadt preferred to go to a place with a more cosmopolitan atmosphere, a place where he could not be reached by those embittered by the fact that he had found shelter and a place of labor. Early in 1530 he left East Friesland and found open hearts and homes in Strassburg. The family von Dornum kept his memory alive, however, by giving a descendant the name Andreas.[11] As will be shown later, Karlstadt's general influence in East Friesland continued and was stronger than he had realized.[12]

3.   Strassburg: Haven of Dissenters

"Strassburg, with its creaking timber bridge, the only one across the Rhine, was a crossroads city of politics as it was of commerce and religion." Strassburg had become a prosperous urban republic with a constitution prepared by the noblemen and guildsmen who were responsible to the emperor alone. It belonged to those free cities which were ready for a reformation when it came and had the distinction which also characterized East Friesland and has been expressed in the words: "He who would be hanged anywhere else is simply driven from Strassburg by flogging." For this reason the city became, from the beginning of the Reformation, the international haven of dissenters, where religious discussions were mild and exile and imprisonment were the severest form of punishment.[13]

The first reformation efforts at Strassburg go back to Matheus Zell, who came to the city in 1518 and soon introduced some changes under the influence of the Reformation. When Martin Bucer and Wolfgang Capito arrived in 1523, they found a fertile soil for their moderate reformation views. A more radical representative was Clement Ziegler, a layman, spiritually related to Karlstadt, who promoted a removal of all "idolatry" of the Middle Ages. He favored a spiritualization of the meaning of the eucharist, baptism, and other practices and ceremonies and, with the peasants, social justice. When Karlstadt came here for the first time in October, 1524, he found supporters of his views and a very attentive audience among the radical reformers. However, he failed to contact Capito and Bucer, the former who, in particular, had been an admirer of Karlstadt. After a four-day stay, during which he successfully promoted a spiritualization campaign of the sacramental system, he departed. Following his departure, Capito wrote a booklet about the split between Luther and Karlstadt, trying to bridge the gap.[14]

When Hofmann arrived in Strassburg in June, 1529, he found there representatives of all shades of the radical Reformation who had come from all directions to the "city of hope" and the "refuge of righteousness" so that it was easy for him to find attachment and a following. However, by this time Strassburg had developed a pattern of its own and was by no means a free-for-all as was evidenced by Karlstadt's brief stay and the many who had been urged gently but firmly to move on. To those that had come, of whom many had soon gone on, belonged Wouter, the "Lutheran monk," and Gerard Geldenhauer of the Netherlands, Balthasar Hubmaier, Martin Cellarius, Wilhelm Reublin, Jacob Kautz, Ludwig Haetzer, Hans Denck, Jacob Gross, Michael Sattler, Pilgram Marbeck, Johann Bünderlin, Caspar Schwenckfeld, Christian Entfelder, and Sebastian Franck. These and other Anabaptists and spiritual reformers were or had been in Strassburg when Hofmann arrived there for the first time. He found indeed a great variety of radical reformers or those representing their views all the way from the somewhat exclusive Swiss Brethren to the extreme spiritualists such as Hans Denck and Sebastian Franck. Among them Hofmann found those who listened to him and those from whom he learned and was inspired to realize his visions.[15]

Hofmann and his family found shelter in the home of Andreas Klaiber, whose wife cared for them and later joined the Anabaptists. Soon he must have called on Bucer, giving him a progress report about the Reformation in Livonia, Holstein, and East Friesland as well as delivering a letter to him written by Karlstadt who was soon to follow. Hofmann must have made a good impression on Bucer who introduced him to his co-workers and also to Schwenckfeld who was a guest in the home of Capito that time.[16] However, Hofmann's first concern, in which he was successful, dealt with the publication of a number of writings.

In Balthasar Beck, whose stepdaughter was the wife of Sebastian Franck, he found a faithful printer and supporter in spite of warnings from the city council. Soon after Hofmann's arrival, his report about the discussion at Flensburg which he and Karlstadt had prepared in East Friesland in the form of a dialogue between Apolitus and Erhart appeared, giving some valuable information about the life of the author and the issues discussed dealing with the Lord's supper. Barely had Hofmann's *Dialogus* appeared when Bugenhagen's "official" two hundred-page report was published, notarized, and signed by the six secretaries. Hofmann never responded to this writing in which he is named *Lügenesel, Lügenschreiber,* and similar "flatteries" of that day. The symbolic interpretation of the Lord's supper was no longer so crucial an issue, either in Strassburg or in East Friesland where he was soon to return.[17]

In Hofmann's *Leuchter des alten Testaments* (1529), he explained symbolically the chandelier of Exodus 25:31-40, interpreting it in the light of the book of Revelation. In rapid sucession he published four booklets devoted entirely to the interpretation of the prophetic and eschatological parts of the Scriptures, all appearing in 1530. The most detailed and best known is his *Ausslegung der heimlichen offen-barung Joannis* which he had been planning and working on for a number of years. Whereas his *Leuchter* . . . was dedicated to his host in East Friesland, Ulrich von Dornum, this one was offered with compliments to Frederick of Denmark, who protected him for two years in his domain. In an interpretation that was concerned with the spirit, not with the letter of the Scriptures, Hofmann asserted that the Lord had chosen Frederick to be one of the two kings mentioned in Revelation, chapter 12, who would protect the spiritual Jerusalem. He belonged to the faithful servants of the Lord who help the pious and are willing to do everything to the glory of God. The role that Luther was assigned was not so flattering since he "has become a new God who condemns and saves." The word, "the first shall be the last," would be applied to him. This book presented Hofmann's eschatolo-gical views in which he interpreted figures and time symbolically, assigning roles to contemporaries as fundamentalist preachers did in the days of Hitler and Stalin.

Among the four writings was one containing seventy-seven visions of Ursula Jost which she had received between 1524 and 1529. The last visions were of an eschatological nature, and Hofmann was con-vinced that God spoke through her as his *Liebhaberin.*[18]

4. A Champion of Anabaptism

Even though the writing of the booklets and pamphlets took most of Hofmann's time during his stay in Strassburg, he must also have witnessed for his faith and ideas in fellowship meetings and in public. Unfortunately, there are very few sources dealing with this significant phase of his life and thus the identity of the people with whom he associated and the circumstances under which he joined the Anabap-tists are uncertain. Even the extent of his association with Karlstadt during this time is unknown. The latter came to Strassburg highly re-commended by Ulrich von Dornum and found shelter in the home of Bucer. First hailed by some as a great supporter of the true refor-mation and later attacked by others as the perverter of the same, his position soon became dubious. On May 9, 1530, the magistrate sug-gested that Karlstadt proceed "to Basel or Zürich where he would be safe." Glad to be rid of this potent force which added to the multiplici-ty of efforts to reform the city of Strassburg, Bucer and Capito recom-mended him highly to Zwingli as he had been recommended to them.

Capito wrote Zwingli that he had great pity for Karlstadt "particularly because of the godless attitude of the Lutherans, who invent the worst deeds of shame against him at the expense of humaneness not to speak of faith, about which they brag so much." [19] Even Strassburg could not keep Karlstadt because of Luther's influence. Although Karlstadt had some linguistic problems in Zürich and Basel, he found a spiritual home and an atmosphere which was free from the pressure of Wittenberg.

Hofmann was influenced by Schwenckfeld during his stay in Strassburg. The latter claimed that Hofmann and Sebastian Franck had "taken their errors from our truth like spiders who suck poison out of a beautiful flower." [20] Franck, and especially Hans Denck, could also have exerted some influence on Hofmann. Clement Ziegler, Strassburg's lay evangelist, should have appealed to Hofmann. If any of the three leading Strassburg Anabaptists, Wilhelm Reublin, Jacob Kautz, and Pilgram Marbeck, influenced Hofmann, it would most likely have been Marbeck. Hans Frisch stated that the Anabaptists of Strassburg were divided into three groups – the followers of Hofmann, of Kautz, and of Reublin – and that the views of the first two were somewhat related. There is no question but that Hofmann was strongly influenced by the various Anabaptist leaders, but it is equally true that he maintained his independence even after he had joined the movement. He left behind a *hoffmännisch* group in Strassburg which continued to exert considerable influence.[21]

The unusual dramatic act through which Hofmann identified himself with the Anabaptists was, as far as the records are concerned, not his submission to baptism, but his petition to the city council in behalf of the Anabaptists that a church be made available to them for public worship. Before he took this bold step he must have realized that he had more in common with the Anabaptists than with the official representatives of the Strassburg reformation. It is true he had no problem regarding the Lord's supper as had been the case in the Lutheran territories. He must, however, have noticed that he was not taken seriously by the officials in regard to his interpretation of the Scriptures. What likely appealed to him most about the Anabaptists were their views pertaining to the covenant or the fellowship of believers and their dedicated Christian life and witness.

Even Capito and Bucer as well as Zwingli in Zürich had originally sympathized with the Anabaptist views, including those regarding baptism. No wonder Hofmann was attracted by them. At last the wandering evangelist had found what he had been searching for. But by now the period of sympathy for the Anabaptists had run its course for Bucer, and he had also drawn the wavering Capito into his orbit. Now that the Anabaptists had separated themselves from the total reformation effort by criticizing its program and effect and by introducing a "second" baptism, they were treated as heretics and tolerated only as objects of a missionary effort on the part of the magisterial reformers in order to win them back to the church. To have someone who was not accepted by the official reformers request that the Anabaptists be granted the privilege of public worship in a church to be graciously made available to them must have struck Bucer and some members of the city council like a thunderbolt out of the clear sky. After all, the Anabaptists had been forbidden through an edict since July, 1527.

On April 23, 1530, the council decided that Hofmann had gone too far. To support their charges they stated that Hofmann had compared the emperor with the dragon in his interpretation of Revelation. Luther and others had done more than that! Hofmann and his printer were to be tried and punished, but when the search for Hofmann was undertaken, he had disappeared, and his printers, Balthasar Beck and Christian Egenolf, knew nothing about him or his wife. Egenolf removed himself to Frankfurt where he printed among others the writings of Sebastian Franck.[22]

Hofmann's escape occurred a few weeks before Karlstadt was asked to leave the city of Strassburg. Unlike Hofmann, Karlstadt's departure did not have to take place during the night, and he went with recommendations from the reformers of the city. In his letter to Zwingli Capito stated that in "doctrines he will agree with you. A hard educator has trained him – the frequent sad experiences." [23] Hofmann went without any recommendation either from the official Strassburg reformers or the Anabaptists. He went as a prophet sent only by God. Before he returned to Strassburg to bear the consequences of life imprisonment, he became an apostle to the North. On his short mission he transplanted the Anabaptism of the South to the North.

B. THE ANABAPTIST APOSTLE TO THE NORTH

1. *The Sacramentarian Background*

It has been pointed out that East Friesland had become the refuge of Sacramentarianism protected by Edzard II and sheltered by Ulrich von Dornum and those under his influence. For Lutheranism spreading rapidly through all of northern Germany and Scandinavia this seemed intolerable and a threat. In 1528 Bugenhagen warned the council of Bremen against the *Sakramentschänder,* that is the Sacramentarians.[24] As a result of this attack the latter published their *Summa* during the same year, attempting to prove that they were neither despising the word of God nor the sacraments. The *Summa* was written by Georgius Aportanus for the ministers of East Friesland and centers around the symbolic views of the sacrament with a strong emphasis on the exclusive mediation of salvation through Christ. The spiritualizing tendency reveals not only the influence of the sacramentarian views of the Low Countries, but also Karlstadt's and foreshadows, and possibly even implies, the extension of the view from its application to the Lord's supper to that of baptism.[25]

Count Enno had no deeply rooted religious conviction, but was sensitive to the pressure of his Lutheran neighbors and feared that he might fall prey to the emperor's policy. He contacted Philip of Hesse at Speyer in 1529. In a letter dated March 25, 1530, he reported to him about the religious conditions and asked for advice. He stated that there was disagreement among the ministers regarding the true meaning of the Lord's supper, baptism, the outward word, the incarnation of Christ, and the power of the Holy Spirit. The Lord's supper was considered to be an outward sign which some thought could be observed even outside of the church. The views along this line seem to have been rather extreme in some instances. That the spiritualizing tendency had affected the view of baptism seems to be evident, for he stated that it was being preached that "it is no sacrament" or that one should receive it at the age of thirty-three and that there were some children five years old who had not yet been baptized. Others maintained that baptism should be discarded altogether. Similarly radical views were being expressed about Christ and the Holy Spirit. It can be assumed that Enno was somewhat generous in describing the radical views of his preachers in order to justify the fact that he had expelled some by the time he wrote the letter.

The fact that in 1530 some children were unbaptized at the age of five has led some historians to assume that Anabaptism had penetrated East Friesland before Melchior Hofmann started baptizing in 1530. This is not necessarily the case. This only proves how well the soil had been prepared for the introduction of adult or believers' baptism by some spiritualizing sacramentarian views. The fact that some pro-

posed to remove the Lord's supper from the church and to observe it
as a fellowship meal and that others wanted to have baptism discarded
also suggests a strong influence of Karlstadt. An indirect influence by
Sebastian Franck may also have taken place. Later he was in touch
with his sympathizers of this area. It is in this light that E. Beninga's
report that the Anabaptist movement started in East Friesland before
Hofmann's appearance must be seen.[26] It must be assumed that the
radical sacramentarian views and the rumors about the spread of Anabaptism everywhere else foreshadowed their appearance in East Friesland and have confused the historians about the exact date of origin
unless some Anabaptists of the Rhine area actually had come to this
country before Hofmann began to baptize in 1530.

2. The Great Commission

What was the situation when Melchior Hofmann came and introduced adult baptism? It is apparent that East Friesland was the haven
of extremists and that Enno inherited grave problems from his tolerant father. Hamelmann has claimed that Melchior Rink, who had
been involved in the Peasant's War, introduced adult baptism in
East Friesland. No other sources support this claim, and modern scholars dismiss it as unreliable.[27] Beninga has reported that in 1528 "the
sect of Anabaptists originated in East Friesland." The Counts Enno and
Johann did publish the Edict of Speyer on January 19, 1530, before
Melchior Hofmann started baptizing in Emden, which stated that "all
whether of spiritual or secular status" if they were "contaminated by
the sect of Anabaptism" had to leave the country.[28]

The denominational bias of the Lutheran and Reformed writers has
clouded the sky of objective historiography. This makes it at times difficult to sift truth and fact from propaganda. The Lutherans, like Hamelmann, blamed the Sacramentarian movement, from which the
Reformed church emerged, for harboring and tolerating the refugee
Schwärmer of Wittenberg such as Karlstadt, Hofmann, and Rink.[29]
In the tradition of Luther they were all not only labeled as *Schwärmer*,
but also as *Wiedertäufer* (Anabaptists) regardless of whether they
were merely spiritualizing the meaning of baptism, advocating a postponement, or whether they actually had reached the point of introducing believers' baptism whereby those were rebaptized who had
been baptized as infants. Thus statements that some children had not
been baptized since 1525 or that Anabaptism was introduced into

East Friesland in 1528 may merely mean that the spiritualizing views were considered a threat and therefore given the Wittenberg label "Anabaptist." The proclamation of the Speyer Edict before adult baptism was actually introduced must also be seen in this light. The proclamation of such an edict could have been inspired by Catholic as well as Lutheran neighbors and actually be a matter of foreign policy and not an indication that Anabaptists were found in any large number in East Friesland. The lack of concrete information about persons and facts regarding the introduction and practice of believers' baptism prior to the appearance of Melchior Hofmann leads us to state that these views were held but not practiced before 1530.

Under the influence of the Lutherans, Enno had accepted a new church constitution prepared in Bremen. This he presented on January 13, 1530, to his ministers who found it unacceptable. Among other questions the sacramental character of baptism and the Lord's supper were emphasized. "We request that the young children do not remain unbaptized nor that the sacrament of baptism is neglected. The ministers must be admonished that it is necessary for every Christian to receive baptism since we are all born into one in Christ-believing church in accordance with the apostle who said: One faith, one baptism, and one Lord." [30]

Enno had become a tool in the hands of Luther and his co-workers of Bremen and Hamburg in an attempt to restore the sacramental character of the church. Of particular concern to the Lutherans was the negligence with which baptism was treated. It would seem that this was really not the time for Hofmann to appear with his newly-won insights in this matter. For example, Karlstadt, as well as other radical ministers, had to leave as reported by Enno to Philip of Hesse in his letter dated March 25. The protest to the new policies by the ministers, Ulrich von Dornum, and Philip of Hesse, however, had an influence on Enno. In addition, on March 6 Enno married Anna of Oldenburg and soon thereafter began preparation for war. The hostilities started in June and lasted a number of years. Religious questions could not receive much attention. The strong Lutheran influence had been stopped. Such a change in events explains the acceptance of Hofmann by many and his success in introducing Anabaptism in Emden and East Friesland in general. [31]

What were the views which Hofmann preached and which appealed to a large number of people and some ministers who shared with him a sacramentarian background? We have no better source of information than his *Ordonnantie Godts* which appeared soon after his arrival in 1530. Unless he brought the manuscript along from Strassburg, he must have found time during his busy schedule to write the best organized theological treatise he ever wrote. It can be assumed that he spent some time with Ulrich von Dornum who was still corresponding with Karlstadt. Perhaps it was during his stay at von Dornum's estate that he wrote his *Ordonnantie*. However, specific information is lacking. He must also have found someone to translate the *Ordonnantie* from the German into the East Frisian language (*Oostersch*). The *Ordonnantie* contains the challenge of the great commission (Matt. 28:18-20) in the light of the Anabaptist views which Hofmann had accepted in Strassburg. In a clear and concise manner and supported by numerous scriptural references, it deals with the essence and the calling of the church of Christ. The great commission goes out from Christ to whom "all power is given" and who even in our day sends out his messengers to unite those in darkness with Christ, the bridegroom, through repentance and the symbol of baptism. Thus those reborn join the church of Christ in the covenant of baptism. The communion is compared with the ring given to the bride by the bridegroom as presented by Hoen. In this close fellowship between the bridegroom and the bride or Christ and the church, discipleship and discipline are practiced. If the member of the covenant does not live up to his promise he is removed as a tree that does not bring forth fruit. A faith that does not bring forth fruit does not justify the sinner. Only in passing does Hofmann speak of the true understanding of the Scriptures by the use of "the key of David". The split hoofs and the horns which are being used by the true Apostolic heralds are his favored phrases in regard to the true understanding and interpretation of the Scriptures. He closes the book with fitting quotations from the gospels.[32]

3. *The Sign of the Covenant*

If this *Ordonnantie* constitutes the essence of the message presented by Hofmann at the time when he inaugurated believers' baptism in Emden, and there is no reason to doubt it, it is not surprising that he found a good hearing. Even the most striking part of it, baptism upon confession of faith, is not emphasized very strongly.

In addition to his having published a popular document, Hofmann was apparently a very gifted public speaker. Enno is supposed to have called him to his castle where Hofmann, through his testimony, moved him to tears. Ministers must have opened churches to him, for there is the report that, in a spontaneous performance, he baptized some three hundred persons in the *Geerkammer* of the *Grosse Kirche* at Emden. This report certainly has a fantastic quality in view of the experiences of such radical reformers at other places, but even if some allowance is made for exaggeration, there remains the fact that numerous sources verify this account of the birth of Anabaptism in the North.[33]

The *Geerkamer* of the *Grosse Kirche* was the vestry which was a room adjacent to the south side of the church near the pulpit. Although the room had been removed, the connecting door was still visible in the wall prior to the destruction of the church during World War II. It is likely that this room was used because it had a container (*Kufe*) with water. That the church was used for the initiation of adult baptism could indicate that Hofmann repeatedly preached in the sanctuary expounding his views as expressed in his writings, particularly in the *Ordonnantie*.

To publicly challenge traditional views regarding the sacraments, including baptism, was nothing new in East Friesland where some children, because of their elders' religious convictions, were growing up without having been baptized. The ministers representing Lutheran views would naturally not have been present nor have cooperated.

The crucial point in a service was reached when Hofmann, in a dramatic way, climaxed his preaching by calling on those who were ready and willing to seal their faith in Jesus Christ by becoming *Bundgenossen* (fellows of the covenant) in his church. He asked such to proceed to the adjacent *Geerkamer* in order to be baptized upon the confession of their personal faith. The response was overwhelming, whether the event occurred only once or at different times. Obbe Philips is one source who states that Hofmann baptized "burgher and peasant, lord and servant in the church at Emden numbering three hundred.[34]

Thus far Wittenberg and the Sacramentarian movement of the Low Countries, the latter supported by Karlstadt and Hofmann, were competing in trying to shape the course of the Reformation of East Friesland. This event in the *Grosse Kirche* was the beginning of a new force in the Reformation in the North which spread rapidly, particularly in the Low Countries. To the endless controversy over the sacrament of the eucharist between the Lutherans and Zwinglians or Sacramentarians in Northwestern Europe was now added the sacrament of baptism which had been a matter of disturbance and persecution in central Germany and Switzerland since 1525.

Although all shades of Protestantism had their roots in the general sweeping Reformation of the 16th century, whether Lutherans, Zwinglians, or Calvinists, all agreed that those who applied the spiritualizing principle to the sacrament of baptism by making a personal faith a prerequisite before its administration placed themselves beyond the pale of Christendom and were punishable by death. There are many factors involved, no doubt, the strongest, however, was the notion of *ex opere operato* whereby the sacrament of baptism automatically regenerates the infant and makes a Christian of him while without it he remains the possession of the devil. To what an extent such notions are innate in human nature, or can be traced to heathen cults, or were due to systematic cultivation in the church of the Middle Ages may be hard to determine and is of little significance. More significant is the fact that this notion is still deeply rooted even in the most secularized Protestantism of our day. Karl Barth, the leader of a group of theologians who challenges the tradition of infant baptism in our day, stated recently that it was a sort of "petrified magic" and that there is "hardly another such deep-seated practice and tradition." One can be a "bad heretic regarding the trinity," demythologize, existentialize, or deny the resurrection of Christ, but it is different with infant baptism, says Barth. It simply "is there mightier than the wall of Berlin and the Cathedral of Cologne or whatever you please. It is a part of the landscape. It takes a heroism to free one's self from it in thought or even to place a question mark behind it." [35]

When these questions were raised nearly 450 years ago, and some answers were found which were as biblically based as the Reformation itself, all of Christendom went up in arms to exterminate the "prodigal" son it had raised. As had been the case with the early Christians, it was declared that Anabaptism was a threat to the church, society, and government. It would constitute an extremely interesting study to show how, to this day, otherwise objective scholarship still uses these criteria and evaluations, often subconsciously. In his otherwise fairly objective description of events, Kochs states that those opposing Hofmann "not only warned from the pulpit but... also went to the government, since not only the church but also the state was endangered." [36] At this point there was no immediate danger in the preaching of Melchior Hofmann as far as state and church were concerned unless uniformity of religious thought and practice are considered to be prerequisites and it is assumed that state and church have to enforce them.

Once again the sources pertaining to the work of the Anabaptist "apostle to the North" and the immediate results and the spread of his message in East Friesland and the Low Countries are extremely scarce and those available are colored by various biases. Most of the information about his activities as an Anabaptist leader was obtained during his imprisonment in Strassburg. It is certain that the most significant and lasting contribution Hofmann made was the transplanting of Anabaptism from Strassburg to the Low Countries. His influence among the Anabaptists of the South remained limited.

Sources of Lutheran origin that tell of the impact of Hofmann's message in East Friesland claim that Hofmann and his followers practically dominated the religious situation immediately after the introduction of believers' baptism. The underlying tendency is to demonstrate that the predominant Reformed Church emerging from the Sacramentarianism of East Friesland harbored and favored views which led to the introduction of Anabaptism while the Lutherans, if they had been in the same position, would never have tolerated such a situation. It is obvious that there is some truth in such a claim, but the significant question here is to what an extent the intention to demonstrate this truth colored the information about the strength and spread of the Anabaptists. The Reformed writers, on the other hand, try to minimize similarities between the Reformed movement and the Anabaptists and their common Sacramentarian background. These sources emphasize the importation of Anabaptism as a foreign element through refugees, who had participated in the Peasants' Revolt, and Melchior Hofmann, a former Lutheran evangelist.[37] To top it all off, one of the chief sources used is the *Confession* of Obbe Philips, a chief promoter of Anabaptism, who defected later and "confessed" his errors in having promoted such "abomination." This very important source is somewhat colored and slanted by his later views. It will be presented later. In this maze of misleading and scattered sign-posts, the contemporary historian must find his way and appraise the meaning of the information and the lack of it.[38]

We must conclude that the activities of Melchior Hofmann during his short visit in East Friesland were an unusual success. This was due to the fact that the soil for his message had been better prepared than anywhere else and that Hofmann possessed an earnest and sincere character and eloquently and convincingly presented his message pertaining to the ordinances of God and his coming kingdom. Soon, however, the introduction of adult baptism and the establishment of the new covenant caused a split among his followers and sympathizers. This occurrence induced his opponents to call on the arm of the government for help. After all, Anabaptism had been declared illegal before it was introduced on such a large scale. It is possible that at this time Hofmann again found a temporary shelter under the protection of Ulrich von Dornum.

Hofmann had foreseen that many of his followers would be persecuted. Persecution seemed to be an extension of his doctrines concerning baptism and the eucharist. For Hofmann baptism was the sign of the betrothal of the believer to the heavenly bridegroom, and the Lord's supper was the marriage feast in which bread and wine symbolized the ring.[39] In living the Christian life as *Bundgenossen* or members of the body of Christ and witnesses of the Lord, those he baptized would have to face the wilderness, persecution, and martyrdom unless the Lord hastened with his second coming to usher in his kingdom. Since the latter did not seem to be part of the Lord's design, the peaceful followers of Hofmann either became wanderers in the wilderness or gave their lives as a testimony for their Lord.

Among the many whom Hofmann had baptized and who now were to live precariously were numerous Dutch Sacramentarian refugees. Jan Volckertsz Trypmaker, who was baptized by Hofmann on November 15, 1530, became well known. After Hofmann's departure, he continued the work in Emden. After he, too, had to leave Emden late in 1530, he gathered Sacramentarians in Amsterdam.[40] Among the women baptized by Hofmann in Emden was Trijn Jans of Monnikendam who was drowned on May 15, 1534. Further evidence that Hofmann's work was continued after his departure is found in the fact that Sicke Freerks was baptized in Emden two weeks before Christmas, 1530, after Hofmann, and likely also Trypmaker, had left.[41]

When the persecution of the Anabaptists in East Friesland began, some of those who had come here as Sacramentarian refugees returned to their homes in the Low Countries as Melchiorite messengers. They found fertile soil, as had Hofmann in East Friesland. Outstanding among those joining the Anabaptists was Menno Simons, who was a priest in the village of Pingjum, Friesland. He had previously come to hold Sacramentarian views. Sicke Freerk's martyrdom led him ultimately to the decisive step of rejecting infant baptism and assuming the leadership of the Anabaptist movement. He accepted Hofmann's

views expressed in the *Ordinance of God* that the Christian must reck-
on with patience and suffering.[42]

The Münsterites, on the other hand, attempted to realize their
eschatological views by trying to usher in the "City of God" if need
be, by force. Hofmann himself never expected this to be done through
„human" force, but by divine intervention in accordance with the
eschatological books of the Bible.

Hofmann's stay in East Friesland was short, as it had been everywhere else. No doubt the situation created through the founding of
the church of the *Bundgenossen* and the resulting pressure exercised
on both Hofmann and Trypmaker had something to do with their
hasty departures from East Friesland. One report, which goes back to
Obbe Philips, states that Hofmann was „driven" to Strassburg by the
"prophecy of an old man" in order to deliberately face imprisonment.
This report, which has not failed to appear in most of the writings
dealing with Hofmann, gives the impression that Hofmann felt that
by such a procedure he could become God's chosen instrument and
fulfill his mission over the entire world. There are reasons to believe
that this event, whatever the facts were, was overemphasized by Obbe
Philips as well as by those who repeated it.[43]

It is not likely that Hofmann proceeded directly to Strassburg as
has been assumed by F. O. zur Linden and others.[44] In December, 1537,
while in prison in Strassburg, Hofmann enumerated all the countries
in which he had preached. He had also preached "in passing through
the Netherlands" before returning to Strassburg.[45] It is true that Hofmann was always "passing through" wherever he labored, but his
activities in the Netherlands may have been of a longer duration than
has commonly been assumed. In an account about the religious situation of Amsterdam called the *Luthereye ende anabaptistereye,* there
is a report "that in the year 1531 there [came] someone named Melchior the furrier, who spoke publicly and initiated the sect of the Anabaptists and baptized Jan Volckertsz with fifty other persons..."[46]
There is no reason to question the fact that Hofmann spent some time
during 1531 in Amsterdam even though the report that Jan Volckertsz
was baptized in Amsterdam is erroneous. If Hofmann was the one who
initiated believers' baptism in Amsterdam, he could have spent some
time after his departure from Emden in East Friesland with Ulrich
von Dornum as previously suggested, or in the Netherlands before he
joined Jan Volckertsz in Amsterdam where the latter had won a group
of sympathizers among the Sacramentarians. In any event, it is likely

most accurate to consider both Hofmann and Jan Trypmaker as founders of the Amsterdam Melchiorite-Anabaptist fellowship.

Hofmann's preaching and baptizing after 1530 was not restricted
to Amsterdam. J. Reitsma has reported that Hofmann "spent some
time around 1532" in Friesland without mentioning the sources of
information.[47] Nevertheless, there are indications that he must have
been in Leeuwarden and other places and that he was not only remembered by his followers but also by the authorities. Even on February
23, 1534, the stadholder Schenck van Toutenburg issued an edict
against a list of Anabaptist leaders topped by "Melchior *Pelser* [fur-
rier], alias Hooftman," who were not to be sheltered and for whom
an award was offered for apprehending them.[48] By this time Hofmann
was already imprisoned for life in Strassburg.

The name of Obbe Philips appeared on the same list. There is a
likelihood that Obbe and Dirk Philips and others of the Leeuwarden
Sacramentarian group met in 1532 with Hofmann. Later Obbe Philips
wrote that he was in close touch with Hofmann and received information "from his own disciples who would daily come and go for him
at Strassburg, and who were my [Obbe's] companions and fellow
brothers. He continues by saying: "We also received his letters every
day."[49] This is an indication of the deep impression Hofmann made on
his followers in the Netherlands, how they looked for his guidance, and
how some risked their lives to get a message from his prison in Strassburg in order to take it home and share it with the brethren and fellow
covenanters. It will become apparent how significant Bucer considered
this influence and contact.

However, the actual physical presence of Hofmann in the Netherlands must have been limited. If this were not the case, the official
records and those whom he had baptized would mention him more
often. His influence continued after the initial personal contact in
Emden, Amsterdam, and other places primarily through his writings
and some limited personal contact while in prison in Strassburg.

Hofmann had now completed his mission as a Lutheran apostle of
the Baltic and an Anabaptist apostle of the North. In his role as an
Elijah to help usher in the city of God, the dream of the ages, he was
as always, too impatient and somewhat too sure of himself. He was a
very gifted Christian layman who achieved much and would perhaps
have made a much greater contribution if he could have exercised
more self-discipline.

4. In the City Chosen by God

Between Hofmann's visit of Amsterdam in 1531 and of Leeuwarden in Friesland, the Netherlands, in 1532, he returned to Strassburg. On December 11, 1531, the city council decided that he was to be "apprehended, if found, and put into the tower" since he "had returned and had published a book and committed other improprieties." The offensive book that he had just published dealt with an explanation that the devil was not confined to hell and death because God planned it that way, but because this was the result of his own will.[50] Hofmann's concealment was apparently so good that neither his own visions about his future role in the fate of the city nor the police of Strassburg were able to satisfy the council's wishes. In the beginning of the year 1532 he published a book explaining his unique view of the incarnation of Christ, containing also the 26th vision of Ursula Jost[51] and a "Joyous Witness Concerning the True, Peaceful, and Eternal Gospel." This writing, which contrasted the free gospel with the one that was based on the view of predestination, was presented by Hofmann to the synod of Strassburg in 1533.[52]

As indicated above, Hofmann had resumed his contact with the prophetess Ursula Jost; he associated, too, with her husband, Lienhart, also a prophet. He continued to be influenced by and to publish the visions of Ursula Jost. In the fall of 1532, a second edition of a previously published edition appeared.[53] The records do not mention him in Strassburg again until May 10, 1533. The interval between could be the time that he was out on another mission, which would have included Leeuwarden in the province of Friesland and possibly another visit in East Friesland. Later when Bucer sent his book against Hofmann to Philip of Hesse he wrote a note stating that since "you have heard him I am sending you this admonition."[54] If Hofmann managed to make himself heard by Philip of Hesse on his missionary journey, that would indicate that he had not lost any of his boldness and great plans of a world mission. In addition, it made Bucer go out of his way to have Philip of Hesse hear also the other side of the story. All this makes us wonder what else Hofmann managed to pack into the short time that was left to him for his public work which has remained unrecorded.

In the spring of 1533 Hofmann was back in Strassburg writing and publishing books, one dealing with baptism and the other the "sword" or the government.[55] He submitted the latter to the city council during the first week of May, requesting a public discussion or hearing. He was staying at the home of Valentin Duft, a goldsmith, where he also conducted meetings. Soon after Hofmann contacted the city council, the police came to get him and he had his first hearing on May 20.[56] According to Obbe Philips, being apprehended by the authorities was for him like a dream coming true: "He thanked God that the hour had come and threw his hat from his head and took a knife and cut off his hose at the ankle, threw his shoes away and extended his hand with the fingers to heaven and swore by the living God ... that he would take no food and enjoy no drink other than bread and water until the time that he could point out with his hand and outstretched fingers the One who had sent him." [57] Granting that Obbe was some-what oratorical in this description, it probably expressed Hofmann's feeling in general when he received an opportunity to witness before the Strassburg members of the council and the clergy.

If Hofmann rejoiced because he had at last been taken seriously and was to be given an opportunity to witness in a hearing, the church and the city council were also pleased to have an opportunity to line him up with others to be heard as dissenters. The complex cloud of radical witnesses that were present in Strassburg at this time, their complaints and testimonies in smaller and larger sessions, and the intention of the magisterial reformers to put the spiritual house in order after "the long-standing and impious clemency" has been excellently presented in a recent monumental study by G. H. Williams.[58] Here we can deal only with some aspects of the total.

The thought of such an all-inclusive campaign was mentioned by the Strassburg ministers, beginning already in February 1531, by sug-gesting to the city council various means to counteract laxity in reli-gious matters and to combat radical tendencies of the "sects." Various steps were taken, but the need for a more general and unified action remained. The same matters were again stressed in November of the same year. Among the seven items to be dealt with, one was the ques-tion of how to cope with the "sects." [59] All this led gradually to an ex-tended synodical session in June, 1533. Prior to this meeting, hearings of Anabaptists and lesser synodical and smaller ecclesiastical meetings took place. The *Landes* or territorial synod took place from June 10 to 14 and was followed by smaller meetings of the magistrate and the clergy which formulated the decisions resulting from the synod. The synod had been prepared by a commission appointed by the city council consisting of ministers and lay wardens (*Kirchenpfleger*) who prepared articles of faith, a church constitution, and an agenda for the meeting. The proposed sixteen articles of faith dealt with internal stabilization of the church and with the "heretical" views of the various radical reformers and refugees of Strassburg. Among them were Schwenckfeld, representatives of the various shades of Anabaptism, including Hofmann and his followers, and even Anthony Engelbrecht, one of the Strassburg ministers.[60]

For Hofmann the result of the synodical session was life imprisonment. With a few interruptions, he spent the rest of his days in Strassburg, crying over the city as Christ did over Jerusalem or as the prophets of old had over a wayward Israel. He persevered in this attitude with a consistent love and devotion and an unshakeable conviction which were unique. Ten years of confinement, during which most of the time he was served bread and water through a hole in the ceiling and his occasional visitors tried to win and influence him to accept their point of view, did not break his spirit nor change his point of view. He can be counted among the bravest martyrs of the sixteenth century. Others in Bucer's school of training surrendered or left the city, but not so Hofmann. He loved this city chosen by God and was willing to give his life for it and for his convictions, which he considered the Lord's sacred trust. If freed and given an opportunity to leave the city, he would likely have come back again because God had chosen this city and him, Melchior Hofmann, to play a significant role in the drama that would usher in the heavenly kingdom and make all earthly kingdoms obsolete.

5. The Trial of the Prophet

Hofmann's first hearing was conducted by two members of the city council on May 20, 1533. He stated that he had preached the word of God for ten years, and a few years ago he had come to Strassburg for the same purpose. He reported that he had returned nine weeks ago and was staying at the home of Valentin Duft, where he instructed those who came to him, emphasizing obedience to the government. He questioned whether the local preachers preached the word of God correctly and expressed his desire to be heard by them. Fearlessly he had come to witness to the truth and was willing to give his life for the cause. Three weeks before he had sent a book *Von dem Schwert* (Sword) and a letter to the preachers. He concluded by saying that he was no prophet but a witness of the highest God. On the basis of this interview the council decided that his books were to be evaluated by the ministers and the *Kirchenpfleger*, that Hofmann was to be given a hearing at the synod, and that his confinement was to be continued in the tower.[61]

However, on May 29 he was exposed to another hearing by three different members of the council who opened the meeting by pressing the question whether he still thought that the "gospel and the true word of God were not being preached" at Strassburg, which he affirmed. This was and remained the crucial question and bone of contention, not only in the case of Hofmann but in general, which determined the outcome of the hearing. Hofmann said that the *predikanten* (ministers) of Strassburg had no right to claim to be apostles since the latter possessed no property and had been willing to travel and proclaim the will of God wherever he called them to do so. Among the other questions raised which remained crucial were Hofmann's peculiar view of the incarnation of Christ, his emphasis on free will versus predestination, and his interpretation of the unpardonable sin. Hofmann stressed his obedience by informing the council members that although he had come to Strassburg to give an account of his faith, he had not preached publicly, but had given instruction only to those who desired it. However, on holidays when too many would come, he would go on a walk in order to avoid the accusation that he was causing insurrection. If he, Hofmann, were to be harmed, it would be done without any justification, for "he has the neck and the lords have the sword." [62]

At the synod taking place June 10 to 14, the articles of faith were presented and discussed first, after which the hearing of the "sectarians" followed. This latter procedure took the major part of the meeting. The accused appeared in the following order: Clement Ziegler, Martin Stör (Storen), Melchior Hofmann, Kaspar Schwenckfeld, and Claus Frey. Others preferred not to present their views, but were expected to have private hearings. This was indeed an unusual way of handling "heresy," differing considerably in spirit and in method from those common in the magisterial Reformation centers of Wittenberg, Zürich, and Geneva, not to speak of Rome. Among the four presidents of the synod was the distinguished Jacob Sturm. Judging by the minutes, Bucer dominated the deliberations. Occasionally the name of Sturm appears.[63]

Although Hofmann received a lengthy hearing the minutes are very brief. His personal summary of his statements appeared soon in print.

Hofmann presented his five points in which he found the Strassburg *predicanten* not truly biblical as follows: Supported by numerous scripture passages, he maintained that Christ, during his incarnation, took none of the flesh of fallen mankind. As "the first man is of the earth, earthy, the second man is the Lord from heaven" (I Corinthians 15:47). In his second statement he presented his claim that God has not created any person from the day of creation until the day of judgment for damnation, but for eternal salvation, and the Son of God has died for all. This opposed the predestinarian view held in a mild form at Strassburg. His third point was closely connected with the preceding; he maintained that man has a free will to choose salvation or to reject it. Regarding baptism, he stated that it constituted the covenant of a believing Christian with God for which faith was a prerequisite; consequently, infant baptism was not scriptural. Unique and objectionable was his strong emphasis on the unpardonable sin on which he elaborated in greater detail than on any of the other issues. He saw the unpardonable sin as being consciously enacted after the gaining of true insight.[64]

Bucer's refutation appeared soon after Hofmann's five statements. He stated that Christ had shared with us in human nature, that man was selected by God unto salvation and had no free will, and that the practice of infant baptism was Christian. Bucer also presented his opposing views on the unpardonable sin.[65] Both writings are indeed helpful in finding out what the differences and contrasts were. In all these deliberations no mention was made of Hofmann's eschatological views and his supposed role in the approaching kingdom of God in which Strassburg was also to play a significant role.

Bucer's extension of the debate beyond the synod was done without the knowledge of the council and surprised the latter.[66] But that did not end the story. By the end of the year Bucer's book was distributed in the Netherlands in a Dutch edition in order to counteract the influence of Hofmann.[67] Bucer was fully aware of the contacts which Hofmann had had in that country and which were to cause some more concern to him. Also, an edition in the Westphalian dialect was prepared by Brixius and published by the city council of Münster. Ironically enough, Brixius was the brother-in-law of Bernhard Rothmann, the great opponent of infant baptism[68] who had been in Strassburg in 1531. His co-workers, Hendric Rol and Gerhard Westerburg, were in Strassburg in 1534, and the latter was a guest of Capito in spite of the fact that he was Anabaptist.[69] But even in May before the synod,

Hendrik Slachtscaep of Wassenberg had written Bucer not to think too highly of infant baptism which the Wassenberg *predikanten* had given up.[70] No wonder Bucer was eager to influence the developments in Münster. Before Christmas of 1533 he wrote Johannes van der Wieck of Münster warning against the consequences of discarding infant baptism. He sent numerous copies of his refutation of Hofmann's views to friends, including Philip of Hesse, as has been pointed out, who had heard Hofmann preach.[71]

The synod's actions also affected the personal lot of Hofmann. Four days after the synod, the council decided to put him into a different "tower" since at his first location, his followers communicated with him through the window. It has been seen that he continued to publish books through the help of his friends. The action of the council was due, furthermore, to a rumor that in the woods near Benfeld a large group of Anabaptists had been seen who intended to "set up a new order" in Strassburg. On June 23 the council took action to lock Hofmann up in still another cell where no one would be able to speak to him because at the new location he had preached through a window the previous day to more than forty persons. He must have reported about his experiences at the synod and interpreted their meaning as he saw it.[72]

At about this time two pamphlets appeared in print in which he dealt in greater detail with the questions he had presented at the synod. The council now decided that he should not get any ink, pen, and paper since he "was continually writing books and now again requested a ream of paper, having written enough of his errors," and there were "many who share his heresy about the incarnation."

Severe measures were enacted against other radicals. Lienhart Jost and the wife of Hans Kropff, both of whom had been prophesying, and all those who sponsored meetings of Melchiorites or Anabaptists and sheltered them, of whom four are named, were to be taken into custody, "particularly so that during the [approaching] fair a rumor will be spread that [Strassburg] does not tolerate all manner of heresy and sects." That these measures were undertaken not only out of zeal for "the purity of doctrines," but also in the interest of public opinion is evident, for it was decreed that "Schwenckfeld should not be admitted to him [Hofmann] so that the people would not get the impression that the *predikanten* were not able to correct his [errors]." The Anabaptist, Hans Adam, who had mounted the pulpit after a sermon by Wolf Schultheiss and who had continued to preach was also to be

taken into custody. Such actions did not deter Adam from doing the
same thing following Christmas after Capito had preached.[73]

Behind the actions against Hofmann and his associates can be seen
the firm guiding hand of Bucer as was evidenced at the synod, in his
ensuing correspondence in connection with the synod,[74] in his refutation of Hofmann's views, and in a letter of Schwenckfeld addressed to
Leo Jud. Schwenckfeld stated that he was very surprised "that you are
wickedly condemning the poor Melchior Hofmann and, as it were,
sentencing him to death, saying that he denies Christ and God – and
who tells you that? He would not admit it since he thinks he has
grasped the true Christ, the heavenly Christ, whose flesh was conceived by the Holy Spirit." He continued by asking whether it was
reason enough to kill him or keep him in prison just because he could
"not yet understand how Christ could have taken on our flesh through
Mary." "He glorifies Christ in ascribing salvation through Christ to the
only begotten son of God and not to the flesh." [75] There was no better
advocate of the cause of Hofmann than Schwenckfeld. No wonder that
the council did not want to have him visit Hofmann. The two had the
same concern regarding the Christology and salvation of mankind
which could not be based on the humanity of Christ but on his divinity. In addition, both had nearly the same view regarding baptism.

One can ask why Hofmann was condemned to spend the rest of his
life in a prison cell while Schwenckfeld went about freely. For one
thing, Hofmann was somewhat more outspoken and also held to eschatological views which ultimately got out of control and, under other
leadership, caused the disaster of Münster. The stigma attached to Anabaptism in general would have been enough to cause his life confinement. In addition, the letter by Schwenckfeld contains a very interesting
observation. He remarked that scholars like Luther and Bucer fought
with their pens, but a "poor fellow must pour out the bath water.
Why? Because he has no one who defends him. He cannot justify
himself and when you are told the truth you cannot stand it and say
that it breaks up the church and destroys unity." [76] Applying this beyond
what Schwenckfeld had in mind, one could say that while Hofmann
remained in prison since he was a poor furrier, Schwenckfeld, of noble
birth and more highly educated, could at least enjoy some freedom or
leave the city.

At the end of October, 1533, a specially appointed commission presented the evaluation of the books handed in at the synod by Hofmann
and Schwenckfeld. The erroneous beliefs of Hofmann were drawn

from seven of his writings and stated in four sentences similarly to Bucer's in his refutation. The four beliefs selected were: The eternal word of God was transformed out of divine nature into human without taking on human flesh through Mary. God has chosen all unto salvation which was available through Christ; thus man had a free will to do good. The unpardonable sin was the knowingly committed sin after the true illumination. Infant baptism was from the devil and was not to be practiced by Christians. After the brief statements followed summaries of each of the books. Having presented the case of Schwenckfeld in a similar manner, the commission stated under what conditions agreements could be reached with him. Less gentle was the final word regarding Hofmann. The "dishonorable and cruel derision which Hofmann has written regarding our teaching ... we are not concerned about, knowing that it will turn out well since the Lord says: 'Blessed are ye, when men shall revile you, and persecute you ...' " [77] No doubt then and during the following years Hofmann found his sole consolation in the same words and with a little more justification, as will be seen. In conclusion, the commission appealed to the council by saying that it pitied the slanderers and the simple people who were turned away from the word of God. It expressed sympathy "that the church is being destroyed, and that the honorable state and you, our lords, are being belittled."

Early in October, Hofmann was reported ill and was granted a warm room during the day and a night cap and slippers. His condition, however, got worse. He wrote to the council numerous times and five times to the warden asking for such things as a light for the night and other comforts. He compared himself to Lazarus at the doorstep of the rich man. At last Matthis Pfarrer of the city council wrote, opening his letter with the prayer that the Lord would lead him to the true knowledge and adding that it was out of place to compare himself to Lazarus and that his condition was entirely due to his stubbornness since he could get hot broth any time he so desired. Evidently Hofmann was still fasting voluntarily, living on nothing but bread and water.

In the beginning of January, 1534, the ministers Caspar Hedio and Mattheus Zell visited Hofmann and found him, as in the past, unmovable in his "error." He was ill, but hoped to get well even on bread and water if he were given a warm room. If the cause he was fasting for did not make progress during the year, he would be willing to reconsider the matter. Hedio and Zell recommended to the council that he be given a room and adequate means so that his life would be spared. They agreed that Hofmann should be kept in confinement so that he would not cause further misery, danger, murder, and damnation of souls in his simplicity. "Who knows, perhaps Satan in him can be tamed through the mercy and patience of the church?" As a result of this petition, the council granted that Hofmann be given a more comfortable room, but one without an outside window.

In the beginning of May Hofmann requested that he be placed in rigid confinement where neither sun nor moon would shine on him because this was the year in which the Lord would end all misery. The ministers came for a visit in the middle of August. In addition to the previous two, Bucer, Matthis Pfarrer, and Georg Pfitzer were along. Hofmann repeated that he was not requesting release, but an opportunity to compare his views with theirs. He was confident that they were not far apart. With joy he offered to go into the dungeon even though no government had the authority to punish anyone for his beliefs. When the ministers referred to Deuteronomy 13:5 according to which passage false prophets are to be stoned to death, he found them bloodthirsty. He insisted that a "breakthrough" from the Lord would occur during the year and that they would do well to come to an agreement with him.[78]

Under September 9, 1534, it was recorded, without stating who interviewed Hofmann, that he admonished the members of the city council that "he was the true Elijah, who is to come before the judgment of Christ." In November, he stated that Strassburg was "the city that God had chosen above all other cities of the world to his glory," and that the lords of this city would establish the banner of justice. Nearly a year later he repeated the same predictions, adding that the city would be besieged, but need not fear anything of the Anabaptists who would not fight but work in the trenches. Ultimately the city would establish the banner of justice. On May 24, 1535 the question was raised as to why Hofmann was really in prison, but no answer to the question was recorded nor was he released.[79]

After the fall of Münster, Bucer reported to Konrad Pellikan that Hofmann was treated more severely. Through the mediation of Philip of Hesse, great efforts were made in an attempt to establish some possible connection between the leaders of the Münster kingdom and Hofmann. The interview with Jan van Leiden during this attempt is extremely interesting, but proved definitely that there was no contact between the master dreamer of the kingdom of God which was to start in Strassburg and his prodigal sons attempting to realize such a kingdom by force in Münster.[80]

6. Hofmann and the Melchiorites

This leads us to the question of what Hofmann's relationship to his followers in East Friesland and the Low Countries was during his confinement in Strassburg. It is obvious that the contact must have been very limited and that the information is scarce. On the other hand, there is enough information available to draw some conclusions.

When the Melchiorites of Emden heard about Hofmann's imprisonment, they petitioned the city council of Strassburg in his behalf on October 9, 1533, representing Hofmann as "a true servant of the eternal word of God, of our Lord Jesus Christ and their industrious servant during night and day." Unfortunately the full text of the petition is not extant. But here is evidence that the fellowship initiated by Hofmann was by no means broken up after his and Trijpmaker's departure.[81]

It has been related that Bucer considered the influence of Hofmann in the Netherlands and in Münster to be so significant that he personally wrote the refutation of Hofmann's views and letters to counteract the same. Not only did he write to Johannes von der Wieck, but the latter also wrote to Jacob Sturm reporting about the developments among their religious leaders. Von der Wieck reported that there were rumors that "Hofmann had won in Strassburg and the whole city had accepted his views." To counteract this report a detailed program was worked out by the city council of Strassburg of writing to the ministers and the council of Münster, sending them information and Bucer's book against Hofmann, and relating to them that he was still in confinement. How closely Strassburg continued to watch the developments in Münster after the collapse of the kingdom has been indicated.[82]

Somehow the Melchiorites of the Netherlands must have remained in close touch with their leader in Strassburg, for it was reported that disciples "would daily come and go for him at Strassburg," and they "received his letters every day." Among those spending a longer time in Strassburg was Cornelis Polderman, who for a while was considered to be the Enoch, next to Hofmann, the Elijah, of the coming kingdom. Others assigned this role to Schwenckfeld. Polderman came to Strassburg when Hofmann was imprisoned and helped him with the publication of his writings. He boldly petitioned the council in the fall of

1533 to grant him permission to see Hofmann regarding his wife and child and some business. He was particularly alarmed because he had heard all over town that the imprisoned Hofmann was ill and that none of his friends were permitted to see him. Besides, Polderman told the council that the views for which Hofmann was condemned in Strassburg were accepted as truths at many places in the Netherlands and publicly proclaimed at Münster. All the pious were complaining about the unfair treatment Hofmann was getting in Strassburg. If Polderman had known that human testimony would be more important in Strassburg than the word of God, he declared that he would have brought several hundred letters along in behalf of Hofmann. In addition to the Netherlands, being "full of his books," Polderman informed the council that the report about Hofmann's part in the disputation had been spread in print "all over the Netherlands." During the hearing of Polderman, which followed this petition, he appeared very much to be a fearless disciple of Hofmann, stating that Bucer's refutation contained nothing but lies which would be properly answered in the Netherlands. Not only did Polderman help Hofmann in having some of his writings published while imprisoned, but he also published some of his own in Strassburg.[83]

Among the many Sacramentarian and Anabaptist Dutch refugees coming to or passing through Strassburg was also David Joris who must have had plans to stay when he arrived there in May, 1535, with wife and child. He had hoped to find shelter and work in Strassburg, but had to leave two days after his arrival. Since Hofmann was in prison at this time, Joris could not have been in touch with him.[84]

7. Basic Views

Before we leave Strassburg it is in place to present some of Hofmann's basic views as far as this has not been done in the course of the discussion. Such a consideration will also involve further mention of his associates in Strassburg. One thing seems to be apparent and this is that he never became fully identified with any of the Reformation groups throughout his career as evangelist – either with the Lutheran or the cause of the Strassburg reformers, or fully with any of the Strassburg Anabaptist groups. Although circumstances under which he was baptized are not known, it must have happened without making him a full-fledged member of the groups led by Kautz or Reublin or Marbeck or Denck.

Strassburg had a number of Anabaptist groups which, for various reasons, worshipped or met at different places. The ministers and the council were far from sharing Hofmann's idea that a church should be made available to them. On the contrary, it was forbidden for Anabaptists to worship separately. Thus their meetings had to take place at different places in small groups, and they had to change the locality of their meetings frequently. In addition to this, their leaders' coming from various backgrounds as far as social status, nationality, Reformation contacts, and Anabaptist origins were concerned did not always succeed in molding their views to the extent that they became fully integrated. Recent studies have somewhat clarified the complex groupings of Anabaptism and the radical reformers of Strassburg. Some became known as followers of Kautz, Reublin, Marbeck, Hofmann, Bünderlin, or Franck.[85] This should, however, not obscure their common basis. The Strassburg *predikanten* and the city council usually spoke collectively of the *Wiedertäufer* (Anabaptists), but often gave Hofmann special attention and treatment or even linked him with Schwenckfeld.[86] This was particularly due to the fact that both shared the concern to trace the saving power of Christ to his divinity and denied that he took on any flesh of Mary during his incarnation and birth. We conclude that Hofmann in joining the Strassburg Anabaptists originated a new fellowship which became known as Melchiorites.

All Anabaptists, including Hofmann and the Melchiorites of the Low Countries, shared views regarding the meaning of the church (*Gemeinde*), the body of believers, and her mission in the world. Closely interwoven were their views of the ordinances or sacraments which were related to the views of the Sacramentarians and Karlstadt. How easily and thoroughly Hofmann integrated the covenantal or ecclesiastical views of the Anabaptists into his own is evidenced by the *Ordonnantie* which appeared in connection with his proclamation of the great commission in East Friesland and the Netherlands. It is of interest to compare his book with the views expressed by Kautz and Reublin on January 15, 1529, in a confession presented to the council of Strassburg when they were imprisoned. "When the merciful God called us out in his mercy through his word . . . from our darkness to his marvelous light we did not reject the heavenly message but made a covenant with God in our hearts, to serve him henceforth in holiness all our days, by his power and to let our intention be known to the fellow covenanters (*Bundgenossen*). Thus while receiving water baptism we were incorporated in the body of which Christ is the head"

(Colossians 1:18). In surrendering themselves to the Lord they began
to proclaim the way of salvation through Christ, which is the true
Gelassenheit (surrender), and baptize in accordance with the commission which Christ gave his disciples when he parted from them (Matthew 28:19 f.). However, before Kautz and Reublin, Hans Denck had
advocated the views centering in the ordinance and covenant which
were later developed by Marbeck for the *Bundgenossen* of South Germany and by Hofmann for those of the North. The expressions used,
such as the body of Christ or the church, the covenant, *Bundgenossen*
(fellow covenanters), *Gelassenheit* (surrender), and the urgency to
proclaim this message remained the basic elements of the laymen's
theology transplanted by Hofmann from Strassburg to the North.[87]
The idea of the covenant was also strongly emphasized by the Strassburg
and Swiss Reformation leaders. A basic difference between them and
the Anabaptists in this matter was that the latter rejected the conclusion that infant baptism must be retained in the new covenant of God.
Marbeck argued against Bucer saying that he identified baptism and
the covenant too strongly; Marbeck claimed that water was merely a
witness and not even a sign of the covenant. He believed that man's
salvation did not depend on baptism nor on the effort of the individual believer, but entirely on the promise of God.[88]

One of the unique characteristics of the radical reformers, including
the Anabaptists, was their expectation of the approaching kingdom of
God on earth. The Reformation in general ushered in a renewal of
the eschatological hope and the awareness of the tension which exists
between the world as it exists and the expected kingdom of God. The
historiography of Sebastian Franck is an example of the strong eschatological expectations during the Reformation. However the eschatological hope to realize a Christian fellowship on earth on an unprece-
dented scale and depth was unique with Anabaptism and particularly
Hofmann. For Luther the Day of Judgment was first of all transformed into a "beloved day" in contrast to the "day of horror" of the Middle
Ages. The eschatologically oriented Luther further neutralized the urgency and significance of the expected kingdom of God by speaking
of a dual or twofold kingdom: one of the world and another one of
God, one being earthly and the other divine, emphasizing that they are
of a different nature and must be kept apart.[89] Luther fought the
Schwärmer whom he accused of mixing the two with ferocity. On the
other hand this division often led the individual to "behave like a

devil in the world and to an escape into the inner sanctuary to play the role of a pious Christian."[90]

Luther emphasized the inward kingdom within the individual soul while Calvin fought for a theocratic view of the kingdom of God which is to be realized in the stress and storm of the world. The immediacy and urgency of the coming of this kingdom was neutralized by Luther by restricting the place of operation primarily to the realm of the individual soul, Calvin went far beyond this view. For him the kingdom of God begins with the theocratically realized church of Christ growing from day to day.[91]

Some of the radical reformers, including the Anabaptists, dared to make their eschatological expectations of the realization of the kingdom of God based on the biblical prophecies the basis of their total reformatory effort. "Chiliasm suppressed by all churches broke out into a big and bright flame in Anabaptism." Melchior Hofmann was one of the major representatives spreading this flame. "The failure of this holy experiment in no way diminishes its magnitude." [92]

Hofmann, originally a Lutheran evangelist, remained evangelical in his concept of the gospel of salvation and its proclamation as has been pointed out in connection with his *Ordinance*. As far as his eschatological views are concerned they were based on the content and spirit of the New Testament including the apocalyptical writings or Revelation and Daniel. Hofmann applied the "predicted" future events to the religio-political situation of his time. A brief summary of these views and their application follows.

The time of grace was running out and tribulation had set in. The two witnesses, to be identified as Elijah and Enoch, would prophecy 1260 days, but their real calling would not be recognized before their message was ended when the beast or dragon would kill them. At this time, emperor, pope, and church, and even the biblical literalists would deny Christ. In the fluctuation and perils concerning the cause of the kingdom, the spiritual Jerusalem would be protected by two powers, one of which was to be Strassburg. The sign of Christ, being that of the cross and the suffering of the children of God, would appear. The spiritual Jerusalem would be built like the temple of Zerubabel and destroyed again. At last Christ would appear and rule forever. The seven years within which this was to transpire were originally set for the time from 1526 to 1533. That made this year of Hofmann's imprisonment so crucial and caused his rejoicing. Details were flexible in the interpretation of the coming last days, but there was one inflexible stand in the total drama. That was Hofmann's unshakable faith and enthusiasm regarding the victorious coming Lord and the word of God giving him the general outline of the approaching events.[93]

The major "heresy" of Hofmann, which led to disastrous consequences unforeseen by him, was his "split hoof" theory of hermeneutics and his interpretation of the eschatological scripture passages whereby he did not heed sufficiently the Lord's word: "But of that day and that hour knoweth no man..." (Mark 13:32). He stayed within the scope of the imagery of the Bible, but he overreached himself in his zeal to apply it to the happenings of his day. In the pose of an Old Testament prophet he assigned too freely to contemporary rulers, countries, and cities roles which they were to play in the final drama of the struggle between the forces of darkness and light. There is no doubt some connection between the impatience of the evangelist when his witness does not immediately produce the expected results and of the prophet who proclaims the approaching day of judgment and the kingdom of God and finds that the Lord is tarrying. Hofmann's problem was that of lack of patience and self-control and not so much error in doctrine.

In passing it should be mentioned that Hofmann furnishes a unique opportunity for a case study of the early Anabaptist relationship to the government. From his early days as a follower of Luther to his last days in prison, he longed for recognition by the authorities, be this in Sweden, Denmark, Emden, or Strassburg. At last he had the assurance that God had chosen Strassburg in his divine plan to play a significant role. He did not tire in his desire to impress this on the council and the *predikanten*. Their ridicule did not shake his faith either in the plan of God or in the role of Strassburg and its government and church. The cosmopolitan foreigner had developed a messianic patriotism centered around Strassburg which was unshakeable. One is under the impression that Hofmann would never have left the city chosen by God if freed, not to speak of trying to harm her safety. To be sure, that was not the view which Bucer and others had of him.

Milder characters and less extreme reformers had failed to find a permanent home in Strassburg and had to continue the search for "a city not built by hand." Even Denck, Franck, Schwenckfeld, not to speak of Karlstadt, could not stay very long. Strassburg, like other cities and countries, was just emerging from the Middle Ages in which uniformity of religious views, on one hand, and the coordination of church and state, on the other, were taken for granted. To achieve this goal, it is true, no machinery of inquisition was set up in Strassburg patterned after those of the past, but a modern method of Christian education was employed – and with success. Bucer succeeded in winning many. He even used the severe criticism issued by the "sects" to improve the ethical and disciplinary standards of the church. The prospective convert had to show some progress in the direction intended by the educational program of which the synods and hearings were a part. Many stubborn believers had to leave the city never to return again. Hofmann was given neither a chance to leave nor to become an outright martyr. He was doomed to become a slowly dying victim whose faith in his Lord and his mission were not shaken.

One is tempted to close this chapter with a word from a letter by Bucer written to Margaretha Blaurer in connection with his attempt to win Schwenckfeld to his point of view. He wrote: "Dear God, each one thinks that he is the one whom the world should follow! May God grant us one whom we all will follow!" Meanwhile Bucer did his best to meet the emergency through his semirigid program of education and coercion.[94]

V

ANABAPTISM AT THE CROSSROADS

J. G. de Hoop Scheffer has stated that "with few exceptions the history of Anabaptism constitutes the history of the Reformation in our country [the Netherlands] from 1530 to 1566." This statement has been repeated many times, and, more recently, it has also been challenged.[1] Nevertheless, it contains enough truth to be repeated even in our day. Anabaptism absorbed the Sacramentarian movement to a large extent and dominated the Dutch Reformation at various places for a number of decades.

It has been pointed out that Hofmann had accepted chiliastic views before he joined the Anabaptists in Strassburg. This eschatological emphasis remained a characteristic of all Melchiorites. Nevertheless, one distinction soon became apparent. After the imprisonment of Hofmann in Strassburg, his followers in the Low Countries gradually developed two distinct schools of thought. With Hofmann, some continued to emphasize disciplined Christian living, enduring all suffering for Christ until his expected second coming. Under the leadership of Jan Matthijsz and Jan van Leiden a movement emerged which attempted to speed up the coming of the Lord by calling on the "saints" to help with the establishment of the New Jerusalem. Although the demarcation lines between the two movements were flexible at first, these peaceful and militant chiliastic views soon became controversial issues of Dutch Anabaptism. As far as Hofmann was concerned, he never approved of a militant chiliasm, but expected that the second coming of Christ would usher in the Kingdom of God on earth.

A. IN SEARCH OF THE CITY OF GOD

1. Centers of Melchioritism

The rapid spread of Anabaptism in the Netherlands was not so much due to a previously unheard-of message as to the fact that this message was anticipated and, consequently, found immediate large scale acceptance. This was true in regard to adult baptism, for which a large part of the population had been prepared by the Sacramentarian movement, to the emphasis on the Christian life and purity of the church, and to eschatological expectations. J. Lindeboom states that there was "an Anabaptist spirit preceding the introduction of [adult] baptism" so that Sacramentarianism and Anabaptism merged to a large extent. All this appealed to the masses and even to some burghers and persons in government circles, especially in Amsterdam. Anabaptism, being a popular movement, found "followers in various strata of society." It was not merely a trend within a spiritually elite group or a school of thought practiced by theologians or the clergy. And not only did these views find a large following among the Sacramentarians, but also in circles strongly influenced by Luther. The message of Melchior Hofmann and his prophetic sons was "challenging and strongly propagandizing. It appealed through promises of a near by eschatological bliss, sharply distinguished between those who are saved and those who are lost, and emphasized the priesthood of all believers." Large masses of people were engulfed by these glad tidings which spread like a fire, which, to be sure, in some instances was like a straw fire, but which also at places and at times left behind a "calmly burning inextinguishable glow." And thus "for a while Anabaptism became predominant in some cities and some areas of the Netherlands." [2]

It has been pointed out that Hofmann and his co-workers established fellowships of covenanters (*Bundgenossen*) in Emden, East Friesland, and in some parts of the Low Countries. Favorable conditions predestined Amsterdam to become a metropolis of Anabaptism in the Low Countries. The work, influence, and exile of Wouter Deelen and Jan Sartorius has been related. In accordance with the *Memorie* record of Amsterdam, Hofmann himself had an active part in the establishment of an Anabaptist fellowship in this city when he baptized some fifty persons in 1531; his follower, Jan Volkertsz Trypmaker, also baptized "many and divers persons." When, in the fall of that year, the Court of Holland at the Hague found out about the activities of the latter and the spread of a new heresy, the city magistrate of Amsterdam was urged to arrest Jan Volkertsz Trypmaker. The sheriff, Jan Hubrechtsz, wanted only to warn Jan but he voluntarily submitted himself for arrest and was sent to the Hague. As a result, seven others were arrested and all were beheaded on December 5. Their heads were sent to Amsterdam to be exhibited. Displeased, one of the burgomasters

said that they would send "no more to the butchershop." When told
that the heretics had renounced their beliefs, the burgomaster asked:
"Did they also deny God?"

As far as the Court of Holland was concerned, it was bad enough
to deal with such heresies as *Lutherye* and Sacramentarianism. Now
"anabaptisterye and all that goes with it," namely a spiritualization of
the traditional meaning of baptism and Hofmann's view of the incarnation of Christ increased the confusion. The fearless witness and the
willingness to suffer for beliefs, on the one hand, and the ruthlessness
with which the inquisition machinery set up by Charles V in Brussels
and the Hague operated, on the other hand, were essential factors in the
dispersion and spread of Anabaptism and also in the tragic course it
took. Amsterdam not only attracted Anabaptists from nearby places,
but also from distant provinces such as Brabant and Flanders. Jan
Hubrechtsz and the burgomasters were accused by the Court of Holland of tolerating Sacramentarian preachers and attending their services. When the burgomaster, Jan Ruysch, was asked to prosecute
those who blaspheme the sacrament, he responded that he would not
be able to handle all cases. After the execution of Jan Volkertsz
Trypmaker and some of his fellow covenanters, there was comparative
quiet during the years 1532 and 1533.[3]

Among those baptized by Jan Volkertsz Trypmaker were Pieter de
Houtzager and Bartholomeus Boekbinder. In turn, de Houtzager baptized Jacob van Campen, who had a leading position among the Anabaptists of Amsterdam. Early in 1534 de Houtzager and van Campen
baptized more than one hundred persons on one day in and around
Amsterdam. Jacob van Campen exercised a wholesome influence in
the days when militant Anabaptism began to gain a foothold in Amsterdam. One of its promotors was Jan Matthijsz, a baker from Haarlem who had been a Sacramentarian for some time. Melchior Hofmann
must have baptized him during his short stay in Holland in 1531,
possibly in Amsterdam when he baptized some fifty persons there.
Little is known about the others and who they were.[4]

The spectacular activities of Jan Matthijsz started in Amsterdam at
about the time when Hofmann was imprisoned in Strassburg in 1533.
Jan Matthijsz now assumed the role of one of the two prophets or
witnesses who were to come to announce the second coming of the
Lord. Visions and zeal made him an outstanding propagandist of Melchioritism, albeit in a modified form. Exaggerated reports have it that
when Hofmann ordered baptism to be suspended, Jan Matthijsz over-

ruled this order. Hofmann likely suggested a temporary halt of baptism, which, however, was never fully carried out; Mellink has pointed out that Matthijsz at first sent out only four or five apostles and not twelve.[5]

One of the early centers of Anabaptism in Amsterdam was the home of Jan Paeuw. Some martyrs maintained that some three hundred persons had been baptized here while others said between forty and fifty. According to the records, the following administered numerous baptisms in Amsterdam: Jacob van Campen, Jan Matthijsz van Middelburg, Hans van Leeuwarden, and Meynart van Emden.[6]

Another significant center of Anabaptism was Leeuwarden, although it never gained the importance of Amsterdam. It was the first place reached by followers of Hofmann who came from Emden, East Friesland. Hofmann could easily have come to Leeuwarden and other places in Holland twice. It has been pointed out that even in 1534 an edict was issued against Hofmann and that Obbe Philips wrote that there was a time that they "received his letters daily." In 1532, or before, when Hofmann visited the city, he must have baptized some Sacramentarians.

Late in 1533 Jan Matthijsz sent Bartholomeus Boekbinder and Dirk Kuiper from Amsterdam on a mission to Leeuwarden, where they met with fourteen or fifteen Melchiorites. Most of them were baptized. One of them was Obbe Philips. The following day Obbe and Hans Scheerder were ordained elders to proclaim the message and baptize believers. When, eight days later, Pieter de Houtzager visited the group, the elders were out preaching in the vicinity. Now Obbe's brother, Dirk Philips, who later became a faithful co-worker of Menno Simons, was baptized. The message presented on this occasion must have made a deep impression on all, including the authorities, for the meeting ended with de Houtzager being "severely pursued and sought after . . . so that he could only narrowly escape." When Obbe Philips returned, his distressed wife met him, begging him to leave at once since he was in danger. This vivid account in Obbe's *Confession* and the involvement of his wife in it makes one wonder whether the meeting possibly took place in their home.

This event caused such public excitement that the government took steps to crush the growing Anabaptist movement. The stadholder Schenck van Toutenburg issued an edict listing six leaders of Anabaptism including Melchior Hofmann, Pieter de Houtzager, Jacob van Campen, Obbe Philips, and Melchior Hofmann, who headed the list.

Jacob van Campen had also been in Leeuwarden. The edict was repeated so that Obbe found it safer to leave Leeuwarden. He spent some time in Delft where he baptized David Joris and in Amsterdam where he discussed some hermeneutical questions on the "split-hoof" theory with Jacob van Campen.[7]

Groningen also became an early Anabaptist center. It is likely that Jans Volkertsz Trypmaker did not pass through the city without stopping on his way from Emden to Amsterdam. In 1534 Obbe Philips and Jacob van Campen labored there. Particularly the former must have been successful in winning followers.[8]

One of the most rapidly growing centers of Anabaptism was Münster in Westphalia. Although not a part of the Low Countries, the fate of Anabaptism in this city and the Netherlands was most closely interwoven for this period of time. Münster was soon to attract not only Sacramentarians and would-be-Anabaptists from Wassenberg at Julich-Cleves and Cologne and its environs, but also the major parts of the Low Countries. What Melchior Hofmann predicted for Strassburg, some of his followers tried to realize in Münster. The "City of God" was to descend on Münster, and Christ himself would turn it into a millennial "New Jerusalem."

The religio-cultural and political situation in the bishopric of Münster during the early years of the Reformation period has been briefly presented. Contacts between the radical reformers of Strassburg, including Hofmann, and those of Münster on November 11, 1533, have been mentioned. The city council of Strassburg took note of a letter by Johann van der Wieck of Münster in which he stated that it was rumored that "Melchior Hofmann had here won [in Strassburg] and that the whole city had accepted his views." The writings of Hofmann must have been reaching Münster directly and indirectly via the Netherlands which was "full of his books." In addition to this, Rothmann, Rol, Westerburg, and others had been in Strassburg.[9] What an exaggerated significance the city council of Strassburg and Philip of Hesse ascribed to the role of Hofmann in the tragedy of Münster will be seen later.

The chief evangelical reformer of Münster was Bernhard Rothmann, whose early significance and reformatory views have been "misunderstood" because he was tragically caught in the unescapable outcome of the Münster kingdom. Recent studies of his theological development and its relation to Anabaptism in general have restored more favorable features of his image.[10]

Rothmann received his education at the cathedral school in Münster and at Deventer with the Brethren of the Common Life. His preaching after 1529 at St. Mauritz Church outside of Münster had great appeal and reflected some influence of the Reformation. In 1531 he visited such Reformation centers as Marburg, Wittenberg, and Strassburg; in the last city he stayed in the home of Capito. Here he received some lasting influences. In 1532 he led in the introduction of a reformation in Münster. Hendric Rol, a Wassenberg *predikant* with Anabaptist views in regard to the Lord's supper and baptism, had great influence on Rothmann.

By August 19, 1532, the evangelical preachers had taken over all of the churches in Münster except the cathedral. Soon the expelled Wassenberg *predikanten* from Julich arrived in Münster and joined in the reformation effort. By February, 1533, there were evangelical preachers with strong Anabaptist leanings. By now the Melchiorites were being attracted to Münster. The city council election strengthened the influence of the guilds and the evangelical party. Rol and Rothmann began to question the validity of infant baptism which led to a division of the reformation forces into a conservative group led by Johann von der Wieck and a popular group backed by the guilds and led by Rothmann and the Wassenberg *predikanten*. On August 7 and 8, 1533, a debate was held, the outcome of which was that unbaptized children were to be baptized and Rothmann was dismissed.

Rothmann now wrote his first Anabaptist treatise, *Bekentnisse...* in which he advocated believer's baptism and a symbolic view of the Lord's supper. When it was published November 8, 1533, it bore also the signatures of a number of the Wassenberg *predikanten*. The *Bekentnisse* constitutes a milestone in the reformation history of Münster and Westphalia and a signpost for Anabaptism. It stated radical evangelical views and, without intending to do so, it opened the gates of Münster to radical chiliasts. They were soon to take over Münster's reformatory movement, which had a better start than in many another city, in order to lead it to a tragic end.[11]

The Münster disputation of August 7 and 8, 1533, and the publication of Rothmann's *Bekentnisse* were taken note of far beyond Münster. Early in March, 1534, the Strassburg ministers sent to Münster their *Bericht auss der heiligen geschrift...* in which they defended infant baptism and other views under attack. A special effort was made to counteract views expressed in Rothmann's *Bekentnisse* and thus to help Münster solve its reformation problems. This effort was so much appreciated elsewhere that the writing was published in Augsburg.

The *Bekentnisse*, which was used by the leaders as a basis to usher in the Anabaptist movement in Münster and by the opponents as a basis for its defeat, was also used by the South German Anabaptist leader, Pilgram Marbeck, as a basis to rally the divergent Anabaptist groups of his day. He used it extensively in his well known *Vermanung* (1542).[12]

Returning to the situation in Münster we observe that the outcome was still indefinite. Would Catholicism regain its former position or would Lutheranism win? Or would the victory go to the Sacramentarian-Anabaptist wing? The Wassenberg *predikanten*, Rothmann, and Rol had committed themselves to the latter in the *Bekentnisse*. The only question that needed an answer was when and how their ideals could and should be realized. The answer came sooner than had been anticipated. On January 5, 1534, Batholomeus Boekbinder and Willem de Kuiper, representatives of Jan Matthijsz, arrived in Münster and initiated adult baptism. It must be assumed that Rothmann and his followers knew little about these representatives of chiliastic Anabaptism nor did the "apostles" know what the end of the "kingdom" would be. The next to come was Jan van Leiden, the later "king" of the "New Jerusalem." The path of no return had been entered.

2. The Spread of Melchioritism

Amsterdam was and remained the center of Anabaptism in the Netherlands proper whence it spread to the various parts of the country and beyond. From here lines of communication went everywhere. Many people persecuted elsewhere found a temporary haven here. North of Amsterdam, in the Zaan River area, evangelical Sacramentarians were strongly represented, and Anabaptist messengers from Amsterdam found a field ripe for harvest. They proclaimed the news brought to the Low Countries by Hofmann. Their message appealed to the common people who were deprived of material and cultural goods enjoyed by others and who longed for a more meaningful religious experience. Hofmann's views about the closely knit fellowship of believers that could enter into a covenant with God as *Bondgenoten* and share in the blessings of his kingdom in the immediate future impressed them. The spiritualization of the meaning of the sacraments – the Lord's supper and baptism – had paved the way for a spontaneous acceptance of baptism upon confession of faith as a symbol of the new covenant with God through Christ. The resulting persecution height-ened the expectancy of the Lord who would come to meet his faithful and usher in his kingdom of perfection.

One of the successful messengers in the Zaan River area was the former priest, Jan Jooste, who had come to Amsterdam from the province of Zeeland. He was sent on his mission by Jacob van Campen, who was the "head" and had "sent out others into the various provinces to preach and baptize." As the result of Jooste's work Westzaan alone had some one hundred fifty to two hundred baptized Melchiorites. Jan Jooste paid dearly for his success, for he was beheaded in the Hague on February 10, 1534.[13]

Reynier Brunt of the Court of Holland in the Hague, who received little cooperation from the authorities of Amsterdam in locating Anabaptists, had a free hand in North Holland. But on February 10, 1534, Brunt was not so successful in his efforts. On the same date as Jooste's execution he reported that twenty officers sent to one of the villages during the night to arrest Anabaptists found none of them at home, except one who lived outside of the village.[14]

In a report of the Court of Holland to Regent Maria dated February 17, 1534, it was stated that the apprehended Anabaptists, when examined, confessed that they were "seeking the kingdom of God" and that "in their meetings they read and discussed the gospel after which one of them broke the bread, which he distributed to all, knowing that it is not a sacrament but only partaken of in memory of the suffering of our Lord." Not so favorable was the report about another group of four to five hundred in North Holland among whom were "many simple and coarse people" who had no views of their own. They had only heard a few sermons in which they were told that "they would be saved through baptism and now realize that they have been misled and deceived and regret it to the extent that they cry and howl." Execution of all of them seemed, to the court, too severe and might cause trouble among the population. Consequently, the officials recommended that these simple people be given an opportunity to repent.[15]

Anabaptism spread throughout North Holland during the first years and was represented in such towns as Alkmaar, Hoorn, Enkhuizen, and even the Island of Texel. Haarlem, the home of Jan Matthijsz, baker and prophet, does not seem to have had many Melchiorites during the first years of spread. Jan Matthijsz, who suffered for Sacramentarian views as early as 1528, was baptized by Hofmann and now assumed a leading role after the latter's imprisonment in Strassburg. From his "headquarters" in Amsterdam he sent out apostles to preach and baptize. Haarlem Melchiorites enjoyed some security, for the city fathers, like those of Amsterdam, were reluctant to turn their citizens over to the Court of Holland.[16]

Utrecht, the see of the bishopric, a center of the Sacramentarian movement, and the home of men like Hinne Rode, Wouter the "Lutheran monk," and Hendric Rol, did not develop a strong Anabaptist movement. However, the nearby town of IJselstein, under the protection of Dirk Weyman, questioned the validity of infant baptism as early as 1530. Here Ghijsbrecht van Baeck had an Anabaptist fellowship of which Rol was the domestic chaplain. Van Baeck's wife, Elsa van Lostadt, an Anabaptist, was imprisoned from 1544 to 1548.[17] Some of van Baeck's group accepted Münsterite tendencies.

In Delft many of the evangelical Sacramentarians gradually joined the Melchiorites. Obbe Philips spent some time in Delft during the year 1534 preaching and baptizing. Among those whom he baptized was David Joris, who as a leader of the evangelical Sacramentarians had been exiled from Delft in 1528. Joris soon made a trip to Strassburg but returned. He had numerous followers (Jorists) of whom many were martyred. Other Anabaptist leaders in or from Delft were Meynart van Delft (or Emden) and Jan Claesz Cock.[18]

Both Dordrecht and Rotterdam revealed some Anabaptist influence. Dordrecht was reached by Bartholomeus Boekbinder and Willem de Kuiper in 1534. An edict of January of that year indicates that Anabaptists had established themselves at that place. Sources of information show that Jan van Leiden and Gerrit Boekbinder must have baptized some persons in Rotterdam around Christmas time, 1533. In April, 1534, Johan Schot was executed in the Hague for baptizing in Rotterdam. During the summer Jacob van Campen was in the city. The link between the provinces of Holland and Zeeland constituted Den Briel which was also visited by Gerrit Boekbinder and Jan van Leiden. They preached and baptized at Briel and Rotterdam. Meynart van Emden was also active here.[19]

Zeeland, Flanders, and Brabant, however, were not reached by Anabaptism during the first years to the extent that the North was. A. L. E. Verheyden maintains that by "1530 Melchiorite teachings had penetrated into the cities of Bruges and Gent, and spread rapidly in the Southern Flemish cities and villages" but continues that the "first indications are too vague to determine with certainty from what area the new faith first came to Flanders."

Jan van Geelen reached Antwerp in the spring of 1534 and won some followers. During the same year a former priest Cornelis Leenaart Boekbinder, and Jacob van Herwerden also promoted Anabaptist teachings.[20] The last named some thirteen Anabaptists of Antwerp. There was a close contact between the Anabaptist group of Maastricht founded by Henric Rol and that of Antwerp. Amsterdam also exerted an influence on the Anabaptists at Antwerp.[21]

3.   Some Views of the Melchiorites

Some of the basic views of outstanding Anabaptist leaders of the North, such as Hofmann and Rothmann, have been presented. An attempt will be made to relate some of the beliefs their followers cherished. Since few recorded them, we must rely primarily on the records of trials at which the accused were made accountable for their "heresy."

It has been pointed out that the Sacramentarians were quite regularly referred to as followers of "Luther." This continued even after the baptism of the covenant was introduced and the courts in reality faced "Melchiorites." The Melchiorites, in turn, soon disagreed in the matter of defending their faith with arms or being willing to suffer punishment and death for it. Even though the lines between these two stands are not and cannot always be drawn sharply, they were one of the most significant distinguishing marks during the years 1533-35. Would the kingdom of God be ushered in by him with or without the help of his saints? Was it permissible to help the cause of God by other than spiritual means?

Basically Melchior Hofmann and his followers, as well as Rothmann in Münster, were heirs of the Lutheran Reformation. Both Hofmann and Rothmann had been Luther's followers and admirers. The *sola fide* may not have remained in the center, but it did stand at the beginning of the movement. Although there was a difference between Rothmann and Hofmann and the followers of each, their common basis was their view pertaining to the ordinances or sacraments, justification, and their desire to live a life of personal and social holiness, as C. A. Cornelius has pointed out.[22]

The small fellowships of Melchiorites mushroomed everywhere, moving from house to house for meetings in order to remain inconspicuous. "Seeking the Kingdom of God ... they read and studied the Gospel during their meetings" and had a meal of fellowship or commemorated the Lord's supper. Although all members were constant witnesses, they had elders or bishops to preach and baptize believers. The office of deacon was as important as that of preacher, elder, or bishop. "Those who received baptism denounced the vices and heathen ways of the world and promised to do the will of Christ." In a confession obtained by the Court of Holland, it was stated that those who baptized "administer an oath to those to be baptized that they will not go to any church, since idolatry is practiced there, and that they will not get drunk and will say no evil about others." When this question was presented to Jan Paeuw, he stated that some weak believers were cautioned about attending the Catholic Church, but that "nothing is said to those who are strong enough in their faith since it is clear that the papal tradition and what is done in the Catholic Church is against true Scripture and the teachings of the apostles." According to Jan Paeuw, baptism was a sign of assurance or of the covenant with God and a promise to follow Christ. In most cases the promise not to attend the Catholic Church would not have been necessary, and the administration of an oath must have been an exception, if it occurred, since the oath was not considered scriptural. On the other hand, the fellowship was to be "without spot and wrinkle." The emphasis on the true Christian fellowship as the body of Christ was so strong that there was a tendency to practice community of goods or, at least, to share material goods with those who had a lack thereof.[23]

In addition to these basic views, the Melchiorites perpetuated Hofmann's emphasis on his unique incarnation theory and the split-hoof concept of the scriptures. They followed an old tradition whereby some passages were interpreted literally and others figuratively. Being of a more speculative nature the latter did not cause so much public and official resentment as the believers' attitude toward the sacraments. The greatest stigma was attached to their spiritualization of baptism and its postponement or repetition at a mature age. Making the validity of baptism and the Lord's supper dependent not only on the giver of grace but also on the recipient's faith was too great a break in the theological and folk tradition, both for Catholics and Protestants.

A similarly great, or even greater disturbance, was caused by the chiliastic views, which assumed more and more realistic form and application among some of the Melchiorites. The sharp distinction between "believer" and "unbeliever" and the identification of the covenanters or believers with the few chosen saints who would meet the Lord at his second coming and participate not only in eternal bliss with him but also in the revenge of the "unbelievers" became more and more the distinguishing characteristic of the militant Melchiorites. It was at this point that the break between the peaceful and biblical Anabaptists and the chiliastic and militant Melchiorites occurred. All were eschatologically oriented, but the latter took God's plan and work into their own hands, determining the stage of events and the time schedule for his final action with his creation and man.

For all Melchiorites the corner stone of their imagery was scriptural and traditional. The "holy city," the "new Jerusalem," came "from God out of heaven" (Revelation 21:2) and was "not made with hands" (II Corinthians 5:1). The dream about the heavenly city which was expected to descend to earth and renew all aspects of life was as old as the recorded visions of the prophets. Augustine's *Civitas Dei* was conceived in days when there seemed little hope for earthly powers such as the eternal city of Rome. Eschatological hope has always prospered best when it has been hope against hope. Melchioritism rooted to a large extent in a population with little hope for this life. The eternal hope gave the followers a new meaning in life.

This new hope and challenge gave them not only something to look forward to, but also made them critical of the society and the church of which they had been a part. Both had deprived them of their legitimate rights. The new city of Revelation, which they would soon enter, would make up for what they had been deprived of. Not only did they have an unshakeable hope in the future, but they also had a sense of satisfaction, knowing that "the Babylonian whore" would be fully punished for all the injustice and evil which they had experienced here (Revelation 17:1, 15, 16; 19:2). This charge was directed not only against the Catholic Church, but because of the close identity of church and state, encompassed them both.

4. *The Eschatological Hope and Persecution*

The Melchiorites' severe attack on the church was based on the reading of the Scriptures, the records of the early church, and the prophecy about the coming church. They found that the church they were a part of had little resemblance with the ideal they discovered in the Scriptures and the kingdom of God to come. Deeply disillusioned by what they saw daily and greatly inspired by the hope of things to come through the power of God, particularly when he would make "a new heaven and a new earth," they ventured out by faith in the direction of that coming city of God for which others had looked in past days and in their own way.

Like Hofmann they now looked for signposts leading them to that city which would open its gates and whose citizens would open their hearts to receive the coming Lord to be preceeded by the prophets, Elijah and Enoch. Here the persecuted saints would find the city "not made with hands" but by God himself (Revelation 11:33ff.).

It has been pointed out with what steadfastness and loyalty Hofmann looked first to the king of Denmark and later to the city council of Strassburg, expecting them to become willing to receive the coming king and his messengers. Although the imprisoned Hofmann remained steadfast to the end, his distant followers in the Netherlands began to look for another place, more conveniently located, where the prophecy would be realized, depending at times on some very human and earthly combinations of local, political, and religious developments and the inspirations and "prophetic" insights of the leaders. It is understandable that Amsterdam and Münster were seriously considered as the choices of God in the final drama that was to usher in the kingdom of God.

All Melchiorites, like the early Christians, expected the Lord to come in their lifetime. The stronger the persecution and suffering of the faithful, the greater was the hope and expectancy. However, most of them had no clear conception as to how the kingdom was to be established. As noted earlier, one of the crucial questions in connection with the coming of the Lord and the establishment of the millennium was whether he would smite his enemies without human aid or whether his saints would help him. Menno Simons, who was fervently opposed to armed resistance, expected with Paul "that the saints will judge the world" (I Corinthians 6:3).[24] Like him, many other peaceful and sober Anabaptists did not look for short cuts in the coming of the kingdom by pointing at cities, persons, and definite circumstances which the Lord would make use of in this eschatological event.

Unfortunate circumstances which speeded up the attempt in the realization of the expected kingdom were the following: The Anabaptist movement was primarily a movement of the common people. Some of the humanistically trained leaders of the Sacramentarian movement, who would have been in the position to furnish leadership, had died the death of martyrdom or had fled. Hofmann, the father of the movement, was imprisoned for life. The movement found no attachment to or sponsorship by ecclesiastical authorities or territorial or city governments as this was the case with the more moderate reformers. Such conditions did exist for B. Hubmaier who, for a while, enjoyed the protection and church membership of the counts Liechtenstein. As a rule, however, the flock of sheep without a shepherd was persecuted more severely than any other reformation group. When tolerance and possible sponsorship loomed as a possibility on the horizon, this was often considered a sign of the Lord indicating that his coming was at hand at this concrete moment and under these particular circumstances. It is perhaps fair to say that if there had been no miscalculation, or if the bishop of Münster had not been helped by his Catholic and Protestant rulers to crush the kingdom, then this movement might have become as settled, acceptable, and honorable as any of the reformation churches that were established by combining religious and political powers to defeat opposition. Most of the cities and countries established such a combination of forces during the sixteenth century regardless of how loudly they sang *Mit unsrer Macht ist nichts getan.*

The longing for a city of God was strengthened through many factors. Many sailors, fishermen, small business people, and workers in the Dutch towns had experienced unusually hard times because of a combination of unfavorable political and economic developments. They were open for news that would give them a new outlook and hope for the future. The hope of the underprivileged and deprived was greatly stimulated by the prophets of the coming kingdom.

This new hope and expectation of the underprivileged received a severe shock through the inhuman persecution, suffering, and martyrdom that set in. As an accompaniment of the eschatological stigma, the elements of the persecution tended to identify the Anabaptist movement with revolutionary and insurgent forces aiming to overthrow the government. Some equated Anabaptism with the Peasants' Revolt. During these times of trial, meek and weak men and women, and even teenagers, became heroes of faith, giving their lives as a testimony for the truth revealed to them through Jesus Christ. The *Martyrs' Mirror* is the monument erected in memory of those who gave their lives for the faith they were not willing to renounce. The testimonies were collected to inspire later generations who did not need to endure such suffering for their faith.

A survey of how heresy was combated has been presented. The first imperial edict dealing with the Anabaptists was issued January 4, 1528. It was confirmed at the Reichstag of Spires on April 23, 1529.

and incorporated into the imperial legal code. All governments were now obligated to prosecute all Anabaptists "whether man or woman, if of age, by executing them by fire, sword, or other means, depending on the person, without the use of the spiritual inquisition." [25] This edict was expected to be made public and enforced by all countries and imperial cities. Some applied it with all rigidity, while others maintained a certain independence and enforced it when unavoidable or suitable. As has been seen, the Court of Holland was most rigid in its application and even tried to enforce it in towns and areas which had been granted the right of law enforcement. The edict made provision for a centralization of imperial effort in suppressing the heresy of Anabaptism by bypassing the ecclesiastical inquisition machinery.

Even though the trials were conducted by secular imperial courts, the accusations were primarily in the category of ecclesiastical crimes. They were labeled as „heresy" in the Catholic territories and "blasphemy" or "insurrection" in some Protestant countries. But even with the charge of insurrection the primary purpose was to protect the religious *status quo*.

During the Middle Ages "heresy" was looked upon as holding to views "deviating from those of the church." Governmental authorities were often called upon to inflict the more severe punishments such as the death penalty even if it was an ecclesiastical offense. The death penalty consisted of burning at the stake, drowning, or beheading. A "blasphemy of God" was considered an "offense to God or the saints" committed by scolding or offending God or the saints by damaging crucifixes or pictures of saints. Punishments consisted of fines, whipping, torture, exile, and the death penalty. An offense against ruling majesties was considered insurrection. In severe cases the death penalty was the verdict. [26]

The first Anabaptist martyr of the Low Countries was Sicke Freerks (Snyder), who was condemned by the court of Friesland and beheaded publicly in Leeuwarden, March 20, 1531. Just before Christmas he had been baptized in Emden by Melchior Hofmann and sent out to preach the gospel. From this Anabaptist fellowship of Leeuwarden emerged such prominent leaders as Obbe and Dirk Philips and, in a way, also Menno Simons. The public execution of a pious and God-fearing citizen made a deep impression on those present. Menno Simons, a priest in the vicinity, after hearing about it, "examined the Scriptures assiduously and meditated on them earnestly, but could find nothing in them concerning infant baptism." Jan Volkertsz Trypmaker, who had also been baptized by Hofmann in Emden and who was, with him, co-founder of the Amsterdam Anabaptist fellowship, was very active and baptized many. The court of Holland at the Hague summoned the magistrate of Amsterdam to arrest him. Trypmaker and seven other Anabaptists of Amsterdam were beheaded on December 5, 1531. Jan Jooste, a former Catholic priest, who was very successful in his work north of Amsterdam, was also beheaded in the Hague, as was reported previously.[27]

These and many other pioneers of Anabaptism in the Netherlands were followers and promoters of the "ordinance" or "commission" of Hofmann to proclaim the glad tidings of the new covenant with God and the hope of the approaching kingdom of God. With many others they lived disciplined Christian lives in closely knit fellowships. Many of them became martyrs in the truest sense of the word, witnessing from day to day in word and deed and joyfully giving their final and ultimate testimony by pouring out their life as apostles of peace. Many who had never heard of the movement were so deeply touched by this unselfish testimony that they could not do otherwise but join the witnesses and disciples of Christ.

The turning point came too soon. Because of the removal of a balanced leadership through the death of martyrdom, radical elements started to exploit the situation. Others, although sincere, lacked the spiritual and intellectual maturity needed in a crisis situation.

The initiator of a new trend was Jan Matthijsz of Haarlem who was baptized by Hofmann and who assumed a leading role after the imprisonment of the latter. He sent out prophets to preach and baptize. In this connection, most of the historians strongly emphasize the suspension order pertaining to baptism which Hofmann gave after his imprisonment and the stigma attached to rebaptizing which led to a more severe persecution. A reference to such a suspension can indeed be found in the *Bekentenisse* of Obbe Philips and is confirmed in the confessions by Jan van Leiden. However, in all of his writings, Hofmann himself makes no reference to it which is rather surprising. Neither does he refer to it when he speaks of Jan Matthijsz. This should not necessarily lead us to the conclusion that he never made any suggestions of this nature. However, the significance of the recommended suspension seems to have been blown up entirely out of proportion to its original intention. C. A. Cornelius, the well-informed archivist, expert in the field, and writer of books dealing with the Münsterites, was very dramatic in his presentation of the Münsterite tragedy. He seems to have over-dramatized this "suspension order." It would seem more likely that Hofmann never "ordered" a suspension of baptism but suggested it. It, furthermore, is probable that there was never an actual suspension of the administering of baptism.[28] This does not mean that, with the assumed leadership of Jan Matthijsz, there was not a renewed zeal in fulfilling the ordinance of teaching and baptizing.

The Sacramentarian Jan Matthijsz started his activities as the prophet in November, 1533. One of his most far-reaching missions was a visit to the home of Jan van Leiden in Leiden where he spent two weeks discussing matters pertaining to baptism. The result was that he convinced Jan van Leiden that "nothing can go above truth" and thus van Leiden was baptized. Some of the plans which the two were soon to realize may have been conceived at this occasion. Following Jan van Leiden's baptism, he was sent out as an "apostle" by Matthijsz. Together with Gerrit Boekbinder he made an extended evangelistic tour to Amsterdam, Hoorn, Enkhuizen, and Alkmaar.

Jan van Leiden, rhetorician, merchant, innkeeper, and a man of many talents, was not only persuaded to be baptized during the two weeks that Jan Matthijsz was in his home, but must also have shared some information and aspirations with his guest. Having lived in England for four years, traveling to Flanders, Lisbon, and Lübeck, he could inspire the imagination of the prophet. With the awareness of this background of Jan van Leiden, one realizes that he was not the only one to gain insight when Jan Matthijsz visited him in his home and baptized him. Matthijsz gained new ideas and information which he did not previously have.

Disillusioned in business matters, Jan van Leiden had become interested in the religious situation at Münster. He had heard that the word of God was being preached best at that place. Thus he had made a trip to Münster and other places in Westphalia at the end of May, 1533. In Münster he had stayed in the home of Herman Rammen.[29] Walraven Herbertsz confessed in 1535 that he, Hendrik van Maren, and Jan Boecksten, likely Jan Bockelszoon (Jan van Leiden), came to Münster, where they associated with Knipperdolling and Rothmann. Rothmann had sent van Maren to Warendorf at the end of May to help the local pastor.[30] Jan van Leiden was, indeed, in a good position to give Jan Mathijsz an eyewitness account of the conditions in Münster, which both were to enter soon.

Jan van Leiden had witnessed crucial days in the development of

the religious, social, and political life of Münster. Those were the days
when the evangelical Lutherans and the evangelical Sacramentarians
had been competing for leadership in the religious life of the city. The
Wassenberg *predikanten* from Julich had arrived and were helping
Rothmann with the preparation of the *Bekentnisse* which were soon
to come off the press. Sent by Jan Matthijsz, Jan van Leiden, along
with Gerrit Boekbinder, now again arrived in Münster on January 13,
1534. However, when they arrived Bartholomeus Boeckbinder and
Willem de Kuiper, who had arrived there on January 5, had already
introduced believer's baptism by baptizing Rothmann, Kloprys, Vinne,
Rol, Stralen, Staprade, and others.[31] The great question regarding baptism, raised long ago, stimulated by Hofmann and opposed by Bucer,
had been answered in favor of adult baptism.

B. MÜNSTER: THE NEW JERUSALEM

1. *The City of God*

The relationship between the City of Münster and the ruling bishop,
Franz von Waldeck, elected June 1, 1532, had been strained from the
start. On July 12, Charles V had demanded that the evangelical ministers be dismissed, which the city refused to do. This led to reprisals and
an arming against the city by the bishop. The matter was settled
through mediation by Philip of Hesse in February, 1533.

Soon, however, the bishop realized that no permanent settlement
had been reached. The introduction and practice of adult baptism,
which was an act of insurrection according to imperial law was being
continued. On January 23, 1534, von Waldeck issued an edict that
the Anabaptists be imprisoned. Meanwhile the city hall had been
seized and Bernhard Knipperdoling had become mayor of Münster.
The radical Melchiorite and evangelical parties had united against the
bishop. Many who did not agree with the radicals left the city. Rumors
about large-scale arming of the bishop increased the restlessness in the
city. After the bishop had unsuccessfully attempted to take the city
on February 10, he established his headquarters at Telgte and appointed a war council and field marshals. A blockade of the city was started
in order to prevent the entry of soldiers and food supplies. The first
reaction of the city was the destruction of the fort St. Moritz located
east of the city and, on February 27, the expulsion of all those who

had not been baptized.[32] The siege of the New Jerusalem had started although not all contacts with the outside world had been cut off. In fact, for a while these contacts and the movement of people in and out of the city were very lively, causing much excitement all over Western Europe.

It has been pointed out previously that the evangelical movement had spread over a large part of Westphalia. At many places this evangelical movement assumed the characteristics of the Sacramentarian movement which was the seed bed of Anabaptism. The Wassenberg *predikanten* and some leaders from Cologne, who had come to Münster, were representative of the growth of the movement. Communities influenced in this manner were attracted by the developments in the city of Münster.

Rothman had been an evangelical leader for Münster and some surrounding communities for some time. During this time he leaned more and more toward Anabaptism. It was pointed out that he placed Hendrik van Maren as assistant minister in Warendorf. The bishop expressed his concern about the fact that van Maren "made weekly trips to Münster with a group." Hendrik van Maren was later baptized in Münster and returned to Warendorf where he baptized thirty persons.[33]

Hendrik Slachtscaep was the evangelical leader at Coesfeld. After his baptism in Münster he baptized more than a hundred at this and other places. Another place and center of Anabaptist activities was Schöppingen. Bartholomeus Boekbinder, Willem de Kuiper, and Jan van Leiden had stopped here in connection with their trip to Münster. This was the residence of Hinrich Krechting whose brother Bernhard was already in Münster. Jan van Leiden shared some plans with him. Hinrich Krechting was in the service of the bishop and as such received orders from him to arrest all evangelicals. He resigned and went to Münster with his family where he joined the Anabaptists and became the "chancellor" of Jan van Leiden. He was likely the only leader who survived the Münster catastrophe.[34]

The Anabaptists and sympathizers began to move to Münster in large numbers. Münster had taken the place of Strassburg as the location where the Lord would meet and protect his faithful children. It was a refuge of the persecuted faithful Christians. The "unbelievers" had fled or had been expelled from Münster, and the believers were being invited. The judgment of the Lord was expected to be at hand. The threatening siege of Münster resulted in sending out Jacob van

Ossenbrug (Osnabrück), Peter Schomecker, and Gyse Scheffen with letters inviting Anabaptists to come to Münster. Johann Kloprys gave directions and letters to his daughter, in particular, inviting her to join him. The group proceeded via Wesel and Venlo to Dremmen and Odenkirchen, gathering men and women to follow them to Münster.

A group of thirty-seven traveling Anabaptists was arrested and tried in Düsseldorf on February 28. The confession which the simple blacksmith, Jacob van Ossenbrug, gave reveals what impressed, appealed to, and concerned common people in their search for the kingdom. First of all, the supposed signs, miracles, and prophecies supporting the chiliastic views of the leaders predominated. Jacob van Ossenbrug named Jan van Leiden as Enoch and Hofmann as Elijah and stated that he expected the second coming of the Lord to take place before Easter at which time "the world will be cruelly punished so that not even one tenth of the population will survive... Only in Münster will there be peace and security, since it will be the city of the Lord and the New Jerusalem, where the Lord will save those who belong to him and they will all have enough." The message which van Ossenbrug brought to those who followed him was that the Christians in Münster were building homes for all those who would accept the invitation. All churches were expected to be occupied, and ultimately the homes of the godless, as well as their goods, would be used. Asked about baptism Jacob stated that a person must have faith and then be baptized in order to be saved, renouncing "the world, pomp, the devil, and all lust of the flesh." His confession includes reference to Hofmann's unique Christology.[35]

The major instigators of the invitations were Jan Matthijsz and Jan van Leiden, who had taken over leadership in the New Jerusalem. The letters, however, were written by men like Rothmann who knew the communities in which the Anabaptists and Melchiorites lived. The hope to survive the approaching "Day of Judgment" within the walls of the city of God was one of the main reasons for the response. In the middle of February, Heinrich Krechting of Schöppingen arrived in Münster with a number of followers, finding shelter in a monastery. In the same month Hendrik van Maren of Warendorf received a written invitation to proceed at once to Münster with those who had been baptized. When this group arrived on February 25, they found shelter in the St. Johanni monastery. Among the comparatively large group was the goldsmith, Johann Dusentschuer, who played a significant role in the development of the "kingdom." The homes and the

property of those who went from various places to Münster were as
a rule confiscated and sold. In Coesfeld alone some 35 homes were
confiscated. Karl-Heinz Kirchhoff names seventeen places around
Münster from which individuals and groups moved to the New Jerusalem.[36]

It would, however, be misleading to consider the entire action as a
mere attempt to save a few "chosen" people from a physical death.
Back of all of this was still the sense of mission expressed in Hofmann's
Ordinance inviting unbelievers to accept salvation by entering a covenant with God. This accounts for some of the daring, courageous, and
foolhardy missionary and evangelistic undertakings of the Münsterites
and the numerous writings by Rothmann which now appeared in
rapid succession. This sense of urgency induced people to prophesy,
to see signs which were to precede the coming of the Lord, to utter
woes, preach, and to testify regardless of threat, imprisonment, and
martyrdom.

An illustration of this is the action taken during a commemoration
of the Lord's supper at the courtyard of the cathedral at Münster. The
prophet Johann Dusentschuer rose and proclaimed that it had been
revealed to him that a number of messengers were to be sent out into
the world at once to proclaim the approaching kingdom. During the
same evening the brotherhood led out twenty-seven messengers by
torchlight who proceeded to Osnabrück, Soest, Coesfeld, and Warendorf, symbolizing the four corners of the earth. The king, Jan van
Leiden, seemed not immediately convinced of the advisability of re-
alizing this plan, but consented in view of the fact that "the spiritual
sword must precede and the secular will follow." All succeeded in
getting through the bishop's camp, but all, with the exception of
Heinrich Graess, lost their lives under cruel torture, among them
Johann Kloprys. The movement had been deprived of some significant
leaders.[37]

2. Life in the New Jerusalem

From the time of the arrival of Jan Matthijsz and Jan van Leiden
early in 1534, life in Münster was dominated largely by these two
foreign prophets. All their doings were supposedly based on the revelation of God, be that found in the Scriptures or discovered personally.
Up to his death, Jan Matthijsz had the leading role.

Few of the native Münster citizens remained in leading positions, with the exception of Bernhard Knipperdolling who became mayor on February 23, 1534, and Rothmann who functioned as the sole theologian, writer, and pamphleteer of the kingdom. Both survived to the end only because they adjusted themselves considerably to the notions and visions of the prophetic leaders, who established a ruthless theocratic rule.

In the early days of the siege an apologetic pamphlet series appeared in rapid succession. The first was entitled *Bekentones des globens und lebens der gemein Christi zu Monster*.[38] The contents played a very significant role as promotional literature. Apostles and evangelists used the booklets on their trips into Westphalia and into the Low Countries. They contained more about the ideals and aspirations than actual achievements and conditions in the besieged city. The pamphlets were not only used to guide friends and sympathizers to the chosen city, but also to win foes who were fighting them on the other side of the city wall. The tracts were thrown into the camp of the besieging forces, telling them that the occupants of Münster had not started the war, but that they had been attacked without a declaration of war. Through prayer and legitimate means they were defending the word of God. Addressed to "all nations" as coming from "the Christian city of God," the tracts stated that the residents "believed in the one true and living God" and that they "do not tolerate evil deeds and horrible sins as they are being falsely related about us ... If you do not believe that this confession of faith is true, we will permit a certain number of you to come and examine everything yourselves." Most or a large number of the besieging forces consisted of mercenaries. The Münsterites therefore "hoped that among them will be many pious ... who will not conduct a war against God and truth for the sake of money." Some must indeed have joined the city's populace in its fight "for truth."[39]

Rothmann's second Anabaptist booklet, entitled *Eyne Restitution . . .*, appeared in October, 1534.[40] In this work he outlined his views regarding the true apostolic church, urging its restitution. In December his appeal, *Van der Wrake . . .*[41] (Concerning Revenge), to take up arms in defense of the church at Münster followed. This constituted a significant point in the development of the Melchiorite Anabaptist movement which had a very unusual record of suffering without revenge. Besieged by a strong army, the "children of Jacob" now felt called not only to defend themselves but also to help God punish the "children of Esau." Their fate and the plan of God were so closely identified that they were certain that victory was on their side because they were on God's side.

The spirit of Rothmann's writing had been anticipated by an action of Jan Matthijsz. On April 4, 1534, Matthijsz had been seized by a foolhardy inspiration to go outside the city walls with a few armed followers in order to disperse the besieging army, as it had happened under Gideon in the days of Israel. Jan, the prophet, and his companions lost their lives. A similar attempt to re-enact the drama of Israel was made when Hille Feickes attempted to go into the camp of the bishop in order to kill him as Judith had done in Israel when she went to the camp of Holofernes and beheaded him. Hille Feickes, too, lost her life.[42]

The shift of a peace-loving pacifist Melchioritism waiting for the Lord to usher in his kingdom to a militant community supposedly defending God's truth and kingdom had been completed partly by design and partly by compulsion. In the design was the bold assumption that God had chosen Münster for the establishment of his kingdom at this point of history. The march of the "saints" to this city and the control taken by the "forerunners" (Enoch and Elijah) of the Lord were seen as part of the plan. Once this action was begun there was not much else to be done but to continue on this path unless a complete retreat was preferred. Since this was not the alternative chosen and the city was besieged, its defense was the only method left. These and later writings of Rothmann "reflect the fact that the city was under siege, which might be seen as self-defense rationalized within the ideology." The dialectic between ideology and historical developments must be seen in this way.[43]

Another basis for the development of Melchioritism of Münster was its complete reorientation as far as its Scriptural basis was concerned. Swiss and Melchiorite Anabaptism was Christ- and New Testament-centered. Christ was the fulfillment of the old covenant and the norm and center of orientation of the new covenant. Melchiorites started out as *Bundgenossen* (fellows of the covenant). So did Rothmann.

The shift from the New Testament basis to the Old Testament and the exchange of the Anabaptist ideal of the disciplined apostolic church for the New Israel went hand in hand with the change that took place in the inner structure of the community life, its religious, social, economic, and political aspirations. The introduction of the community of goods still had a New Testament orientation, but with the introduction of polygamy and Jan van Leiden's rule in a theocratic fashion as the Second David in Zion or the New Jerusalem, the shift was completed. In Jan van Leiden's ambition to rule the world, the basically biblical and eschatological orientation in regard to the second coming of Christ had been given up and replaced by the self-centered messianic ambition of Jan van Leiden, the king, and his Israel. Out of the suffering fellowship, which aimed to follow Christ, a militant theocratic and secularized chiliasm had emerged.

The basic change found expression in the transformation of the structure of government and the social life. The co-mayor Knipperdolling, became, on the basis of a prophecy, the *Schwertführer* (executioner) of Jan van Leiden. Similarly, an Israelite constitution was revealed to the people. The former council was replaced by Twelve Elders of the Tribes of Israel. After they had been appointed, Rothmann preached a sermon based on the new constitution. Now Jan van Leiden handed to each of the twelve elders a sword stating: "Take the right to carry the sword which has been given to you by God through me and use it in accordance with the command of the Lord."

"Although all of us in this holy church of Münster, in whose hearts the law and the will of God are inscribed by the finger of God . . . should readily fulfill them, we, twelve elders of the nation, shall nevertheless summarize them briefly in a list in order that the new state may be protected so that each one may see what to do and what not to do." This is the introduction of the thirteen statements of the "order of life" issued by the twelve elders based primarily on Scripture passages from the Old and New Testaments giving the citizens guidance and an ethical code of behavior. A similar code was presented in regard to public behavior and responsibilities by even listing job assignments. The citizens were referred to as Israelites, and the threat of death penalty was used freely.[44]

The Münster Anabaptists developed a unique characteristic otherwise only fully developed among the Hutterian Anabaptists. This was the principle of sharing to the point of having all or at least all major property in common. In the case of the Münsterite group it had two purposes: one was ideological and the other practical. The first was rooted in Christian Anabaptist tradition and the second in the unique situation in which the besieged Anabaptists found themselves. The question as to whether the Münsterites actually practiced a communistic way of life has been answered in this way by Hans Ritschl: "The community of goods actually existed and was realized as a communistic system as far as this was possible on the existing economic level." However, that the idea of the community of goods originated even before the siege of Münster has been pointed out by Hans von Schubert. He refers to Rothmann's *Bekentnisse* which appeared in the fall of 1533. Here Rothmann speaks about the Lord's supper, referring to Acts 4:32 and stating that the early Christians "gave each one what he needed because they had all things in common."[44] For Rothmann the fellowship meal at the Lord's table was only one aspect of Christian sharing.[45]

Prior to the city's being taken over by the Anabaptists, it had a strong and influential guild system which was a significant factor in the democratization process. The guilds had fought successfully the competitive enterprises of the monastic industries. One practical reason which led to the communal living in Münster was the fact that surplus property became available when some prosperous "children of Esau" had preferred leaving the city instead of joining the "children of Jacob." Others were ultimately expelled, leaving their property behind. The emergency situation of the city was another reason for the rapid development and the application of the principle of the community of goods. The possessions of the deserters and those expelled, as well as the property of the church and the monasteries, became public property which was managed in accordance with the newly developed laws and regulations. Many refugees from the surrounding places as well as the Netherlands arrived in Münster; these people had left all their possessions behind. They found shelter in the various monasteries and were cared for out of public funds. Community living was a natural development.

The next step was that all money had to be brought to the city hall and that all personal property was listed and surplus food supplies were taken to the community homes located at every gate of the city. Public eating places were established, particularly for those working in connection with the defense of the city. Knipperdolling's motto is supposed to have been: "One God, one pot, one egg and one kitchen."[46]

Deacons were sent around in the early stage distributing goods where they were needed and collecting them where there was more than enough. Private trade was forbidden and survived only on a very limited scale. Property as well as debts were taken over by the government. The accumulated silver and gold were used for foreign trade which was in the hands of the state. All labor was done free of charge since everybody was getting what he needed free of charge. The twelve elders assigned the work to the citizens.

The possessions such as clothes and household goods of someone who died, as well as property acquired in combat, were turned over to the community and redistributed where needed. During the final stage of the siege, some of the aspects of the practice of the community of goods were altered in order to adjust to the circumstances. Ritschl summarizes the experiment by stating that "this communism originated as a religious ideal and not as required by economic needs. It found expression in a complete community of all goods . . . and in a just and even distribution of products, of labor, and of supplies." Rothmann, the chief originator of this practice, put it this way: "We hope that the fellowship among us is so strong and glorious that community of goods will be practiced with a pure heart through the grace of God as it has never been practiced before. Not only do we have our goods in common under the supervision of the deacons, but also we praise God with one heart and courage through Jesus Christ and are inclined to serve one another in all manners." He continued by giving the following reasons for their practice of the community of goods: "All that have served self-seeking and the owning of property, such as purchasing and selling, working for money, interests, or speculation, even with unbelievers, and drinking and eating the sweat of the poor, who are our own people and neighbors, through whose labor we fatten ourselves, . . . and all this has disappeared completely among us through the power of love and fellowship.[47]

The polygamy practiced in Münster has received more publicity than any other aspect of the kingdom and has also been given some serious study regarding the reasons for its introduction. Some have pointed out that Jan van Leiden forced it upon the community for personal reasons. Others have maintained that it was an emergency measure caused by the loss of men during the siege. It is true that Jan Matthijsz left his wife in Haarlem and married another in his early career as a prophet. Jan van Leiden had a wife in Leiden and married a daughter of Knipperdolling in Münster; after the death of Jan Matthijsz, he added his widow to the growing list of his wives, later making her queen Divara. Nevertheless, Ritschl comes to the conclusion that it would be wrong to blame the introduction of polygamy entirely to the promiscuity of Jan van Leiden.[48]

The theologian Rothmann treated the question of matrimony in great detail in the *Restitution* published in October, 1534. In the New Israel, Old Testament regulations and examples played a significant role. The patriarchal role of the husband and the right to marry more than one wife were mentioned. The Lord's exhortation to Adam and Eve to "be fruitful and multiply" was interpreted as a blessing issued primarily for the purpose of multiplying. "If, therefore, a man is so richly blessed that he is able to fructify more than one woman, he is free, and even advised to have more than one woman in matrimony." Outside of marriage, however, the practice became adultery.[49]

In appraising the appearance of polygamy among the Münsterite Anabaptists, one must not lose sight of the Old Testament orientation of the leaders. The male member of the community was not only expected to give protection to the weaker sex, but through him the female member found access to the spiritual blessings of the Lord. The leaders of the New Israel found this confirmed by Paul who said "the head of every man is Christ; and the head of every woman is the man." Developing this thought, the Münsterites, and later the Latter Day Saints, came to the conclusion that every woman must be attached to a man in order to be saved, just as a man is subject to Christ.

Another fact not to be overlooked was that there were about three women to one man. Men had fled and died in larger numbers. This posed the problem of providing for the women. Although this was by no means the first and main reason, it was indeed significant. Some scholars have come to the conclusion that this led to a twofold level of marriage. In one case the women became regular wives, more than one regular wife being permitted, and in the second they became house partners or co-sisters. In the first case the husband had a more intimate relationship which, however, was not necessarily excluded in the second case. The house partnership provided protection for the female partner. Thus no marriageable girl or woman was to remain unmarried. Following an early period when marriage for all was rigidly enforced, it was later officially decreed that "no one is to be forced to marry because marriage is a free union." With this new freedom unmarried women could take the initiative and ask men to become their partners of protection.[50]

The notion that promiscuity and lack of standards made all ethical and sexual traditions obsolete is, to a large extent, based on some loose reporting and imagination. Within the framework of the ethic of the New Israel, the regulations and their enforcement were rigid. Sexual offences were punished by inflicting even the death penalty.

On August 31, 1534, a second attack of the bishop's army was repulsed and many of his mercenaries deserted him. Johann Dusentschuer, on the basis of a vision and the scriptural passages of Jeremiah 23:2-6 and Ezekiel 37:21, declared Jan van Leiden the "King of the

New Zion." The new king had a throne erected in the market square where he held court. Medals were struck to symbolize his new status as ruler of a kingdom which was to spread all over the world. Around his neck he had a chain with a golden ball symbolizing the world with the inscription: "A King of Justice over all." The second David of the New Israel enjoyed the climax of his power and kingdom.[51]

At the height of his rule the king and his co-workers continued their efforts to keep in touch with the outside world in proclaiming the approaching spread of the kingdom and inviting believers to come up to the New Jerusalem in order to be counted among the 144,000 who would escape annihilation at the day of judgment which was at hand. The apostles that were sent out took along books written by Rothmann, including *Van der Wrake* (Concerning Revenge). Reference has already been made to Jan van Leiden's sending out twenty-seven apostles, including Kloprys, Vinne, Slachtscaep, and Stralen, most of whom were put to death soon after their departure.

3. Münster and the Netherlands

Early in the year 1534 the persecution of the Anabaptists and Sacramentarians was extremely severe in the Netherlands. Many were tortured, beheaded, burned, or drowned. "Flying columns" were sent by the Court of Holland in the Hague to imprison by night those who had been rebaptized. On February 27, a special decree was issued according to which those who would repent within twenty-four days would save their lives. This was the calm before the storm. Many people had to make momentous decisions. Should they repent and consequently return to the Catholic Church or should they choose the death of martyrdom? It was into this situation that the written and personal invitation to come to Münster was brought. Münster, the city of God, offered a refuge for all persecuted and oppressed.[52]

In one of the tracts addressed to "All Believing Covenanters in Christ," it was stated that "the day of deliverance is at hand" since "God has made known to us that all should get ready to go to the New Jerusalem, the city of the Saints, because he is going to punish the world ... No one should neglect to go along and thus tempt God, because there is an insurrection all over the world." Therefore, the readers were urged: "Flee out of Babylon, and deliver every man his soul ... for this is the time of the Lord's vengeance" (Jeremiah 51:6). This was not merely a friendly, pleading invitation from Münster, but a command of the Lord's prophet: "I do not simply tell you about it but command you in the name of the Lord to obey without delay." Those concerned about their relatives and the property they were to leave behind were told that they should not be concerned about unbelieving relatives and that "there were enough supplies for the saints and therefore they should take nothing along except money, linen, and enough food for the trip." A little more than parenthetically it was added: "and he who has a knife, or a sword, or a gun take them along, and if he does not have them, buy them, because the Lord is going to save us through his mighty arm . . ." Precise designations of time and place for the departure to Münster were given.[53]

Those who chose to follow the invitation extended from Münster thought they were escaping not only the severe persecution of tyrants but also the great judgement day of God. In large numbers they started moving toward the designated places. General orders were to meet at the Bergklooster near Hasselt in the province of Overijssel at noon on March 24, 1534. From here a prophet would give them direction and protection on their way from the Netherlands to Münster. The messages about the trip to Zion were spread by mouth and in writing; some of the latter were signed "Emmanuel." They were to be secret messages. The whole plan and its execution, however, was so fantastic and naive that it could remain no secret.

Even though it was suggested that weapons be brought along, the whole movement did not, at this point, have the characteristics of an insurrection against authority and government. The people involved were without any earthly possessions and hope. They were persecuted because of the faith and hope they had. Like simple children they naively believed and hoped that somehow they would escape their misery and persecution by joining those on their way to the promised city of Zion in Münster.[54]

From North Holland they came by the hundreds. From South Holland, Utrecht, and even from Zeeland they came to the harbors of the Zuiderzee to cross it by boat and to proceed to Hasselt. From other parts of the country they came by foot or with horse and cart, men, women, and children moving in the direction of Münster. Even from Emden, where Hofmann had introduced adult baptism, some followed the call of the new leaders. Not only from the nearby Gelderland but also from Brabant did some come. Some sources speak of as many as fourteen to sixteen thousand pilgrims on their way to the city of God in Münster. Later some leaders stated in their confessions that only those had been invited who were under severe pressure and persecution. It had not been foreseen "that there would be that many." A mass movement like this could not remain a secret.[55]

It was on March 24, 1534, that twenty-seven boats had reached the designated place with some three thousand men, women, and children waiting for the prophet Jeremiah to take them to the promised land. Instead they were met by officers of the surrounding towns, including Kampen, who had been notified by the Court of Holland and other authorities about the large movement of Anabaptists. Although the occupants of the boats had brought along some 1500 weapons in accordance with instructions from Münster, no resistance was offered when a handful of officers arrested them. Kühler takes this as an indication that the step toward an armed resistance was not even considered at this time. Certainly it was not contemplated when the refugees left home. As a whole they were not "revolutionaries" at this point.

Kampen inquired at the Court of Holland what to do with these "poor and innocent people." Even the stadholder Schenck van Toutenburg of Friesland-Overijssel appeared to investigate the matter. He was very much interested in the fate of Münster, as will be seen later. Some of the leaders of the group were put to death, while the others were deprived of their money and valuables and sent back to the places from which they had come. According to Kühler, about a hundred of those who returned were put to death by the Court of Holland.[56]

The outcome of this mass movement to Münster does not mean that none reached their destination. Münster was still accessible to individuals and smaller groups. The mass movement was only one expression of the great unrest and apprehension of Anabaptism and a large part of the population. Other expressions and results of the ecstasy, tension, and pressure occurred at the same time.

On March 22, 1534, while many were on their way to Münster, five of the leading Amsterdam Anabaptists used a unique method of announcing the approaching judgment. They ran along the streets of Amsterdam with swords in their hands shouting "repent" and "woe, woe to all godless." Three of them were seized, tortured, and put to death by the Court of Holland. Obbe Philips went to see them executed because he "was curious to know which in the heap those three were who had baptized" him and others and had given them their "calling." But of a total of seven executed, he could not identify them, "so frightfully were they changed by fire and smoke, and those on the wheels"

were not recognizable either. The three Obbe Philips looked for were
Pieter de Houtzager, Bartholomeus Boekbinder, and Willem de Kuiper. The latter two had baptized and commissioned Obbe Philips and
his group in Leeuwarden.[57] Although this group had used a drastic
method of announcing the Lord's coming they had not intended to
follow the call to join the pilgrims to Münster.

A similar scene had occurred earlier in the streets of Amsterdam.
During the night of February 10, 1534, seven men and women appeared nude on the street shouting their "woe" and proclaiming the "naked
truth" to the godless. Thoughts Melchior Hofmann expressed combined with mystical piety could easily have led to such drastic application. In his *Ordinance of God* Hofmann had spoken of the victors
who would enter the kingdom of God here and now and come to "the
Sabbath and the true rest completely naked and resigned," when "the
old Adam is put off completely, the individual, quite naked, is rid of
all." Having burned their clothes, the group ran about with their cry
of "woe" until they were caught and imprisoned. How catching these
notions could be is illustrated by the fact that one of the women of
the group was still a Catholic but was carried away by the action of
the others. When the group entered the prison cell, Hendrik Hendriks,
the leader, ordered Jan Paeuw, who was in the prison when they came,
to follow their example, and he did.

During their trial they called Reinier Brunt of the Court of Holland
and his helpers "bloodsuckers," but referred to the lenient mayors of
Amsterdam, Heyman Jacobs, P. Colijn, and G. J. Reekalf, as "our
brethren." All the men, including Jan Paeuw, and some of the women
were executed. Kühler has stated that outbursts like these caused a
more rigid application of the edicts even in tolerant Amsterdam.[58]

Even though the mass movement to Münster had found an abrupt
end, it was not stopped altogether. Gresbeck related that the Hollan-
ders and Frisians entered Münster "day and night" and that the Anabaptists came from all countries. Even if this is an overstatement, those
besieged in Münster did their part to make this come true. As the ring
around the city tightened, as the bishop pleaded for help from all over
Western Europe, and as the Lord's help seemed further away than it
ever had been, king David saw his kingdom in great danger. Following
the pattern of worldly diplomacy, he once more sent secret agents out
to the surrounding cities and the Netherlands equipped with literature
and money to obtain military aid and forces which would attack the
bishop from the rear and end the siege. Now it was not so much a

matter of finding a refuge in the city of God but a call to arms to free the city of God in danger of being destroyed by the godless.

The theological spokesman, Bernhard Rothmann, made this clear in the book *Van der Wrake* (Revenge) which appeared in December, 1534. Rothmann started his book telling the reader that "To everything there is a season, and a time to every purpose under the heaven" (Ecclesiastes 3:1). He complained that among those coming to them daily from the outside world there were so many who "have barely gotten beyond the suffering in Christ" and were not prepared "to endure the majesty of Christ." Some were still waiting that "God himself would come with his angels from heaven to revenge the godless. No, dear brother, this is not so. He will come, that is true, but the revenge must be executed first by the servants of God." Numerous quotations from the Old Testament and Revelation were used in support of this change. The verse about making plowshares out of swords was reversed (Micah 4:3). Rothmann admonished the reader not only to be "armed with the humble arms of the apostles to suffer (II Corinthians 10:4), but also with the armor of David to revenge with the help of God all Babylonian power and to extinguish all godlessness..." In closing he says: "Watch out; do not make a sin of something that is no sin and do not try to be wiser than God himself is in his Word." [59]

Jan van Geelen, one of the most militant and diplomatic Münsterites, and three others were sent to the Netherlands by Jan van Leiden on December 24, 1534, with a thousand copies of *Van der Wrake* and a large sum of money. Antonie Kistenmaker and Jacob Kremer went to Groningen and Hendrik Cramer to Deventer. Jan van Geelen chose the province of Holland. Van Geelen not only contributed toward the transformation of some long-suffering Anabaptists to a militant and revolutionary wing of Münsterites, but also toward the establishment of "zions" at various places for the coming Lord as centers of resistance and revolution. [60]

First of all, another attempt was made to direct the Melchiorites to the New Jerusalem at Münster. Jan van Geelen invited them to gather at places like Deventer, Groningen, Amsterdam, Leiden, and Delft. Amsterdam, in particular, was recommended, where the banner was to be erected and where the sound of the trumpet was to be heard. With the money he had brought along, weapons would be bought. The convenanters of the whole country would then march to Münster. Here they would attack the bishop's army from the rear and, while

Jan van Leiden attacked from the inside, the army would be dispersed. Jan van Geelen claimed that the deliverance of the saints was to occur before Easter, 1535.

Rothmann's *Van der Wrake* was distributed in a short time and proved to be a successful means of propaganda for the new line. Wherever this "armor of David" philosophy was proclaimed, heated discussions followed.

In a group of twelve to fourteen in North Holland, this disturbing question was discussed after the group had had a meal and read the controversial book. All present, with one exception, agreed with Damas Jacobs that a brother in need must be helped even to the point of taking up arms. The representative of the peaceful Melchiorites was David Joris, who had risked his life to come and defend his views.

A larger meeting took place in Spaarndam, North Holland, when 32 leaders from various parts of the northern Netherlands met at the end of December, 1534, or early in January. The topic of the discussion was the same. "They could not come to an agreement in their teaching" pertaining to the question of taking up arms to defend their faith. Kühler is of the opinion that those opposing this view were in the majority. A strong promoter of the Münsterite views was Meindert van Emden. The opponent, Jacob van Campen of Amsterdam, was not present but had sent his views to the group in writing.[61]

In the meantime, Heinrich Graess, who had saved his life as one of the twenty-seven apostles by becoming a secret agent for the bishop, had returned to Münster and obtained valuable information about the king's plan to be executed by Jan van Geelen and his group. Provided with information and money, Graess was sent on another mission by the king but went directly to the bishop with his information. As a result of Graess' betrayal, a number of Anabaptists, including Hendrik Cramer, were put to death in Deventer and in Wesel. Only Jan van Geelen escaped.[62]

4.   Menno and Münster

Melchiorism had spread from Emden to Antwerp, from Strassburg to Münster, from Cologne to London, and from Amsterdam to Danzig. It had retained some common features at all the geographical locations to which it had spread, but had not remained a homogeneous movement. As Marxism in our day claims the right for various countries to develop its own brand and system, so did Anabaptism. Particularly its chiliastic views led to basic differences in regard to the coming of the kingdom of God. The question of where and when God would choose to gather his saints has been referred to. Hofmann originally suggested that it would be in Denmark and then shifted to Strassburg which remained the "chosen city" to the end of his life in prison. However, he must have followed the early developments of Münster with interest.

Münster played a very significant role in the history of chiliastic Anabaptism, but was by no means the only place designated as God's choice for his kingdom. Some Melchiorites looked for signs through which God would make his chosen city known. Such an expectation made Jacob van Campen reluctant to follow the path of Jan van Leiden. Jacob van Campen related during his trial that Jan van Geelen had urged the covenanters to take up arms in defence of their lives. He and Cornelis uit den Briel were waiting for God to announce his will through "visible signs as it happened at Münster, when the city was taken while the opponents fled the city without being pursued by anybody and all this was accompanied by visible signs in the sky." Jacob van Campen was convinced that God did not want the saints to take up arms in defence of Münster or Amsterdam. Persistently he avoided all meetings at which he suspected that this question was to be discussed.

Next in prominence to Münster, Amsterdam was looked upon as a possible city of God. Adriaan van Benschop prophesied that Amsterdam would soon be turned over to the covenanters, stating that there were already five thousand in the city. Another prophet, Dirck Tasch, predicted that "there would be a darkness in the city for three days and that the Lord would then turn it over to his saints without bloodshed." It was natural that Amsterdam, the city which had had a tolerant government for years, was considered by those who looked for a place of refuge and by the prophets who were in search of the chosen city. However, other cities were also being considered. Among them were Deventer, Wesel, and London. As will be seen, even smaller places were used as a base for the spread of God's kingdom.[63]

Jan van Geelen, who went from Münster to the Netherlands to win support for the besieged city of God, seemed to be uncertain about the place chosen by God. He proved his disloyalty to Münster by negotiating with authorities who were interested in turning the city over to the emperor. For this act, he, for some time, was granted safe conduct for his activities. Jan van Geelen was ready to see God's finger pointing at another city and eventually died in an attempt to take over the city of Amsterdam for the saints.

Jan van Geelen traveled extensively (Antwerp, Utrecht, Groningen, Friesland) trying to stir up the population and to establish centers of militant Anabaptism. He succeeded in taking over the monastery Olde-klooster near Bolsward, Friesland, on March 30, 1535, with some three hundred followers. The imperial stadholder, Georg Schenck van Toutenburg, besieged the monastery and had to use heavy artillery. Only after repeated assaults and a final heavy battle did van Touten-burg succeed in retaking the monastery on April 7. Many of the Ana-baptists had perished in the battle, thirty-seven were beheaded at one time, and 132, both men and women, were taken to Leeuwarden, of whom fifty-five were executed. Nevertheless, Jan van Geelen escaped.[64]

This tragic development of Anabaptism greatly affected the spiritual development of a young priest in the nearby village, Witmarsum. When Anabaptism was transplanted to this area by Jan Volkertsz Trypmaker, which led to the martyrdom of Sicke Freerks in Leeuwar-den, Menno Simons had become disturbed in regard to infant baptism. As early as 1532, some persons around Witmarsum had been baptized. In addition to his consideration of adult baptism, Menno Simons ac-cepted some Sacramentarian views pertaining to the Lord's supper. He made these doctrinal changes and sympathized with the Anabaptists without leaving his Catholic parish. When radical Münsterites came into his community, he was deeply disturbed. Early in 1534, he had public and secret discussions with "two fathers of the rotten sect," one of whom could have been Jan van Geelen. In any event, "the report spread" that he "could silence these persons beautifully. Everybody de-fended himself by reference" to him. According to Menno Simons, the Oldeklooster tragedy occurred "through the ungodly doctrines of Mün-ster, and in opposition to the Spirit, Word, and example of Christ; they drew the sword to defend themselves, the sword which the Lord commanded Peter to put in its sheath." The Oldeklooster incident speeded up Menno's conversion and development. "The blood of these people, although misled, fell so hot on my heart that I could not stand it," he reflected later.[65]

During the following nine months before he left his parish, he preached "the word of true repentance publicly from the pulpit," reproved "sin and wickedness, all idolatry and false worship," and pre-sented "the true worship." He also "faithfully warned everyone against the abominations of Münster, condemning king, polygamy, kingdom, sword, etc." But his work was not restricted to preaching. Among his many writings the first one was addressed "to all the true Brethren of the Covenant scattered abroad, against the great and fearful Blasphemy of Jan van Leiden, who poses as the joyous King of all ... so Usurping the Place of God." This "Plain and Clear Proof from Scripture, Proving that Jesus Christ is the Real, Spiritual David of the Promise, the King of Kings ... Spiritual King of Israel, that is, of His Church" was the first Anabaptist tract pointing out the fallacies of the radical Münster-ite views. The first part of the writings called on the "true covenanters" to reject the views of Jan van Leiden who was an "antichrist," since he had put himself in the place of Christ. God, who had placed Christ as the head of the church, could not tolerate giving this place to someone else. In the second part of the booklet Menno presented the view, that the Christian has no other weapon but the Scriptures, to which he has to conform. His primary call was to discipleship. The judgment over the church belongs to the Lord, whose coming the Christian should anticipate in long-suffering. He pleaded with his readers when he said: "This only I would learn of you, whether you are baptized on the sword or on the cross? So foolish are ye, having begun in the Spirit, are ye now made perfect by flesh? Have you suffered so many things in vain?" [66]

This strong warning against the Münsterites and the call to an evangelical view of the church and the Christian life did not reach the covenanters in a printed form before the collapse of Münster. Nevertheless, it clearly stated and reflected the issues involved between the peaceful and militant Melchiorites. For a while it seemed as though the latter were predominant, particularly in leadership. The writing of Menno Simons against the "Blasphemy of Jan van Leiden" and other publications that followed in rapid succession proves that there was a core of covenanters who had always opposed the radicals, and if they had wavered, they now became thoroughly disillusioned and, as sheep without a shepherd, willingly followed the leadership of such men as Menno Simons, and Dirk and Obbe Philips. Others op-posing the radicalism were David Joris and, to some extent, Jacob van Campen.

Jan van Geelen had escaped once more and had soon proceeded to Amsterdam. While negotiating with Pieter van Montfoort, represen-tative of the Brussels government, about a surrender of Münster to the emperor, he secretly prepared an attack on the city hall of Amster-dam. Feverishly he went to work trying to win the Anabaptists of

Amsterdam as well as those in the neighborhood for his cause. He was particularly interested in winning the influential leader, Jacob van Campen, whom he had repeatedly made an effort to win for his revolutionary cause. Just before the attack he asked Jacob van Campen through Fije Danen to come to him at once. He refused to comply since he "did not approve of the plan" which would indicate that he had some idea what Jan van Geelen intended to do.

The daring attack was planned for the evening of May 10, 1535, at the time that the burgomasters were celebrating with a guild in the city hall. It was expected that a surprise attack after the alcoholic beverages had been served would assure a success. Since the burgomasters were warned in advance, the attack was not a complete surprise. During the struggle, burgomaster Colijn, who had been sympathetic toward the evangelical cause, and others were killed. The attackers succeeded in taking over the city hall for the night, but in the morning during the counterattack, one after the other, was killed. Jan van Geelen climbed on the tower, exposing himself to the bullets, and then threw himself on the street in order to escape torture and execution. Approximately forty had participated in the attack. Three hundred came from Benschop when it was too late. Jan van Geelen had miscalculated the willingness of the Anabaptists to take the city by force. If he had counted on sympathy for such a plan among the government circles, he was mistaken.

This was the end of whatever tolerance had been practiced during the last years. Hunting up of Anabaptists, using all cruelties known and inventing new ones, became the competitive enterprise of the magistrate. Jacob van Campen, although he had opposed the attack, was apprehended and condemned to die. He was put on display in the square in front of the city hall; his tongue, which he had used "to spread false teachings," was cut off, his right hand, "which he had used in baptizing," was cut off, and after this he was beheaded. His head and hand were displayed at the Haarlem Gate to warn others. Jan Matthijsz van Middelburg, who was also sought, escaped to England. He was accused of having helped Jan van Geelen but must have escaped before the attack.[67]

Whatever suspicion there was that the Anabaptists of the Netherlands had become radical and revolutionary was not proven during the uprising in Amsterdam. In a city with between three and five thousand Anabaptists who had been exposed to much propaganda by Jan van Geelen, only some forty were ready to participate in trying to make Amsterdam a city of God. The comparative lenience with which the magistrate had treated the dissenters could have had something to do with Jan van Geelen's failure.

5. The Battle of the New Jerusalem

Little has been said about the physical struggle over the New Jerusalem. Some of the "Children of Jacob" had thought foolheartedly that the besieging army could be dispersed by the sword of the Lord. Jan Matthijsz and Hille Feickes, who tried to imitate Old Testament heroes, were examples. The saints now turned into a tenaciously fighting, well-organized unit, still confident that they were fighting the Lord's battle even if he did not perform many miracles and not much outside help could be expected. How well fortified the city was can be seen by the effort it took on the part of the bishop and the surrounding rulers to conquer the city. The most detailed account of the political and military background of the struggle has been presented by Karl-Heinz Kirchhoff in "Die Belagerung and Eroberung Münsters 1534/35." [68]

The ruling bishop, Franz von Waldeck, was in charge of the siege of Münster that defeated the New Jerusalem. He had been bishop of Minden since 1530 and was elected to the same office in Münster and Osnabrück in 1532. Only in 1540-41 was he consecrated priest and bishop. Although it became his task to defeat the radical Anabaptism which in Münster had grown out of a reformation effort supported by the reformers, he was and remained interested in a moderate reformation of the church. Nevertheless, religious questions were for him subordinated to political and personal interests. The Anabaptist incident gave him a chance to test his diplomatic skill. He managed to involve friend and foe, Catholic and Protestant rulers, and even imperial representatives in the support of his cause by skillfully playing them off against each other in his political moves. Only after the defeat of Münster, when he aimed to exploit his victory for personal ends, did he have to retreat. [69]

As soon as the Anabaptists arrived in Münster, the bishop called his noblemen to take up arms and prepare for the siege. In addition to those subject to service, mercenary soldiers were won, by the bishop and even by the city. By the summer of 1534, the bishop had hired between seven and eight thousand mercenaries from surrounding countries for which he had to pay 34,000 Emden guilders monthly.

By May, 1534, five camps had been established around Münster which gradually closed in the city. Forty cannons and other military equipment had been borrowed from far and near. But what was this in comparison to the eighty-two cannons placed strategically on the walls of the city? The besieged Münsterites made attempts to hinder the work on the fortification around the city by attacking the workers. Thousands of peasants were drafted by the bishop to help with for- tification of the approaches to the city and the draining of the moats. Taxes were levied to raise money. Although the bishop found much resistance and refusal by many of his subjects, he always found new ways and means to increase the income in order to be able to meet the ever increasing cost of the war and keep the mercenaries who, without pay, threatened to leave. Markets were established where the besieging forces could purchase what they needed. This helped peas- ants and merchants to dispose of their goods which they were accus- tomed to take to the markets of Münster.[70]

On May 19, 1534, a four day attack on the city with thirty-five cannons was started. Soldiers and cavalry were to storm the wall at a place where the moat had been drained. But on the evening before the attack, drunken soldiers alarmed the city and the plans had to be given up. The bishop, who had figured on a surrender of the city within a short time, had to seek help for a longer siege. He could expect help from Philip of Hesse who was very much interested in the fate of the bishopric of Münster. It was in danger not only from the Anabaptists but also from Charles V who aimed to gain it as he had obtained some areas of the Low Countries. This alarmed all local rulers, including the rulers of Cologne, Cleves, and Gelderland. Already in December, 1533, Philip had received word from Franz von Waldeck that he had rejected "favorable offers" from Charles V. The bishop had had a visit by the Burgundian representative Georg Schenck van Toutenburg who offered him imperial help in his struggle. The fact that aid from Charles V might result in the bishop's having to turn his bishopric over to Burgundy remained a significant bargaining factor in the nego- tiations for help which Franz von Waldeck conducted among his neighbors. The greatest supporter of the Catholic bishop was Philip of Hesse, one of the staunchest promoters of Protestantism. Gradually the others also helped but remained suspicious and extremely cautious. Even the good relationship with Philip of Hesse became strained when the bishop ordered the murder of Johann von der Wieck, a strong promoter of an evangelical reformation of Münster and an opponent of Anabaptism who had fled the city.[71]

In June the Burgundian government of Brussels sent two representatives to the bishop, expressing surprise that Münster had not yet been taken and saying that the present condition could cause insurrection in the Netherlands. The Regent Maria was willing to help the bishop to the full extent of her powers. This "unlimited offer" disturbed Philip of Hesse very much. He urged Cologne and Trier to help the bishop so that Münster would not become Burgundian. Frightened by this development Cologne and Cleves actually began to help with the war effort, but this did not prevent the bishop from accepting very substantial aid from Burgundy. Especially disturbing was the fact that in July, 1534, the Burgundians also negotiated with the Anabaptists of Münster through Pieter van Montfort, who was also in contact with Jan van Geelen in Amsterdam.[72]

Constantly out of funds, the bishop wrote form letters to the following, pleading for help: King Ferdinand, elector of Mainz, Trier, Saxony and Brandenburg; the dukes of Braunschweig, Lüneburg, and Saxony; the bishop of Lüttich; and Philip of Hesse. Most of them declined, but the fact that Cologne and Cleves sent help prevented the unpaid mercenaries from leaving before the planned attack on Münster. After a four-day attack on August 27 to 31, although the walls had been reached, the bishop's forces had to withdraw. Again more funds were needed to conduct the war. The army of mercenaries was dissolving. Only half of the six thousand remained. In addition, a large part of the cavalry had been dispersed.

An interesting peace mission was attempted by Theodor Fabricius who was sent by Philip of Hesse to the king of the New Jerusalem. The king invited him to stay over night and showed him the city. When the Münsterites were asked to surrender, Fabricius was told that the city had been attacked without reason, and "they would rather die than accept the Catholic Church." Before he departed the next morning, the council told him that they were willing to negotiate with a secular ruler but could not surrender to the bishop because in that case "they feared that they would all die."

Support for the bishop came from the Upper and Lower Rhine areas and Westphalia while Philip of Hesse continued negotiations with Münster. At the *Kreistag* of Koblenz the bishop's representatives presented their request for speedy aid on December 13, 1534. Funds to cover the expenses of the war for six months were granted provided the *status quo* of Münster was guaranteed. Meanwhile, the Hanseatic cities, in February, 1535, attempted to negotiate between the bishop and the king but failed.[73]

Under a new commander in chief, Count Wirich von Dhaun, a wall was to be constructed and a moat was to be dug around the city as preparation for the attack. Reports reached Dhaun from within the city that the Münsterites expected help from the Netherlands by Easter, 1535, at which time they intended to break through the ring of the besieged city to unite with the foreign help. This was the time of the climactic activities of Jan van Geelen.

At the Koblenz *Kreistag* Bishop Franz was instructed to invite the ten imperial districts (*Reichskreise*) to a *Kreistag* at Worms for April 4, 1535. At this latter *Kreistag* funds were insufficient because not all contributions had come in. King Ferdinand, speaking for the emperor, requested more aid. It was decided that the war effort be financed for another six months, that Count Dhaun continue as commander in chief, that he be entitled to accept a surrender of the city, and that the emperor, king, electors, princes, and the states of the empire be entitled to establish the new order in Münster. When some of the free cities protested against the handing over of Münster to the princes, they were granted the privilege of negotiating a surrender with Münster. The Münsterites turned down their offer on May 10.[74]

6. *The Fall of the Kingdom*

In April, 1535, the last gaps in the siege of the city had been closed which cut it off completely from the outside world. But most of the artillery on loan from princes and cities had to be returned in accordance with the terms. Instead of taking the city by force, it was decided to try it through treason.[75]

Now old people, women, and children began to leave the city because of shortage of food. In order to prevent the escape, four were beheaded on April 26 by the besieging forces and the bodies placed at the gate as an example of what would happen to others who would leave the city. Philip of Hesse advised dealing with the refugees in accordance with conscience and reason. He suggested that not all be killed but that each should be examined and only those who were guilty be punished. Between April 22 and June 15, at least fifteen hundred men, women, and children fled, but almost all of the men were killed. Even former mercenaries of the bishop who had entered the city and wanted to surrender were killed without mercy. Those in Münster had reasons to turn down requests to surrender. To add to the pressures of the moment, in this final stage of the conquest of Münster the bishop feared that Karel van Gelder, who was arming for some purpose, was intending to take Münster as he had taken Groningen.[76]

As expected, the conquest of the New Jerusalem was made possible through a betrayal from within. On May 25, Heinrich Gresbeck abandoned his post as a guard at the *Kreuztor* and surrendered. His life was spared and he made information available which led to the entry of the bishop's army into the city. He and Hans Eck, who had also escaped, showed the way into the city on the night of June 24. Under Wilken Steding five hundred mercenaries entered the city through the *Kreuztor*. However, the Münsterites succeeded in closing the *Kreuztor*. The next morning Dhaun entered through the *Jüdefeldertor* and thus the murder of the saints began in full swing. An escape was impossible. In accordance with the bishop's policies of war, there was no mercy for the conquered except for pregnant women, priests, and churches.

The surviving eight hundred armed men of Münster faced three thousand soldiers who had been waiting for this occasion for sixteen months, having gotten no booty and receiving no pay for two months. They did not only want to do justice to their occupation but also to get what they could. The indescribable killing continued for two days. The last three hundred survivors, who had withdrawn into the Wagenburg, were promised that they could leave the city. Hinrich Krechting and twenty-four men were permitted to leave. All others, in spite of the promise, were killed. According to one report 450 of the armed men had been killed during the fighting and an additional two hundred by the soldiers afterwards when they searched the cellars and the attics day after day. On June 27 Dhaun gave orders to stop the killing. Numerous men and women were gathered at the cathedral square where many were condemned and executed. The bodies of those killed and starved to death which were lying on streets and in homes were buried by peasants from the surrounding area in the cathedral square. The stench was unbearable.

On May 23, 1535, a month before the final struggle, the total population of Münster was estimated to be 9500 of whom about nine hundred were men, able to defend the city, 5500 were women, and the rest children. These men, with few exceptions, lost their lives during and after the struggle. Some 3500 to 4000 women and an unknown number of children survived the conquest of the city. Some of the women were among the executed at the end of June, and the others had to leave the city within three days. Those from other places often found shelter among relatives. Those from Münster were promised to be pardoned if they would renounce their Anabaptist views. A large number must have refused to do this. A year later there were 216 women and nineteen men in the city who were "Münsterites" who had renounced their views and had proven to be innocent.[77]

Bernhard Rothmann must have perished in the city unless he escaped. No definite reports about his fate are available.[78] Details are given about Jan van Leiden, B. Knipperdolling, and B. Krechting. Bishop Franz personally came to the city to receive his share of the booty including the king's insignia and the three captive leaders of the New Jerusalem. He could barely stand the three days in the city because of the conditions and stench in it. The bishop claimed half of the total booty, which included all the property of the Anabaptists, while the mercenaries received the movable property. Since they had not received all their pay, a considerable unrest was the result. The citizens of Münster who had been driven out by the Anabaptists had the right to buy back their own property.[79]

Jan van Leiden, Knipperdolling, and Krechting became a public spectacle and were interviewed for various purposes; among their interviewers were theologians. Philip of Hesse showed particular interest in these interviews. Antonius Corvinus and Johannes Rymens had lengthy discussions with the three leaders about which they reported by stating the leaders' views and refuting them. Ironically enough, when Corvinus and his friends used scriptural evidence to show that they were not doing God's will in establishing themselves in Münster and when they admonished the king that Christians cannot take up arms to defend their faith, they sounded more like true Anabaptists than representatives of Luther and Philip of Hesse.

From the report of the first interview with van Leiden, it becomes apparent that Jan van Leiden had been influenced strongly by the views held by Rothmann and also by Hofmann, including the latter's Christology. Jan van Leiden agreed that the Christian must be obedient to the government in all temporal matters but must obey God more than men. Other matters discussed were justification by faith, the Sacraments, the incarnation of Christ, and marriage.

After their first session with van Leiden at Bevergern near Rheine, Corvinus and Rymens went to Knipperdolling and Krechting at Horstmar but were notified after eight days that Jan van Leiden wanted to have another discussion with them at which occasion he would be more cooperative. After having obtained approval from Philip of Hesse, they returned to spend two more days with him. He let it be known to them that he was hopeful that his life would be spared and that he was willing, with the help of his wives and Hofmann, to do his utmost to persuade all Anabaptists everywhere to "be silent and obedient, to refrain from insurrections... to baptize their children until the government achieves unity in matters of religion." The interviewers now formulated Jan van Leiden's views stating "that the kingdom at Münster was a vain and dead structure" and that he had become king not out of his own desire, but because of the prophecy of Dusentschuer. He now admitted that one must obey every government whether by "Turks or good-for-nothings" since it was "ordained by God." He still believed that faith must bring forth fruit and that infant baptism was not right but was willing to advise the Anabaptists that their offices of "bishops, prophets, and baptism be discontinued... and that nothing should be taught about [adult] baptism which is not permitted by the government." Similarly he expressed himself about the Lord's supper, the incarnation of Christ, and marriage. This document ends "I, Johann van Leiden, signed with my own hand."[80] It is hard to tell of whom this end result was more characteristic, of the price that the king thought he had to and was willing to pay or the inspiration that the two examiners gave him to make of the government, any government, a supreme idol, if not a god. It was a long way from these Lutheran views of the relationship of Christianity and government to those of Karl Barth and Dietrich Bonhoeffer.

As indicated above, the matter of marriage and polygamy was also discussed. When Jan van Leiden claimed that they had merely followed the pattern of the Old Testament patriarchs, he was told that even contemporary society forbade this practice for social and political reasons. It seems incongruous that these ministers of Philip of Hesse, who not only practiced bigamy but had received permission for it from Luther, were sent to the Anabaptists to teach them ethical standards.

The interviews with Knipperdolling and Krechting were similar. An additional item was the matter of whether the mortification of the flesh preceded or followed faith. The Münsterites claimed that they are as inseparable as the light and heat of the candle.[81]

But Philip of Hesse was not satisfied with these interviews. He ar-

ranged for the Strassburg patrician, Bernhard Wurmser, to interview
Jan van Leiden to find out what relationship there had been between
him and Melchior Hofmann who was still in the prison at Strassburg.
He was hopeful that such an interview would yield considerable information about the international threads of the spider web of Anabaptism. On September 25, 1535, he urged that the execution should be
postponed for this purpose. The interview took place late in November of 1535, also at Bevergern near Rheine. Wurmser presented Philip's crucial concern: whether Jan van Leiden and Knipperdolling had
sent Hofmann to Strassburg to start a similar kingdom as they had
done in Münster. To this van Leiden replied that he had never met
Hofmann nor did he ever have any contact with him except through
his writings which he had seen and read some time ago. This conversation, which included a discussion about van Leiden's other activities
and wives, continued into the night; the next day they had dinner
together, at which time van Leiden was again pressed about possible
contacts with Hofmann which he denied. Instead of going to Horstmar
to interview Knipperdolling, Wurmser went to do some sight-seeing
in Münster and even saw the cage into which Jan van Leiden was to
be put after his death. The jewels of the king were already on display
at that time. But as far as the real purpose of his trip was concerned,
it had yielded none of the information Philip of Hesse had sought.
The fact that Philip also admonished the Strassburg city council to
look out for Jan van Geelen, who was supposed to have gone to this
city, and that even after the fall of Münster Hofmann remained a
great concern to all and was kept in more rigid imprisonment indicates that religious and secular leaders feared that another kingdom
would be established.[82]

That Hofmann was aware of the Münsterite kingdom but was
hardly in touch with it is indicated by the fact that he told the city
council of Strassburg on November 23, 1534, that "Münster has a
prophet, Jan Matthijsz, who claimes to be a witness of God." That
he had died in April seemed to be unknown to Hofmann. "Münster
shall not be molested," Hofmann said. But for him Strassburg remained the city "chosen by God above all cities of the earth to his praise."
There were considerable differences between Hofmann and some of
his radical followers, including the fact that he remained a visionary
dreamer of God's kingdom to be established in Strassburg while others
were more pragmatic in shifting from town to town depending on the
possibilities of achieving their goals. Even in 1539 when visited by

Konrad van Bühel Hofmann admonished his followers to "be pious and live quietly," keep "the marriage intact and create no mobs," and to keep in mind the outcome of "the Peasants' War, of Zwingli in Switzerland, and the Münster rebellion." [83]

This brings to a close one of the most unusual and adventuresome chapters in Anabaptist history. One aspect could be related, in more detail and that is the personal fate of the leaders who were dealt with in a special way. As indicated earlier, Rothmann most likely perished in the final battle although his body was never located which caused rumors that he had escaped. Jan van Leiden was found hiding and so was Knipperdolling. B. Krechting was found in the Aegidius monastery. Although the killing and execution of the "pale" looking Anabaptists went on for eight days, according to Kerssenbroch, these three were kept alive for special treatment. With rings around their necks they were chained to the saddles of horses and were taken walking to Iburg where they were kept in a prison.

The main spectacle, the execution, was in line with medieval tradition and brutality. It took place in front of the cathedral where the throne of King David had stood. On the 20th of January they were transferred to Münster and interviewed. For a second time, Knipperdolling was pressed for answers under torture. The examiners were again particularly interested in finding out about underground international Anabaptist contacts, but the answers yielded little information. Each one minimized his responsibility in the role he had played. [84] The day before the execution Jan van Leiden availed himself of the consolation of Johann von Siburg who spent the night with him. According to Kerssenbroch, who relied heavily on A. Corvinus, an eyewitness to the torture and execution, he must have repented of his errors and admitted that he deserved to die ten times.

The bishop, who had also interviewed Jan van Leiden, watched the event from a window of a house. Jan van Leiden fell on his knees and prayed. Johann Wesseling proclaimed the death penalty against all three since they "had sinned against God and the government." Jan van Leiden admitted to having "offended" the government but not God.

On the elevated stage of execution was a container with hot glowing coal and pincers for torture purposes. The victims were strapped against posts with iron rings around their necks. Jan van Leiden was the first to be tortured. When Knipperdolling witnessed how the hot glowing pincers were used to burn the body of Jan van Leiden, he attempted to end his life by hanging his head over the iron ring around his neck. The executioner tied his head against the post with a rope through his mouth in order to prevent his attempts. After the final act of torture, which consisted of pulling out their tongues with the hot pincers, they were put to death by piercing their hearts with a glowing hot dagger. The stench in the air was almost unbearable.

The executed were put into large iron cages and hung up on the tower of the St. Lambert Church, where replicas of these cages hang to this day, and the pincers were attached to a column of the city hall. This was done so that "all insurrectionists who refuse to obey proper authorities would see in this an example and warning."[85]

The tale of the kingdom and its end has been told by serious scholars, artists, and literary writers in all ages and has remained popular to the present. It is not surprising that special attention has been given to Münster as well as to Thomas Müntzer by Marxian historians.[86]

VI

GATHERING A CHRISTIAN FELLOWSHIP

The failure to establish a visible kingdom of God on earth did not end the attempts to do so. Eschatological expectations and severe persecution had spurred the attempts. Without the latter the saints would likely never have taken up arms in defence of the kingdom. Among some surviving radical Anabaptists the thought of executing the wrath of God remained a significant factor even though the religious and eschatological aspect of the kingdom of God gradually disappeared. The revenge motif for persecution suffered personally or by relatives continued to play a significant role. Jan van Batenburg, a man of noble background, took this position. He defended righteousness and acted as a criminal at the same time. Although it is usually pointed out that the feared Batenburgers deteriorated to a status of gangsterism, there was, at times, a sense of justice noticeable among them. Like the famous Volga Cossack, Stenka Razin, they aimed to punish evil and help the oppressed.

However, the faith, hope, and dedicated discipleship of early Melchioritism, although in modified form, survived and were intensified among those who had not participated in attempts to establish an earthly kingdom but were willing to endure persecution for the sake of Christ. Even many of those who had been carried along by the prophets to immediate action returned in disillusionment to the home base of peaceful Melchioritism. The hope of Christ's return remained, but the where, when, and how were left in the hands of the Lord.

One more result of this development must be called to attention. In the court hearings, trials, and verdicts, as well as the contemporary reports and histories of Anabaptism, very little effort was made to distinguish between the various Anabaptist groups whether they were peaceful, militant, or insurrectionist. Just to practice *ana*-baptism, that is, to rebaptize adults, carried with it the stigma of blasphemy against God and of insurrectionist activities against the government, be this in Catholic or Protestant countries. This made the peaceful surviving Anabaptists even more emphatic on the quiet and withdrawn Christian life. In their emerging historiography they distanced themselves from the source of the stigma, militant Anabaptism or the Münsterites.

A. SIFTING AND GATHERING

1. *Appraising Differences*

It has become apparent that many of the leaders opposed the radical development of Anabaptism leading to incidents like those that had occurred in Amsterdam, Münster, and other places. Menno Simons, although still a Sacramentarian priest, did his utmost to counteract this development. Jacob van Campen, Obbe and Dirk Philips, David Joris, and others resisted Jan van Geelen and other apostles of Münster. It will never be possible to evaluate the unrecorded witness in quietness against this radicalization. At places like Amsterdam where several thousand Anabaptists were found, only a few aimed to establish themselves in that city by force. But only the testimony of those tried was recorded, and above all those were apprehended, tried, and examined who were preaching and practicing the use of force.

It would, however, be misleading to assume that there were already at that time always noticeable, clear-cut lines between the peaceful and violent Melchiorites. Self-defense by the use of spiritual, psychological, and physical means is a human characteristic that no one ever gives up completely as long as he lives. Suffering for the cause of Christ was strongly emphasized by most, but the desire to live was never absent unless it was sublimated by the desire to live with Christ in the glory of the heavenly kingdom. In this situation some were challenged to suffer for Christ in the establishment of his kingdom on earth after which the reward would be forthcoming.

How flexible the lines still were in 1536 is demonstrated by the fact that representatives of most of the divergent Anabaptist groups met at Bocholt in order to discuss their differences and, if possible, reach some agreements. The representatives were primarily from the center of the Anabaptist groups. Neither Obbe and Dirk Philips, on the one hand nor Jan van Batenburg, on the other, were present. David Joris emerged as the dominating mediator between the extremes. Probably no one could have played this role better than he did.

The Bocholt meeting of Anabaptists convened in August, 1536.

Bocholt is located near Wesel and Emmerich in the province of West-phalia. The financial convener of the conference was an English Ana-baptist known as Henry. The group consisted of some twenty leaders coming from far and near. Among them were Jan Matthijsz van Mid-delburg and Johan van Utrecht from England; Johan van Maastricht and Johan van Schoonhoven from the province of Holland; Matthias van Balk, Tiardus van Sneek, and Stewerdus Klerick from Friesland; and Jan van Gulik, Christoffel and Hendrik van Zutphen from Gel-derland. The presence of David Joris enabled his son-in-law, N. Bles-dijk, later to give a detailed report about the meeting.[1]

The representatives could be classified as Melchiorites, Münsterites, and Batenburgers. They shared views in matters of baptism, the Lord's supper, the incarnation of Christ and, to some extent, also in regard to the second coming of Christ. The Melchiorites could under no circum-stances accept the views of the Münsterites in regard to polygamy and the earthly kingdom of God, not to speak of the acts of crime which the Batenburgers engaged in. David Joris proved to be a successful mediator, establishing an understanding between the Melchiorites and Münsterites. In view of the fact that they "are one on many important points and that there are only differences in two major areas, they agree to abstain from bitter controversy and to pray to God to give them light and to show them the way to unity." The conference was, how-ever, probably more important in assessing existing differences than in achieving unity. The Batenburgers found no sympathy and were advised to refrain from pillaging churches and from killing those who had done them wrong.

Anabaptism did not disappear from the province of Westphalia with the fall of Münster. Not all had moved to the city; neither had all those who had gone to Münster perished. The number of surviving men was small, but a large number of women and children found shelter among relatives and friends. Some who had not gone to Mün-ster had never been afflicted by some of the radical views. Others continued to adhere to Münsterite expectations and even Jan van Ba-tenburg had some followers in the province. Some of the places that had had Anabaptists continued to remain centers. Jasper Smedes of Coesfeld, who rejected the views of Batenburg, held to views of Ana-baptism including the establishment of a kingdom of David and Solo-mon. He is reported to have known between two and three hundred Anabaptists.[2]

The city of Münster again housed Anabaptists and even attracted some from Groningen who arrived in the fall of 1538. One of this group had married a Münsterite girl who had survived the fall in 1535. From the Groningen group's confession it became apparent that they had stopped on the way at Oldenburg where they intended to check up on the present status of the views of Hinrich Krechting, who had escaped from Münster and was the leader of a group. They also related that a prophet had said that by 1540 Münster would again be conquered by the Anabaptists.[3]

Nevertheless, the spirit of the Münsterites did not survive in West-phalia, but the *Mennisten* did. On July 18, 1607, a petition of "all Fellow believers, commonly called *Mennisten,* appealed to the city council of Bocholt declaring that they had nothing in common with the Münsterites of 1533 and that everybody could testify that they were quiet citizens for which reason they begged that the edicts against them be annulled." This was the general development of Anabaptism in Westphalia as far as it survived the persecution.[4]

It has been observed that Hinrich Krechting and a few others were given the opportunity to escape from Münster after its defeat. Krech-ting had fled to Oldenburg where he gathered a fellowship of Anabap-tists. Batenburg called him a "great commander of David Joris." He listed Krechting with the "Anabaptist Bernardus, a great man,"[5] who, some assume, was Bernhard Rothmann. He had not been identified among the dead nor living after the battle of Münster. David Joris attended an Anabaptist meeting in Oldenburg in May, 1538, consisting of followers of Krechting. Another meeting followed in August at-tended by some one hundred Anabaptists. They still dealt with such questions as to where and when the Lord's second coming was to be expected. In the form of a prophecy it was revealed that this would take place at the end of December, 1538, at Münster, when it would be fulfilled that the "holy city shall they tread under foot forty and two months."[6] However, Krechting soon left Oldenburg and settled in Gödens, East Friesland, where he became an honorable member (*Vor-steher*) of the Reformed Church under the influence of John a Lasco, the reformer of East Friesland.[7]

Reference has been made to Jan van Batenburg, who after the fall of Münster assumed leadership among the most radical Münsterites, particularly in the Netherlands. He was a descendant of the noble van Batenburg family of Gelderland and was the mayor of Steenwijk before he joined the Anabaptists. Little is known about his connections with Anabaptism before and during the Münster episode, but after the fall of Münster, he succeeded in gathering many radicals. When he was arrested and tried in 1538, he related how he received a call to destroy Babel (Burgundy) and the Babylonian whore (papacy) by sword. During his trial he was a little too cooperative, blaming the committed atrocities on others and naming many Anabaptist leaders, most of whom had no contact with his radical group. Kirchhoff says that he "gave the names of approximately one hundred Anabaptists of all shades but did not betray his own followers." Topping the list were David Joris, and Obbe and Dirk Philips. Menno Simons, although active in gathering the peaceful Anabaptists, was not mentioned in the list.[8] It so happened that these four became the major leaders of peaceful Anabaptism. The Batenburgers and other radical Münsterites gradually disappeared from the scene after the execution of Batenburg in 1538.

2. A Leadership Emerges

In "Menno and Münster" the encounter of Menno Simons, the parish priest of Witmarsum, Friesland, with Jan van Geelen was related. The factors leading to Menno's conversion to Sacramentarianism and Anabaptism have also been recounted. In his writing against Jan van Leiden he took a courageous stand not only in regard to the Münsterites but also in connection with the errors of the Catholic Church from which he withdrew early in 1536. He now wrote tract after tract laying the biblical foundation for a disciplined Christian church. At about the time of Batenburg's trial and death, when some of his followers turned to David Joris, Menno wrote in his *Foundation Book*: "Is it not a grievous error that you suffer yourselves to be woefully seduced by such worthless persons, and so sadly misled from one unclean sect to another: first to that of Münster, next to Batenburg, now Davidian...? You are ever learning but never able to come to the knowledge of the real truth. You suffer yourselves to be led about by every wind of doctrine."[9] It was evident, at this point, that Menno Simons did not fully approve of the views of David Joris. This became even more apparent later as their ways parted.

On the other hand Menno, the shepherd and gatherer of erring sheep, had tender words of love when he addressed "the corrupt sects" in the early edition of *Foundation Book* by saying: "My chosen brethren, but not in Christ Jesus, because those are brethren in Christ Jesus who remain steadfast in his Holy Word and are... born of

God." He therefore admonished them to "give up their errors and to seek Christ again, your only and true shepherd, whom you have lost...". Thinking of the many who were on the verge of being misled and those who followed the call to Münster, Menno continued: "'I do not doubt but that our dear brethren who have formerly transgressed a little against the Lord, when they intended to defend their faith with arms, have a merciful God. I hope they were not tainted by the previously mentioned [Münsterite] heresies. They sought nothing but Christ Jesus and eternal life, and for this cause they forsook all their possessions, their own kindred, yea, their own lives, although afterwards they erred a little, as said above, ... namely, they used weapons other than patient endurance and God's word. And it is not to be wondered that they erred at that time, for in those times they had not yet examined the spirits" (I John 4:1).

These were the cautious words written by one who had opposed the Münsterite trend with all his power of persuasion and who had lost some members of his own parish. The words were written at the time when the sifting of the spirits took place and when the call to a return to the sound foundation was extended by Menno Simons and his coworkers. They were the words of a shepherd gathering the flock scattered by the wolf. Later when this task had been accomplished, Menno ommitted and altered the passages in a revised edition of the *Foundation Book*.[10] Menno Simons did more than any other leader of Dutch Anabaptism in gathering the Melchiorites. Because of his courageous work in preaching and writing in the most crucial moment of Anabaptism's development, some attention should be given to his early life and religious development.

Menno Simons was born in the little village of Witmarsum, Friesland, likely in 1496. Since he knew Latin and some Greek, it can be assumed that he received his training in a monastery in Friesland or Groningen. Albert Hardenberg, who received his training at the Aduard Monastery near Groningen and whose path crossed with that of Menno's repeatedly, was not very flattering when he said the following about the latter's education: "One who has had stupid teachers during his studies hardly teaches with understanding. Those who have left monasteries without study and without correct understanding or are self-taught have done much damage to the church. Such a one is a certain Menno Simons, whom I knew as a rural priest." It has been conjectured that Menno was educated at Aduard and he and Hartenberg met there. In this event, Hardenberg's remarks would not have been very complimentary in regard to his alma mater, and they are not in line with his writing a biography of Wessel Gansfort, the founder of Aduard. Thus it is doubtful that Menno was an alumnus of Aduard. Hardenberg, a student at Aduard (1527-30), may have learned to know Menno as a priest at Witmarsum who had accepted the Sacramentarian views. Hardenberg was soon to accept the same views.

The following additional testimony of Hardenberg in regard to Menno is an unintended credit to the latter in spite of the lack of his education. Menno Simons "after reading fanatical books indiscriminately and taking the Bible into his hands without judgment and formal education, has done much harm among the Frisians, Belgians, Menapiers, Saxons, and Cymarians, over all surrounding countries, so that posterity will not be able to shed sufficient tears on this account." [11] That Menno became an influential leader among the Anabaptists was true, although Hardenberg probably made an overstatement. Furthermore, a statement in the first cited testimony of Hardenberg needs to be corrected. Menno Simons did not leave the Catholic Church by running away from a monastery, but by leaving the parish as a priest.

In 1524, at the age of 28, Menno was ordained priest at Utrecht. He first served as vicar at Pingjum near Witmarsum. He complained later that he joined his fellow priests in "playing [cards], drinking, and in diversions." His co-workers had "read the Scriptures a little," but he "had never touched them" because he feared that if he would read them he "would be misled." Now he exclaimed: "Behold, such an ignorant priest was I for nearly two years." "And when [they] touched upon the Scriptures," he could not speak a word with his colleagues "without being scoffed at." The first jolt that made Menno open the Scriptures and study them was the Sacramentarian question as to whether bread and wine are actually transformed into the body of Christ. His problems were quickly resolved, and he whole-heartedly accepted the Sacramentarian views along this line after discovering the Bible. Even Luther, in whose writings he found that "human injunctions cannot bind unto eternal death," [12] helped him. Thus Menno served his parish as a Sacramentarian priest for a number of years and gradually developed into an evangelical preacher, although he complained in retrospect that "the world loved him and he the world."

When, in 1530, Sicke Freerks Snijder, who had been baptized in Emden, was put to death in Leeuwarden, Menno faced the problem of investigating the essence of another sacrament he had grown up with and had been administering. He "examined the Scriptures diligently and pondered them earnestly, but could find no report of infant baptism." After consulting Luther, Bucer, and Bullinger, he came to the conclusion that they "varied greatly . . . among themselves" and that he was "deceived in regard to infant baptism." Thus he "obtained a view of baptism and the Lord's supper through the illumination of the Holy Ghost, through much reading and pondering of the Scriptures," and not through "the erring sects" as he was accused. Nevertheless, Menno continued as an evangelical preacher in his parish. When the "sect of Münster made its appearance," he faced new problems. "Many pious hearts in our quarter were deceived." It has been pointed out that he opposed them through his evangelical preaching and debated with some leaders so that is was said that he "could silence these persons beautifully."

The indicents at the *Oldeklooster* nearby and at Münster brought Menno Simons' struggles to a climax. He described this in the following words: "I prayed to God with sighs and tears that He would give to me, a sorrowing sinner, the gift of His grace, create within me a clean heart, and . . . bestow upon me wisdom, Spirit, courage, and a manly spirit so that I might preach His exalted adorable name and holy Word in purity, and make known His truth to His glory." This constituted the decisive hour in the life of Menno. He continued his report by stating: "I began in the name of Christ to preach publicly from the pulpit the word of true repentance." He preached and wrote against the "abominations of Münster," which at this moment were reaching their final stage. This he continued for nine months, that is from May, 1535, until January, 1536. At this latter date, Menno, "without constraint, of a sudden renounced all . . . worldly reputation, name, and fame . . . and willingly submitted to the distress and poverty under the heavy cross of Christ." Between the lines of Menno's report we must read that his evangelical preaching and his views had developed to a point that he was in danger of being apprehended. Consequently, he withdrew and went underground. This meant that he "sought out the pious" and that he "found some who were zealous and maintained the truth, . . . dealt with the erring, and through the help and power of God with His Word, reclaimed them from the snares of damnation and gained them to Christ," leaving "the hardened and rebellious . . . to the Lord." [13]

After Menno's withdrawal from Witmarsum, he "secretly exercised" himself "in the Word of God by reading and writing." Some of the earliest writings after the pamphlet against Jan van Leiden were *The Spiritual Resurrection* (c. 1536), *The New Birth* (c. 1537), and *Meditation on the Twenty-Fifth Psalm* (c. 1537). He now wrote these tracts for which the conceptions and basic thoughts had been on his mind for some time. These practical devotional writings found their crowning in the *Foundation of the Christian Doctrine* (1539). This *Foundation Book,* enlarged by the preceding and some following writings, became one of the most significant means to gather the scattered Melchiorites, Obbites, and even some Münsterites on a more solid and stable Christian foundation than had been the case since Melchioritism swept the Low Countries. This was symbolized by the fact that every writing from the first to the last bore on the title page the motto of Menno: "For other foundation can no man lay than that which is laid, which is Jesus Christ" (I Corinthians 3:11). In simple language Menno Simons presented basic doctrines and ethical standards based on the New Testament to a bewildered, seeking group of covenanters, who found in these writings the guide they needed and were looking for.[14]

Leaving Witmarsum Menno found a temporary shelter in Groningen. Here he must have done his first "reading and writing" and here he was likely also baptized and married to Gertrud, his faithful companion in the following years of tribulation and persecution. He was baptized by Obbe Philips. One of the most far-reaching steps taken while Menno was "secretly" engaged in "reading and writing" was initiated by the call extended to him by "some six, seven, or eight persons" who urged him "to put to good use the talents" which he had received from the Lord. After a period of searching prayer he consented "to teach and to baptize, to till the vineyard of the Lord...., to build up His holy city and temple and to repair the tumble-down walls." At least some members of the delegation urging Menno to assume the responsibility of leadership among them must have been from Leeuwarden. With these, as well as with Obbe and Dirk Philips, he must have been in contact while he served in Witmarsum. Obbe Philips who had baptized him, now also ordained him for his field of service. This happened early in 1537 in or near the city of Groningen. That Menno never referred to Obbe Philips in this connection must be due to the fact that Obbe later renounced his calling and left the fold he had helped to bring into being.[15]

In writing his valuable and detailed account about his calling, Menno Simons emphasized that he "was not called by the Münsterites

nor any other sect as it is falsely reported," but that he was called
"by people who had subjected themselves to Christ and His Word,...
served their neighbors in love, bore the cross, sought the welfare and
salvation of all men." [16] Could this be said about Obbe and Dirk
Philips? Or were they also tainted by the Münsterites? Obbe Philips
stated in his Confession: "God knows that [Dirk] and I could never
find it in our hearts that such onslaughts were right; we taught firmly
against this... The false brethren whom we punished and spoke out
against vowed our deaths... Were it not for the love I felt for the
simple hearts who were daily misled by the false brethren, I would
long ago have left them... We were never in our hearts given over
to such seditious inspiration and false prophecy. Indeed, I may well
say with truth that my love of the brethren in the zeal for the house
of the Lord very nearly engulfed me." Dirk Philips who was ordained
by his brother, Obbe, expressed himself similarly. Obbe Philips also
baptized and ordained David Joris, who similarly disapproved of the
Münsterite radicalism. [17]

Obbe and Dirk Philips were sons of a priest in Leeuwarden. The
former became a barber-physician and the latter became a Franciscan
monk, whereby he acquired some knowledge of Latin, Greek, Hebrew,
and theology. How the two were won for the Sacramentarian and
Anabaptist cause has been related previously. Both became traveling
evangelists due to persecution and their zeal to witness. As has been
seen, both were strong opponents of the Münsterite development and
suffered great inner agony because so many did not heed their warning.
Obbe Philips was imprisoned but succeeded in escaping. Not much information is available about his activities after he had ordained Menno
in 1537. By 1539 he was in Rostock where he had gathered a circle
of followers.

During the following year the list of Anabaptist leaders speaks of
Obbe Philips as having "renounced the faith." Menno Simons reported in a writing in 1554 in which he related his conversion and ordination that "Obbe has become a Demas." Obbe himself gave a detailed
account of the reasons for his withdrawal in A Confession. He emphasized not having had a valid calling without stating whether he joined
another denomination. It is generally assumed that he became a religious individualist without any denominational ties, similarly to Sebastian Franck. There is a likelihood that he joined the Lutheran Church. [18]

In regard to Dirk Philips, Menno Simons said that "the followers of
Dirk and we agree, and I trust through the grace of God, we will ever

continue so." [19] Although there were differences of emphasis at times, they continued as co-workers. Not so David Joris. His contribution will be presented in the following chapter.

Even though Menno spent some time in Groningen reading and writing, where he could have been baptized and married and where he was installed elder "by people who had subjected themselves to Christ and His word," his real work started in the neighboring province, East Friesland, where Melchior Hofmann had initiated Anabaptism a few years ago. For a number of years this was the center of the renewal of Melchioritism or Anabaptism. Neither in his native Friesland nor in Groningen could Menno Simons spend any length of time. Menno himself stated in 1544 that he "could not find in all countries a cabin or hut in which my poor wife and little children could be put up in safety for a year or even half a year." [20] Herman and Geeryt Jansz from his native Witmarsum were accused on October 24, 1536, of having sheltered Menno Simons. This indicated that he had returned to his home community. Tyaard Renicx of Friesland was executed in Leeuwarden in January, 1539, because he had sheltered Menno. Numerous other Anabaptists were put to death during these years. Thus Menno Simons "came to Friesland once or twice a year," as stated in a document of Leeuwarden dated May 19, 1541. The following year a hundred guilders were offered by the authorities of Leeuwarden for the apprehension of Menno Simons who continued to appear by night at different places to preach and baptize. [21] There was no permanent place for residence available to him in his native country after his renunciation of the Catholic Church.

The situation was not much better in the neighboring province of Groningen. On June 7, 1536, Charles V himself was royally received in Groningen by Schenck van Toutenburg; this procedure added another province to Burgundy. Maria, regent at Brussels, complained on March 22, 1537, that Anabaptists were being tolerated in Groningen. The mayor and city council responded that they were doing everything possible to enforce the imperial mandates. [22] Obbe Philips was imprisoned and Dirk Philips and Menno Simons had left, at least temporarily.

3. A Refuge in East Friesland

Peter Jansz confessed on June 14, 1540, that Menno had baptized him at Oldersum, East Friesland, "about four years ago." This indicates

that Menno reached the shelter and center of the activities of Melchior
Hofmann and Karlstadt soon after his withdrawal in Witmarsum. The
sponsor, Ulrich von Dornum, however, died in the early spring of
1536 so that Menno may not have met him upon his arrival. The tradition of hospitality, however, was continued by his brother, Hero
von Oldersum, so that Menno and others found shelter here.[23]

Before Ulrich died he had left the Oldersum castle and established a
new residence at Tergast where his three daughters lived after his
death. In 1551 Margarethe married Christoffer van Ewsum from Groningen, who lived for some time in East Friesland, and continued the
spiritual heritage of Ulrich by providing shelter to radical reformers
including Menno Simons. A son was named Andreas, likely after
Karlstadt. Essa married a Johan Gerdsema, an Anabaptist refugee
from the Netherlands. There are some indications that Imele was also
married to an Anabaptist.[24]

To what extent East Friesland was still an open field for cultivation
is evidenced by a letter of Sebastian Franck written in 1541 or 1542
to the "Dear Brethren" of East Friesland who are compelled "to live
like sheep among wolves." Johan van Bekesteyn from the Netherlands,
who resided in East Friesland, had visited Franck and begged him to
write this letter and help them with their problems. This he did by
saying not "to search for Christ here and there and to send messengers
everywhere but to look for him where he can be found, namely in
yourselves and in the temple of your hearts... As far as the fellowship of the saints is concerned..., have confidence in all those, who
grant you freedom in your faith and of your conscience." [25] These are
some of the words of admonition sent to a place that threatened to
become a battle ground between those coming from Wittenberg and
the native Sacramentarians more inclined to accept the views of the
emerging Reformed Church or Anabaptism. Both were greatly strengthened by Dutch refugees finding temporary or permanent shelter in
East Friesland.

Keeping in mind Menno's statement that he had no permanent
home between 1536 and 1544, it must be assumed that he spent most
of the time at different places in East Friesland, going from time to
time to Groningen and Friesland and other places of the Low Countries. The books he started writing in Groningen he continued in
East Friesland. Linguistically they were written in an "eastern" colored
dialect (Oosters gekleurd), which means that they were influenced by
the linguistic peculiarities of these provinces. Dirk Philips was with

Menno Simons in East Friesland spending considerable time in the city of Norden. Joachim Kükenbieter, who succeeded Gellius Faber in Norden, had a religious discussion with Dirk Philips, whereby he, from his Lutheran point of view, found Dirk's views pertaining to baptism, the Lord's supper, and the incarnation of Christ objectionable.[26] Among other religious refugees coming from the Netherlands to East Friesland was David Joris, who spent a number of years here.

When Hofmann brought the seed of Anabaptism to Emden in 1530, Count Enno I (1528-40) was engaged in a war which prevented him from paying full attention to the religious questions of his country. A small local war led to an involvement with Karel van Gelder, who defeated him in March, 1534. East Friesland had been dominated for a while by the Lutherans. The unpopular Lutheran church constitution of Bremen (1529) had been replaced by one from Lüneburg which was now enforced. Now Karel van Gelder threatened with the restoration of Catholicism. Under pressure from Karel van Gelder, Count Enno issued an edict in accordance with which all Sacramentarians or Reformed were to leave the country. This included the Anabaptists. Oldersum and some other places again became the shelters of the persecuted. The rigid enforcement of Lutheranism met strong opposition. With the death of Karel van Gelder in 1538, a retreat of the Lutheran influence set in. When Enno died in 1540, his widow, Anna of Oldenburg, who was more tolerant, became regent (1540-62). Under her, John a Lasco, a Calvinist, transformed the reformation efforts of East Friesland in the pattern of the Reformed Church. Anabaptism also experienced a breathing spell for a number of years.[27] During this time Menno Simons, Dirk Philips, David Joris, and others found limited freedom for their work and even had religious discussions with their opponents.

4. A Lasco and the Anabaptists

John a Lasco (1499-1560), of Polish noble background, had received his humanistic training in Bologna and Basel. At the latter place he was in close touch with Erasmus, Froben, and other humanists (1523-25). During his stay in Poland, Mainz, and Louvain, he broke more and more with the Catholic Church and arrived in Emden in 1540 as a Sacramentarian and Zwinglian. Although a stranger, he soon won the confidence of the Frisians, and in 1543 he was appointed superintendent of the church in which capacity he established the Reformed Church. First attention was directed against the forces aiming to retain or re-establish the Catholic Church. Disturbed by the promotion led by monks that images be used in worship services, he turned to Countess Anna, who gave instruction that the images "be removed by night" so that "the mad people cannot get at them ... The mayors and churches shall be informed about it, and it shall be execut- ed without noise." John a Lasco had a great influence on the countess, but she gave the orders, or approved them, to reform the church.[28]

One of the great concerns of a Lasco was the matter of church dis- cipline. Like Bucer and Capito in Strassburg so was a Lasco in Emden challenged by the Anabaptists to emphasize disciplined Chris- tian living. Many serious members of his church were attracted by the dedicated life and the brotherhood practice of the Anabaptists. This caused the following appeal: "I told the city council that we would always have sectarians as long as we would be rigid against others and tolerate vice in our own midst... We must make in our own churches a distinction between those who live up to the standards of the church and those who despise the church of God and its dis- cipline." Gradually a Lasco succeeded in introducing deacons, who helped the ministers raise the standards of Christian living in the local congregations.[29]

More and more Anabaptist refugees from the Low Countries found asylum in East Friesland. This did not remain unnoticed to the Court of Brussels. Having extended its sphere of influence to Groningen, East Friesland was next. In 1534 Countess Anna was asked to take action against the Anabaptists. This request was repeated in another writing to her and also to the magistrate of Emden. Back of this action was Count Johan, the brother of Enno, who was in imperial service in the Netherlands and was interested in the throne of East Friesland. Before the following action of Brussels is presented, the relationship between a Lasco, his co-workers, and the Anabaptists will be taken up.[30]

Valuable information about the various Anabaptist groups and their views during this time has come to light in the letters from Herman- nus Aquilomontanus to Heinrich Bullinger. The former was minister first at Borssum near Emden and later in Oldersum under the patro- nage of Hero von Oldersum. He complained that Sebastian Franck's *Paradoxa* was popular in his community. Above all he requested sug- gestions about how to deal with the Anabaptists. Among them were the peaceful followers of Menno Simons, those adhering to the views of David Joris, the Münsterites, and the Batenburgers. His great problem was that Hero von Oldersum and his neighbors were much too tolerant and mild toward the refugees. The result was that more and more of them were coming to his community from the southern Netherlands. H. Fast concludes that the urgent request of Aquilomontanus for advise and council did not remain unheeded. It could have been one of the reasons that Bullinger later wrote his well-known *Der Widertäufferen ursprung...* (1560).[31]

John a Lasco was also alarmed about the growing Anabaptist movement. He was particularly concerned about the problem that among the "orthodox refugees from the Low Countries were also Anabaptists and others who had in some doctrines gotten off the right way." He hoped to win some by discussing with them the controversial questions. Having numerous followers in East Friesland, a Lasco, with consent of his colleagues, called on the "most prominent and humble" among the followers of David Joris for a meeting in a home in January, 1544. In a winning way, he explained briefly his basic Christian teachings and asked his guests to express themselves openly along these lines. They dealt with such questions as justification, the Lord's supper, baptism, polygamy, and the magistrate. At the close of the discussion, a Lasco drew up a statement in regard to the discussed basic beliefs which was signed by the followers of Joris under the condition that no disadvantages would result from it for their leader. When Joris heard about it, he entered into a correspondence with a Lasco whereby the latter hoped that a discussion between the two could be arranged for. However, it never materialized.[32]

A similar disputation took place between Menno Simons and a Lasco on January 28 to 31, 1544, in the former Franciscan monastery at Emden. After having received permission from Countess Anna and the approval from his colleagues, a Lasco invited Menno Simons in writing to come to Emden for this occasion. The discussion was attended by numerous witnesses, including Gellius Faber and most likely also followers of Menno. The disputation centered around five points: 1) the incarnation of Christ, 2) infant baptism, 3) original sin, 4) santification, and 5) the calling of the ministers. Even though no agreement was reached on points 1), 2), and 5), Menno Simons reported later that he had been treated in a friendly manner and was allowed to leave the city in peace. Keeping a promise he had made, three months later Menno submitted to a Lasco a written statement dealing with the incarnation of Christ and the calling of the ministers. He promised to send a treatise on baptism later. It was embarrassing for Menno when the ministers of Emden published his booklet without his consent.[33]

Menno Simons also published the same writing, a *Brief and Clear Confession*..., during the same year. A year later, it was followed by a Lasco's counter report devoted to the incarnation of Christ. Menno's views in this regard differed considerably from those of a Lasco as well as the Orthodox Christian views in general. Menno Simons considered this matter significant enough to write another treatise in response to a Lasco's even though nearly a decade elapsed between the appearance of a Lasco's *Defensio verae*... *doctrinae de*... *incarnatione* and Menno's reply.[34] Menno had accepted and developed the views pertaining to the incarnation of Christ held by Melchior Hofmann in which a strong emphasis was placed on the divinity of Christ which, at times, led to a corresponding de-emphasis on his humanity.[35]

Another radical who can hardly be classified as Anabaptist was Heinrich Niclaes (1502-1580), the founder of the "House of Love" or the Familists. An opponent said "David George [Joris] laid the egg and Henry Niclaes brought forth the chicken." He shared with Joris not only some views but also the skill and mastery to conceal the real beliefs in order to prevent persecution. Common beliefs led him to carry on a literary dispute with David Joris.

Born and educated in Münster, Westphalia, Niclaes moved to Amsterdam (1529) for religious reasons and around 1540 to Emden where he became a prosperous businessman and gathered members for the "House of Love." The members of this "House of Love" promoted a mystical enlightenment and divinization. Niclaes wrote over fifty pamphlets dealing with his prophecies and mystical pantheism, most of which were printed in Antwerp by his follower, Christoffel Plantijn. When, in 1560, the city council of Emden discovered his "real business," he fled and spent some time in the Netherlands, London, and Cologne.[36]

5. In the Pincers of Charles V

Meanwhile Maria of Austria, regent of the Low Countries, kept informed about the developments in East Friesland. The jealous Count Johan and tortured Anabaptists furnished information about Anabaptist refugees sheltered in East Friesland. Thus, while a Lasco and his helpers were trying to win them to their church, Maria of Austria, in the name of the emperor, complained (1544) to Countess Anna and her council that Anabaptists were still being tolerated in her country. They were reminded in no uncertain terms that those who sheltered and tolerated Anabaptists must, as enemies of God and the emperor, be put under the ban. As a result the government speedily issued an edict stating that all members of "sects," the Anabaptists included, had to leave the country at once and that no one dare shelter them or rent them any property such as homes or land. The edict made no distinction between those who were natives and refugees or between degrees of sectarianism. All this became noticeable and disturbing when the application of the mandate followed. As a result of a suggestion by a Lasco, a second edict was issued which made provision for all "sectarians," including the Anabaptists, to report to a Lasco or the ministers and subject themselves to an examination in regard to their attitude toward the church and its doctrines. Whether a person could remain in the country or would have to leave was to depend on this interview. In a letter to his friend Albert Hardenberg dated July 26, 1544, a Lasco stated that the church was being purified not for the sake of God, but because of the emperor and with such a severity that he had begged Countess Anna to have only those expelled as heretics who would be designated as such by him and his co-workers.[37]

The *Kirchen- und Polizeiordnung* of 1545 had a detailed statement in regard to religious life, including a provision for the treatment of the sects. The reason for the decree was stated thus in the introduction: "Because we are generally being suspected of tolerating the insurrectionist sect of Anabaptists, we consider it advisable, in view of the present rumors, that an investigation be carried out in every city, village, and county and on the estates of noble men to determine whether there are any [persons] tainted with evil and insurrectionist sectarianism who have arrived just recently." Such persons were to report about the place from which they had come, and reports of their conduct were to be sent in so that a Lasco, the superintendent of the churches, could examine them. Even if these persons did not comply with all the principles of the examiner, they were to be tolerated unless they were of the "insurrectionist sects." Since the confessions of the followers of Joris and Batenburg could not be trusted, they were to be condemned without examination. Followers of Menno Simons were to be examined, and if they were not willing to be instructed by Scriptures, they were not to be tolerated. Those who had come to the country as refugees for the "sake of the Gospel," were to be permitted to remain.[38]

A Lasco had his hand in the shaping of this regulation. Much depended now on its interpretation and application. No doubt many of the Anabaptists remained on the estates where they had found work and shelter. Not so Menno Simons and Dirk Philips. They had left in 1544 when Maria of Austria sent in her urgent request to expel the Anabaptists and when Countess Anna complied with it.

When Charles V, by means of the *Interim* of 1548, aimed to restore Protestant areas to Catholicism, East Friesland was not bypassed. Again and again he urged Countess Anna to cooperate or threatened her with bearing the consequences. Now it was a Lasco's turn to leave. In 1549 he accepted a call by Thomas Cranmer to serve the refugee church of London. To further ease the pressure from Brussels, a new edict was issued in East Friesland on April 6, 1549, in which it was forbidden to give shelter and sustenance to Mennonites, Davidites, Obbites, and Batenburgers and, in particular, to refugees who had come from imperial countries. However, this was likely more a gesture to appease the emperor than to exile the Anabaptists. A core of Anabaptists had been established in East Friesland and remained there for decades to come. It must be added that East Friesland also continued to be the outpost of the Reformed Church which was ultimately also established in the Low Countries. The primary result of the edict was a temporary withdrawal of leaders most of whom later returned.[39]

6. *Anabaptism in the Liege-Cologne Area*

In May or June, 1544, Menno Simons and possibly also Dirk Philips went to the Cologne area. Nothing is known about the route they took or where they stopped. In any event Menno Simons left East Friesland just in time, leaving his wife and children behind. How rigidly the edicts concerning the Anabaptists were applied is shown in an incident reported by Menno Simons. "In 1546 at a place where they boast of the Word, a four-room house was confiscated because the owner, unknown to anyone else, had for a short time rented one of the rooms to my poor sick wife and her little ones." [40]

Menno Simons likely had many reasons for going to the Lower Rhine area. One was the tolerant policy of Herman von Wied, archbishop of Cologne, who at this time was assisted by Albert Hardenberg in the introduction of a moderate reformation. There were also numerous Anabaptists in this area. The chapter "In the Embrace of a World Revolution" revealed the growth of the evangelical Sacramentarian movement in the bishopric Liege (Luik) in the southeastern part of the Low Countries and the archbishopric of Cologne. This territory between the cities Liege-Aachen-Cologne-Cleve-Liege was the seedbed for Anabaptism. Many Sacramentarians had gone from there to Münster either to stay or to receive baptism and to go out as evangelists. This was particularly the case with the *predikanten* from Wassenberg near Aachen as has been related. This area continued to remain a center of Anabaptism after the disastrous end of the Münsterite kingdom.

Menno Simons very likely had some contact with some of the Anabaptists of this area and may himself have been here before. He and Dirk Philips ordained Gillis van Aken, Antonius of Cologne, Frans Reines de Cuyper, Adam Pastor, and Hendrik van Vreden. The first two were of the area Menno was now visiting. Either he, and possibly also Dirk Philips, commissioned them during this visit or had done so previously. The same could be said about the latter two. According to the *Successio Anabaptistica* and the *Copia der Outsten,* Pastor and van Vreden were ordained or commissioned between 1542 and 1547.[41] Since the field of labor of Adam Pastor and Hendrik van Vreden was Westphalia, they could have received their assignments from Menno (and Dirk) on their way to Cologne or on the return trip. In any event, Menno was in contact with Gillis van Aken and Antonius van Ceulen (Cologne) and possibly ordained them during his stay in this area between 1544 and 1546.

Gillis van Aken was born about 1500 in or near Susteren in the Jülich district (now Limburg). He was likely a priest, but by 1531 he was a traveling Anabaptist evangelist in Iimburg and Aachen. He was ordained by Menno Simons and became his close co-worker. Many of the martyrs named him as the one who baptized them during his extensive travels between Aachen, Antwerp, and Amsterdam. Antonius of Cologne was baptized by Hendric Rol in Münster, but escaped to the Rhineland and continued his work as an Anabaptist leader attending various conferences.[42]

Another outstanding leader was Theunis van Hastenrath, who preached in the duchy of Jülich and in Maastricht and Cologne. When, in 1551, he was examined to be burned at the stake, he stated that fifteen years ago he had learned to read and to study the Scriptures and finally received baptism and started to preach. The first baptismal service he conducted in a barn. He insisted that he was not administering a *re*-baptism but a baptism since infant baptism was not founded on Scriptures. "Man must be taught first, accept Christ, and then be baptized." He stated that he had been "asked by the brethren to assume his office." Hastenrath related that Menno Simons was in Visschersweert in 1546, and that he did "not like the teachings of David Joris" but knew Gillis van Aken well. He also reported that Adam Pastor from Odenkirchen, Westphalia, had moved to Welle a year ago. Among the twenty places of Pastor's activities and centers of Anabaptism, Illikhoven, Aachen, Cleve, Goch and Welle were named.

Liiske Snyers was baptized by Theunis von Hastenrath in the name of the Father, the Son, and the Holy Ghost by taking water out of a well and pouring it on her head. She confessed to have heard Gillis van Aken, Menno Simons, and Adam Pastor preach. When asked about her beliefs she stated that they were in conformity with Menno and his followers' convictions. Other Anabaptist leaders named in the examinations of the Anabaptists were Lenart van Ysenbroeck (van Tongeren), Lemke Cremer, and Reinicken Radermecher.

Meeting places were named, but many of the meetings took place during the night at hidden places. For example, one night in 1544 or 1545 Menno Simons preached in a pasture near Visschersweert.[43] Vos considers Menno the founder of the group of believers of Visschersweert and the surrounding territory. At this time Menno Simons was nearly fifty years old. Jan Neulen, who ferried him across the Maas River to Roermond, described him as a "thick, fat, and heavy man with a wry facial expression and a brown beard who had difficulty walking." Later Menno Simons often signed his letters "Menno, the cripple." It is not definite whether the above description leads to the conclusion that he was already crippled at this time.

Repeatedly the Anabaptists were asked about books they read. The Bible or New Testament was mentioned most. However, the *Acta Adolphi Claerenbach* and writings of Menno Simons were also referred to. When asked during the trials how they recognized each other, they answered by saying, "The peace of the Lord be with you" to which the reply was "Amen." After this they shook hands and kissed each other.[44]

At this point the question about the origin of Anabaptism in the Cologne-Maastricht area should be dealt with. It is obvious that Menno Simons and his co-workers were not the founders but, at best, its gatherers and sustainers. The pioneer historian of Anabaptism of this territory, Karl Rembert, stated that "with few exceptions the history of the Anabaptists from 1530 to 1550 coincides with the Reformation of these areas" in general and that the "Anabaptist movement of Jülich up to 1534" led to the tragedy of Münster in 1535.[45] Following somewhat the thesis of Vos and Mellink pertaining to the origin of Anabaptism in the Netherlands, J. F. G. Goeters has recently challenged Rembert's approach and conclusions. He points out that the actual practice of re-baptism, or adult baptism, prior to the Münster catastrophe was minimal and concludes that the early reformatory movement of the German Lower Rhine was a popular movement containing humanistic, Lutheran, and spiritualistic-sacramentarian elements. Anabaptism did not stand at the beginning of this reformation movement, according to Goeters, but entered midstream and helped to clarify concepts. It constituted a radicalization of the spiritualistic-sacramentarian movement.

To this it must be added that it has become apparent in the study of the origins of Anabaptism in the total range of the Low Countries, that the evangelical Sacramentarian movement from the beginning carried within itself the potential of Anabaptism in some form as well as it did of the Reformed Church, later to be established in these territories as well as in the Netherlands. Thus, Goeters, after having pointed out the weakness of Rembert's pioneer study, goes too far when he, based on Mellink's thesis, concludes that "early Anabaptism of the Lower Rhine stands completely in the shadow of Münster" and that it, generally speaking, "originated in Münster."[46] One can say that it is equally wrong to claim the seedbed of the evangelical Sacramentarian movement solely for the Anabaptist movement, or the later Reformed Church. Both sprouted side by side in the same soil. "Münster" ended the prospects for Anabaptism to continue its popularity, but was in no wise the source of its origin, be that in the Low Countries or any other place. The combined forces of imperial and territorial governments and of Catholicism and Protestantism crushed its popularity and potential without distinguishing between the original peaceful and later militant wings of Anabaptism. Only on the fringes of the evangelical Sacramentarian seed bed did Anabaptism survive while the rest was occupied by the old church, Catholicism, and some of it by the Reformed Church, closest related to the original Anabaptist potential.

After this general observation it is appropriate to present a few highlights from the emerging Anabaptist movement in the Cologne-

Jülich area. Similarly to the occurrence in the Netherlands, the application of the principle of the spiritualization of the sacraments led from one discovery to another one. As has been pointed out, the Sacramentarian view of the Lord's supper reached this area from the Netherlands and Saxony through Karlstadt via Gerhard Westerburg of Cologne by 1522-23. As had been seen the Wassenberg *predikanten* not only advocated early the symbolic view of the Lord's supper, but raised similar questions in regard to infant baptism. By 1533, the development had reached such momentum that an official inquiry was conducted including questions in regard to baptism. Although no *re-baptism* of adults was recorded, spiritualized views were strong. Johannes Campanus and Hendrik Slachtscaep von Tongeren were accused as early as November 1, 1532, of "writing and preaching disparagingly about the holy sacrament and the traditional use of infant baptism." [47]

An example of the development from Sacramentarianism to Anabaptism is the step taken by Henric Rol and with him the Wassenberg *predikanten* with whom he associated at the time he wrote his outstanding Sacramentarian tract, *Die Slotel van dat Secreet des Nachtmaels* (1531). He totally rejected the Catholic and Lutheran views pertaining to the Lord's supper and described it as a meal of rejoicing in which the redeemed of the Lord may partake. By 1533, he was minister of the St. Ilgen Church of Münster, opposing infant baptism and signing Rothmann's *Bekentnisse* which rejected both the sacramental character of the Lord's supper as well as infant baptism and thereby introduced the practice of believer's baptism in Westphalia and the Rhineland. Believer's baptism had been advocated in theory by Müntzer, Karlstadt, and the Wassenberg *predikanten* for some time. Rol was baptized early in 1534 and after having baptized Gerhard Westerburg, both returned to the Rhineland, now including in their reformation effort the practice of believer's baptism. Rol baptized numerous Sacramentists in Wesel, Maastricht, and other places and died a martyr's death on September 2, 1534. Gerhard Westerburg and his brother Arnold, who also had been baptized in Münster, established or promoted the Anabaptist congregation in Cologne. Already on July 11, 1533, the Anabaptist Martin von Iffenen had been summoned by the authorities. [48] Apparently there were some pre-Münster Anabaptists in this area, although small in number.

However, the action of the authorities in issuing edicts against Anabaptists sometimes seemed to precipitate their appearance. This would indicate that the local authorities were willing and, at times, eager to demonstrate their loyalty in proclaiming imperial edicts passed not only to extinguish Anabaptism but also to prevent it. On the other hand, as the term "Lutheranism" was often extremely vague in edicts, so it was with "Anabaptism." Both, or either, were used at times to fight "heresies" which tended to undermine the sacramental character of the Lord's supper as well as baptism in the awareness that one can, and often does, lead to the other. It is in this light that measures taken in Cologne must be viewed. First the Spires mandate of April 23, 1529, against the Anabaptists was cited. On August 24, 1530, and in 1532 Anabaptists were again officially referred to in decrees. Most of the time actually all Protestant groups – Lutherans, Zwinglians, and Anabaptists – were condemned. However, with the concentration of Anabaptism in Münster and its appearance in Cologne and the neighboring places, the Anabaptists did receive special attention. Herman von Wied issued a severe edict against the Anabaptists dated August 23, 1534, which initiated the persecution and martyrdom of the Anabaptists in this territory.[49]

On the other hand, the early mandates against the Anabaptists in the Cologne area may have had some very concrete reasons not known to us today. There is a possibility that Anabaptism reached Cologne from the Upper Rhine area. An Anabaptist martyr was put to death at Kreuznach as early as 1529. The sources dealing with the spread of Anabaptism along the Rhine River have not yet been investigated.[50]

By the time Menno Simons arrived in the Cologne area in 1544, the spirit of Münsteritism among the Anabaptists, whatever there had been of it, was thoroughly dispersed, but the stigma attached to all forms and shades of Anabaptism as a result of the Münster incident was not. Not even a Lasco in East Friesland, lost sight of Menno Simons. On July 26, 1544, he wrote to his friend Hardenberg, who at this time helped Archbishop Herman von Wied introduce a moderate reformation, that Menno was "misleading many" in this area. Hardenberg, whose account was based on personal observations, reported in a similar vein to Vadian on March 22, 1545, that through Menno, the "bishop of the sects," all their congregations were being tainted.[51] That Menno Simons' influence was lasting and that the contacts he made were continued is evidenced by a number of incidents. He remained in contact with Lemke Cremer, with whom he worked and in whose home he stayed overnight. Through Cremer and Zyllis, he was also in contact with the South German Mennonites, as will be seen later. Matthias Servaes von Ottenheim still spoke highly of Menno when Georg Cassander of Cologne tried to persuade him to return to the Catholic Church. Steadfastly Matthias Servaes chose to die because he did not want to betray the doctrines for which Menno Simons stood.[52]

Less pleasant were Menno's memories in regard to a Lasco and Hardenberg. J. a Lasco stopped in Cologne twice to meet Hardenberg and Herman von Wied. He even had his *Defensio* against Menno published in Bonn. All this, judged by the letters referred to, did not work out in Menno's favor. Ten years later, in *Reply to Gellius Faber,* Menno wrote the following: "In the times of Archbishop Herman, the elector of Cologne, of blessed memory, I offered this same thing [a discussion] at their request to the learned men of Bonn, but my offer was rejected because these good sirs were dissuaded by John a Lasco and A[lbert] H[ardenberg]." The rejection was made by Heinrich Zell of Bonn under the pretext of three reasons which were "obvious falsehoods." Menno had a similar experience with the ministers at Wesel, who "made our people believe they would furnish me safe conduct... but when I signified my willingness in writing, I received an answer that they would let the executioner treat with me, and other tyrannical and unchristian words."[53]

In spite of this disappointing experience, Menno speaks of Herman von Wied favorably. There are indications that the archbishop made a distinction between peaceful Anabaptists and the Münsterites whom he actively helped defeat. In line with the policy of his advisors, Bucer and a Lasco, he aimed to win them back to the fold instead of putting them to death.

J. F. G. Goeters has recently discovered a confession of faith written by the Anabaptist leader, Thönis von Sasserath (Jüchen) of Kempen. This source adds additional information to the understanding of Anabaptism in the general Cologne area. Kempen is the place of birth of the well-known Thomas à Kempis. The information and the writing of the confession of faith coincide with Menno's visit to this area. The confession was presented to the pioneers of the Reformed church of Kempen, Wilhelm von Rennenberg, an official, and Dietrich Vollebier, a minister, who arranged for a hearing of the Anabaptists on March 28, 1545. The Reformed theologian at this hearing was Heinrich Zell with whom Menno dealt during his visit. Anabaptist spokesmen were a goldsmith, Georg, and a mason, Tewes Ruebsam, both from Kempen. They remained steadfast during this cross-examination.

The original handwritten Anabaptist confession presented at this occasion was hitherto unknown and represents a significant first formulation of the faith of the Anabaptists of this area. It deals with the incarnation of Christ, baptism, the Lord's supper, the true ministry, the government, and non-resistance. The statement insists that only true believers can receive the seal and symbol of baptism and only ministers from the midst of such fellowships can be true shepherds of the flock. Although it is written ten years after the collapse of the Münster kingdom, it strongly denounces revolutionary Anabaptism and emphasizes the legitimacy of government. This emphasis furnished significant evidence that all Anabaptists were still suspected of revolutionary tendencies in their effort to demonstrate that they were blameless.

A document estimates the number of Anabaptists of the Gladbach area as being a thousand. This includes towns like Kempen, Krefeld and Rheydt west of the Rhine River between Duisburg and Düsseldorf. Menno Simons must have visited this area. The formerly named Tewes Ruebsam confessed that he had been baptized on November 11, 1544, "by an unknown bearded man from Friesland" in the home of Reynar Piper of Kempen in whose home the meetings convened. It could be that this unknown man was Menno Simons. Goeters comes to the conclusion that the spirit of Menno Simons is expressed in the confession of the Kempen Anabaptists. The Anabaptist fellowship continued in this area. When Albert Hardenberg became Reformed pastor at Kempen, he is supposed to have been successful in winning many to his church.[54] A more thorough study of early Anabaptism along the present day German Lower Rhine will be possible when the Anabaptist source material located in archives will be published.

John a Lasco in East Friesland and Herman von Wied in Cologne had to leave their positions at about the same time, namely, when Charles V had gained enough power to launch his counter-reformation. That Menno Simons, Hardenberg and Bucer left the Rhineland at about the time that archbishop Herman von Wied was excommunicated and had to give up his position was no mere coincidence.

Menno left the Lower Rhine area in 1546 but was back again in Goch in the following year to attend a meeting which dealt with Adam Pastor's deviating christological views.[55]

B. THE COVENANTED CHURCH OF GOD

1. *The Renewal of the Covenant*

It has been pointed out that Melchior Hofmann accepted the covenant idea from the Anabaptists of Strassburg. Hans Denck and other
South German Anabaptists took over the concept of the covenant
from mystical literature and, to some extent, also from Thomas Müntzer. The *Bund* (covenant) played a significant role in Müntzer's struggle
for the kingdom of God and his attempt to usher it in. During the
Peasants' Revolt the peasants entered the covenant outlined in a *Bun-
desordnung.* In the final struggle, Müntzer told the peasants that when
they would see the rainbow in the sky, that would mean that they
were "in God's covenant." He confessed before his death that those
with him were members of the covenant (*Verbundnis*) and therefore
Bundgenossen.[55]

Lowell H. Zuck has investigated this subject in the "Anabaptist
Revolution through the Covenant in Sixteenth Century Continental
Protestantism." He emphasized the concept of the covenant as a most
basic element in the radical reformation and points out that "the radical Anabaptist covenanters, like Thomas Müntzer... believed that
allegiance to their covenant would inaugurate the eschatological
Kingdom of God on earth." Zuck defines Müntzer's concept of "Anabaptism" as a "fanatical religious idealism centered in the hope for a
completely new Church, state, and society. Though the new order will
be ushered in by God, the elect believer is sworn into a revolutionary
covenant." He makes allowance for the "violent Anabaptists," who
anticipated a more expansive social role for themselves, and "their
withdrawn non-resistant associates."[56]

A study by Peter von Zahn dealing with the social ideas of Thomas
Müntzer and the early Swiss Anabaptists describes how Müntzer, the
mystic, developed the covenant idea coupled with an eschatological
expectancy and a social and ethical concern for the peasantry of his
day. Patiently waiting for God to act, Müntzer gradually became an
eschatologically oriented radical revolutionary calling his fellow-cov-
enanters to take up arms to help God usher in his kingdom.[57] The
shift from the *Gelassenheit* of the mystics to a militant covenantism
had taken place.

The Swiss and the South German Anabaptists were indeed strongly influenced by Müntzer's covenant idea, but their attempt to establish a true Christian brotherhood also constituted a renewal or revision of the covenant idea and its eschatological implications. Jacob Kautz and Wilhelm Reublin, imprisoned in Strassburg, presented a confession to the city council on January 15, 1529 in which they stated, "As the merciful God has called us ... through his grace to his marvellous light, we were not unheeding toward the heavenly message, but made a *covenant* with God in our hearts, to serve him henceforth in holiness all our days ... and to make our intention known to the covenanters." [58] Similarly, Hubmaier expressed himself in regard to the covenant: "O, my Lord Jesus Christ, re-establish the two bands with which you have outwardly girded and covenanted your bride, the church, namely, the proper water baptism and the Lord's supper." [59]

Hans Denck repeatedly referred to the covenant. He said, "The covenant of God and the yoke of his son are heavy only for those who have never entered them." In regard to baptism he stated that "this covenant means that who ever is baptized be baptized unto the death of Christ, so that as Christ died, Adam die in him ... Wherever this covenant is, the spirit of Christ enters and ignites the fire of love." [60]

It was this purified idea of the covenant that Hofmann transplanted to Emden which spread throughout the Low Countries. Reference has been made to his *Ordinance of God*. Here Hofmann speaks of the covenanters who "wed and bind themselves to the Lord Jesus Christ, publicly, through that true sign of the covenant, the water bath and baptism" and the covenanted who is "detached from his own will, and, through God's covenant, absorbed into the will of the exalted Father." [61]

The writers of early Dutch Anabaptism and the martyrs in their confessions spoke freely about the *verbond* (covenant) and the *bondgenooten* (covenanters). The radical Münsterites returned to Müntzer's militant concept of the covenant. Jan van Geelen appealed to the followers that "each one of the covenanters should purchase arms." Rothmann's *Van der Wracke* bore the term *Bundtgenooten Christi* on the title page. [62] Since this radicalization of the idea of the covenant stripped it of its original idealism, it came into disrepute. Menno Simons reacted against the concept of a militant covenant by stating: "May the almighty God protect all true covenanters, and give them wisdom and prudence to keep the covenant of God, and to be mindful of what kind of spirit Christ wants his disciples to be" (Luke 9 : 55). [63] In the process of renewing the concept of the covenant, the term was used less frequently. One of the martyrs, when asked at the trial wheter he was a covenanter, answered that he was not of the *bond* but of the *evangelie*.[64]

Zuck's observation is correct when he says, "The Anabaptist view of the church covenant enforced vigorous internal discipline, an imitation of Christ including believer's baptism, the Lord's supper, a ban against association with unbelievers, non-resistance, non-swearing, cross-bearing in martyrdom, and a vocation for each member in carrying out the Great Commission." [65] The peaceful Anabaptists of the Low Countries aimed to restore the pure concept of the covenant. Menno Simons, as a writer and preacher, and his co-workers, Obbe and Dirk Philips, Adam Pastor, Gillis van Aken, David Joris, and others risked their lives many times to visit those in need of counsel and spiritual guidance. Many others lost their lives in an effort to cleanse the fellowship of believers of the stain which the Münsterites had caused. By 1545 hardly a trace remained of the radical views and the thought that the covenant obligated and included the establishment of a visible Anabaptist kingdom by taking up arms. The militant covenanters had disappeared and the covenant of sufferers (*Gelassenheit*) had been re-established.

This, however, did not mean that an ideal brotherhood and a pure church representing the body of Christ without spot and wrinkle, the goal of those entering the renewed covenant, had been achieved. Some who were weak and could not endure the weight of persecution and painful martyrdom were tempted to deny Christ and compromise their beliefs. Others harbored views deviating from those which were considered scriptural. Menno Simons and his co-workers had to deal with these problems within the renewed covenant.

Although the radical eschatological implications of the covenant idea were softened to the degree that the word itself lost its original meaning, the ideal of the gathered, dedicated, and disciplined fellowship of Christ was not given up. In the literature the term *gemeente Godts* became more prominent while the term "covenant" was limited to the usage in connection with baptism. But the concept of the church of God (*gemeente Godts*) was very different from that of Catholicism and any of the other Protestant churches. It still retained enough of the eschatological and exclusive element contained in the covenant idea to prevent the movement from becoming absorbed or "adjusted." It is true that the immediacy of the establishment of the kingdom, which God would usher in and whereby the wicked world was to be punished, had been softened considerably. Nevertheless, the martyrs, as well as the surviving witnesses, still had enough of a sense of mission to risk all for the cause of Christ and his *gemeente*.

The concept of the church (*gemeente Godts*) was a revival of the early Christian meaning of the *ecclesia*. With the early Christians the Anabaptists felt called out of the world of sin and doom to an entirely different level and newness of life in which each believer became a member of the body of Christ who, as the head of this church, motivated, moved, and disciplined every member of the covenanted church (Ephesians 5:25, 27, 30). The early Anabaptist ecclesiology read like this: "The divine and heavenly church, which is the separated holy flock and people of God, originated upon earth at the beginning of the world, has existed through all the ages up to the present time, and will continue to the end of the world." Even though the early Anabaptists traced the origin of the church back into the old covenant, it was in the new covenant and in the apostolic church where they found the pattern for the restitution of the true church.[66]

Although Menno Simons did not devote any particular book to this subject from the time of his first writing and preaching to the end of his life, this was and remained the theme of his concerns in all his writings. His life's motto on his title-pages, "For other foundation can no man lay than that is laid, which is Jesus Christ" (I Corinthians 3:11), makes this clear. It was the convenanted church which he and his co-workers aimed to gather on this foundation. Particularly Menno's *Foundation Book* of 1539, studded with Scripture quotations, was influential as a guide and source of information and inspiration. Dirk Philips wrote a book on the church, *Van die Ghemeynte Godts,* which later became a part of his own *Enchiridion. Gemeinte Godts* was the name in the church record of the Mennonite Church of Danzig of which Dirk Philips was the first elder. So devoted was Menno Simons to the gathering of the believers into a fellowship, the church, that even when he suffered agony and experienced disappointments because of this church, he still maintained that there was "nothing upon earth which my heart loves more than it does the church." [67]

The ideal of this church was delayed to be realized on earth to its fullest potential until Christ's second coming. The call extended to the individual to become a member of this body implied a radical break with the past and the world. Not only was the individual called out of the general political, social, and economic entanglements with the world and what had been considered "church" in the past, but this call might also imply or necessitate a break with former friends and even family members. Through the act of the covenant of baptism, the individual entered the closely-knit and disciplined fellowship. After the individual had become a member, he was to continue to live in harmony with the body of which Christ was the head. He practiced discipleship so that he would not be in danger of severing himself from the body of Christ. This church-covenant took into the close fellowship those who had become followers of Christ and rejected those who had severed their ties and had failed to remain in the disciplined fellowship.[68]

The Anabaptist sense of mission, contained in the *Ordinance* which Hofmann proclaimed on the basis of Acts 1:8 and Matthew 28:18-20, was still in force. Discipleship was expressed in the dedication of the individual to Christ and his fellow-believers as well as in his effort to win those to Christ who were outside. Discipline became necessary when the believer or disciple lost the sense of awareness of the demarcation line between the body of believers and the doomed and sinful world around him. The following cases will illustrate the attempt in the post-Münsterite period to realize Christ's church in the world as a disciplined and covenanted fellowship.

2. David Joris: Spiritualizing Tendencies

Barely had the peaceful wing of Anabaptism drawn the lines of demarcation against militant Anabaptism when new problems arose. David Joris, who had been baptized and ordained by Obbe Philips, had never turned into a model Anabaptist leader. He had played a significant role at Bocholt and had won numerous followers including some from the ranks of the radicals. As long as possible he lived in the Low Countries. He had been in Strassburg and spent some time in Oldenburg and East Friesland. In many ways he was the most brilliant among the Anabaptist leaders. He had always had a flair for doing things on a big scale and addressed such rulers and religious leaders as the Court of Holland, Philip of Hesse, Luther, and others. In his voluminous writings he took the pose of a seer and prophet very close to Christ with whom he at times vaguely identified himself. Seeking shelter and a hearing in established church circles, he made a daring and drastic move by appearing in Basel in 1544 and claiming a noble background under the assumed name of Johann van Brugge. He managed to be accepted by the Basel patricians by compromising sufficiently and cooperating religiously with the Reformed Church fathers.

This did not prevent him from keeping in touch with his followers in the Low Countries and supplying them with the nourishment of his mystic and chiliastic prophecy. One of his most faithful followers was Nicolaas Meyndertsz van Blesdijk, later his son-in-law, who promoted the spread of his thoughts and writings. After the death of "Johann van Brugge" when the city fathers and religious leaders discovered that he really was David Joris, they dug up his grave, burned his body and books, and made his family and followers vow not to promote his views.[69]

Menno Simons had his misgivings about the character and the spiritual leadership of Joris at a rather early stage. Already in his writings in 1539 he took issue with him stating that under the followers of David Joris "evil, Godless, and carnal fruits and works were found." He objected particularly to their willingness to compromise with the world by taking part in social and religious activities which for Menno Simons and his followers seemed forbidden. The more biblical Anabaptist leaders objected primarily to Joris' arrogant, messianic conscientiousness through which he claimed a special divine authority. They were too much reminded of the King David of the New Jerusalem at Münster, although Joris was more brilliant and refined, and managed to sublimate and veil his ambitions and his identifications so that they were not always apparent.

Joris challenged Menno Simons by saying, "Put on your sword, Menno. Take up your arms because I have decided to fight you." Menno Simons responded to this by stating that his weapons were the "teachings of the Gospel ... which you, David, have given up and instead are using your imagination, figures of speech, philosophy ... Rightly you are considered ... a false prophet ... I am surprised over your arrogance and shamelessness in your writings and the blasphemy which you are spreading in your books over so many years ..." Menno particularly objected to David's hinted and suggestive implications that his "service was above that of Jesus Christ, the Son of God, and his teaching above the teaching of the apostles."

Menno Simons, Dirk Philips, Adam Pastor, and other leaders found that the imagination of David Joris was running away with him in the manner of a prophet who had lost his footing on the solid ground of the Scriptures. The parting between them was a matter of choosing between the authority of the Scriptures and the validity of prophetic dreams.[70]

Since David Joris was in Basel, Blesdijk represented his work and

followers in East Friesland and the neighboring territories. Although
the edicts of East Friesland, and elsewhere, were severe for the followers of Joris, they survived. Their leaders permitted them to compromise by taking part in the religious and social activities of their respective communities side by side with their own activities in smaller
fellowships. This must have attracted some of the more rigid Anabaptists and caused their leaders to take steps against David Joris and
his followers. In 1546 a debate was held in the city of Lübeck between
Blesdijk and his followers on one side and Menno Simons, Dirk Philips, Gillis van Aken, Adam Pastor, and Leenaert Bouwens on the other.
One of the basic questions dealt with religious honesty and integrity on
the one hand and the possibility of compromising with the environment
on the other hand. The followers of Joris emphasized that what really
mattered was the purity of the "hidden" faith. Attendance of the worship services of Catholics and Protestants, including the baptizing of
children, was an insignificant outward manifestation. Menno Simons
and his group could not accept this view. If the lines between the views
and practices of the followers of Joris and the more biblically orientated Anabaptists had not always been clear, they were now clarified. In
spite of the disillusionment that set in when the identity of "Johann
van Brugge" was discovered, his followers survived for a while. The
greatest setback came when Blesdijk himself denounced everything he
had taught after the death of David Joris and joined the Reformed
Church.[71]

3. Adam Pastor: Christological Issues

Another controversy arose in connection with Adam Pastor's christological views. Anabaptism of the Low Countries had accepted the
unique views of Hofmann in regard to the incarnation of Christ whereby, according to orthodox standards, the divinity was emphasized at
the expense of the humanity. Pastor could not share this view and
moved into the opposite direction by emphasizing the humanity at
the expense of the divinity. Already during the discussion with the
followers of Joris, the difference must have become apparent.

Adam Pastor, formerly a priest in Westphalia under the name of
Roelof Martens, had been ordained by Menno Simons and Dirk Philips
in 1542. A special meeting took place at Emden in 1547 attended by
Menno Simons, Dirk Philips, Gillis van Aken, Hendrik van Vreden,
Antonius van Ceulen (Cologne), Adam Pastor, and Frans de Cuyper.

The latter two, particularly Pastor, differed in their views regarding church discipline and Christology. The meeting was continued at Goch during the same year, where the elders and "their followers and disciples" met in a large basement at which occasion Menno Simons preached a sermon. No agreement could be reached at this meeting nor at another one at Lübeck in 1552. At this latter occasion the parting of the followers of Pastor and those of Menno Simons and Dirk Philips was sealed.[72] Pastor stated that he was "confessing the same that he had done in East Friesland five years ago." In 1550, Menno Simons had written his *Confession of the Triune God* and Dirk Philips a poem to counteract the "errors" of Pastor. In the introduction to his book Menno wrote that "during the last four years, Christian love and peace have become pretty thin with some, on account of much pernicious arguing and bickering about the divinity of Christ and of the Holy Ghost; also about angels and the devils, and about the ban." He stated that he had "been troubled not a little" by it because he hated "such bickerings and disputings" and that he "loves peace and unity which are in conformity with the Word of God," more than his "own life." Two years after the meeting in Lübeck Menno wrote Gellius Faber, who had challenged Menno in regard to the divisions among the Anabaptists, stating that "we could not help it that Adam Pastor left us."

Pastor, on the other hand, said about Menno and his co-workers, who excommunicated him, that they were refusing to have anything to do with him. Pastor quoted from Menno Simons' *Foundation Book* where the latter declared himself willing to discuss matters of faith with any scholar. Pastor argued that this should include himself also who, although excommunicated, was still a member of society and this world.[73]

Menno Simons, Dirk Philips and their co-workers were of the opinion that Adam Pastor and his followers were holding views which were not "in conformity with the Word of God" and that they were dealing with them in accordance with Matthew 18:15 ff. and II Thessalonians 2:14 f, in order that the purity of the body of Christ might be established and maintained. Excommunication and ban were considered a means not only of maintaining the purity of the *ecclesia* but also of winning back to the fold those who were in error. This was not achieved in the case of Pastor.

Soon after the Lübeck meeting Pastor published a book dealing with *The Difference Between the Right and False Doctrine* in which he presented his Christology and a report about the controversy in this matter.[74] A careful analysis of the arguments and writings reveals that Adam Pastor had a good Biblical knowledge, a fairly good theological training, and was intellectually equal, if not superior, to the other Anabaptist leaders.

In church discipline matters and practices Pastor, and with him also Frans de Cuyper, were more liberal. In dealing with David Joris, Pastor had agreed that the Scriptures must be the basis of the Christian faith and life. Now it became apparent that for him they were the authority for all questions. Menno Simons and his co-workers had a Christo- and ecclesio-centric approach to the Scriptures while Pastor's could be considered theocentric. For Menno and his followers, who based their doctrine on Hofmann's views, salvation was guaranteed only through Christ who became flesh without accepting the stain of sin. Salvation was anchored in the strongly emphasized divinity of Christ. Pastor, on the other hand, in his views of the trinity, Christology, and salvation was very much interested in preserving the oneness and the unchangeable character of God, who can neither be born nor die. Christ was for him the divinely endowed Son of God who retained the qualities of mediator and savior of man. It is apparent that the strong emphasis on the divinity in the incarnation of Christ and Pastor's view of God and Christ could not be harmonized during the first generation of Anabaptism and had to lead to a parting of the groups. This time it occurred in the realm of thought and doctrine. In the case of David Joris it had happened because of Joris' speculative approach to the Scriptures and because of his laxity in ethics that insisted that "for the pure everything is pure." [75]

In 1554, Frans de Cuyper, who had been active in Friesland and attended some meetings, withdrew from Anabaptism. Although there are indications that he was not in full agreement with some of the leaders, the main reason was likely the pressure of persecution. He renounced his Anabaptist views and obtained pardon in 1554 from M. Hyppolytus Persijn, president of the Court of Friesland, after "casting out and swearing off Menno's errors and promising henceforth to live by the faith of his fathers which had made him during his first baptism heir of life eternal." [76]

4. The Covenanters in the Arena

Some leaders of Anabaptism who were most sought after left the Low Countries proper in order to continue their work elsewhere. They spread all the way from Antwerp to Danzig and even went to London.

Jacob van Campen of Amsterdam was ready to escape to Königsberg, East Prussia, when he was apprehended and put to death in 1535. Most of the Anabaptists, however, remained in their homeland, and many of them suffered a martyr's death. N. van der Zijpp estimates that the total number of Anabaptist martyrs in the Low Countries was 2,500.[77] The reasons for the persecution and the martyrdom of some of the Sacramentarians and the radical Anabaptists have been presented. The following are samples of the inner motivation, the faith, and courage of some peaceful Anabaptists of the Low Countries primarily during the first decades.

The first collection of the accounts of the Dutch Anabaptists who died for the faith was a book entitled *Het Offer des Heeren* (1562) which can be translated as "Sacrifice unto the Lord." The expanded collection by Thieleman Jansz van Braght bore the following title translated into English, *The Bloody Theater or the Martyrs' Mirror of the Defenseless Christians ... who suffered and died for the testimony of Jesus their Savior ...* Characteristically, the illustrated title page of the first Dutch edition (1660)[78] had Christ as cross-bearer whom his disciples followed all the way by suffering death by crucifixion, burning at the stake, beheading, drowning, and horrible tortures. For the early Anabaptists, the suffering of a Christian for his Lord was not only an integral part of discipleship but also a continuance of the life and death struggle of the early Christians in the Roman arena. They were participants in a struggle between the forces of light and darkness, *De Civitate Dei* (city of God) and *De Civitate Diaboli* (city of Satan).[79] Boldly, some seemed to imply that their suffering was a continuation of the suffering of the Lord. In any event, a glimpse into the *Martyrs' Mirror* convinces the reader that this suffering was not the result of a passive, fatalistic attitude of resignation. On the contrary, it was an aggressive act of love filled with conviction and hope that the light would conquer darkness and truth would ultimately prevail. Balthasar Hubmaier, burned at the stake in Vienna, expressed it this way, "Divine truth cannot be killed although it may be apprehended, punished, crowned with thorns, crucified, and placed in a tomb, it will, nevertheless, arise victorious on the third day and rule and triumph throughout eternity." [80] The convenant of baptism by water implied and obligated a willingness to receive the ultimate baptism by blood. This is expressed in song 608 of the *Ausbund,* the German collection of martyr testimonies.

"Drei Zeugnisse sind uns hier beschieden,
Die zwei man heisst Wasser und Geist,
Der dritte, Blut, das ist Leiden."

An example of the boldness of faith of the Sacramentarian period was the testimony of a widow named Weynken (Wendelmoet) Claes burned at the Hague in 1527. When told that she would be "subjected to an intolerable death" if she would not give up her error, she replied, "I am ready to suffer." When asked whether she did not fear death, she answered, "I shall never taste death, for Christ says, 'If a man keep my saying, he shall never see death'." To the question as to what she thought about the sacrament, she replied, "I hold your sacrament to be bread and flour"; and concerning the saints, she said, "I know no other mediator than Christ." Threatened with the death sentence she said, "I know how I stand with my Lord." [81] It was in this soil of Sacramentarianism that Anabaptism, and later also the Reformed Church were rooted.

5.   Letters from Prison

An unusual Anabaptist martyr was Anneken Jans of Rotterdam, a follower of David Joris, who had fled to England with her husband in 1536. She returned with her son and was arrested because she was singing an Anabaptist hymn. After a trial and courageous testimony before the court, she was drowned in Rotterdam on January 24, 1539. Nippold considered Anneken's testament for her fifteen months old son, "one of the most worthy witnesses of the self-denying, sacrificing, steadfast piety of the Anabaptists." [82] The following are some excerpts: "My son, here are the instructions of your mother; open your ears to hear the words of my mouth (Proverbs 8:11). Behold, I go today the way of the prophets, apostles, and martyrs, and drink of the cup of which they all have drank (Mathew 10:23). I go, I say, the way which Christ Jesus, the eternal Word of the Father, full of grace and truth, the Shepherd of the sheep, who is the Life, Himself went, and who went this way, and not another, and who had to drink of this cup, even as He said: 'I have a cup to drink of, and a baptism to be baptized with; and how am I straitened till it be accomplished!' Having passed through, He calls His sheep, and His sheep hear His voice, and follow Him whithersoever He goes; for this is the way to the true fountain (John 10:27; 4:14). This way was traveled by the royal priests who came from the rising of the sun, as we read in Revelation, and entered into the ages of eternity, and had to drink of this cup (I Peter 2:9).

"This way was trodden by the dead under the altar, who cry, saying: 'Lord, Almighty God, when wilt Thou avenge the blood that has been shed? White robes were given unto them, and it was said to them: Wait yet for a little season until the number of your brethren that are yet to be killed for the testimony of Jesus be fulfilled' (Revelation 6:9-11). These also drank of the cup and are gone above to keep the eternal, holy Sabbath of the Lord. This is the way in which walked the twenty-four elders, who stand before the throne of God, and cast their crowns and harps before the throne of the Lamb, falling down upon their faces, and saying: 'Lord, unto Thee alone be praise, glory, power, and strength, who shalt avenge the blood of Thy servants and ministers, and shalt through Thyself gain the victory. Great be Thy name, Almighty, which was, and is, and is to come' (Revelation 4:8, 10).

"Behold, all these could not attain to this, without first suffering judgment and chastisement in their flesh; for Christ Jesus, the eternal truth, was the first, when it is written: 'The Lamb slain from the foundation of the world' (Revelation 13:8). So Paul says: 'Thus it pleased the Father, that all whom He predestined from eternity, He called, elected, justified, and made to be conformed to the image of His Son' (Romans 8:29, 30). Our blessed Savior also says: 'The servant is not above his Lord; but it is sufficient for him, that he be like his Lord and Master' (Matthew 10:24)."

"If you, therefore, desire to enter into the regions of the holy world, and into the inheritance of the saints, gird your loins, and follow after them; search the Scriptures, and it shall show you their ways" (John 5:39).

"O Holy Father, sanctify the son of Thy handmaiden in Thy truth, and keep him from the evil, for Thy name's sake, O Lord."

The account concludes "Thereupon she sealed this with her blood, and thus, as a pious heroine and follower of Jesus Christ, she was received among the number of the witnesses of God who were offered up." [83]

Jan Claesz was baptized by Menno Simons and had six hundred copies of one of Menno's books published in Antwerp of which two hundred were sold in the province of Holland and the rest were shipped to Friesland. He was an Anabaptist leader in Amsterdam where he was beheaded January 19, 1544. He wrote six "testaments" to this wife and children which bear witness of his faith and love. He also gave a courageous testimony before his execution. To his wife he wrote: "Affectionate salutation in the Lord, to my beloved wife whom I no longer love after the flesh, but after the soul. Hear my admonition ... Take Christ for an example, and behold the way in which he went before us, and know that we must through much tribulation enter into the kingdom of heaven. (James 5:10, II Timothy 3:12) ... Pray to God for faith that you may overcome. And I will willingly give myself to the Lord in the same manner as he comforts my heart by His grace ... Persevere with a firm confidence in the Lord; he will help you in everything for the best."

To his children he wrote, "My dear children, Claes Jansz and Geertge Jansz, I leave you this as a testament when you come of age ... 'If any man will come after me, let him deny himself' ... if you will do this, the Holy Spirit will teach you all that you ought to believe. ... My dear children, surrender yourselves to that which is good, and the Lord will give you understanding in all things. I give you this as my last farewell. ... I, Jan Claesz, your father, have written this while in prison for the Word of the Lord. May the good Father grant you His grace. Amen."

When Jan Claesz and Lukas Lambertz were to be burned at the stake, the former said to the latter: "Fear neither fire nor the sword: Oh, what a joyful feast will be prepared for us before the clock strikes twelve!" When he had ascended the scaffold, he addressed the people with these words: "Hear, ye citizens of Amsterdam ... we suffer not as thieves or murderers. ... We die for no other reason than for the true Word of God. ... However, do not understand me as justifying or exalting myself; but I come as a prodigal son and depend only on the pure Word of God." [84]

In the year 1544, Maria van Beckum and Ursula, the wife of Jan van Beckum, were brought to Deventer to be tried and punished because of their Anabaptist faith. When led to the stake to be burned, followed by many people they sang for joy and said, "Weep not on account of what is inflicted upon us." Maria said: "We do not suffer as witches or other criminals, but because we adhere to Christ, and will not be separated from God; hence be converted, and it shall be well with you forever." Maria's final prayer was: "To Thee, O Christ, I have given myself; I know that I shall live with Thee forever. Therefore, O God of heaven, into Thy hands I commend my Spirit." This event not only moved the hearts of the pious but also relatives in East Friesland to protest. [85]

6. *The Theology of Witnessing Laymen*

A later martyr, Jacob the Roore, a chandler by trade, was burned at the stake at Brugge, Belgium, on June 8, 1569. He was baptized by Gillis van Aken in 1554 and was a minister in Flanders. He was imprisoned in Brugge in 1569 and severely cross-examined by the Franciscan monk, Cornelis, and tortured. He wrote nineteen letters from prison to his wife, children, and the congregations he had served. The interview between Jacob and friar Cornelis, as well as some of the letters are found in the *Martyrs' Mirror.* They are typical in regard to the procedure followed as well as some of the knowledge of the scriptures of Anabaptists who, just a few years before, knew nothing about the content of the Bible. The friar was extremely irritated by his victim's constant reference to the scriptural basis of his faith, the source of the boldness of Jacob. The following are some selections from the discussion between friar Cornelis and Jacob.

Friar Cornelis. Well, I've come here to see whether I can convert you (Jacob, I believe, is your name) from your false and evil belief, in which you are erring, and whether I cannot bring you back to the Catholic faith of our mother, the holy Roman church, from which you have apostatized to this damnable Anabaptism. What do you say to this, eh?

Jacob. With your permission, as regards that I have an evil, false belief, this I deny; but that through the grace of God I have apostatized from your Babylonian mother, the Roman church, to the members, or the true church, of Christ, this I confess; and thank God for it, who has said: "Come out of her, my people, that ye be not partakers of her sins, and that ye receive not of her plagues" (Revelation 18:4; Isaiah 52:11).

Friar Cornelis. Is it true? And do you call our mother the holy Roman church, the whore of Babylon? And do you call your hellish, devilish sect of Anabaptism the members, or the true church of Christ? Eh! Hear this fine fellow once. Who the devil has taught you this! your accursed Menno Simons I suppose...

Jacob. With your permission, you talk very wickedly. It was not necessary that Menno Simons should have taught us as something new that the Babylonian whore signifies your mother, the Roman church, since John teaches us enough concerning this in his Apocalypse, or Revelation, in the 14th, 16th, 17th, and 18th chapters.

Friar Cornelis. Ah, bah! What do you understand about St. John's

Apocalypse? At what university did you study? At the loom, I suppose; for I understand that you were nothing but a poor weaver and chandler before you went around preaching and rebaptizing out here in the Gruthuysbosch. I have attended the university of Louvain and studied divinity so long, and yet I do not understand anything at all about St. John's Apocalypse; this is a fact.

Jacob. Therefore Christ thanked His heavenly Father, that He had revealed and made it known to babes and hidden it from the wise of this world, as it is written, Matthew 11:25.

Friar Cornelis. Exactly; God has revealed it to the weavers at the loom, to the cobblers on their bench, and to bellows-menders, lantern-tinkers, scissors-grinders, broom-makers, thatchers, and all sorts of riff-raff, and poor, filthy, and lousy beggars. And to us ecclesiastics who have studied from our youth night and day, He has concealed it. Just see how we are tormented. You Anabaptists are certainly fine fellows to understand the holy Scriptures; for before you are rebaptized, you can't tell A from B, but as soon as you are baptized, you can read and write. If the devil and his mother have not a hand in this, I do not understand anything about you people.

The conversation between the two continued in regard to the pope as the vicar of God; Cornelis made reference to Peter to whom Christ said: "Feed my sheep" and to whom he gave "the keys of heaven, and all priestly authority to loose from sin and to bind." To this the answer of Jacob was that "Christ said that upon this rock (i.e. upon such a faith as Peter confesses, Matthew 16:17) he would build his church; he said nothing about his seat or about vicars, popes, or priestly authority." The constant swearing of the friar led Jacob to say that Christ said, "Do not swear an oath, but let your communication be yea, yea, nay, nay; for whatsoever is more than these cometh of evil."

When asked about the sacrament of the altar, Jacob said, "I have never seen nor read this name in the holy Scriptures; hence, I can say nothing about it," and since the sacrament is not "once mentioned in the Scriptures," Jacob said, "you have only seven too many." The friar said, "Bah, you certainly have the Scriptures at your fingertips; and because you Anabaptists will read nothing but simply the holy Scriptures, that is why you never read about the sacrament of the altar ... You flatly refuse to hear by way of instruction, anything that the old fathers or teachers of the holy Catholic church write; such as St. Ambrose, St. Jerome, St. Augustine, St. Gregory, St. Chrysostom, St. Bernard, St. Anselm, and many others. Yea such as are more ancient yet: Irenaeus, Cyprian, Basil, Cyril and Tertullian... But you Anabaptists would rather delve and root in the accursed, damnable books of your arch-heretic, Menno Simons. And therefore, you do not know anything of the sacrament of the altar – is not this a fine thing?" But Jacob claimed to be "satisfied with the simple holy Scriptures; for all that is necessary for us to know, for our salvation, we find abundantly contained in them, and we need not to search the doctrines of men."

In regard to the question whether "Christ is truly present in the consecrated host with his natural flesh and blood," Jacob replied that "nothing is taught in the holy Scriptures of a consecrated host" and they used bread and wine as the "memorials of the Lord's body." In desperation Cornelis shouted, "Bah, what monsters are these memorials? This begins to sound quite Zwinglian and Calvinistic; and are you, Anabaptists, also Sacramentarians? I suppose so... My Lord, what do you think of this accursed, hellish, devil's crew? for they are Anabaptists and Sacramentarians." This discussion continued with the friar getting angrier so that Jacob finally told him to "consider that Paul says to Titus in the first chapter that a teacher must not be angry, snappish, or contentious."

Friar Cornelis exclaimed in desperation, "Bah, you have preached enough now; for my head begins to ache severely from it. Hence let us now dispute about Anabaptism and infant baptism, and be done with it... Why is the sacrament of baptism not necessary for children for their salvation as you Anabaptists preach and teach?" To this Jacob said "that infants are nevertheless saved, although they die unbaptized: for they are baptized and cleansed in the blood of Jesus Christ" (John 1:7). A long discussion about the necessity of baptizing infants followed. Finally, the friar exclaimed, "Bah, Jesus, Jesus, how well you can talk, how well your tongue is hung! Bah, never in all my life did I hear the Scriptures expounded so strangely contrary to the views of my mother, the holy Roman Catholic church, and the ancient teachers and fathers. Bah, now I am not surprised that the Anabaptists have made you their teacher, preacher, and bishop."

In support of infant baptism, Cornelis stated, "We Catholics baptize them upon the faith of the Holy Church, and because they have believing parents; therefore they need not be taught first." Jacob quoted, "Go ye into all the world, and preach the Gospel to every creature. He that believeth and is baptized shall be saved" (Mark 16), and "Go ye therefore, and teach all nations baptizing them" (Matthew 28). Here the dialogue between the two ended abruptly and with a finality.

Friar Cornelis. Well, I have no desire to dispute any longer with you. I shall go my way, and let the executioner dispute with you, with a burning fagot... and afterwards the devil in hell, with burning pitch, brimstone, and tar, see.

Jacob. No; for Paul writes (II Corinthians 5:1): "If our earthly house of this tabernacle were dissolved, we have a building of God, a house not made with hands, eternal in the heavens."

Friar Cornelis. Bah! in hell, in hell. Expect nothing else than to go through this temporal fire into the eternal; hell yawns and gasps for your soul you accursed, damned Anabaptists that you are, see.[86]

Most of the martyrs and Anabaptist witnesses of the covenant were simple laborers, many of whom learned to read and write when they accepted the message presented to them. This changed their life completely and gave them the motivation to learn to read, to study the Bible, and to share this experience with others. Their disciplined and covenanted Christian life was as much of a witness in spreading the message as their spoken word. Most impressive, however, was their willingness to seal their witness with their own blood. This made Hubmaier's statement about truth that cannot be crucified come true in the spread of the Anabaptist movement and in the disarmament of the inquisition machinery which did everything possible to stop the spread. The blood of the martyrs, which was the seed of the church, was the primary cause for the renewal of the covenant after the perversion of it at Münster.

VII

GROWTH AND MOLDING OF THE
BROTHERHOOD

A. FROM ANTWERP TO DANZIG

When Melchior Hofmann died in the Strassburg prison in 1543, his *Ordinance of God* had won followers throughout the Low Countries, across the channel in England, along the North Sea in East Friesland, and along the Baltic Coast from Schleswig-Holstein and Mecklenburg to Danzig at the mouth of the Vistula River. This rapid spread was due not only to a strong sense of mission on the part of all those accepting the call of the ordinance, but also to the severe persecution of the Anabaptists and their resulting dispersal. The persecution was strongest under Charles V and Philips II in the southern part of the Low Countries, the present Belgium. The regent representing the emperor resided in Brussels. In its effort to exterminate Anabaptism, the influence of the court of Brussels on the stadholders of the various provinces was, as a rule, strongest in the south, in Flanders, and Brabant.

1. The Final Struggle in the South

The fact that all cities along the North Sea and Baltic coast from Antwerp to Danzig belonged to the Hanseatic League provided the Reformation, as well as the Anabaptist movement, with channels of communication which enhanced the rapid spread. In spite of the rigid applications of the edicts, for some time merchants and travelers could spread their message as strangers unnoticed at the seaports. Antwerp's significant role during the early days of the Reformation and the spread of Sacramentarians has been indicated. Antwerp continued to be the publishing center of the Low Countries; even one of Menno Simons' books was printed there. Being a cultural center of the Low Countries with direct contact with most of the cities of the world, it offered other advantages for Anabaptism and underground activities in general. How this was exploited even after the fall of Münster is exemplified by the edict issued in Antwerp on February 19, 1536: "Images, pictures, prints, or engravings of Jan van Leyden, . . . books containing the biographies of such heretics and delinquents are not to be sold."[1]

Around 1545 there was a great need for leadership in the Gent area. In a letter written to the brethren at Antwerp it was stated that the Gent Anabaptists were "sincerely troubled and grieved by the great distress, . . . that poor weak brethren tragically wander about like sheep without a shepherd" while "the harvest is great and the laborers are few."[2] This not only indicates that there was a lack of leadership and that Antwerp was looked up to as a place from which help could come, but also that the field was ripe for the harvest everywhere.

An outstanding leader of the Gent Anabaptists had been Hans van Overdam who escaped arrest in 1545 and went to Antwerp. However, he found frequent occasion to return to Gent. In 1551, he was deeply moved as he watched the execution of four members of the Gent congregation and consequently posted protests at various places: "Oh, you spiritual Babel, how shall the Lord visit vengeance upon you for the innocent souls and blood of his witnesses!" Betrayed, he was arrested and executed with eleven others on July 9, 1551.[3]

Gent was visited sometime between 1554 and 1556 by the courageous Leenaert Bouwens who had been ordained by Menno Simons in 1553. During his 1554 to 1556 visit, Bouwens baptized 225 people in Antwerp, Brussels, Tournai, Gent, and other nearby places. He repeated his visits in 1557 to 1561 and 1563 to 1565, adding 367 more names to his baptismal list.[4] How daring and bold he was is evidenced by the edict issued in Antwerp in 1558 with regard to Leenaert Bouwens and Joachim Vermeeren:

Whoever delivers or denounces one of these two Anabaptists so that they can be arrested, the same shall receive from the city three hundred carolus-guilders and furthermore shall be amnestied if he is an Anabaptist.[5]

Peaceful and militant Anabaptism reached Flanders and Brabant during the first years of its spread. Jan van Geelen and Batenburg had followers there. The mandates of October 10, 1535, January 24, 1539, and December 14, 1541, were directed against the Anabaptists. According to A. L. E. Verheyden,[6] the number of Anabaptist martyrs who died for their faith in this area was greater than the combined total of Lutherans and Calvinists.

Among the early leaders coming from the north to Flanders to promote the movement and establish congregations was Jan Mattijs van Middelburg, who attended the Bocholt meeting and was burned in

London in 1538. Another outstanding promoter of Anabaptism in Flanders was Gillis van Aken. No other is named as frequently by the martyrs as Gillis van Aken, the one who baptized them. In 1557, while preaching near Antwerp, he was captured and beheaded.[7] Hans Busschaert, who was ordained by Menno Simons in 1555 and became Menno Simons' close co-worker, was a leading native elder (bishop) of Flanders. However, not much is known about his work in Flanders.

The severe persecution and the execution of Anabaptists in the mid-century caused many to flee from the south to the northern parts of the Low Countries, including East Friesland. Antwerp, where many found underground shelter, did its utmost to prevent the flow of refugees to the city. An edict issued in 1550 read: "Foreigners suspected of heresies, and in particular the Anabaptists, are not to be admitted here without an attestation from the parish of their last place of residence." Later an even more drastic measure was taken when an ordinance was passed stating that "foreigners having lived here less than two years are to leave..." Some Anabaptists crossed the channel and found shelter as foreigners in London and the port towns of the east coast of England.

Yet Anabaptism seems to have increased in numbers even during the severest oppression. Pieter Titelman, one of the inquisitors, stated in 1561 that the Anabaptists were "increasing at several places," and a little later he reported that Flanders was completely infested by Menno Simons' teachings.[8] Menno Simons himself, unlike Leenaert Bouwens, never came to Flanders.

After 1550 Calvinism began to spread rapidly in the southern and northern provinces of the Low Countries; it penetrated the regions from France and Geneva to Frankfurt a. M., East Friesland, and London.[9] Now Anabaptism, Sacramentarianism, and Calvinism occupied the same regions of the Low Countries. Calvinism, however, was typified as a well-organized new form of the Reformation that allied itself with a strong militant nationalism. This alliance ultimately sought the independence of the new movement in the Low Countries. The clash came soon after Philip II, son of Charles V, became king of Spain and consequently ruler of the Low Countries. The Habsburg empire was now divided into two parts. Ferdinand, brother of Charles V, received Austrian Habsburg and Philip II, Spain and Burgundy. Philip II continued the policy of strengthening his position in the Low Countries in an attempt to make this region an integral part of Burgundy. A part of his strategy was to exterminate any form of Protestantism in the Low Countries. Charles V had had some advantage in his execution of this policy since he had been reared in the Court of Brussels; but Philip was a Spaniard and extremely unpopular from the start. He followed a policy of rigid subjugation of the Low Countries to his will and the throne of Spain. In 1559 he departed for Spain, leaving his sister, Margaret of Austria, duchess of Parma, as governess in charge of the country. He reduced the power of the States General and saw to it that heretical views would be suppressed. The formation of the Confederation of Nobles in 1565 led to uprisings in the following year in the form of "iconoclasms" sweeping from the south northward and marking the entry of Calvinism and national independence. Philip met the challenge by sending the Duke of Alva with troops to suppress the uprising. This move led to the Eighty Years War and resulted in the establishment of the independent Orange monarchy with a Reformed state church, the creation of the present-day Netherlands, and the emergence of a Catholic monarchy in the southern Low Countries, known as Belgium.[10] The end result was that neither Anabaptism nor Calvinism survived in Belgium.

It is estimated that more than eight hundred Anabaptists died, while the remainder fled to the north or recanted. The information that there were two thousand Anabaptists in Antwerp, seven hundred in Brugge, and a corresponding number in other parts of Flanders at the peak of Anabaptism must be overstated, although the movement was popular.[11] That Anabaptism was non-resistant at the time of the Calvinist uprising is without question. On the other hand, it can be assumed that individual Anabaptists may have joined the forces of militant Calvinism although no study along this line has been made. With the rise of this liberation-reformation movement, the popularity of Anabaptism decreased. Its first setback had occurred when a radical wing of the Melchiorites took up arms in order to help the Lord usher in the kingdom of God, and failed. In the same soil of Sacramentarianism a victorious militant, national and reformed movement replaced the popularity of Anabaptism. From a national and military point of view, it must be said that the Anabaptist military attempts lacked the experience, the political and military backing, and the leadership which Calvinism had. Furthermore, neither the religious and eschatological utopian aspect nor the proletarian uprising had as much general appeal as militant Calvinism found under the leadership of the Confederation of Nobles. The backgrounds of oppression, persecution, and deprivation were similar in 1530 to 1535 and 1565 to 1566, but the utopian notion of a heavenly kingdom on earth had been replaced by the concrete objective of the liberation of a country for national and religious reasons. Experienced leaders were at the head of the movement instead of fanatical utopians. These were some of the main reasons for the failure in the first case and the success in the second instance. Anabaptism survived as a tolerated branch of Protestantism while Calvinism became the state church of the northern Low Countries.

At the beginning of the second half of the sixteenth century, Anabaptism had still been the largest non-Catholic group in Flanders. The preceding mandates and the one of 1555 now made it increasingly difficult for the Anabaptists to survive.[12] Gradually the evangelical Sacramentarian movement came more and more under the influence of Calvinism which at times was ready to promote its cause by iconoclastic and violent means. However, in their escape from persecution and their attempts to find a refuge in the northern provinces of the Low Countries or on foreign soil, the Anabaptists and the Reformed went the same roads and often met again at the same places.

2. A Refuge in the North

Many of the southern Anabaptists sealed their faith and made their last witness by giving their lives as martyrs. The number of those who escaped, however, was not negligible. A. A. van Schelven estimated that sixty thousand religious refugees may have fled from the south to the north; some historians give even higher figures. The same author has pointed out how strongly the Flemish and Brabant Reformed refugees influenced the establishment of the Reformed Church in the north and how they contributed to the refinement of the culture of the nation and the promotion of art and literature as well as the weaving and textile industries and business.[13] Although no specialized study has been made in regard to the Anabaptist contribution in these areas, it can be assumed that it was equal to that of the Reformed in most areas. Before the general influence and the history of the Flemish and Brabant refugees in the north is presented, a few outstanding individuals will be named. Those selected were second generation Anabaptists, who personally went to the north as religious refugees.

Hans de Ries was born December 13, 1553, at Antwerp. After being influenced by Protestantism in his native city, he was soon drawn to the Anabaptists and, because of persecution, went to Alkmaar, Holland, where he became a Mennonite minister and wrote the first Dutch Mennonite confession of faith. He traveled extensively as a minister throughout the Low Countries and had a profound influence on the Dutch Mennonites, particularly the Waterlander branch. He helped in the shaping of the religious thinking among the Mennonites far beyond his time and the borders of the Low Countries through his numerous writings and personal contacts. In a time during which the religious controversies were strong, he exerted a unifying influence. He was instrumental in publishing numerous books, including a revised edition of *Het Offer des Heeren* which was used by T. J. van Braght as the basic collection for the *Martyrs' Mirror.*[14]

Another individual worthy of mention is Christiaen van Eeghen (*de Oude*) 1595-1669) who was born at Cortemerck near Brugge in Flanders and migrated to Aardenburg, Zeeland, were he became a leader in the Mennonite church. Other members of the family made their contributions here and also became influential at Middelburg, Zeeland. Jacob van Eeghen, son of Christiaen van Eeghen (*de Oude*), was born at Cortemerck in 1631 and went via Aardenburg to Amsterdam in 1662. From this family came the founders of the well-known *Handelshuis van Eeghen*. Rogge in the book *Het Handelshuis van Eeghen* says of Christiaan Pieter van Eeghen (1816-1889) that he "was one of the greatest of all in his family." He embodied the family tradition as a good businessman, had strong religious interests, and promoted philantropy and the fine arts (Rijksmuseum, Vondelpark).[15]

The greatest Dutch poet, Joost van den Vondel (1587-1679), was the son of a refugee by the same name who came to Amsterdam from Antwerp via Cologne. The poet's literary works, among which were a number of biblical and historical plays in verse, are considered treasures of the Dutch literature. His parents belonged to the Flemish Mennonite church while he joined the Waterlander congregation of Amsterdam in which he served as a deacon (1616-1620). However, he was gradually estranged from the congregation and in 1641 joined the Catholic Church.[16] He continued his Mennonite connections and friendships and gave expression to them in his literary work.

Another outstanding Mennonite was the artist Carel van Mander who was born in 1548 in Meulebeke, Flanders. In 1583 he left his home for religious reasons and went to Haarlem where he became the head of the Haarlem school of art. He was the teacher of some noted Dutch painters and a man of varied gifts. He published some writings of Virgil, and a collection of his poems in *De Gulden Harpe* (Haarlem, 1599) which was used as a Mennonite hymnary in Holland and even in Prussia. Most famous was his *Het Schilderboeck,* a book of biographies of artists which is in use to this day. French and German translations soon followed.[17]

A general observation is in place at this point. Swiss Anabaptist leadership was at first predominantly in the hands of individuals who had some training in the religious and humanistic tradition of their time. Because of severe persecution, the Swiss Anabaptists soon lost this leadership and survived only in remote areas where they pursued agricultural endeavors and had little contact with the cultural life of their environment, be it in Switzerland, France, South Germany, or Austria. Dutch Anabaptism, on the other hand, was originally a popular movement with only a few leaders who had some religious training. Since it had its strong-hold in cities and was ultimately tolerated, it soon became *kulturfreundlich* and began to make a significant contribution to the economic, cultural, and religious life of the country. Cultured leaders in these areas joined the Anabaptists, greatly strengthening the group and its mission.

Returning to the large number of Flemish and Brabant Anabaptist refugees which came to the north, we must observe that they found new homes in the various provinces from Zeeland to East Friesland. They sought and obtained spiritual fellowship and acceptance among their brethren of the north. The bonds uniting both were the Christian fellowship and the cause of Christ for which they suffered. Brotherly love and mutual aid had always been among the characteristics of the *bondgenoten* of Christ. In this emergency the practice was deepened and extended to include the brethren from far away. A relief service was born spontaneously. Homes were opened to the homeless and jobs were found for those without work. Goods were shared with those who did not have any.

On the other hand, those coming from the south soon began to make contributions to the brotherhood and the national life in general, as has been illustrated in the case of the outstanding refugees. The chambers of rhetoric so common in the south gained in popularity in the north and were strengthened by the efforts of these refugees. As shown by the examples, the Flemish and Brabant refugees made significant contributions in numerous areas, including the religious life (Hans de Ries), business (van Eeghen family), and the fine arts (Joost van den Vondel and Carel van Mander). These refugees also made a substantial contribution in the weaving and textile industries at various places, including Leiden and Twente, Overijssel.[18] At Twente these industries were developed on a large scale similar to the practice started and promoted by Mennonites across the German border in the cities of Gronau and Krefeld.

We cannot overlook the fact that the difference in background also caused cultural and religious divisions. The seventeenth century historian, G. Brandt, related that the "Flemish neglected their household goods but were particular about their clothes" while the Frisians "wore simple clothes but emphasized cleanliness and good appearance as far as their linen and household goods" [19] were concerned. This outward difference, which is understandable, was duplicated many times in Mennonite history and in general contributed to disagreements and misunderstandings in the spiritual effort to present to the Lord a "church without spot and wrinkle." However, it would be wrong to state that the development of the very far-reaching division between the Frisians and the Flemish was entirely due to this difference in cultural traits and ethnic background. These were simply the areas in which differences became noticeable as the groups attempted to mold the true Christian life within the household of Christ. That the division between the "Flemish" and "Frisians" was caused primarily by religious views was evidenced by the fact that it spread rapidly with little regard to ethnic and cultural backgrounds. The tags "Frisian" and "Flemish" were soon used to designate certain characteristics and views in the realm of spiritual and ethical behavior. These groupings spread from Friesland through all provinces of the Low Countries and along the North Sea and the Baltic coast wherever Mennonites resided. They became so deeply ingrained that even in 1788 when Mennonites from the Danzig area intended to migrate to Russia, they were urged by the Russian representatives to give up their differences as Flemish and Frisians so that they could come to the country of their choice as one group of Mennonites. [20]

3. The Escape: London and Danzig

From 1528 onward, persecuted Sacramentarians, Reformed, and Anabaptists from the Low Countries, particularly artisans, found shelter and work in England under Henry VIII. Many resided in London; others were employed in the factories of Norwich and other cities. Thus London became a center for all three dissenting groups; for a while a Reformed Church existed here under the leadership of J. a Lasco and Martin Micron.

A. H. Newman states that by 1560 there were about ten thousand refugees in England and that two years later the number had increased threefold. In the years of Alva's persecution (1568-73) the number was at least fifty thousand. When Antwerp was taken by Spain in 1576, many businessmen settled in London.[21]

It must be assumed that soon after the spread of Anabaptism in the Low Countries in 1530, some members of this group fled to England even though no definite information is available. Irvin B. Horst states that "not only the literate but also the masses of the people, at least in London, had the opportunity to learn about the Anabaptists early in the 1530's." The first known reference is dated 1538. In this, a royal proclamation, it was stated that "divers and sundry strangers of the sects and false opinion of the Anabaptists and Sacramentarians" had "lately come into this realm" who "lurk secretly in divers corners and places" and aim to "provoke and stir the king's loving subjects to their errors and opinions."[22]

The flow of Anabaptist refugees continued. Reference has been made to Anneke Jans, an Anabaptist who for sometime resided in London and who was put to death after her return to the continent. Henry, an English Anabaptist, was the sponsor of the Bocholt meeting of 1536. Philip of Hesse, one of the best informed rulers about Anabaptist movements and trends, wrote Henry VIII in 1538 calling his attention to the fact that German Anabaptists were in touch with those of England. As a result, Henry VIII urged Cranmer to "search for and examine Anabaptists" in England. Consequently, Archbishop Cranmer sought out Anabaptists for execution; he attempted to persuade them to give up their views before they were put to death.[23] Because of this persecution some Anabaptists who fled from Flanders to England met their death on foreign soil. Among those burned in London in 1538 was Jan Mattijsz van Middelburg.

Anabaptism did not survive in England in the form in which it was transplanted by the refugees. In the early seventeenth century John Smyth and other English separatist refugees in the Netherlands were influenced by the Mennonites of Amsterdam in founding the Baptist or independent churches. Irvin B. Horst concludes his article dealing with the Anabaptists in England by saying that they "deposited a ferment of religious ideas which were finally absorbed into English and American church and secular history."[24]

The spread of the Anabaptists from the southern provinces of the Low Countries into the northern and the development of Anabaptism in the Cologne area and in East Friesland have been presented. Before the spread into the German provinces of Schleswig-Holstein and Mecklenburg is taken up, the beginning of Anabaptism in the area of the Vistula Delta on the Baltic Coast will be presented. The Anabaptist refugees of the first decades who settled in the Vistula Delta came primarily from the Low Countries and particularly the southern part where the persecution was most severe. Some, no doubt, went via the northern provinces including East Friesland and later also Holstein and Mecklenburg. The first Anabaptist refugees to come to this area settled in the delta because this gave them an opportunity to follow their occupations under conditions similar to those to which they were accustomed. Although they were dissenters living under Lutheran or Catholic sponsors, they were usually tolerated because of the great economic contribution they made through their skill in draining swamps or through their occupations as farmers, weavers, or other artisans. As the delta area between Danzig, Marienburg, and Elbing became occupied, newcomers proceeded along the Vistula River, establishing themselves on land in the vicinities of Graudenz, Culm, and Thorn and ultimately even near Warsaw. About half of the Mennonites of the world today originally came from the Vistula River area directly or via Russia where a large number settled during the eighteenth and nineteenth centuries.

The territory under consideration was originally occupied by the Teutonic knights. The western part of the possessions of the Teutonic knights, West Prussia, on both sides of the lower Vistula, was ceded to Poland in 1466. This area from Danzig to Thorn later became the center of the Dutch settlements. East Prussia, the eastern part of the territory of the Teutonic knights and adjacent to West Prussia, was secularized by Duke Albrecht (1525), who promoted the Lutheran Reformation. The duke tolerated such Sacramentarians and semi-Anabaptists as William Gnapheus, Gerhard Westerburg, Christian Entfelder, Caspar Schwenckfeld, and others of non-Lutheran persuasion, at least temporarily. In 1527 the duke established a Dutch settlement east of Preussisch-Holland near Bardeyn through the mediation of Hendrik Claasz of Alkmaar and Thomas Lorenszoon of St. Maarten and in 1529 through Gert Johanszoon of Wormer. At a later date some Anabaptists came to this area, but this particular attempt of settlement was not successful.

Another settlement which involved Anabaptists was established later at Rossgarten near Königsberg, East Prussia, the fate of which was somewhat similar. In both cases the problem was the same. The newcomers were located on land not suitable for the type of agriculture to which they were accustomed in their home country, and when it was discovered that they were Anabaptists, they were as a rule ordered to leave. Most of them ultimately went to the Danzig Werder (lowlands).[25]

Danzig itself had attracted Dutch businessmen and settlers since the Middle Ages. In the Artushof, the guild house, the Dutch had their own bank. But business with religious dissenters was one thing and granting them a domicile another. With the same concern that Antwerp had displayed, the city council of Danzig requested that Amsterdam, Antwerp, Enkhuizen, and Emden prevent Anabaptists from boarding ships destined for Danzig. This urgent request in 1535 indicated that some had arrived as refugees. Other Protestants had been put to death in Danzig as early as 1526.[26]

An unusual refugee and agent for recruiting settlers was Jan van Sol of Dordrecht, who had gone to Danzig in 1530. He was likely a Sacramentarian who associated with Mennonites. He contributed to the persecution of the Anabaptists by revealing much information about them when he went to Brussels in 1550. He proposed a plan to combat Anabaptism and returned to Prussia.[27]

After Danzig rejected religious refugees, the dissenters, and later on primarily Mennonites, found their way to the Danzig suburbs of Neu-Schottland and Hoppenbruch where they were tolerated. These places which were under the jurisdiction of the bishop of Leslau had been destroyed by fire. Therefore, the bishop welcomed artisans and the prospect of rebuilding the towns and developing industries. The weaving and lace making industries were soon a strong competition for the guilds of Danzig. Mennonites settled in numerous other settlements or suburbs of Danzig where they were visited by Menno Simons, Dirk Philips, and Leenaert Bouwens.

Once the various authorities of the lowlands saw what the skill and diligence of the Dutch refugees accomplished in making waste land useful and valuable, contracts were offered to them to invite others in their homeland to join them. A great drainage program was initiated to conquer the Vistula Delta area between Drausen Lake and Elbing. Philip Edzema (Frese), a Mennonite, was sent to invite settlers from the Low Countries, and he and another Mennonite, Herman van Bommel, acquired land in the Danzig Werder for settlement.[28]

Felicia Szper reports that a large stream of Dutch religious refugees reached Elbing in 1531. It can be assumed that they were mostly Sacra-

mentarians. In 1536 another group followed. At this time the Sacramentarian Willem Gnapheus was a teacher at the Elbing gymnasium.
He was compelled to leave in 1541. In 1550 jealous citizens complained to the king that the Dutch Anabaptists were doing damage
to their business. When the Anabaptists were asked to leave this time,
they requested permission to settle in Ellerwald near Elbing on land
that was still uninhabited. This request was granted.[29]

In Prussia, as in England, the coming of the Anabaptists was preceded and paralleled by the Sacramentarians. The lines between the
two, as in the homeland, were not always drawn sharply. The Sacramentarians of the city of Danzig formed the nucleus of the Dutch
Reformed Church as was the case in Emden, London, and Frankfurt.
As has been seen, the Anabaptists were not tolerated in the city of
Danzig and consequently settled in the suburbs. Whatever the number
of the Sacramentarians may have been in the rural areas, most of them
must have joined the Anabaptists. This merging, among other things,
must have caused some frictions and conflicts which were dealt with
by Menno Simons during a visit in 1549.[30]

On October 7, 1549, Menno Simons wrote a letter to the "Elect
and Children of God in the Land of Prussia." He started by saying
"what grievous solicitude, care, trouble, labor, and sorrow we experienced in your midst this past summer," and expressed concern for
the outcome. Before he came to the brethren in Prussia "for a long
time, alas, a severe quarrel" had existed among them. It is hardly
possible to conclude from this letter of what nature the cause of the
"severe quarrel" was. Neither is it possible to determine whether this
was a quarrel which affected all "children of God" or one congregation only. It was likely in Menno's presence that they "again received
one another with the kiss of peace and ... saluted each other as brethren." But having "seen with my eyes and heard with my ears the heath-
en impurity of many a heart," he hurried to write this letter in which
he begged the recipients to become filled with the love of Christ and
to strive toward peace. Even though the letter does not reveal much
factual information about the Mennonites of the Vistula Delta, it
constitutes one of the best writings of Menno Simons. A copy of the
letter was preserved in the Thiensdorf-Markushof Mennonite Church
and has been published recently with the writings of Menno.[31]

Just prior to Menno's visit of the congregations in the east, a letter
was received in Amsterdam from a brother in Danzig which caused
much discussion in regard to church discipline.[32] It is hard to tell

whether there was any relationship between the "quarrel" among the "children of God in Prussia," the letter written from Danzig to Amsterdam, and the heated discussion of the question of church discipline which was to become an even greater issue among the brethren of Amsterdam.

Questions about how long Menno's visit lasted, whether he was accompanied by Dirk Philips or someone else, what congregations he visited, whether he made these trips repeatedly, and whether the restored peace lasted cannot be answered on the basis of the available factual information. It is also not known how many congregations had already been organized at this time or whether Menno helped with the organization of additional congregations, with baptismal services, and with the ordination of ministers.

The list of ministers of the *Gemeynte Godts* of Danzig is headed by Dirk Philips. It is stated that he went from Danzig to Emden in 1567 where he died the following year.[33] Leenaert Bouwens also visited Danzig. Faithfully the followers of these leaders aimed to build the church of God under the pioneer conditions of members coming from all provinces of the Low Countries and representing various social and economic strata and occupations. Among them were Sacramentarians, Melchiorites, and even those who were suspected of having belonged to the militant Anabaptist wing. Menno's letter to these children of God is an example of the attempts to mold a brotherhood into the pattern of the apostolic church. That was a great task under unusual conditions.

The flow of Anabaptists to the *Oistlandt* continued and increased depending on the pressure of persecution in the crown lands of the Low Countries. On December 23, 1550, Jan van Sol estimated that a hundred had arrived that year. He made the interesting observation that the Anabaptists liked to deal in small businesses to be foot-loose and free in order to be able to move when it was necessary. He claimed that many managed to bring along letters of recommendation from their former places of residence in the Low Countries. Many went back again in order to teach and preach, having letters of recommendation and making full use of Anabaptist hospitality. The brotherhood had a well-functioning system of mutual aid administered by the deacons of all congregations, which was used both to grant aid in emergency situations and also to start businesses.[34]

Walter Kuhn estimates that between 1527 and 1578, some 750 families or a total of three thousand Dutch refugees and settlers came to Danzig and East and West Prussia, most of which were Mennonites. A later survey indicates that of 567 Prussian Mennonite names, at least five hundred were of Dutch background and could be traced to the various provinces of the Low Countries.[35] Dutch ships and business dominated the traffic and trade between the Dutch ports and the cities of the Baltic coast up to Danzig and Königsberg during the major part of the sixteenth century. Large numbers of Dutch business men, crafts- men, sailors, and farmers established themselves in these cities and rural areas.[36] The Dutch language and traits of Dutch culture were preserved into the eighteenth century and lasted longest in Danzig be- cause of a continued contact with the home country.[37] One exception to this predominantly Dutch emigration was the settlement in the Culm and Graudenz area in 1535 of some Moravian Anabaptists.[38]

The contact between the Anabaptists of Amsterdam and those of Danzig was particularly strong, as evidenced by the trial records of 1539-52. Many of the Amsterdam Anabaptists were sailors who made repeated trips to Danzig. Others had relatives living in Danzig. The place *Rametsteegje* in Amsterdam was known as a meeting place of "strangers from various places leaving every morning to travel east." [39]

By the end of the sixteenth century the settlement of Dutch refugees in rural areas was nearly over. The trek to the Danzig area continued for some time, and a return to the Low Countries even took place.

4.   The Hanseatic Cities, Schleswig-Holstein and Mecklenburg

Centers of Anabaptism were not restricted to the Low Countries, East Friesland, the German Lower Rhine, Westphalia, and the Vistula Delta, but were also found in and near the German Hanseatic cities of Hamburg and Lübeck, throughout Schleswig-Holstein, and in Wismar and Rostock in Mecklenburg. The origin of Anabaptism in these areas is still obscure in many cases. Gradually centers were formed by refu- gees coming from the Low Countries. Many stopped only temporarily on their way to the Vistula Delta area. Others left Friesland and Gro- ningen to come to East Friesland with Menno Simons and Dirk Phi- lips. Dirk Philips had a debate with the Lutheran Joachim Kükenbieter in Norden, East Friesland in 1537. Soon some of the Anabaptists went to Schleswig-Holstein and Mecklenburg.[40]

The Reformation at Rostock, Mecklenburg, started under J. Slüter (1523) and became established under J. Oldendorp (1532) in the form of a moderate Lutheranism. Bugenhagen, Luther, and Rhegius played a significant role in counteracting Sacramentarian views spreading from the west. Particularly Lübeck felt responsible for the neighboring city and the course of the Reformation it took. Whether as a trick or an act based on rumor, or both, the Lübeck city council warned Rostock on June 6, 1537, that Bernhard Rothmann, who supposedly had escaped from Münster, was in their city and that Hinrich Techen of the *Marien-Kirche* knew of it. The strategy worked, and an edict was passed to examine all refugees that had come from the Low Countries to see whether there were some with Anabaptist leanings.[41] This was the situation which Obbe Philips and some Anabaptists encountered when they came to Rostock. It was as precarious here as at most other places.

Obbe Philips, who must have continued his profession here as a barber-physician with some success, gradually reached the stage of a more mellowed type of Anabaptism by attending worship services of moderate Lutheran ministers. He likely continued meeting with Anabaptist refugees until he came to the point where he could no longer "serve two masters" and withdrew from the Anabaptists around 1540. Later he wrote his *Confession* which has been referred to repeatedly. Menno Simons and his co-workers, who were not far from Rostock and who must have met Obbe occasionally, gradually began to consider him a "Demas" who, just like the followers of Joris, found nothing wrong with a dual church membership as long as the "faith in his heart" remained intact.

The presentation of the development of Obbe's religious views differs here from those usually presented, namely that he became an individualist not affiliated with any group. The basis for the view presented here is obtained by reading his *Confession* as well as the preface by the unnamed Reformed publisher. The reasons for assuming that Obbe Philips, at least outwardly, affiliated with and possibly joined the Lutheran Church are as follows. The writer of the *Confession* was not a Catholic. Living in Rostock he could not have been Reformed. Significantly, the Reformed publisher of the *Confession* states in the preface: "Herewith we do not intend to say that he was converted from a bad religion to a better one." It was not the publisher's intention to relate in what faith Obbe Philips lived and died after that, leaving that up to God.[42] Obbe Philips could not have had a long-standing business and a livelihood in Lutheran Rostock without being at least considered a Lutheran. In his credo he emphasizes that he was never connected with the Münsterites and that he had now withdrawn

from Melchioritism because it had no legitimate call from God or
the Scriptures to start a new church. With this credo and an attendance
of the Lutheran church, he was tolerated in Lübeck. He would also
have been accepted in Reformed Emden and other places under these
conditions. He died in 1568, the same year that his brother, who had
remained a "bishop" of the brotherhood, died in Emden.

Some Anabaptists must have been present in Rostock when the city
took repeated action against them in 1555 and in 1561 to 1563. A
group of Anabaptists coming directly from Groningen was detected in
Ribnitz near Rostock in 1556, carefully examined, and expelled.[43]
When, in 1567, refugees from Antwerp arrived fleeing Alva's bloody
rule, the gates of the city were closed. Not only the Anabaptists but
also the Sacramentarians and Reformed were feared. Even during the
following century Anabaptists were expelled if recognized as such.

Wismar, located between Rostock and Lübeck, has already been
referred to in connection with the Anabaptist discussions with followers
of David Joris (1546), with Adam Pastor (1552), and with Martin
Micron and his group (1553-54). Menno Simons and a large group
of Anabaptists resided there for a longer period of time. Wismar
played a significant role in the history of early northern Anabaptism
in general, not just locally. This was particularly the case in regard
to the Wismar Resolutions agreed upon at a large meeting in 1554.
Wismar's significance is in part due to the course which the Reformation took in this Hanseatic city.

Wismar had a popular evangelical Sacramentarian movement which
started in 1524. It was supported by the middle class and led by the
Franciscan Hinrich Never, who was assisted by Clemens Timme. The
Sacramentarian Zwinglian views in regard to the Lord's supper became apparent when Never stated that it did not constitute a sacrament but was in "memory of the perfect and eternal sacrifice of
Christ." His views brought him into conflict with Bugenhagen who
was in Hamburg at this time.

The radical development at Münster in 1535 had some influence
on the development of the Reformation in the Hanseatic cities of
the north. At a convention in Hamburg on April 15 of that year, representatives of the cities agreed to take action against Anabaptists, Sacramentarians, and Catholics. The worship was to be strictly Lutheran.
Wismar and Rostock, however, declined to issue this mandate in their
cities. Among the cities of Hamburg, Lübeck, Lüneburg, Bremen,
Wismar, Rostock, and Stralsund, the latter three were considered black

sheep because they did not cooperate fully. Even Danzig was threatened and asked to make the mandate known and apply it. Wismar was asked to stop the activities of Never and his co-worker Hinrich Timmermann. An examination of Never was conducted in regard to baptism and the Lord's supper which revealed once again that his views were extremely spiritualistic and could in no way satisfy the Lutherans. He considered infant baptism in conflict with Christ's teaching. Even Luther was asked to examine Never's written confession. For him it was a "foolish thing without any Scriptural foundation." After many examinations and negotiations Never and Timmermann received the verdict on December 26, 1541, inflicting on them "eternal silence" because they were "Sacramentarians and Anabaptists."[44]

It was in this environment that Anabaptists felt relatively at home and may even have had a friendly relationship with the two accused of being "Anabaptists." Herman van Tielt was the local Anabaptist minister. There are some indications that Obbe Philips could have come here from Rostock and gathered some followers who considered it permissible to attend the Lutheran churches. When Obbe went underground, he is supposed to have assumed the name Aelbrecht. In 1554 the request was made in Wismar that the barber-physician Aelbrecht, an Anabaptist, be exiled. Was this a coincidence or was this actually Obbe Philips?

The year 1554 contained other noteworthy events. During this year Micron and his Reformed group arrived and found temporary shelter, but they had to leave as "Anabaptists and blasphemers of the Sacrament" in spite of their protest. Also occurring in 1554 was the convening of the Anabaptist meeting which formulated and adopted the Wismar Agreements. Immediately after this meeting Menno Simons and many of his followers took up permanent residence at Fresenburg near Oldesloe between Hamburg and Lübeck. The time during which Wismar was a safe place for Anabaptists and Sacramentarians belonged to the past although a small number of them continued to live there.[45]

Little definite information is available about the origin of and early conditions among the Anabaptists of the Free and Hanseatic city of Lübeck. Unlike the situation in Wismar, the development of the Reformation was not strongly challenged by exponents of evangelical Sacramentarian views. Early guidance came from Wittenberg and Bugenhagen in Hamburg. The latter came to Lübeck in 1530 to organize the Lutheran Church.

The proud city of Lübeck had been ruled by a council consisting primarily of patrician family heads. Under the leadership of Jörgen Wullenwever, a rise of the middle class took place which resembled the events of that time at Münster under the leadership of Knipperdolling. And yet the reasons for and results of this development were very different. Wullenwever favored a democratic government promoting the evangelical cause and the strengthening of Lübeck's position as a leading power on the Baltic Coast. While he was trying to achieve the latter in a war with Denmark, he lost the popular support at home and consequently his life. His chief foe, the archbishop of Bremen, caught him and turned him over to the archbishop's brother, Duke Heinrich of Braunschweig, who did the bloody work of having Wullenwever beheaded in 1537. In those days rulers saw connections with Münster everywhere. Under torture Wullenwever "admitted" that he had had plans for Lübeck similar to those which miscarried in Münster. Leopold von Ranke observed that Protestants did not think of disturbing the foundations of the political and social life but were concerned only with emancipating themselves from a secularized hierarchy claiming divine authority. In any event, it will be difficult to determine to what an extent, if at all, Wullenwever had any Anabaptist leanings. Both the theory that he was more tolerant with dissenters and the conjecture that he looked at Münster at some stage of its development as an ideal and inspiration are doubtful.[46]

Anabaptists found shelter in this lively and vital port city for both short and long periods of time and made various uses of the location. Many went on from here to Danzig; two sons of Coord Roosen, of whom more will be mentioned later, even went to Riga. Lübeck became a significant meeting center of Anabaptism, for here in 1546 Menno and his followers conducted a discussion with the followers of David Joris, and in 1552 the parting of the ways with Adam Pastor was sealed. It is likely that Menno Simons, after his return from the Cologne area, spent his time in Lübeck and Wismar when he was not traveling. His numerous writings of this time must have been printed in Lübeck where the Anabaptists maintained a printshop.

This printshop has an interesting history in connection with Menno Simons. Likely as a result of one of the many mandates against the Anabaptists, a *doper* (Anabaptist) and his printers, in danger of being discovered, attempted to move this underground printshop and some books to Fresenburg but were caught in Oldesloe. The resulting examination of the *doper,* his printers, their printshop, and their product shed some significant light on a number of questions. The three theologians interviewing them for two hours had to give up since they found the Anabaptist "a despiser of God, his word, and his holy sacrament," denying the necessity that infants had to be baptized in order to be saved. It became apparent that the *doper* had had "many tons of books printed" in his printshop in Lübeck. Ten tons had been brought along to Oldesloe and fourteen had been sent to Antwerp. The books were copies of an edition of the Bible, a Dutch translation of the Luther version with a concordance of the Zürich Bible. Such an ecumenical product was too much for the Lutheran examiners of that day. Nevertheless, the *doper* and the printers must have been given permission to continue their journey, seemingly even with the printshop. The Bibles, however, were confiscated.

The three examining theologians, Balthasar Schröder, Cornelis Grocken, and Gunarris Tuelens, submitted a report to King Christian III of Denmark on November 28, 1554. The report concluded with the sad note that Bartholomäus von Ahlefeldt had meanwhile built a house located *up den heidenschen walle* (on the heathen dam) on his estate at Fresenburg for Menno or the printer and that the printer had a "printshop and all the necessary equipment." In addition to this, the owner had Anabaptists in his own house, many had settled on his estate, and "more and more [were] coming daily." [47]

Bartholomäus von Ahlefeldt had inherited the estate Fresenburg located near Oldesloe between Lübeck and Hamburg in 1543. He must soon have opened his estate to the persecuted Anabaptists whom he had learned to appreciate while in the Low Countries. Since they settled at *Wüstenfelde* (waste land), some of his land must have been unoccupied. Soon many trades and occupations were brought to Fresenburg by settlers coming from far and near.

That Menno Simons had a printshop at Fresenburg after his arrival is an old tradition, and the Menno House and Linden Tree have become landmarks known far beyond the community of Oldesloe. Now we are inclined to ask whether the *doper* who transferred the printshop and printers from Lübeck to the growing center of Anabaptism was no other than Menno himself. The question must also be raised why no names, either of the *doper*, who was the spokesman, or of the printers, of whom there must have been at least two, were recorded. Were they permitted to hide their identity? One of the printers stated that he was from Gent. Whether the *doper* was Menno Simons or not, the amazing thing is that none of Menno's writings printed in Lübeck were found among the many tons of books. In any event, his books did continue to appear at the Fresenburg printshop which was a thorn in the flesh for many. One of the neighbors on a large estate kidnapped the printer, but Menno's protector saw to it that he was freed again.

The above mentioned report disturbed the Lutheran king, Christian III, considerably. He communicated his concern to his brothers, Hans and Adolf, who shared in the government of Schleswig-Holstein which at that time was subject to the king of Denmark. One of them suggested that Bartholomäus von Ahlefeldt should be ordered to remove the Anabaptists from his estate, while the other maintained that that would do no good since they had by now spread over the whole country. The latter favored a general edict forbidding their stay anywhere. Such an edict, issued September 29, 1555, did not seem to change anything for Fresenburg. Even after the death of the owner in 1558, this place remained a refuge for the persecuted until a free city with better economic possibilities opened its gates for them. This was Altona near Hamburg.[48]

It is not known just how many Anabaptist leaders besides Menno Simons, Michael Steffens, and Dirk Eggerat ever spent some time there. The congregation was served by these three men. In 1709, at the age of 98, Gerrit Roosen dictated a brief memoir in which he stated that his grandmother, Elisabeth Roosen, had been a member of Menno Simons' congregation at Fresenburg near Oldesloe. He also stated that he personally knew Mennonites residing at Lübeck where he had served a congregation. This memoir was a pious admonition for his grandchildren.[49]

The family and descendants of Coord Roosen deserve particular mention at this point because records of this family are in existence and reveal geographical movements typical of the ancestor of a leading Mennonite family. Coord Roosen was forced to flee persecution in the duchy of Jülich-Cleves with his four children. Roosen's first wife had died, and he had married again before he escaped, but he left his pregnant wife with her parents in Korschenbroich. He established himself at Steinrade near Lübeck where he farmed and produced gunpowder. This occupation was continued in the family for a number of generations. The claim that Coord Roosen left his home as an Anabaptist cannot be substantiated since Anabaptists were not found in Jülich-Cleves before 1534.

Apparently Coord Roosen and his second wife never saw each other again, but the son Geerlinck born after the father's departure came to Steinrade in 1554 just after the death of his father. It could be that

Geerlinck Roosen, who married Elisabeth nèe van Sintern in 1565, was the first of the family to become Mennonite. Geerlinck's youngest son, Paul, lived for some time in Oldesloe and fellowshipped with the Fresenburg Mennonites. He was the first of the Roosen family to move to Altona, where his son Gerrit was born in 1612.

The Roosen family near Lübeck rented the *Hof* Holzkamp. The Mennonites of that area also had a loose affiliation with the Rensefeld Lutheran Church where for generations they had pews in the church and a burial lot in the cemetery to the dismay of an inspector in 1670, who could not understand that such "coarse heretics" could gain such favors. Mennonites were also found at Ovendorf, Haffkrug, and other places into the 17th century.[50]

But not only in the cities and suburbs along the Baltic Coast did Anabaptists seek and find places of refuge. As they had sought the rural areas along the Vistula River and in East Friesland, so they settled in rural Schleswig-Holstein between Hamburg, Lübeck, Kiel, and the marshes of the North Sea. That refugees settled here at various places is not only apparent because of the edicts issued, which were often a matter of routine, but also because of specific cases and names mentioned. Bertram Ahlefeldt (Anevelde) complained in 1554 that at Lütjenburg near Kiel, an Anabaptist meeting had taken place during the night attended by 900 people at which occasion they "thanked God that he had enlightened their mind and led them to the true faith."

Dutch Anabaptists were also located between Oldesloe and Hamburg. Particularly attractive were the Wilster marsh lands north of the Elbe River. The Eiderstedt peninsular district between Heide and Husum attracted not only Anabaptists but also followers of David Joris. They were dealt with as early as 1557 when the prosperity of both groups became the envy of the surrounding Lutheran neighbors, causing disputations and extra taxations. King Christian I established Glückstadt in 1616 on the north side of the Elbe River and invited businessmen of all nationalities and denominations to settle here. Many Mennonites accepted the invitation. The Anabaptists were also permitted to settle in the newly founded town of Friedrichstadt east of Eiderstedt where they enjoyed full freedom after 1623.[51]

A brief reference should be made to the beginnings of the Hamburg-Altona Mennonite Church. Although it should be expected that Anabaptists would have reached such a strategic city as Hamburg on their way from the Low Countries during the first years of persecution, no records confirm this except that Hamburg issued edicts reg-

ularly with the other Hanseatic cities starting in 1535, the crucial year
in early Anabaptism. The first Anabaptists recorded here in 1575
among the many Dutch Reformed refugees was the de Voss family,
soon to be followed by other refugees. Among the Anabaptists was
François Noe from Antwerp, whose son, François Noe II, secured from
Count Ernst von Schauenburg of Pinneberg a document permitting
Mennonites to settle in Altona, adjacent to Hamburg in 1601. The
Mennonites settled in the district known as *Grosse Freiheit*; this name
referred to the rights secured, namely to follow any occupation they
chose. This presupposed religious freedom was extended to Catholics,
Reformed, and Jews. The little town of Altona grew rapidly, attracting
many Mennonites not only from rural Schleswig-Holstein, but also
from Friedrichstadt and Glückstadt, which had admitted the Mennonites on the same basis but did not offer the same economic advantages. Many came from the Low Countries. Most of the Fresenburg
Mennonites moved to Altona.[52] The worship service remained in the
Dutch language up to the beginning of the nineteenth century. Among
the most prosperous families were the Roosens,[53] van der Smissens,
Goverts, and de Vliegers. Shipping, whaling, and weaving were some
of the common industries. Gysbert van der Smissen had escaped as
an Anabaptist from Belgium around 1576 and had gone to Haarlem.
One of his sons moved to Friedrichstadt and his son, Gysbert II,
moved from there to Glückstadt and ultimately to Altona, where he
started a bakery. His ninth child, Hinrich I, laid the foundation for
Altona's prosperity and became known as the "city builder."[54]

Even though not always on the same scale, similar contributions
were made by Mennonites in other cities where they were given an
opportunity. The cities and the areas of contribution are as follows:
Danzig-business; Emden and Norden, East Friesland-grain trade, mill-
ing, shipping, whaling, and distilling; Gronau, Westphalia-weaving
and spinning; Almelo, Overijssel, Netherlands-textile industry; and
Krefeld, Lower Rhine-linen weaving and silk industry. The Mennonites of the Vistula Delta in Prussia and Poland and later in the steppes
of the Ukraine made significant contributions in agriculture and industry. The great industries in Gronau, Almelo, and Krefeld which
originated in the homes of Flemish refugees who settled at those
places were gradually tolerated and ultimately considered great assets
to their respective communities. Flemish weavers and velvet makers
were found everywhere from the northern Netherlands to Danzig,
but their enterprises did not always develop into large industrial

centers as was the case with those mentioned. Developments and similar contributions made by southern refugees and Anabaptists in general in the northern Netherlands have been treated previously. It should however, be pointed out that Anabaptists settling in rural areas in East Friesland and Schleswig-Holstein either did not remain here or did not persevere in their religious persuasion. Most of them went to the cities and industrial centers, partly because of continued pressure, while others joined the Lutheran and Reformed churches.[55]

B. DEFINING AND DEFENDING THE FAITH

1. Wismar: Agreements and Disagreements

Anabaptism spread via the witness of many who gave their testimonies in spoken word, in writing, and in martyrdom. One of its most vigorous promoters was Leenaert Bouwens (1515-1582). In spite of the fact that his daring and repeated evangelistic journeys spanned the area between Antwerp and Danzig, he survived. K. Vos says of him that no single "Calvinist, Lutheran, or Anabaptist preacher was able to harvest as much fruit from his labors." [56]

Leenaert Bouwens was born in Sommelsdyk, South Holland. Like several Anabaptist leaders, he had belonged to a chamber of rhetoric. After he had been an active preacher for some time, he attended the Lübeck conference in 1546. He was also present when the Wismar Agreements were adopted in 1554. Occurring between these two dates was his ordination at Emden by Menno Simons, which has already been mentioned.

Leenaert Bouwens lived in a neighboring village of Emden called 't Falder from where he undertook evangelistic trips throughout the Low Countries. When his wife complained to Menno Simons about her daring and absent husband, he encouraged her to support her husband and added that he could not relieve him from his ministry.[57]

A carefully kept record of the places Leenaert Bouwens visited and the number of individuals he baptized between 1551 and 1582 has been preserved. No other similar record pertaining to the Anabaptists is extant. This record shows that he conducted baptismal services at 182 places all the way from Antwerp to Danzig; he visited many of these places five times. In many instances he must have been the founder of the congregation. The total number baptized between 1551 and 1582 was 10,386. In Antwerp, for example, he baptized 584 persons and in Harlingen, Friesland, over 2,000. He also baptized more than 500 in Dokkum and Emden. From 1551 to the death of Menno Simons in 1561, the period of severest persecution, he baptized 2,234. His baptismal journeys were broken up as follows: between 1551 and 1554, the total was 861; 1554 to 1556, total 693; 1557 to 1561, total 808; 1563 to 1565, total 4,499; 1568 to 1582, total 3,509.

It can be assumed that Menno Simons, Dirk Philips, and David Joris performed more baptismal services than most of the other leaders. But it can hardly be expected that any of them accomplished more than Leenaert Bouwens. There seems to be no place or province that he did not reach. It is true, however, that he baptized the largest number of persons toward the end of his lifetime when persecution was no longer so severe.

Bouwens' list reveals that there was a period from 1565 to 1568 in which he recorded no baptism. This was a time when silence was imposed on him by his co-elders, particularly Dirk Philips who died in 1568. Both Leenaert Bouwens and Dirk Philips were rigid disciplinarians who attempted to mold the brotherhood into an ideal Christian community. A dispute between the two was climaxed when Leenaert Bouwens was accused of domineering ambitions, of accepting money for spiritual services as elder, and of drinking wine. After the death of Dirk Philips, Leenaert Bouwens resumed his work and added another 3,509 to the brotherhood during the last four years of his life.[58]

Any history of Anabaptism must deal with some of the problems and issues encountered in the attempt to mold the Christian brotherhood. Some controversies centered around the leadership of David Joris and Adam Pastor and their seemingly deviating views. The issues and questions raised were discussed person-to-person and also dealt with at small conferences at Emden and Goch in 1547 and Lübeck in 1552. Other unrecorded meetings certainly took place from time to time. One of the most significant small conferences of leading ministers convened in Wismar in 1554. Seven leaders or elders gathered together, among whom were Menno Simons, who resided in Wismar at this time, Dirk Philips, Leenaert Bouwens, and Gillis van Aken, who had just been reinstated after an excommunication. The noteworthy agreements which were reached became known as *Besluyt tot Wismar* or *Bespreck van Wismar* (Wismar Agreements).[59]

The basic issue which occasioned this meeting, and many to follow, was how a truly Christian brotherhood could be realized on earth.

The Münsterite attempt had been defeated by force and a remnant inflicted by Münsterite views had been won back to the brotherhood. The paramount issue was how to establish a church "without spot and wrinkle." Some basic characteristics of a brotherhood had been introduced, but disagreements arose as to the degree to which a Christian community can be realized in a world of sin and imperfection. At Wismar nine agreements were reached which dealt primarily with questions concerning the relationship of the church and the individual Christian to the world. The first decision stated that a member of the church who married someone who was not a member must be "put out of the congregation." If the person continued to live a "truly Christian life before God and the brethren," he could be reinstated to full membership. Secondly it was decided that the members of the church should shun an excommunicated member and avoid business transactions with him. The third article stated that husband or wife should shun their excommunicated marriage partner unless they could not agree to this because of a "weak conscience." Articles four and five dealt with the marriage of a believer to an unbeliever. Under certain conditions separation was possible and if the unbeliever remarried, it was permissible for the believer also to remarry. Under six, an attempt was made to regulate the marriage of children of believers and unbelievers. The children were advised to get the consent of their parents and to avoid "secret marriage feasts." Under seven, it was stated that it was permissible to "collect a just indebtedness, if no ungodliness results." In the next statement permission was given to "carry a stick or sword on the shoulder while on a journey," as customary, but the developing principle of non-resistance was evident in the elders' withholding permission "to handle weapons on orders of the magistrate."

The last agreement was "that no one [had] the right to go from congregation to congregation teaching and preaching unless he [had] been sent or ordained by the church or an elder." This would indicate that the early Anabaptist tendency for each member to be a witness or evangelist, which was one of the reasons for the movement's rapid spread, also had some negative results which were to be curbed by this measure.

These were some of the issues which needed attention at the mid-century. They grew out of the attempt to answer a basic question: how can the church of Christ, not being *of* this world, be *in* this world and remain untainted? The guide lines drawn up at Wismar were helpful but did in no way solve all problems. Now remained their application in the various fellowships and in daily life.

In 1555 Menno Simons received a letter written by "five brethren of good report" from Franeker, Friesland, asking for advice and help in regard to church discipline. From Menno's answer we learn of two views that were held in the congregation of Franeker. One insisted that "no sin or work of the flesh" should be punished with excommunication without being preceded by three admonitions. The other group insisted that "all works of the flesh (John 5) are to be punished with excommunication without any previous admonitions at all, and that all penitence must take place outside the church." Menno Simons found both views "altogether contrary to the words of Christ, of Paul, and of James." He considered a threefold admonition before an excommunication necessary, unless a crime had been committed which was prosecuted by law. In this case he advised immediate excommunication.

Another question presented to Menno Simons was whether a brother to whom a sin had been confessed by another brother was obligated to report the same to the congregation. This Menno considered "not only unheard of, but also ... clearly against all Scripture and love" (Matthew 18; Colossians 2; Ephesians 5). Unfortunately, the answers which Menno Simons sent to the brethren did not end the disagreements.[60]

The preliminary action leading to forgiveness and reinstatement of the offender on his excommunication was not the only matter of controversy. What about the relationship of the congregation and of the family to the member who had been excommunicated? A case in point was that of Swaen Rutgers who belonged to the Emden church of which Leenaert Bouwens was the elder. Her husband had been excommunicated, and now she was expected to shun him. Since Swaen refused to do this, she herself was threatened with excommunication. When the case was presented to Menno Simons, he wrote a pastoral letter dated November, 1556, to the congregation of Emden. He stated that he had been "distressed with great fear concerning this matter" for more than twenty years and that he could not bring himself "to agree with the extremism which [was] in evidence in the Netherlands." He suggested that if the person married to an excommunicated member "is permitted in all matters to keep the faith, and is moreover bound in conscience so that he dared not leave such mate," he be permitted to remain with his marriage partner. Menno Simons stressed that he desired "to teach a Gospel that builds up, and not one that breaks down."

Menno Simons considered the Wismar Agreements as guide lines to be used with love and moderation. Consideration was to be given to the circumstances and the conscience of the individuals involved. Leenaert Bouwens and Dirk Philips were inclined to follow a more rigid disciplinary course. Representatives of the most moderate course were Hendrik Naaldeman and Joriaan Heyns of Franeker and Jacob Jans Scheedemaker of Emden. The latter was excommunicated in Emden and consequently, went to Holland.[61]

2. "Without Spot and Wrinkle"

The desire to establish a disciplined fellowship or body of Christ had been the basis and reason for the break with the Catholic Church. The development of radicalism which led to Münster made it even more important that the body of Christ be cleansed by means of biblical discipline. Menno Simons and Dirk Philips were in agreement on the necessity of discipline to maintain an effective brotherhood and leadership, and for this purpose they had won Leenaert Bouwens to carry on the work they had started. N. van der Zijpp has summarized Bouwens' work as follows: "Leenaert Bouwens travels through the congregations, organizes them, encourages them, inspires and cleanses them, disciplining and trimming them as an energetic worker in the vineyard of the Lord." [62] Because of his rigid views on discipline, some Anabaptists began to long for the more experienced and understanding guidance of Menno Simons. But Menno could no longer travel as he had done in his younger years when the persecution was much more severe. For some time now his letters that answered the many requests for help and advice had borne the signature: "Your brother and servant, who is crippled." [63]

And yet when the call came to attend a meeting in Harlingen in order to settle a crucial question, Menno Simons accepted the invitation. On the way he stopped in Franeker where he met Hendrik Naaldeman, with whom he had corresponded, and Naaldeman's followers. Menno was pleased with the unity that he found in Franeker and expressed his desire that the group here would "remain brethren." He enthusiastically stated that he would "jump for joy on his cane" if there would be such agreement in Harlingen.

After his arrival at Harlingen, Menno tried to promote understanding and a moderate view in disciplinary matters; he was supported in this stand by Naaldeman and his group. They were opposed, however, by Leenaert Bouwens and Dirk Philips. Menno Simons did succeed in persuading them that no one was to be forced to share with the congregation the information about sins confessed to him by another member. But no agreement could be reached on the matters of excommunication and shunning. Naaldeman and his group insisted that no excommunication, regardless of the nature of the offense, could take place before the offender had been admonished three times. Their opponents advocated rigid views in regard to shunning or avoiding excommunicated members, particularly in family life. The side advocating moderation was outnumbered by the group following the more vigorous and dominating Leenaert Bouwens. A cleavage resulted, and Naaldeman became a leader of the moderate Waterlanders, named after an area in North Holland. Leenaert Bouwens referred to the group as *drekwagen*, implying that they took in all excommunicated members from the strict congregations.[64]

Broken-hearted and physically exhausted, Menno Simons left his native Friesland for the last time. He wrote to his friend Reyn Edes: "If the omnipotent God had not preserved me last year as well as now, I would already have gone mad. For there is nothing upon earth which my heart loves more than it does the church; and yet I must live to see this sad affliction upon her." His concern was best expressed in the words: "Brethren, beware of discord. Follow after love and peace with all your heart." [65]

As was the case in Wismar, the exact proceedings in Harlingen were never recorded, possibly because no agreement was reached. Conclusions have been drawn from Menno's references in his later writings and from the transmitted oral report by Apollonia Ottes, who listened in an adjacent room to what was said during the meeting. Although this unofficial report has the earmarks of having been slanted in favor of the Franeker representatives, it is helpful for the information it does present. The aging Menno Simons was caught between the two resulting groups, while Dirk Philips, at least temporarily, sided with Leenaert Bouwens.[66] A younger man had taken the lead.

3. Relationship to the German Mennonites

What happened in Emden, Franeker, and Harlingen was significant enough to be watched carefully by all Anabaptists of the Low Countries and also by those in the Cologne area, in Strassburg, Switzerland, and Moravia. Lemke Cremer, Zylis, and Heinrich [Krufft] had called on Menno Simons at Wüstenfelde in April 1556. Hans van Tielt and Hans S[ikken] were also present. The group had spent two days together discussing matters pertaining to church discipline. Menno Simons seems to have been pleased with the outcome even though the visitors were not fully convinced by his views and arguments. Apparently enough agreement had been realized to lead Menno to expect that the practices he followed would also be introduced in the Cologne area and in the southern countries.[67] He submitted to his visitors a written statement concerning their discussion.

Menno's yielding to Leenaert Bouwens and Dirk Philips at Harlingen prevented the High German Mennonites along the Rhine River from accepting his views. His position of weakness was related by Carel van Gent. He tells that Leenaert Bouwens, after having persuaded Menno Simons to accept his stricter views, caused him "to travel to Cologne in his old age with Leenaert Bouwens and others in order that they might persuade the German congregations to accept their views."[68] In Menno's detailed account of the ensuing controversy between him and his former friends at Cologne, there are no indications that this meeting took place in 1557 as has been repeated by many writers.[69] Nevertheless there was a very lively written exchange of thought between the north and the south during the years 1555 to 1557.

Already in 1555 the High German Mennonites had sent a friendly admonition to their brethren in the Low Countries in regard to the Melchiorite Christology. The view of the incarnation of Christ held by Melchior Hofmann had caused little controversy in the Low Countries except with the Reformed theologians. This was not the case in Strassburg. Schwenckfeld's and Hofman's views were well known and accepted by many, but they were by no means the only concepts common among the Anabaptists here. In any event, Hofmann's Christology was an extremely offensive heresy for the Lutheran, Strassburg and Reformed theologians. The Christology played later a prominent role at the Frankenthal Disputation (1571).

Edicts that were issued and the *Formula of Concord* give evidence that some Anabaptists of Middle and South Germany held Hofmann's views. Disagreements along this line led the "Brethren and Elders," who many times had been urged to express themselves along these lines, to formulate some statements. The immediate reason for issuing the "Agreement of the brethren and elders congregated at Strassburg regarding the question and source of Christ's flesh" was that "the followers of Hofmann, as well as the Dutch brethren," had requested it. This carefully worded statement said that the Bible had numerous references indicating that Christ had received "his flesh from heaven" and also that he received it from Mary. For this reason no attempt was to be made "to know more than can be known" and "reason was to be subordinated to the obedience of Christ." [70]

More impressive and significant was the meeting at Strassburg in 1557 of some fifty elders or leaders representing at least that many congregations located in Switzerland, Moravia, Württemburg, and Alsace, of which some had as many as five or six hundred members. It was stated that the congregations whose representatives gathered here were "all one in their faith and confession of God and his Son, the Lord Jesus Christ." After the salutation in the document drawn up, the writers said that they were expressing the consensus of the brethren present who asked the Dutch brethren, in this manner, whether they agreed with them. The first brief statement suggested that all types of work and business enterprises were permissible for Christians if they were not offensive and were not contrary to the Scriptures. The second item dealt with the shunning of backsliders. On the one hand, the congregation had to be kept pure and, on the other, the erring brother and sister had to be won back to the fold if possible. The writers expressed the hope that "we will become one people that will have unity and peace with each other so that all of us will praise God in one accord through Jesus Christ." A closing message followed.

However, a postscript was added in which it was suggested that man and wife should not be separated by shunning because the commandment in regard to matrimony had greater significance than that of shunning. The Dutch brethren were informed that the conference also dealt with the question of original sin which had caused some disagreements. It was emphasized that some of the conference representatives had associated with the Swiss martyr, Michael Sattler, and that others had suffered severely through imprisonment. The closing contained the assertion that the document was being sent not only at the urging of Lemke Cremer and Zylis, but that all joined in expressing the wish that Menno Simons and all elders and ministers serving the churches of God in the Netherlands would "seriously and with diligence turn to peace, love, and unity." Menno Simons was especially admonished not to go to extremes in matters of discipline and shunning.[71]

These were wise and brotherly words spoken at the right time and in the right direction. The leaders who had spent a lifetime cleansing the church from various spots and wrinkles had not realized that their zeal was not being matched by the necessary brotherly love, patience, and forbearance. Following these admonitions the aging pioneers of the faith could not sit idle and let their pens rest. It was felt that Zylis and Lemke Cremer had betrayed Menno. These two had promised to respond to the statement Menno Simons wrote following the discussion in April, 1556. They had instead misrepresented the Dutch views at the Strassburg conference and then had made the conference responsible for the answer.

Dirk Philips was the first to respond and Menno Simons followed. When Menno maintained that the "celestial marriage between Christ and our souls" had to remain unbroken even if it were at the cost of family relationships, he may not have expressed anything basically new. But he was admitting the development of a more rigid, practical application of his ideals under the influence of his co-workers and because of the circumstances. Menno was to close his last writing with these fitting words: "Chosen children, this is my final farewell to you all. Know God, love the brethren, and beware of dissension!"[72]

The discussion was not ended. Herman Timmerman, a representative of the moderate group, responded first to Menno Simons' writing.[73] Although Menno had not mentioned them, Zylis and Lemke Cremer in 1559 also wrote a pamphlet against him which has not been preserved. From Menno's response we can conclude that they were rather outspoken. On December 15, 1558, Menno Simons had written a well-composed letter to "some brethren" on marital avoidance.[74] In his "Reply to Zylis and Lemke" of January 23, 1560, Menno was not at his best.[75] He refuted the accusation of the two and explained that he could no longer consider them as brethren unless they repented.

According to some sources the negotiations among the various groups continued. Dirk Philips and Leenaert Bouwens are supposed to have gone to the Cologne area to continue the debate. The contact is reported to have ended by their excommunicating the High Germans.[76]

4. *The Struggle for Religious Freedom*

The Anabaptists' concentration on problems of an internal nature did not imply that there were no disagreements and struggles with the outside world. After the northern provinces of the Low Countries had become independent and the Reformed Church was officially recognized, relationships to the new government and to the state church had to be established. The relationships between the leaders of the Reformed Church and the Anabaptists in East Friesland have been touched upon from time to time.

The early refugee churches, Anabaptist and Reformed, had a number of things in common in spite of their differences. Their roots had usually been established in the soil of the same evangelical Sacramentarian tradition. They became "churches under the cross," suffering persecution under the same ecclesiastical and governmental authorities and often finding refuge in the same countries and places. One of the major differences was that the Reformed Church stopped short of applying the principle of spiritualization to the concept of baptism and retained infant baptism, although with an altered meaning. Another difference concerned the church-state relationship. After the Münster catastrophe, Anabaptism emphasized even more the purity and the withdrawn character of the biblical church. On the other hand, the Reformed Church emerged from the struggle of the nationalistic forces for independence from Rome and Spain. The new church desired the preservation of the traditional church-state relationship whereby the state was not only obligated to defend and protect the visible and established church, but also to help the religious group maintain its purity in its struggle against sectarian infiltrations. In its early history the Dutch Reformed Church in the diaspora did not have the supporting arm of the government except in East Friesland, and even there it was not always a steady arm.

However, it is in place to express caution at this point. Since radical Anabaptism in its various forms aimed at the establishment of the kingdom of God on earth, these attempts would by necessity have developed wholly integrated or theocratic church-state relationships if given an opportunity. This would have been the case in Münster as well as with Thomas Müntzer. Hubmaier and the Liechtenstein counts in Moravia practiced such relationships for a while. And even Menno Simons was very grateful to find a protector for himself and his followers in Bartholomäus von Ahlefeld. Thankfulness and gratitude for such protection became as much a Mennonite characteristic as any other soon after Münster. Such an attitude developed even while Anabaptism's enemies continued to express fear and blame in regard to the group's supposed insurrectionist intentions. Menno Simons and his co-workers were the chief molders of this spirit and acted as the apologetics who addressed themselves to the leaders of the churches and governments, asking for tolerance and protection.

Under the authority of Philip II of Spain, William, Prince of Orange, served as governor of Antwerp from 1566 to 1568. The Reformed and Anabaptist groups petitioned him to cease persecution. The Anabaptists of Antwerp stated that they had been severely persecuted but had now been granted religious freedom since September 2, 1566. Since that time the interest in Anabaptist meetings had increassed greatly. The Anabaptists went on to state their view on loyalty toward the government. They believed that the government was ordained by God, and they were willing to obey but declined to take the oath since Christ had forbidden it. They stated further: "We consider it right that no one should be persecuted because of his faith as long as it does not cause evil; the Lord has said in Matthew 13 to let the wheat and weeds grow until the day of judgment. The Lord alone wants to be the judge of conscience in matters of faith. He has not taught that the unity of faith is to be maintained through the sword of tyranny. The Lord himself spoke about a divided household because of faith in Mathew 10." Information found in the account by A. A. van Schelven seems to interpret the Reformed and Anabaptist plea as unnecessary. This authority relates that the Prince of Orange was already at that time "tolerant to all sects without discrimination." Alva sent by Philip II moved in and delayed the application of the principle of tolerance.[77]

Later, in 1577, the Anabaptists of Middelburg appealed to William of Orange to protect them. The magistrate of the city, supported by Marnix van St. Aldegonde, claimed tolerance for the Reformed Church but oppressed the Anabaptists by closing their shops and molesting them in other ways. William of Orange stated on January 26, 1577, that the Anabaptists did not need to swear oaths, that their shops should be permitted to be opened, and that the magistrate was not to interfere with "someone's conscience." Throughout the following years William of Orange continued to oppose intolerance and persecution for religious reasons, "fearing that on this road the rule of the new [Reformed] Church would shove on the neck of its members a new yoke in the place of papacy from which the church had just been freed." The Dutch States-General did not always agree with William of Orange on this matter. Inspired and challenged by the theologians and church leaders, particularly by Marnix van St. Aldegonde and Gaspar van der Heyden, the States-General advocated that in the United Netherlands only the Reformed Church should be allowed to meet publicly, being the state church. Again and again William of Orange protected the Anabaptists against the religious and political zealots.[78]

The question has been raised as to what influences William of Orange encountered that made him favor religious freedom. A. A. van Schelven has questioned the possibility that William of Orange was influenced by Sebastien Castellio or Erasmus and has concluded that he was persuaded by the French Huguenots. The fact that an influence from France took place would not necessarily preclude others. Could it not be that the native evangelical Sacramentarian environment, molded by men like Erasmus and Sebastian Franck, which brought forth the Anabaptists could also have affected the Prince of Orange? And why would not petitions like those of the Anabaptists of Middelburg in 1566 and 1577 have influenced the future ruler of the Netherlands? Little credit in matters of tolerance can be given to the court preachers, Jean Taffin and Pierre Loyseleur de Villers, and the theologians named previously. And the sources of William of Orange's tolerance cannot be traced to rigid Calvinism or to Calvin himself, as has been suggested by some.[79]

The Reformed Church continued to seek action against the Anabaptists wherever possible. The numerous synods furnish a record of action and means taken no defeat Anabaptism.[80] Such leaders as Gaspar van der Heyden wished to deny the Anabaptist ministers the right to preach. From time to time such a policy was also pursued by the magistrates. Others favored the arranging of disputations between representatives of the Reformed Church and the Anabaptists. Menso Alting of Emden, who was in touch with Gaspar von der Heyden and Marnix van St. Aldegonde, took the lead in organizing such a disputation in Emden. Alting had been at Heidelberg when the Frankenthal Disputation took place, and he was so impressed that he patterned Emden's after it. A later and similar disputation took place in Leeuwarden.[81] All of these disputations had to be approved or sponsored by the state. Before they are presented in greater detail, some literary duels will be taken up.

5. *Literary Duels and Religious Disputations*

The Reformed Martin Micron had some theological discussions with Menno Simons. He wrote to Bullinger stating that Menno's "authority extends through the entire country of Belgium and all eastern countries," and again "Menno's authority extends widely along the coastal regions from Flanders to Danzig." [82] Having dealt with internal problems of the brotherhood in 1550 and then with church discipline and doctrines, Menno now, as a shepherd of the flock, wrote *A Humble and Christian Apology... Concerning... False Accusations Against the Anabaptists* (1551). He found it necessary, after more than fifteen years, to point out once more that the peaceful Anabaptists could not be accused of the crimes of the radical Münsterites. In his travel and work he must have found that this was one of the greatest obstacles for the brotherhood. He pointed out that the form of the outward baptism made the peaceful Anabaptists as little identical with Münster as infant baptism made other Christians identical with criminals who followed this same practice. In regard to being obedient to the government, he said that the Anabaptists were to pay their taxes as Christ taught them to do and to obey the government as Paul had taught. When he responded to the "charge that we have our property in common," he grew oratorical, exclaiming that "the whole Scripture speaks of mercifulness and love, and it is the only sign whereby a true Christian may be known." The following is Menno Simons at his best:

Beloved reader, it is not customary that an intelligent person clothes and cares for one part of his body and leaves the rest destitute and naked. Oh, no. The intelligent person is solicitous for all his members. Thus it should be with those who are the Lord's church and body. All those who are born of God, who are gifted with the Spirit of the Lord, who are, according to the Scriptures, called unto one body and love in Christ Jesus, are prepared by such love to serve their neighbors, not only with money and goods, but also after the example of their Lord and Head, Jesus Christ, in an evangelical manner, with life and blood. They show mercy and love, as much as they can. No one among them is allowed to beg. They take to heart the need of the saints. They entertain those in distress. They take the stranger into their houses. They comfort the afflicted, assist the needy, clothe the naked, feed the hungry, do not turn their face from the poor, do not despise their own flesh. Is. 58:7, 8.[83]

The accusation that the Anabaptists had "wives in common" and were fond of saying, "Sister, my spirit desires your flesh" was labeled rude; Menno countered with the statement that some slanderers may have been "guilty of the things with which they charge us." The Anabaptists were also accused of granting no forgiveness to those who sinned after baptism; they were called "heaven stormers and merit men

who want to be saved by [their] own merits and works." To this
Menno responded: "We trust by the grace and mercy of the Lord that
we are children of God and disciples of Christ." [84]

Menno Simons continued his effort to defend the "Distressed Christians" in *A Fundamental and Clear Confession... Concerning Justification, the Preachers, Baptism, the Lord's Supper, the Swearing of
Oaths... Derived from the Word of God* (1552).[85] On this basis,
Menno undertook to demonstrate that the confession of faith of the
Anabaptists was based on the justification by faith which was obtained
"through Christ alone" and not works, words, and the sacraments. As
indicated in the title of this writing, Menno felt obligated to defend
the Anabaptists in the matter of oaths, for the objection to the swearing
of oaths was held against the Anabaptists already at that time.

Another brief apology was directed "to all pious, benevolent, and
proper magistrates, lords, princes, rulers, and superiors" as *A ... Sup-
plication of Poor and Distressed Christians* (1552).[86] In this writing
he attempted to prove once more that the true believers had nothing
in common with the Münsterites, that they aimed to be true Christians
and were therefore entitled to be given freedom and not to be persecuted. This touching testimony and challenge ended with this appeal:
"May the great and merciful Lord Jesus, who is a Lord of lords and
a King of kings, grant your Noble Highnesses and Honorable Excel-
lences, altogether rightly to know the truth, faithfully to walk in it,
piously to rule your cities and provinces in happy peace, to the praise
of your God and the salvation of many souls! This we wish with all
our heart. Amen."

The series of appeals was continued in *A Brief Apology of Distressed
Christians and Scattered Exiles addressed to all the Learned and Ministers of the German Nations...* Here Menno Simons made a "kind
request for a free discussion of the Scripture." (1552)[87] Like Hofmann
he taught that theologians and rulers could ultimately be convinced
of the truth on biblical grounds as he saw it. As he had found no
hearing in Bonn, so he found no well-established rulers and theologians
willing to listen to his exhortation of the faith based on Scriptures. J.
a Lasco, an exile himself, had been willing to listen to him. A similar
encounter was soon to occur.

Before Christmas, 1553, Menno heard that part of a Dutch Reform-
ed refugee congregation from London had arrived in the harbor of
Wismar and got stuck in the ice. The Reformed leaders, J. a Lasco, Jan
Utenhove, and Martin Micron had tried in vain to find shelter for the

congregation in Lutheran Denmark, but they had been turned down. The Anabaptists living in Lutheran Wismar took some bread and wine to the boat for the sick, brought the group to the harbor, and found employment for some, although their stay was a temporary one. In the meantime, J. a Lasco and Jan Utenhove had gone to Emden; Martin Micron soon followed them.

Now Menno Simons' request for a discussion of the Scriptures was to be fulfilled. On the second Christmas holiday, the Reformed and Anabaptists agreed to have a discussion of religious questions. The meeting was well attended by men and women. Herman Backereel, the leader of the Reformed group, and Menno Simons were the main participants.

Members of the Reformed group invited Micron to return for another meeting, which took place on February 6, 1554. Menno Simons' writings had been submitted to Micron and were to be used as a basis for the discussion. After an eleven hour session the group had a meal together and parted in peace. Another discussion followed on February 15, which turned out to be rather heated. It would be putting it mildly to say that the hospitable Mennonite did not serve a fellowship meal but opened the door at the end of the meeting and asked his Reformed guests to depart. They felt as if they had been thrown out. As in the discussion with a Lasco, the topic which had received most attention was the incarnation of Christ. Again the result was an exchange of writings with accusations hurled at each other. Menno, who had been living in hiding in Wismar, had to leave. The last writing by Micron in the matter was a book of nearly four hundred pages.[88]

While Menno Simons was busy gathering and cleansing, writing his supplications in defense of the church, and writing against Micron, he picked up another challenge not necessarily hurled at him personally. Some Anabaptists had published a letter giving their reasons for not being members of the larger Reformation churches. Gellius Faber (de Bouma), one of the ministers of the Reformed Church at Emden, wrote a response to it which did not remain unnoticed or unanswered by Menno.

Gellius Faber had been a priest in Jelsum near Leeuwarden where he had an experience similar to that of Menno. It is likely that they knew each other from those days. Influenced by Luther and the Sacramentarians, Faber left the Catholic Church at the same time as Menno, in 1536, and also went to East Friesland where he became a minister at Norden, and in 1538 at Emden. He remained there until he died in 1564.[89] In 1544 he took part in the disputation between a Lasco and Menno Simons. He was well acquainted with the Anabaptists. He himself must have had strong Lutheran leanings although he is currently being claimed by the Reformed Church.[90]

In his response to the *Bitter hönischen breeff der Wedderdöper,* Faber outlined the Anabaptist letter and tried to refute the same point by point. The writer of the letter claimed that the ministers of Protestant churches did not have a true calling, that their baptism and the Lord's supper were not scriptural, that their church was not truly a "fellowship of believers" in accordance with the Scriptures, and that its members did not practice church discipline.[91] Menno Simons, who had had contact with Faber, could not remain silent after reading his pointed and personal refutation. Following the outline of the letter and the writing by Gellius Faber, Menno took it upon himself to defend the "poor scattered congregations." In *A Plain Reply to a Publication by Gellius Faber,* Menno pointed out that Faber's writing "will serve to the disgrace of the pious children of God, to the increase of their cross... and to the comfort and strengthening of the impenitent."

With one exception there is nothing particularly new in this lengthy account. In his defense of the Anabaptists' calling to the ministry, Menno took the occasion to give a detailed description of his life as a priest and Sacramentarian and of his conversion and calling to the ministry in the covenanted church of the Melchiorites. This is not only the jewel of this book but the heart of all the writings of Menno Simons. Without it so much less would be known not only about his life, but also about early Dutch Anabaptism. No other part of his writings has been reprinted as many times as his conversion account or the "Renunciation of Rome."[92]

There were other ministers and theologians of East Friesland who concerned themselves with the Anabaptists by trying to win them to the Reformed Church. Hermannus Aquilomontanus has been referred to.[93] Bernhardus Buwo also had contact with the Anabaptists in his work as a Reformed minister in East Friesland and also attempted to win them to his church. In 1556 he published a booklet about Anabaptists with an unusually friendly title for that time. By 1580, four editions had been published in Low German, Dutch, and German.[94]

In spite of the fact that much of the material dealing with the Dutch refugee churches of the Lower Rhine area, Frankfurt, Emden, and London, such as church minutes and correspondence, has been published, no systematic study has been made in regard to the relationship and mutual influence of the Dutch Reformed churches and the Anabaptists who lived and suffered side by side. From the information available, one more incident of note will be presented.

Adriaen Cornelis van Haemstede (1525-62) studied at the University of Louvain and worked in behalf of the Reformation in Antwerp, Emden, and London. While in Antwerp he compiled the well-known collection of martyr stories from the days of the early church to his time which influenced Thieleman J. van Braght in the production of the *Martyrs' Mirror*. Although Haemstede was Reformed, in selecting accounts of martyrs he included some about Anabaptists of which practice stricter Calvinists did not approve. When he fled to London and served as a minister of the Dutch Reformed Church, he soon became suspected because of his lenience toward the Anabaptists. He had much milder views than his Reformed associates in regard to adult baptism and the Anabaptist concept of the incarnation of Christ. In 1560 Haemstede was suspended as minister. He finally signed a statement which was presented to him pertaining to the incarnation of Christ, but refused to make a confession of guilt, whereupon he was excommunicated from the church and expelled from the country. Such an ecumenical stand was unusual in those days on either side, the Anabaptist or the Reformed. W. G. Goeters observes that Haemstede's "influence continued not only in England. In Holland and East Friesland voices were heard in [the Anabaptists'] defense." [95]

East Friesland not only served as an encouraging region for these defending voices, but must have continued to be an asylum and a gateway to the east for the Anabaptists. Additional encounters occurred here between the Reformed and Mennonite groups. In 1556, a three-day colloquy dealing once again with the question of the incarnation of Christ took place between Reformed and Anabaptist representatives at Norden. [96] In spite of Countess Anna's tolerant reign, however, neither a Lasco nor Menno Simons returned to stay here for any length of time. The former went to Frankfurt and back to Poland while Menno spent some time in Wismar and Lübeck and ultimately found a home near Oldesloe.

Two Anabaptist leaders who were active and spent considerable time in this area were Dirk Philips and Leenaert Bouwens. Leenaert's successful evangelical campaigns have been referred to previously. Between 1551 and 1582, he baptized six hundred persons in East

Friesland.[97] Fifty-one of these were baptized just in Emden between 1551 and 1554. Such success was possible not only because of the heavy refugee immigration, but because of Anabaptism's appeal to the native population. As had occurred at Danzig, a large number of Anabaptists lived in the outskirts of Emden known as 't Falder.

Anabaptism's appeal to certain strata of the population influenced public opinion which in turn encouraged the government not to take drastic action against its followers. With the coming of Menso Alting to Emden (1574), who aimed to make this city a northern Geneva, a change in tolerance occurred and a new chapter in Reformed-Anabaptist relations was written.

As mentioned previously, Menso Alting had witnessed the Frankenthal Disputation of 1571. This disputation had been sponsored by the Palatine Elector Frederick III. After Frederick had embraced Calvinism, he tried to win the Catholics, Lutherans, and Anabaptists for the Reformed Church. He found the Anabaptists most difficult to persuade, but he hoped to succeed in doing this by arranging for a disputation between their representatives and those of the Reformed Church. The discussions took place between May 28 and June 7, 1571, at Frankenthal, Palatinate. The invited participants, including the Anabaptists, were entertained royally and free of charge.

Fifteen Anabaptist participants arrived from South Germany and Moravia. Even some Dutch representatives are supposed to have been present. The chief Anabaptist speaker was Diebold Winter who had attended a smaller disputation at Pfeddersheim. Thirteen points were presented to the Anabaptists, including the Scriptures, God, Christ, sin, justification, baptism, communion, the church, the government, the oath, and community of goods. At times the Anabaptists were not specific in their answers. In his concluding statement Rauff Bisch stated that "we do not want to burden our consciences with several articles which we cannot believe with a good conscience; we hope only to answer to God, and we do not know any better way to remain on this position." Although the elector was disappointed he still hoped to win the Anabaptists to the church. The *Protokoll...*, a 710-page summary of the proceedings, was published three months after the disputation.[98]

Now as Menso Alting faced the Anabaptists in East Friesland, he was reminded of the Frankenthal Disputation. He felt that such a method might prove beneficial, not only in stopping the influence and spread of Anabaptism, but also in bringing discipline into his own church. He found the Reformed Church of East Friesland too lax, for it tolerated deviating views and the growth and spread of Anabaptism. It had been found upon examination that some members of the Reformed Church sympathized with the Anabaptists and opposed the persecution of heretics. Some members of the Reformed Church even went so far as to disapprove of infant baptism and to favor stronger disciplinary action. To Alting's great dismay, he discovered that one of his own church council members harbored some Anabaptist views and that Peter Dathenus, whom Alting had admired as the chief leader of the Frankenthal Disputation, had not only read the *Wonderboek* by David Joris but had also been influenced by it.[99]

Thus it was that Alting became the leading spirit in the preparation of the Emden Disputation. The encounter was conducted in 128 sessions starting February 27 and ending May 17, 1578. Menso Alting himself led the Reformed presentation; representatives of the Mennonites were Hans Busschaert, Peter van Ceulen, Paulus Backer, Christiaan Arends, Jan van Ophoorn, and Brixius Gerritsz. The presentations were recorded on the Reformed side by the imperial notary, Dominicus Julius, and on the Mennonite side by Carel van Gent. The records were read and signed by the chairmen, speakers, and recorders. Among the points discussed, which did not differ greatly from those at Frankenthal, were God, man, sin, Christ, justification, the church, the ministry, and communion. The biographer of Menso Alting has summed up the results by saying that the disputation "accumulated new materials for a mutual embitterment." Each side claimed the victory but only one had the power to make use of it. The minutes of the Reformed secretary were published and those of the Anabaptist recorder were confiscated.[100]

The government started a new campaign against the Anabaptists; Menso Alting cooperated in the attack by writing a book against Hans de Ries. The efforts must not have been particularly successful, for when the well-known historian Ubbo Emmius later wrote a book against the followers of David Joris, the latter still had such a strong following among leading people in Emden that it took all the influence Alting could muster to have it published. Menso Alting did not restrict his efforts to combat the left wing movement, which included Erasmian humanism, to East Friesland. As mentioned earlier, he was also in close contact with the developments in the Low Countries.[101]

Although religious tolerance had been established in the Low Countries in 1572, here, too, rigid Calvinism within the Reformed Church tried to combat Anabaptism by the use of various means. At the Synod of Dordrecht in 1574, it was decided to request that the government not tolerate Anabaptism. Giving support to this atmosphere of intolerance was the militant Calvinist Ruardus Acronius. He began a debate with Peter van Ceulen that led to a disputation which took place in Leeuwarden, the capital of Friesland, from August 16 to November 17, 1596. Acronius and Peter van Ceulen were the main speakers who discussed the eleven points involved. The *Protocol* of 502 pages was printed. The foreword, written by the Reformed stated that "the Anabaptists plant and cherish nothing but shameful and terrible errors which overthrow the foundation of eternal salvation and destroy the well-being of the churches." As a result of the debate the Frisian states prohibited Mennonite worship. Only gradually was tolerance granted.[102]

One of the staunchest defenders of rigid Calvinism in the Low Countries was Marnix van St. Aldegonde. Even his friendship with William of Orange did not prevent his attacking the *geestdrijvers* (spiritualizing enthusiasts) and libertines in his *Ondersoeckinge...* Sebastian Franck and David Joris were included in his attack. He did not exactly demand the death penalty for offences in religious matters but wanted to have exile enforced.[103]

The rigid Calvinists were right in singling out Sebastian Franck as one who caused the spiritualizing tendencies of the religious life in the Low Countries. His influence was comparable to that of Luther, Karlstadt and others during the early decisive years of the reformation efforts in the Netherlands. Alfred Hegler claimed that "Franck's writings had the strongest influence in the Netherlands" and Christiaan Sepp stated that "among the writings of foreign scholars and writers that were completely translated [into the Dutch language] belong above all those by Franck." [104]

It has been pointed out that Franck had numerous followers in East Friesland. His writings were not only admired in all of the Low Countries as a source of factual information but they also had considerable spiritualizing influence on the Anabaptists and the moderate representatives of the Reformed Church. M. Duncanus claimed in 1549 that Menno Simons derived most of his factual information from Franck. K. Vos made a study of Franck's *Chronica* and Menno's writings which led him to the conclusion that the latter depended heavily on Franck's writings and that he was strongly influenced by him. There is no doubt that Menno and his co-workers relied heavily on Franck and belonged to the many readers of his writings. The writings spread in the Low Countries and were translated and appeared in numerous editions.[105] Between 1558 and 1621 seventeen of his writings were translated into Dutch. The famous *Chronica* was translated four times during the sixteenth century. *Van het Rycke Christi* (The Kingdom of Christ) exists at present only in a Dutch version. Franck's spiritualizing tendency is clearly expressed in a quotation from this writing: "In the kingdom of Christ there is neither book, nor Scripture, nor sermon, but the Spirit is all, Scripture and Master." [106]

Dirk Volkerts Coornhert (1522-1590) was the "Sebastian Franck of the Netherlands." He was one of the strongest promoters of religious tolerance. He engaged in many oral disputations with Calvinist theologians and in numerous writings attacked such doctrines as predestination and demanded religious freedom for Catholics, Anabaptists, and libertines alike. One of his most important works on religious freedom was *Synodus of van der Conscientien vryheyt* (1582) which was a dialogue devoted to the various questions pertaining to faith and tolerance.[107]

Other champions of tolerance could be named. At times they seemed like voices in the wilderness. The Dutch Calvinists joined the Catholics in pointing out the ever present threat of Anabaptism with constant references to Münster. Among those writers were Guydo de Bray, H. Faukelius, J. Cloppenburg and others.[108] The Dutch also translated Swiss writings against the Anabaptists. G. Nicolai translated H. Bullinger's well-known *Adversus anabaptistas* and added a refutation of Dutch Anabaptism (1569).[109]

Theologians and humanists did not only advocate tolerance for reasons of idealism; others were concerned for practical and economic purposes. Furthermore some magistrates objected to being told by the clergy what policies they were to pursue. It will be remembered that the Amsterdam magistrate had a tradition of tolerance. P. C. Hooft, burgomaster of Amsterdam for many years, considered religious persecution an "economic heresy." A. Geldorp and I. Bogerman translated Beza's *De haereticis a civili magistratu puniendis* ... (Geneva, 1554), (Concerning heretics who should be punished by the government) in order to influence the Dutch authorities to follow the example of Geneva. In their preface the translators complain that some are guided by the fear that intolerance would have a bad influence on business to which they respond: "Must Satan now, instead of God, promote our commerce?" [110] The minutes of the Reformed synods furnish a rich source of information about actions taken against dissenters. A thorough study of these sources in regard to their theological content, the differences of views and the emergence of tolerance has not yet been made.[111]

Religious tolerance was bound to come. Sixty years after the Dutch theologians published a Dutch edition of Beza's book challenging the magistrates to punish heretical citizens, Philip von Zesen published a book in Amsterdam dedicated to the Bernese government appealing that the Swiss should follow the example of the Dutch.[112] By this time the country of the birth of Erasmus had given up severe persecution of dissenters, while the Reformed Church and its government, in the land where Erasmus had lived and labored and had been buried, was still persecuting the Anabaptists. Switzerland, in which Anabaptism originated and had its first martyr (1527), was also the country in which the last Anabaptist martyr died (1614).

However, when the countries Switzerland and the Netherlands, in which the Reformed Church became established as state church, are compared with those countries in which the Catholic and Lutheran churches were established, we can make the following general observation. In Catholic countries neither the state nor the church ever made arrangements for disputations or a dialogue with radical reformers as they occurred in Reformed countries. Only individual cross-examinations by inquisitors in prison took place, and they always ended with the ultimatum of an either-or. Lutherans never entered into a conversation with Anabaptists on the level of a public disputation. Only the Reformed in Switzerland, Strassburg, the Palatinate, East Friesland, and the Low Countries used this method with the objective of winning them to the fold if at all possible. The Catholic and Lutheran churches were so confident that they were in possession of the absolute truth that to negotiate would already have compromised the truth. The Reformed were aware of the fact that both, they and the Anabaptists had, at their respective places, the same spiritual and cultural rootage. Both sides were therefore more inclined to deliberate and discuss those questions in which they held different views. Both hoped to win the opponent to their respective point of view.

The result was that the Anabaptists survived only in the countries in which the Reformed Church had been established, in Switzerland and in the Netherlands. In Westphalia, in Central and South Germany and in Austria they did not survive. They were exterminated, had to flee or had to join the state churches. Some exceptions can be noted such as Schleswig-Holstein and the delta of the Vistula River. Independent rulers occasionally ran the risk of losing prestige with their superiors and their homogeneous religious population by inviting Mennonites to their uninhabited land because of their agricultural skills. This was the case in the areas mentioned as well as in Bavaria and the Palatinate.

Severe persecution often drove the Anabaptists from their homes. This caused their spread. They witnessed wherever they went. The necessity to defend their faith caused them to formulate their basic beliefs even though they did not have many theologically trained leaders. The body of literature of a devotional and theological content was significant and remained the source of inspiration and orientation for many generations. Most significant were the *Martyrs Mirror*, the writings of Menno Simons, and some early statements of faith.[113]

VIII

CONCLUSION

1. In the Context of the Reformation

It is apparent that historically and ideologically Anabaptism and other forms of the Radical Reformation constitute an integral part of the general sixteenth century Reformation movement. Ludwig Keller popularized the view in the second half of the past century that the genius and the roots of Anabaptism could be traced, in a special way, beyond the Reformation.[1] Today it is taken for granted that Swiss and Dutch Anabaptism are part of the Reformation at large. More specifically the Swiss Anabaptists separated directly from the emerging Reformed Church led by Ulrich Zwingli. Dutch Anabaptism originated in the Sacramentarian movement of the Low Countries in which somewhat later the early Dutch Reformed Church also had its origin. It is true that medieval mystic piety as well as Christian humanism furnished the soil and climate in which the seed of the Anabaptist movement began to grow. However, without the influence of the Lutheran Reformation the outcome would have been different.

Dutch Anabaptism is related to Swiss Anabaptism from which Melchior Hofmann indirectly received his Great Commission. On the other hand Anabaptism was closely related to most of the branches of the Radical Reformation as has been demonstrated by G. H. Williams.[2] The use of the term "radical" is appropriate in two ways. The reformers involved were the most radical in their break with the Catholic tradition and the most radical in their use of the biblical norms for the restoration of the church and the Christian life.[3] Within the range of the Radical Reformation were two extremes: the Biblicists, who were related most closely to Zwingli, and the Spiritualists, who tended to rely more on the personally received guidance of the spirit of God for the illumination of the Revelation in the Bible. Within this range the Anabaptists, with few exceptions (David Joris), tended to be Christ-centered Biblicists with a strong emphasis on the gathered fellowship of believers and disciplined Christian living. On the other hand, the Spiritualists emphasized an individual ethical Christianity, rejecting many forms of the ecclesiastical traditions, organizations, and institutions (Sebastian Franck).[4]

2. The Swiss and Dutch Anabaptists

What is the common background of the Swiss and the Dutch Anabaptists? The Swiss originated in the camp of Zwingli (1525) and spread under severe persecution into the neighboring countries including South and Central Germany, Moravia and Tyrol. Numerous cities became centers of Anabaptism, including Strassburg in which most of the persecuted leaders of Anabaptism found temporary shelter. In Strassburg Hofmann joined the Anabaptists and became their advocate and great commissioner in the Low Countries. Anabaptists of Swiss or High German background had contacts with those of the Low Countries and Low German background particularly between Cologne and Strassburg. Similarities and differences became apparent in matters of doctrinal and ethical views. Some differences were due to the soil and the seed which gave rise to both movements. The determination to restore the church as the body of Christ or as a disciplined Christian brotherhood was held in common. There were differences in regard to the degree in which such a brotherhood could be realized in a sinful world, and in connection with their eschatological and Christological views. The unique emphasis on the latter two was Hofmann's contribution to Dutch Anabaptism. Both disappeared gradually after the Münster incident.

There was constant contact between the southern and northern Anabaptists from the earliest days. Some High German Mennonites lived in the Low Countries. The early writings of the Swiss and South German Anabaptists were in use in the Low Countries and those from the Low Countries had great influence in the South. The *Foundation Book* of Menno Simons appeared in a German translation in 1575 and the *Enchiridion* of Dirk Philips was later translated into German and French. The martyr testimonies of the Swiss, Hutterite, and Dutch Mennonites by Thieleman Jansz van Braght were a truly monumental inter-Mennonite collection, used to this day by the more conservative American Mennonite groups. A spirit of genuine brotherhood between the two became apparent when during the early eighteenth century Swiss Mennonites had to leave their country because of persecution and found aid and shelter in the Netherlands. Some stayed and others were helped to proceed to Pennsylvania.

3. At the Crossroads

Various forces had prepared the population of the Low Countries for a great change. Native mysticism and humanism had paved the way. The message from Wittenberg in its various forms had a decisive influence on the future course of the religious development. A traveler through the Low Countries in our day finds road signs everywhere with the precise information as to what destination the well-kept roads will take him, leaving nothing to chance. Neither the road signs nor the certainty about the future course of the religious and national life were charted out in detail in the days when Anabaptism emerged.

The institutionalized church had lost the confidence and authority of many of its members. New thoughts and insights appeared and appealed everywhere. Faith in the miracle of the sacraments had been undermined. Hoen's symbolic interpretation of the Lord's supper became popular. In East Friesland and in the Low Countries many were waiting for the moment to apply this very principle to the remaining sacrament, baptism. If the miraculous transubstantiation of the bread was not real, the Lord's supper was symbolic of what transpires when man accepts the forgiving grace of God offered to him in Christ. But what about baptism? It had become so thoroughly identified with the act of regeneration or rebirth and the removal of original sin that to declare this sacrament a symbol proved to be far less acceptable. In fact if there was anything that could bring together Roman Catholics and the Protestants from Luther to Zwingli, it was the determination to eradicate the *Ana*-baptists (*Wiedertäufer*, *re*-baptizers), who practiceed the most sacrilegious act imaginable at that time. The postponement of baptism to adulthood was for Anabaptism the only logical step to take. For its opponents in all camps it symbolized a pact with the devil.

At no other place than the Low Countries, however, had the conditions become more favorable to introduce baptism as a symbol of a faith in God's forgiving and regenerating grace experienced by an adult believer. So well prepared was the spiritual soil that Anabaptism became a mass movement within the Dutch population prepared by Sacramentarian views. In fact the "calmly burning inextinguishable glow" spread so rapidly that Sacramentarianism and Anabaptism merged at places, making Anabaptism predominant in some cities and areas of the Netherlands. The missionary zeal of those immersed with the spiritual baptism was such that all strata of the population were reached by it. The severe persecution only added to the speed of its spread.[5]

4. Covenanters of Christ

Those who had personally experienced the forgiving grace in Christ became members of the covenant of Christ (*bundgenoten*), initiated through the symbol of baptism. This covenanted and disciplined fellowship, welded together through the love of Christ, established an intimate relationship of sharing in the spiritual, social, and physical necessities of life. In this context the imitation of Christ became a meaningful attitude toward the Lord, who had called them into discipleship, and toward those who followed Christ with them. To those outside they had a witness of a changed life and the invitation to accept the call of Christ: "Follow me!"

The idea of the covenanted fellowship of followers of Christ was not new. It existed in the old covenant of Israel and was renewed through Christ and his disciples in the new covenant. There are some indications that Anabaptism renewed the use of the idea of the covenant which also became popular in Calvinism.[6] Zwingli used the concept of the covenant in support of the practice of infant baptism. For him baptism took the place of circumcision practiced in Israel as a symbol of the covenant. Thomas Müntzer and others, as has been shown, made use of the concept of the covenant as a symbol of a close fellowship with the Lord and those who are the Lord's own. Among others, Hans Denck and Pilgram Marbeck used the idea of the *Bund* (covenant) and *Bundgenossen* (fellows of the covenant) and transmitted it to Melchior Hofmann who introduced it in the Low Countries. After the Münster episode the terms *bond* and *bondgenoten* came into disrepute and the peaceful Anabaptists preferred the use of *Gemeente Gods* (congregation of God).[7] The designation "church" was not acceptable since the covenanters had just left the "church" and dit not care to be identified with anything that would remind them of what they had left – even the name. So deep-seated was this objection that the Dutch Mennonites to this day use the term *gemeente* (*Gemeinde,* congregation) in speaking of their churches and the term *kerk* (*Kirche,* church) in speaking of a state church.

5. The Ministry and the Ordinances

All members of the fellowship of believers were witnesses and were active in the realization, spread and maintenance of the church of Christ. The attempt made to truly establish the priesthood of all believers had two far-reaching implications. Each believer was accountable directly to God through Christ in everything he did or failed to do. The role of the old mediators of grace, the church, the saints, and the clergy had been removed. Each one now had open access to the throne of God. Secondly, each one was challenged in a special way to be his brother's keeper and beyond that to be a witness among those who were not yet believers in the Lord and members of the Christian fellowship.

This does not mean that the Christian fellowship had no specially designated ministers of the gospel but it does imply that their role was very different from the concepts common in the Catholic and the Protestant traditions. Neither recognized the calling of the Anabaptist ministry. Menno Simons and his co-workers spent much effort in defending their biblical calling, which was derived from the word of God and from the fact that the true church which Christ came to establish no longer existed. The Anabaptists found that the Catholic Church did not measure up to the teaching and the life of the ministers of the New Testament church nor did some of the ministers of the Protestant churches.[8]

According to Menno Simons the ministers and evangelists receive their call either directly from God or from the congregation. The early emphasis on the direct divine call later made room for a stronger emphasis on the confirmation of such call by the congregation. The Münster episode and some individualistic an spiritualistic tendencies, as those of David Joris, made a stricter control advisable. The Wismar Agreements illustrate this point.

The zeal to witness and the persecution caused many early evangelists to travel widely. Menno Simons and Leenaert Bouwens were best known as itinerant preachers and elders. The preacher (*leeraar, Lehrer* or *Diener am Wort*) could be an evangelist or interpreter of the Bible but need not be an elder (*oudste, bishop, Ältester,*) who was in charge of a number of congregations and was also entitled to baptize, administer the Lord's supper and ordain ministers. The functions and authority of this elder differs greatly from that of the Reformed-Presbyterian tradition. The role of the deacon was also very important during the beginning and crucial years of persecution and hardships.

The significance of these offices and the authority and duties assigned to each varied and was flexible particularly in the formative years. Basically the Anabaptist view of the church with the concept of the priesthood of all believers was congregational or democratic. Nevertheless in the days of severe persecution when the survival of the fellowships often depended on the ministry of a courageous elder who would risk his life to serve the group, his office and authority could easily become very significant. Again Leenaert Bouwens can be cited as one who, having unusual evangelistic zeal and success, could use such a position to promote an autocratic rule and harsh disciplinary actions not always approved of by the congregations.

The calling of the minister and elder was to preach and lead the congregation and to witness to those who had not yet been brought in contact with the gospel. The preaching in the fellowship consisted of interpretation of the Scriptures and exhortations by the elders as well as preachers. The exhortation was so important that the preacher was spoken of as the *vermaner* (exhorter) and the place of meeting as *vermaning*. Outstanding among the many duties of the elder (*bishop, oudste*) were baptizing and the administration of the Lord's supper.[9] Baptism was administered primarily by sprinkling or pouring upon confession of faith, that is after a person had experienced salvation through Christ. No special saving grace was attached to the act of baptism. This would be in conflict with the spiritualistic views of Sacramentarianism from which Anabaptism emerged. This was also the case in regard to the form of baptism and prevented the question whether one is more biblical than the other. Baptism regardless of the form in which it was administered was a symbol of what Christ had done for the sinner who had been regenerated through faith in Christ.[10]

The Lord's supper was observed as a memorial of Christ's sacrifice for mankind and as a symbol of the believer's appropriation of the grace made available to him by faith. The Anabaptists and the Reformed churches removed all superstitions and the concept of magic from the Lord's supper and referred to it mostly by this name. Since these views changed the former meaning completely, the term sacrament was no longer used. The concept of the sacrament had been altered and as an ordinance it became an integral part of the Great Commission (Matthew 28:18-20) and a sign (*teken*) of grace.[11]

Menno Simons went beyond the emphasis on the symbolic meaning

of bread and wine which the Anabaptists shared with Zwingli and
the Reformed Church of the Netherlands. For him the elements in
the Lord's supper were not merely symbols but also a challenge for
those partaking in them to become conformed to Christ in their daily
life. Thus the ordinances became an invitation and inspiration to follow
Christ as true disciples. This emphasis on discipleship led the early
Anabaptists also to observe the washing of the feet practiced by Jesus
during the last supper. To this day this is being observed by some
American Mennonite groups as a sign of humility and discipleship.[12]

6. *The Disciplined Brotherhood*

The restitution of the true apostolic church or the Pauline "body
of Christ," in which there is a genuine practice of discipleship of
Christ and separation from the world, was the objective of Anabaptism.
All Anabaptists in Switzerland, Germany, and the Low Countries
pursued this as their goal. They differed only at times in their expectations and their efforts to which degree the purity of the true church
could be established and maintained on earth. One measure to achieve
their goal was church discipline consisting in the admonishment of
a member who did not live a truly Christian life. Failure to repent
and show fruits of repentance would result in excommunication and
the shunning of the excommunicated. Differences of opinion as to
what constituted a sin of which a member had to repent sometimes
caused splits within congregations.

Similarly the observing of the border line between the truly Christian life within the congregation or the fellowship of Christ and the
social, economic, and political involvements in the society in which
they lived caused differences of opinion. Is it possible to draw lines
valid in all cases of what constitutes a Christian or a worldly behavior
or deed?

Differences of interpretation in these questions led to disagreements
and divisions not only within local congregations but also on a national scale. References have been made to the differences, originally
based on their ethnic and national backgrounds between the Frisians
and Flemish. Later subdivisions occurred, leading to designations such
as Old Frisians and Young Frisians and Old Flemish and Young
Flemish. The Waterlander under the leadership of Hans de Ries and
the High German group were more liberal than the Frisians and the
Flemish. It took a long time for such divisions to heal and often reunion

came only because of another rift dividing the whole brotherhood and bringing together the old factions. This happened when the Lamists and Zonists separated during the seventeenth century.[13]

The concept of the church and its realization had theological and ethical implications. In the long run the questions and problems resulting from theological issues often became rather practical matters of interpretation of traditions. But purely doctrinal questions could also become the center of agreements or disagreements.

The Christology of Adam Pastor in which he minimized the divinity of Christ and emphasized his humanity was an example. He had to leave the brotherhood. The other extreme was Hofmann's emphasis on the divinity of Christ. He claimed that Christ received a "heavenly flesh" during his incarnation. Mary furnished the womb only and not the "flesh" of Christ. This view of the incarnation of Christ was a deviation from the age-old orthodox view that Christ was equally man and God, and was not entirely new with Hofmann. It was fully accepted among the Dutch Anabaptists, while the Swiss never dealt with it, and the South Germans did not fully agree along this line. Most of them must have remained orthodox.

Menno Simons was the chief promoter of Hofmann's view in regard to the incarnation of Christ and the resulting Christology. Menno wrote repeatedly on this subject but not so much to promote his views within the congregations as to defend them because of the attack from the Reformed representatives. Menno's concern is of a theological or philosophical nature as well as a practical one. Our salvation depends entirely on Christ's sacrifice as the son of God. If Christ received his flesh from Mary, then our salvation would be partly man-made. This, Menno claims, could never have been. Even the church of the "first-born," Christ, would not be perfect. Thus the divine flesh and the body of Christ, the church without spot and wrinkle, can be of divine origin only. God chose Mary as a channel of grace only, as a ray of sunshine penetrates a glass of water without taking on part of the water.[14]

The concept of the church and the disciplined fellowship had some consequences beyond those dealt with. As long as there was a strong sense of mission, the believers were conscious of being *in* the world but not *of* the world. They did not develop peculiarities in appearance, speech or behavior that made them outwardly recognizable. Their inner Christ-filled love which reached out to help others was the distinguishing mark. To be sure there were activities and trades they did

not find appropriate for a Christian. Some guide-lines they worked
out deal with this matter.

7. *The Christian and his Citizenship*

The insistence of the Anabaptists that church and state must be
separated was one of the issues over which Zwingli and the Swiss
Brethren parted. It was a problem in the Netherlands when the Reformed Church misused its state-church relationship by trying to
enforce the suppression of the Mennonites. The Anabaptist concept
of the church did not permit a church – dominated state nor a state –
dominated church.

The Anabaptists were basically opposed to warfare. In this respect
they agreed with Erasmus and Sebastian Franck. Their strong emphasis
on the disciplined Christian life of love did not permit them to participate in bloodshed. The unfortunate Münster incident served only to
reinforce these views leading to the traditional concept of non-resistance
practiced throughout the centuries. The early Anabaptists were willing
to heal wounds instead of inflicting them. But they were also willing
to give their lives as a testimony of faith instead of preserving it at any
price. Some 2,500 Dutch Anabaptists gave their lives for their faith
in Christ instead of compromising with the trend of the day.

This leads us to the question of the justification of promoting spiritual values by the use of physical force. Anabaptism of the Netherlands faced this question twice. Deeply eschatologically orientated,
that is, expecting the Lord himself to help in the establishment of the
kingdom on earth, and severely persecuted, some looked for the city
of God on earth chosen by the Lord. Israel of old found refuge in
certain cities which offered safety for those persecuted. Even the persecuted Huguenots were given this consideration in Catholic France.
Some Anabaptists sought such a city, while others preferred to endure
all injustice and give their lives if need be. The surrender of Münster
to some Anabaptists without struggle made it easy to find the "city of
God," but impossible to keep it without bloodshed. This event was no
different from all other religious wars including those that led to the
independence of the Netherlands and to the establishment of numerous
territorial and state churches in various countries. For non-resistant
Anabaptism this was a test and resulted in even greater withdrawal
from the use of any other than spiritual means to achieve freedom
and recognition.

The second time Anabaptism faced the question of using force was when the Spanish oppression seemed unbearable for the population of the Netherlands and there was a general uprising. It is probably theoretical to ask what would have happened if Anabaptism had assumed the role which the emerging Reformed Church played when national and religious forces fought the war of liberation from the Spanish yoke. Could their number and zeal for their faith have built up a formidable force? However, to fight with a bleeding conscience is not the armor necessary to win a war. Even if the fighter had lost his scruples during the prolonged struggle, the victorious Anabaptist would not have been the same as he was when he entered the combat. The Anabaptist contribution to his nation was in another area.

8. Lasting Contributions

Anabaptism continued some aspects of the Sacramentarian movement of the early days. This does not imply that the early Reformed Church did not do the same. Both emerged from the same Sacramentarian background. The same can be said about Arminianism which constituted a reaction to the strong Calvinistic influence within the later Reformed Church. In Arminianism, Anabaptism discovered a kinship and the common background which all three, the early Reformed Church, Arminianism, and Anabaptism, shared in Sacramentarianism.

With Arminianism and related representatives of the Dutch tradition Anabaptism kept alive a significant heritage of the Low Countries. In an otherwise somewhat stern Calvinistic environment, the Anabaptist view of the voluntary Christian fellowship was maintained and bore fruit. In a country in which the creedal and predestinarian emphasis was predominant, Anabaptism continued to represent a Christian fellowship in which the believer was called to be a co-worker with Christ charged with a strong ethical responsibility.

When the Low Countries had gained their independence, the Anabaptists fully shared in the ushering in of the Golden Age of the Netherlands. This was not restricted to the economic realm as was the case in most of the countries in which Mennonites survived. Dutch Anabaptists were more *kulturfreundlich* than the Mennonites of the rural tradition of Swiss background. They did not only supply Mennonitism the world over with historical and devotional literature but also contributed more than their share to the fine arts of the country for which

the Netherlands is famous. As has been pointed out, as early as the
sixteenth century some of the best writers and artists were members of
the Mennonite church.

Nevertheless the major emphasis of the Dutch Mennonites has
remained on voluntarism in matters of the Christian faith, on the faith
that must find expression in daily life, the separation of church and
state, and tolerance and religious freedom. These were significant contributions in the land that had given Erasmus to the world and had
accepted Calvin in exchange. The Mennonites helped to preserve and
keep alive the legacy of Erasmus and Anabaptism side by side with
that of Zwingli and Calvin.[15]

A final observation is in place. It has become apparent that early
Anabaptism was truly most radical in its break with the religious,
social, economic, and political aspects of Christendom and the society
of that time. It was even more than that. It made the most earnest
effort to restore the potential of Christendom and its message in the
world. A strong eschatological eagerness and missionary zeal characterized the movement. Dutch Anabaptism had its origin predominantly
among the lower classes which responded uncompromisingly to the
newly discovered Gospel. Ultimately, however, piety and industry led
to respectability and prosperity which gradually dimmed the early
vision and led to conformity with the environment.

Contemporary research and the spirit of ecumenicity have contributed to the removal of the stigma under which Anabaptism suffered
in the sixteenth century. What is now needed above all is a concentrated effort to re-study the potential that early Anabaptism presented
in its day and its application to the needs of our contemporary life.
The Anabaptists were radical in their day in introducing changes in
regard to antiquated religious, social, and political traditions. In what
way can their discoveries and legacy be made use of in our day? [16]

NOTES

I. THE LOW COUNTRIES DURING THE MIDDLE AGES

1. John L. Motley, *The Rise of the Dutch Republic* (London: J. M. Dent & Sons), I, 1.
2. Adriaan J. Barnouw, *The Pageant of Netherlands History* (New York: Longmans, Green and Co., 1952), 1 ff.
3. *Ibid.*, 5; Jan Romein, *De lage landen bij de Zee* (Utrecht: W. de Haan), 48 ff.
4. Aug. C. J. Commissaris, *Leerboek der Nederlandse geschiedenis*, I, 's-Hertogenbosch: L. C. G. Malmberg, 1960), I, 15 f.
5. *Ibid.*, 31.
6. Otto Hollweg, *De Nederlandsche Hanzesteden* (Den Haag), 13 ff.
7. "Handel en bedrijf in de middeleeuwen" in Jan Romein, *op. cit.*, 115 ff.
8. Aug. C. J. Commissaris, *op. cit.*, I, 53.
9. John L. Motley, *op. cit.*, I, 50 f.
10. Aug. C. J. Commissaris, *op. cit.*, I, 57.
11. Jan Romein, *op. cit.*, 207; Commissaris, *op. cit.*, I, 58 ff.
12. L. J. Rogier, *Geschiedenis van het Katholicisme in Noord Nederland in de 16e en 17e eeuw*, I (Amsterdam, 1947), 204 ff; Commissaris, *op. cit.*, I, 60 f.
13. General: Paul Rosenfeld, *The Provincial Governors from the Minority of Charles V to the Revolt* (Louvain: E. Nauwelaerts, 1959); J. S. Theissen, *De regeering van Karel V in de Noordelijke Nederlanden* (Amsterdam: Meulenhoff & Co., 1912).
14. C. Busken Huet, *Het Land van Rubens* (Haarlem: H. D. Tjeenk Willink & Zoon, 1905), 86 ff; Jan Romein, *op. cit.*, 244 ff; Adriaan J. Barnouw, *op. cit.*, 53-86.
15. F. A. Vermeulen, *Handboek tot de geschiedenis der Nederlandse bouwkunst* (1928), I, 419.
16. R. R. Post, *Kerkelijke verhoudingen in Nederland voor de Reformatie van 1500 tot 1580* (Utrecht: Het Spectrum, 1954), 509 f.
17. Jan Romein, *op. cit.*, 236.
18. *Ibid.*, 238 f.
19. *Ibid.*, 239.
20. Jan Romein, *op. cit.*, 228 ff.
21. General: L. M. van Dis, *Reformatorische Rederijkersspelen uit de eerste helft van de zestiende eeuw*, (Haarlem: 1937), Pr. van Duyse, *De Rederijkerskamers in Nederland* (Gent, 1900-02).
22. Rosella R. Duerksen, "Dutch Anabaptist Hymnody..." in *Legacy of Faith*, 110 ff.
23. R. R. Post, *op. cit.*, 452 ff.
24. Jan Romein, *op. cit.*, 232; Commissaris, *op. cit.*, I, 70.
25. R. R. Post, *op. cit.*, 515 ff.
26. L. J. Rogier, *op. cit.*, 96.
27. J. Huizinga, *Waning of the Middle Ages* (London: Edward Arnold & Co., 1924), 129, 148 ff.

28. L. J. Rogier, *op. cit.*, I, 76 f.

29. *Ibid.*, 81.

30. C. G. N. de Vooys, *Middelnederlandsche legenden en exempelen. Bijdrage tot de kennis van de prozalitteratuur en het volksgeloof der Middeleeuwen*, (M. Nijhoff, 1900), 79 ff., 92 f., 110 ff, 136, 153.

31. J. Huizinga, *op. cit.*, 263.

32. *Ibid.*, 124 ff, 129 ff.

33. C. G. N. de Vooys, *op. cit.*, 238; J. Huizinga, *op. cit.*, 159.

34. R. R. Post, *op. cit.*, 406 f.

35. F. Pijper, *Het Middeleeuwsch Christendom. De vereering der H. Hostie* (Den Haag: M. Nijhoff, 1907), 26 ff.

36. C. G. N. de Vooys, *op. cit.*, 232 f.; J. Huizinga, *op. cit.*, 139.

37. J. F. M. Sterck, *Onder Amsterdamsche Humanisten* (Amsterdam: Paul Brandt, 1923), 40; J. F. M. Sterck, *De heilige stede in de geschiedenis van Amsterdam* (Amsterdam: Gooi & Sticht, 1938).

38. L. J. Rogier, *op. cit.*, I, 82 f.

39. R. R. Post, *op. cit.*, 405 f.

40. *Ibid.*, 37 ff.

41. *Ibid.*, 44.

42. L. J. Rogier, *op. cit.*, I, 17 f.

43. R. R. Post, *op. cit.*, 49, 52.

44. *Ibid.*, 52 ff., 55 ff., 59.

45. L. J. Rogier, *op. cit.*, I, 41 f.

46. R. R. Post, *op. cit.*, 61.

47. A. H. L. Henson, "Eene Inquisitiereis door Friesland," in *Archief voor geschiedenis van het aartsbisdom Utrecht*, (1897), XXIV, 215-245; J. S. Theissen (ed.), "Reformatie-voorstellen van Letmatius en Sonnius, met de aanteekeningen daarop van den Raad van Friesland" in *Archief voor geschied. v. h. aartsbisdom Utrecht*, (1905), XXX, 321-416.

48. L. J. Rogier, *op. cit.*, I, 18 ff., 56 f.

49. R. R. Post, *op. cit.*, 99.

50. L. J. Rogier, *op. cit.*, I, 32, 35 f., 236.

51. L. Knappert, *Het ontstaan en de vestiging van het Protestantisme in Nederland* (Utrecht, 1924), 87 f.

52. J. G. de Hoop Scheffer, *Geschiedenis der kerkhervorming in Nederland van haar ontstaan tot 1531* (Amsterdam: J. L. Funke, 1873), p. 17.

53. R. R. Post, *op. cit.*, 114.

54. *Ibid.*, 149 f., 165, 167.

55. *Ibid.*, 171 f.

56. *Ibid.*, 173 f.

57. *Ibid.*, 198, 209 ff., 219 ff.

58 L. J. Rogier, *op. cit.*, I, 53 ff.

59. R. R. Post, *op. cit.*, 185.

60. *Ibid.*, 180, 185.

61. Some of the pertinent sources: J. A. Feith, "De Rijkdom der kloosters in Stad en Lande" in *Groningsche Volksalmanak*, (1902), 1-35; D. de Man, "Maatregelen door de middeleeuwsche overheden genomen ten opzichte van het economisch leven der kloosterlingen en leden van congregaties" in *Bijdragen voor de vaderlandsche geschiedenis en oudheidkunde* 5e serie, (1921), VII, 277-292; A. G. Jonghees, *Staat en Kerk in Holland en Zeeland onder Bourgondische Hertogen* (1425-1477), (1942), 82 ff; J. G. Avis, *De direkte belastingen in het sticht Utrecht aan deze zijde van de IJsel tot 1528*, (Utrecht, 1930), 71 ff; J. S. Theissen, *Centraal gezag en Friese vrijheid. Friesland onder Karel V*, (Groningen, 1907), 54 f., 274 ff.; R. R. Post, "De economische positie van de kloosters" in *op. cit.*, 185-225.

62. R. R. Post, *op. cit.*, 1, 13.
63. *Ibid.*, 3 ff, 13.
64. *Ibid.*

II. THE DAWN OF A NEW DAY

1. Karl Heussi, *Kompendium der Kirchengeschichte* (Tübingen, 1949), 248 ff.; Gustav Wolf, *Quellenkunde der deutschen Reformationsgeschichte* I (Gotha, 1915), 250 ff.
2. L. Knappert, *Het ontstaan en de vestiging van het Protestantisme in de Nederlanden* (Utrecht: A. Oosthoek, 1924), 48 ff.; Albert Hyma (ed.), *The Imitation of Christ* (New York: The Century, 1927), X.
3. L. Knappert, *op. cit.*, 28 ff.; W. H. Beuken, *Ruusbroec en de middeleeuwse mystiek* (Utrecht: Spectrum, 1946).
4. *Ibid.*, 33 ff.; Albert Hyma, *The Christian Renaissance* (Grand Rapids: Reformed Press, 1924), 1-190; Gustav Wolf, *op. cit.*, 219-345.
5. Albert Hyma (ed.), *The Imitation of Christ*, XXXI; L. Knappert, *op. cit.*, 49 ff.
6. L. Knappert, *op. cit.*, 21, 33 ff.; Theodore P. van Zijl, *Gerard Groote, Ascetic and Reformer – 1340-1385* (Washington, D. C., 1963).
7. *Ibid.*, 50.
8. We list only: *Het Bijbelsch humanisme in Nederland* (Leiden, 1913).
9. W. J. Kühler, *Geschiedenis der Nederlandsche Doopsgezinden in de zestiende eeuw* (Haarlem, 1932), 23 ff.; N. van der Zijpp, *Geschiedenis der Doopsgezinden in Nederland* (Arnhem, 1952), 27 f.
10. Albert Hyma, *op. cit.*, 175 f.
11. L. Knappert, *op. cit.*, 78-81; R. R. Post, "Johann Pupper van Goch," *NAK*, XLVII, Afl. 2, (1965-1966) 71-98.
12. Basic writings: Edward W. Miller and Jared W. Scudder, *Wessel Gansfort: Life and Writings* (New York and London, 1917); M. van Rhijn, *Wessel Gansfort* (Hague, 1917); M. van Rhijn, *Studiën over Wessel Gansfort en zijn tijd* (Utrecht, 1933), J. Lindeboom, *Het Bijbelsch humanisme in Nederland* (Leiden, 1913), G. H. Williams, *The Radical Reformation* (Philadelphia, 1962), 27-37.
13. Albert Hyma, *Christian Renaissance*, 329.
14. L. J. Rogier, *op. cit.*, I, 121.
15. M. van Rhijn, *Studiën . . .*, 23 ff.
16. L. Lindeboom, *op. cit.*, 55 f.; Albert Hyma, *op cit.*, 191.
17. M. van Rhijn, *op. cit.*, 38 ff.
18. *Ibid.*, 40 f.
19. J. Lindeboom, *op cit.*, 50.
20. Lewis W. Spitz, *The Religious Renaissance of the German Humanists* (Harvard University Press; Cambridge, Mass., 1963), 197.
21. L. J. Rogier, *op. cit.*, I, 107.
22. F. Pijper, *Erasmus en de Nederlandsche Reformatie* (E. J. Brill: Leiden, 1907), 9 f.
23. J. Huizinga, *Erasmus* (New York, 1924), 9.
24. L. W. Spitz, *op. cit.*, 209.
25. *Ibid.*, 199.
26. *Ibid.*, 221.
27. J. F. M. Sterck, *Onder Amsterdamsche humanisten* (Paul Brandt; Hilversum, 1925), 2 ff; F. Pijper, *op. cit.*, 11 ff.; J. G. de Hoop Scheffer, *Geschiedenis der kerkhervorming in Nederland van haar ontstaan tot 1531* (Amsterdam, 1873), 54, 267 f., 405.
28. J. J. Woltjer, *Friesland in de Hervormingstijd* (Leiden, 1962), 103.
29. J. Huizinga, *op. cit.*, 52.
30. A. F. Mellink, *De Wederdopers in de Noordelijke Nederlanden* (J. B. Wolters: Groningen, 1954), 329.

31. John P. Dolan, *The Influence of Erasmus, Witzel and Cassander in the Church Ordinances and Reform Proposals of the United Duchies of Cleve during the Middle Decades of the 16th Century* (Münster, 1957), 1 ff.

32. J. F. M. Sterck, *op. cit.,* 5 ff., 31 ff., 53 ff., 88 ff.

33. *Ibid.,* 91 ff.

34. Adriaan J. Barnouw, *op. cit.,* 64 ff.; H. A. Enno van Gelder, *Erasmus, Schilders en Rederijkers* (P. Noordhoff: Groningen, 1959), 5 ff., 37 ff.

35. Jan Romein, *op. cit.,* 405 ff.

36. Leonard Verduin, "The Chambers of Rhetoric and Anabaptist Origins in the Low Countries" in *MQR,* XXXIV (July, 1960), 3, 193.

37. L. Knappert, *op. cit.,* 133 ff.

38. J. G. de Hoop Scheffer, *op. cit.,* 475.

39. L. Knappert, *op. cit.,* 135 f.

40. See articles in *Mennonite Encyclopedia,* – "Leenaert Bouwens," "David Joris."

41. Christiaan Sepp, *Verboden lectuur* (Brill, 1889), 95. Other literature: G. Kalff, *Geschiedenis van de Nederlandsche Letterkunde in de 18e eeuw* I, 62-185; L. M. van Dis, *Reformatorische Rederijkersspelen uit de eerste helft van de zestiende eeuw* (Haarlem, 1937); J. te Winkel, *Geschiedenis der Nederlandsche Letterkunde van Middeleeuwen en Rederijkerstijd* (Haarlem, 1922), Vol. I and II; Quirinius Breen, "Some aspects of humanistic rhetoric and the Reformation," *NAK,* XLII, Afl. 1 (1959), 1-14; Karl Hagen, *Deutschlands literarische und religiöse Verhältnisse im Reformationszeitalter . . .,* (Aalen, 1966).

42. M. E. Kronenberg, "Uitgaven van Luther in de Nederlanden verschenen tot 1541," *NAK,* XL, Afl. 1 (1953) 1.

43. L. Knappert, *op. cit.,* 164, 166.

44. John P. Dolan, *op. cit.,* 1 ff.; W. Bax, *Het Protestantisme in het bisdom Luik en vooral te Maastricht,* 1505-1557 ('s-Gravenhage, 1937), 37 ff.; "Edzard I" in *ME,* II, 157.

45. M. E. Kronenberg, *op. cit.,* 23 f.

46. L. Knappert, *op. cit.,* 163-173; J. Lindeboom, *De confessioneele ontwikkeling der Reformatie in de Nederlanden* (Hague, 1946) 8 ff.

47. W. Bax, *op. cit.,* 15.

48. L. Knappert, *op. cit.,* 123 f.

49. W. Bax, *op. cit.,* 15: Christiaan Sepp, op. cit., 40-46; Lindeboom, op. cit., 8.

50. Cornelius Krahn, *Menno Simons . . .,* (H. Schneider: Karlsruhe, 1936), 41 ff.; K. Vos, *Menno Simons* (Leiden: E. J. Brill, 1914), 234 f.

51. A. F. Mellink, *op. cit.,* 327 f., 330.

52. R. R. Post, *op. cit.,* 518 f.

53. *Ibid.,* 519; J. G. de Hoop Scheffer, *op. cit.,* 332, 504.

54. W. Bax, *op. cit.,* 8 ff.; 17 f.

55. *Ibid.,* 37 John R. Dolan, op. cit., 1, ff.

56. W. Bax, *op. cit.,* 42-64; Heinrich Forsthoff, *Rheinische Kirchengeschichte* (Essen: Lichtweg-Verlag, 1929), 110-153; Albert Wolters, *Reformationsgeschichte der Stadt Wesel . . .,* (Bonn, 1868), 30-62.

57. C. Varrentrapp, *Hermann von Wied and sein Reformationsversuch in Köln* (Duncker & Humbolt, 1878), 56-60; G. Drouven, *Die Reformation in der Cölnischen Kirchenprovinz zur Zeit des Erzbischofs und Kurfürsten Herman V., Graf zu Wied* (Köln, 1876).

58. H. Forsthoff, *op cit.,* 76-109; Karl Rembert, *Die "Wiedertäufer" im Herzogtum Jülich . . .* (Berlin, 1899), 125-136.

59. C. Varrentrapp, *op. cit.,* 61-65; Hermann Barge, *Andreas Bodensteun von Karlstadt* II (Leipzig, 1905), 17-20, 205 f.; "Gerhard Westerburg" in *ME,* IV, 930. A general treatment is: J. F. G. Goeters, "Die Rolle des Täufertums in der Reformationsgeschichte des Niederrheins" in *Rheinische Vierteljahrsblätter* (Jahrg. 24, Heft 3/4, 1959), 221-227.

60. Ludwig Keller, *Geschichte der Wiedertäufer und ihres Reiches zu Münster* (Münster, 1880), 68; Josef Niesert, *Beiträge zu einem Münsterischen Urkundenbuch* I (Münster, 1823), 116; G. Franz, *Der deutsche Bauernkrieg* (Darmstadt, 1956), 235-238.

61. C. A. Cornelius, *Historische Arbeiten vornehmlich zur Reformationsgeschichte* (Leipzig, Duncker & Humbolt, 1899), 1-33; D. Reichling, *Johannes Murmellius. Sein Leben und seine Werke* (Nieuwkoop, 1963).

62. E. Kochs, "Die Anfänge der ostfriesischen Reformation" I, *JGKAE*, XIX, 1, 167-172.

63. See "Oldersum" and "Ulrich von Dornum" in *ME*, IV, 53; II, 94; Gerhard Ohling, *Junker Ulrich von Dornum und das Oldersumer Religionsgespräch* (Aurich, 1955).

64. C. A. Cornelius, *Der Anteil Ostfrieslands an der Reformation bis zum Jahr 1535* (Münster, 1852) 8-11; E. Meiners, *Oostvrieschlandts kerkelyke Geschiedenisse* I (Groningen, 1738), 479 ff; E. Kochs, *op. cit.*, II, 204-216, 231 ff.

65. E. Beninga, *Volledige Chronyk van Oostfriesland* (Emden, 1723); *ME*, II, 122; E. Meiners, *op. cit.*, II, 352 ff.; C. A. Cornelius, *op. cit.*, 12 f.; E. Kochs, *JGKAE*, 216-223

66. This is based on calculations by Walther Köhler, *Zwingli und Luther* ... I (Leipzig, 1924), 61 ff. for Switzerland and C. A. Cornelius, *op. cit.*, 19 for Norden. He says, "1926 ist er in Friesland, heirathet und wird Predicant zu Norden." The date given by Knappert, *op. cit.*, 140, and J. Lindeboom, *Het Bijbelsch humanisme* ..., 160 ff., namely that he came to Norden in 1527 cannot be right. This is also confirmed by Capito's letter to Zwingli dated Sept. 26, 1526 in which he states, "Johannes Rhodius uxorem duxit apud Frisios"; C. A. Cornelius, *op. cit.*, 19.

67. E. Meiners, *op. cit.*, I, 114 ff., II, 346; C. A. Cornelius, *op. cit.*, 20 f.

68. E. Meiners, *op. cit.*, I, 108, II, 367.

69. E. Meiners, *op. cit.*, I, 53 ff.; E. Beninga, *op. cit.*, 631., C. A. Cornelius, *op. cit.*, E. Kochs, *op. cit.*, II, 256 ff.

70. C. A. Cornelius, *op. cit.*, 19; E. Kochs, *op. cit.*, II, *JGKAE*, 256.

71. J. G. de Hoop Scheffer, *Geschiedenis der kerkhervorming* ... 109. See Alardus van Amsterdam in A. J. Kölker, *Alardus Aemstelredamus en Cornelis Crocus. Twee Amsterdamse priester-humanisten* (Utrecht: Dekker & van de Vegt, 1963), 138.

72. J. Lindeboom, *De confessioneele ontwikkeling* ..., 29.

73. *Complete Works of J. W. Goethe* (New York), Vol. V, 134. This could also be applied to the prince of humanism, Erasmus, who had a hard time disassociating himself from the child fathered (to a certain degree) by Humanism.

74. George H. Williams, *The Radical Reformation* (Westminster Press: Philadelphia, 1962), 849 f.; Heinold Fast, *Heinrich Bullinger und die Täufer* (Weierhof, 1959), 92-106.

75. An example is Fritz Heyer, *Der Kirchenbegriff der Schwärmer* (Leipzig, 1939).

76. See "Historiography," *ME*, II, 751 ff., 758 ff.

77. A. J. Kölker, *op. cit.*, 136, 138.

78. W. J. Kühler, *Geschiedenis* I, 36.

79 R. R. Post, *op. cit.*, 491.

80. J. G. de Hoop Scheffer, *op. cit.*, 115 f.; L. Knappert, *op. cit.*, 162.

81. M. E. Kronenberg, *op. cit.*, 1, 4-25.

82. W. J. Kühler, *op. cit.*, 38.

83. H. Barge, *Andreas Bodenstein von Karlstadt*, II (Leipzig, 1906) 18; J. de Hoop Scheffer, *op. cit.*, 405 f., 464.

84. K. Vos, *Martinus Luther* ..., 185.

85. W. F. Dankbaar, *Martin Bucer's Beziehungen zu den Niederlanden* ('s-Gravenhage, 1961), 5, 8-12, 20-26.

86. K. Vos, "Karlstadt of Zwingli?" *DB*, 54ste Jaarg., 1917, 92 ff.; K. Vos, "Luther tegen Karlstadt en de Wederdoopers" in *Martinus Luther in zijn leven en werken van 1483-1525* (Amsterdam, 1917), 198.

87. Christiaan Sepp, *Verboden lectuur. Een drietal Indices Librorum Prohibitorum* (E. J. Brill; Leiden, 1889), 12.

88. *Ibid.*, 53.

III. THE EVANGELICAL SACRAMENTARIAN MOVEMENT

1. A. J. Kölker, *Alardus Aemstelredamus en Cornelis Crocus. Twee Amsterdamse priester-humanisten* (Utrecht: Dekker & Van de Vegt, 1963), 132 ff., 110 f.

2. For these and other designations of the Sacramentarian period see G. H. Williams, *The Radical Reformation* (Philadelphia: Westminster Press, 1962), 27 f.; J. Lindeboom, *De confessioneele ontwikkeling...*, 35; J. J. Woltjer, *Friesland in Hervormingstijd* (Leiden: Universitaire Pers, 1962), 102.

3. Leonhard Fendt, *Die katholische Lehre von Messe und Abendmahl* (Lüneburg, 1954), 124; Hans Preuss, *Die Geschichte der Abendmahlsfrömmigkeit in Zeugnissen und Berichten* (Gütersloh, 1949), 11-13, 172, Canon 3.

4. Fendt, *op cit.*, 164.

5. Hans Preuss, *op. cit.*, 14; L. Fendt, *op. cit.*, 165.

6. Hans Preuss, *op. cit.*, 15, 84-86; G. H. Williams, *op. cit.*, 207 ff.; H. Preuss, *op. cit.*, 166, 169, f.

7. Karl Heussi, *Kompendium der Kirchengeschichte,* 10th ed. (Tübingen, 1949), 235 f.

8. L. Fendt, *op. cit.*, 168, Canon 2.

9. L. Fendt, *op. cit.*, 167 f.

10. *Het Bijbelsch Humanisme...*, 39.

11. Albert Hyma, ed., *The Imitation of Christ,* 176.

12. Albert Hyma, *The Christian Renaissance,* 209 f.

13. *Documenta Reformatoria I,* 9; G. H. Williams, *op. cit.*, 30-33.

14. M. van Rhijn, *Studiën over Wessel Gansfort en zijn tijd* (Utrecht, 1933), 85.

15. *Ibid.,* 86-89. *Documenta Reformatoria I,* 9, has only a Latin excerpt from *De sacramento eucharistiae.* E. W. Miller and J. W. Scudder, *Wessel Gansfort: Life and Writings* (New York and London, 1917), II, 1-70 have an English translation.

16. R. R. Post, *Kerkelijke verhoudingen in Nederland voor de Reformatie van 1500 tot 1580* (Utrecht: Het Spectrum, 1954), 405 f.

17. K. Vos, "Wessel Gansforts invloed," *Groningsche Volksalmanak voor het jaar 1920,* 143 ff.; M. van Rhijn, *op. cit.*, 38 ff.

18. M. van Rhijn, *op. cit.*, 47 f.

19. H. A. Enno van Gelder, *Erasmus, Schilders en Rederijkers* (Groningen: P. Noordhoff, 1959), 153 ff.

20. M. van Rhijn, *op. cit.*, 42.

21. H.A. Enno van Gelder, *The two Reformations in the 16th Century,* 156.

22. Walter Köhler, *Zwingli und Luther. Ihr Streit über das Abendmahl nach seinen politischen und religiösen Beziehungen,* I (Leipzig, 1924), 51 ff., 63 ff.

23. Lewis W. Spitz, *The Religious Renaissance of the German Humanists* (Cambridge Massachusetts: Harvard University Press, 1963), 227.

24. H. A. Enno van Gelder, *op. cit.*, 157.

25. Walther Köhler, *op. cit.*, 52.

26. Stated in a letter to the author dated March 13, 1964. The unpublished dissertation is entitled "Die Abendmahlslehre der Erasmus von Rotterdam und seine Stellung am Anfang des Abendmahlstreites der Reformation" (Erlangen, 1955).

27. Lewis W. Spitz, *op. cit.*, 191, 227.

28. Walther Köhler, *op. cit.*, 52.

29. *Ibid.,* 4, 6, 49 ff., 53 ff., 57 f., 60, 63 f.; See also in general John P. Dolan, *The Influence of Erasmus, Witzel and Cassander in the Church Ordinances and Reform Proposals of the United Duchies of Cleve during the Middle Decades of the 16th Century* (Münster, 1957), 5 f.; Robert Stupperich, *Der Humanismus und die Wiedervereinigung der Konfessionen* (Leipzig, 1936) and Gottfried G. Krodel, *op. cit.;* I. B. Horst, *Erasmus, the Anabaptists and the Problem of Religious Unity* (Haarlem, 1967).

30. "Karlstadt," in *RGG,* III, 1154-55; E. Freys und H. Barge, *Verzeichnis der gedruckten Schriften des Andreas Bodenstein von Karlstadt* (Nieuwkoop, 1965).

31. H. Barge, *Andreas Bodenstein von Karlstadt* I (Leipzig, 1905), 170; On March 28, 1519 Luther wrote to Erasmus: "Greetings from Andreas Karlstadt, who admires Christ in you." See also 175 ff.

32. *Op. cit.*, II, 150; See also the outdated arguments by J. G. de Hoop Scheffer, *op. cit.*, 100, footnote 4.

33. Walther Köhler, *Dogmengeschichte als Geschichte des christlichen Selbstbewusstseins*, II (Zürich, 1951), 275, 27 ff.; Erich Roth, *Sakrament und Luther* (Berlin, 1952), 45 II, 4.

34. Walther Köhler, *Zwingli und Luther*, 49-72; M. van Rhijn, *op. cit.*, 41-44; G. H. Williams, *op. cit.*, 35-44.

35. Walther Köhler, *op. cit.*, 72; About the Swiss Anabaptists see Hans J. Hillerbrand, "The Origin of Sixteenth Century Anabaptism: Another Look" in *AfR*, Jhrg, 53 (1962) Heft 1/2, 161-178; H. S. Bender, *Conrad Grebel 1498-1526...* (Goshen, 1950), 108 ff., 103 f., 119 ff., 196 ff.

36. Eduard Meiners, *Oostvrieslandts kerkelyke geschiedenisse* I, 168; II, 367; C. A. Cornelius, *Der Antheil Ostfrieslands...*, 21.

37. M. van Rhijn, *op. cit.*, 74-76; J. G. de Hoop Scheffer, *op. cit.*, 61 ff.; G. H. Williams, *op. cit.*, 30 ff.; Hans Preuss, *op. cit*, 84-86.

38. K. Vos, *Menno Simons* (Leiden, 1914), 221 ff. has convincingly demonstrated that the source for this information is unreliable. Nevertheless it is being repeated by Knappert, *op. cit.*, 116; Reitsma-Lindeboom, *Geschiedenis van de Hervorming...*, 28; J. Lindeboom, *De confessioneele ontwikkeling...* 37 and others. An exception is J. J. Woltjer, *op. cit.*, 96 f.

39. L. Knappert, *Het ontstaan en de vestiging van het Protestantisme in de Nederlanden* (Utrecht: A. Oosthoek, 1924), 115 f.

40. Wouter, the "Lutheran monk": L. Knappert, *op. cit.*, 115 ff., 137, 142; Wouter Deelen; J. F. M. Sterck, *Onder Amsterdamsche Humanisten* (Hilversum, 1923), 97-107.

41. L. Knappert, *op. cit.*, 170 f.

42. J. G. de Hoop Scheffer, *Geschiedenis der Kerkhervorming...* 83.

43. *Divisie-Kronyk* published August 17, 1517; See also J. G. de Hoop Scheffer, *op. cit.*, 51 f.

44. R. R. Post, *op. cit.*, 473 f. This chapter dealing with "De aflaat en de aflaathandel" presents a thorough treatment of the sale of indulgences in the Netherlands (473-484).

45. Published in *Corpus Reformatorum*, XCI (Leipzig, 1927), 512-519; A. Eekhof, *De Avondmaalsbrief van Cornelis Hoen* (facsimile ed.) ('s-Gravenhage, 1917); *Documenta Reformatoria*, I (Kampen, 1960), 33-36; Discussion in L. Knappert, 138 ff. (See also footnotes 2 and 3); J. G. de Hoop Scheffer, *op. cit.*, 93-98. "Those who partake of the eucharist without faith seem to prefer the manna of the Jews to Christ."

46. *Documenta Reformatoria*, I, 33-36.

47. Knappert, *op. cit.*, 141 f.; Kölker, *op. cit.*; Rogier, *Geschiedenis van het Katholicisme...*, I, 130 f.

48. Sterck, *op. cit.*, 90-107; H. F. Wijnman, "Wouter Deelen..." in *Amstelodamum*, XXVII, (1930), 43-65.

49. J. F. M. Sterck, *op. cit.*, 2-101; L. Knappert, 141 f.; A. J. Kölker, *op. cit.*, 194-196.

50. J. F. M. Sterck, *op. cit.*, 39-46; A. J. Kölker, *op. cit.*, 60-66.

51. H. F. Wijnman, *op. cit.*, 44-46; J. F. M. Sterck, *op. cit.*, 98 ff.

52. J. F. M. Sterck, *op. cit.*, 98 ff.

53. H. F. Wijnman, *op. cit.*, 45-64; J. G. de Hoop Scheffer, "Beschuldigingen tegen Meester Wouter te Amsterdam in 1536" in *Studiën en Bijdragen* II, 1872, 470-474. G. Grosheide, "Verhooren en vonnissen der Wederdoopers, betrokken bij de aanslagen op Amsterdam in 1534 en 1536" in *BMHG*, XLI, (1920) 154 ff. Among the writings of Wouter Deelen are: A revised Vulgate edition of the N.T. (London, 1540) in which he

said that the O.T. was to follow; A Dutch translation of Sleidanus, *De religionis statu* (Emden, 1558). See Wijnman, *op. cit.*, 55-57, 62, 64.

54. Johannes Sartorius treated here died in Basel in 1557 and not in Delft as stated by many. His son-in-law Henricus Junius Gouda erected a tombstone on his grave during the same year. In Delft was another Sacramentarian leader by the name of Johannes Sartorius. See Sterck, *op. cit.*, 107.

55. J. F. M. Sterck, *op. cit.*, 2, 9, 23 ff.; A. J. Kölker, *op. cit.*, 14, 16 f.; A general treatment of the influence which humanism exerted on the development of education in the Low Countries is P. N. M. Bot, *Humanisme en onderwijs in Nederland* (Utrecht, 1955); F. J. Dubiez, *Op de grens van humanisme en Hervorming* (Nieuwkoop: B. de Graaf, 1962); D. Reichling, *Johannes Murmellius. Sein Leben und seine Werke* (Nieuwkoop: B. de Graaf, 1963).

56. *Biogr. Wb.*, III, 269-272; J. G. de Hoop Scheffer, *Geschiedenis der Kerkhervorming in Nederland...*, (Amsterdam, 1873), 31, 351, 354, 359 f., 372-375, 538-540.

57. J. G. de Hoop Scheffer, *op. cit.*, 91, 362-79, 389; L. Knappert, *op. cit.*, 150-154; F. D. J. Moorrees, *Geschiedenis der Kerkhervorming in Noord-Nederland* (Groningen, 1905), 41-44.

58. L. Knappert, *op. cit.*, 123.

59. W. J. Kühler, *op. cit.*, 42 f.

60. L. Knappert, *op. cit.*, 124. General treatments: H. van Druten, *Geschiedenis der Nederlandsche Bijbelvertaaling*, I (Leiden, 1895-96), II (Rotterdam, 1897); J. G. de Hoop Scheffer, *op. cit.*, 256-278.

61. F. C. Wieder, *De schriftuurlijke liedekens* ('s-Gravenhage, 1900), 77.

62. *Ibid.*, 11.

63. *Het Offer des Heeren* in BRN, II, 429.

64. J. G. de Hoop Scheffer, *op. cit.*, 432 ff.

65. D. F. Scheurleer, *De Souterliedekens* (Leiden, 1898); Eliz. Mincoff-Marriage, *Souterliedekens. Een Nederlandsch psalmboek van 1540 met de oorspr. volksliederen die bij de melodie behooren* ('s-Gravenhage, 1922); L. Knappert, *op. cit.*, 128-132.

66. *Documenta Reformatoria*, I, 39 f.

67. J. G. de Hoop Scheffer, *op. cit.*, 117 f., 121.

68. *Ibid.*, 135.

69. *Ibid.*, 137.

70. J. te Winkel, *Geschiedenis der Nederlandsche letterkunde van de Middeleeuwen en Rederijkerstijd*, II (Haarlem, 1922), 323.

71. J. G. de Hoop Scheffer, *op. cit.*, 431, 475.

72. J. te Winkel, *op. cit.*, II, 454 f.

73. *Ibid.*, 456, 458.

74. *Ibid.*, 446-451. For general information see also G. Kalff, *Geschiedenis der Nederlandsche letterkunde in de 16de eeuw*, I (Leiden, 1889) particularly "Rederijkers en Volksdichters," 86-185.

75. Menno Simons, *CW*, 668; *Opera Omnia*, 256 a; Cornelius Krahn, "The Conversion of Menno Simons," *MQR*, X, 1 (January, 1936).

76. Cornelius Krahn, *Menno Simons* (1496-1561), Karlsruhe: Schneider, 1936), 17-21, 41-44; M. E. Kronenberg, "Uitgaven van Luther..." 14, Nr. 56.

77. K. Vos, *Menno Simons, op. cit.*, 13 f., 234 f.

78. J. J. Woltjer, *Friesland in de Hervormingstijd.* (Leiden, 1962), 80.

79. *Biogr. W.*, I, 542-544.

80. J. J. Woltjer, *op. cit.*, 57-63.

81. *Ibid.*, 78 f.

82. J. G. de Hoop Scheffer, *op. cit.*, 484, 488 f.

83. *Ibid.*, 282-312, 458 ff.

84. *Ibid.*, 314-316.

85. *Ibid.*, 441-448; J. Prinsen, *Collectanea van Gerardus Geldenhauer Noviomagus* in UHG, 3e Serie, 16 (Utrecht, 1901).

86. R. R. Post, *op. cit.*, 3 ff.

87. J. G. de Hoop Scheffer, *op. cit.*, 91, 101, 316-332; F. D. J. Moorrees, *op. cit.*, 39 f.

88. *Ibid.*, 335-338.

89. *Ibid.*, 339, 597 f.; C. A. Cornelius, *Aufruhr*, II, 403, 413.

90. J. G. de Hoop Scheffer, *op. cit.*, 332.

91. A. M. C. van Asch van Wijck, *Bescheiden betreffende het eerste tijdvak van de geschiedenis der Hervorming in de stad en provincie Utrecht, 1524-1566* in *BMHG*, IV, 2, 1851, 117.

92. A. F. Mellink, *op. cit.*, 343.

93. J. G. de Hoop Scheffer, *op. cit.*, 581 f; W. J. Kühler, *Geschiedenis der Nederlandse Doopsgezinden* . . . I, 46.

94. J. G. de Hoop Scheffer, *op. cit.*, 460; G. J. Boekenoogen, "Een veroordeling van Jan Matthysz. in 1528" in DB, 56ste Jrg. (1919), 213-217.

95. J. G. de Hoop Scheffer, *op. cit.*, 553 ff., 557.

96. *Ibid.*, 540 f., 544 f.; A. F. Mellink, *op. cit.*, 340.

97. J. G. de Hoop Scheffer, *op. cit.*, 503 f., 513 f.

98. M. E. Kronenberg, *op. cit.*, 20-24; Paul Kalkoff, *Die Anfänge der Gegenreformation in den Niederlanden*, I, 59 f.

99. M. E. Kronenberg, *op. cit.*, 5-6, 9, 14, 20.

100. K. Vos, *De Doopsgezinden te Antwerpen in de zestiende eeuw* (Brussel, 1920), 5 f.

101. Paul Kalkoff, *op. cit.*, 19 ff.; A. L. E. Verheyden, *De Hervorming in de zuidelijke Nederlanden in de XVI eeuw* (Brussel, 1949), 38 f., 43, 49.

102. *Ibid.*, 55.

103. *Ibid.*, 53.

104. R. R. Post, *op. cit.*, 546.

105. Camilo Henner, *Beiträge zur Organisation und Competenz der päpstlichen Ketzergerichte* (Leipzig, 1890).

106. Karl Heussi, *op. cit.*, 292.

107. P. Fredericq, *Corpus documentorum inquisitionis haereticae pravitatis Neerlandicae* (Gent, 1884 ff.) III, 59-76; Paul Kalkoff, *op. cit.*, 17 ff., J. G. de Hoop Scheffer, *op. cit.*, 153-155; R. R. Post, *op. cit.*, 542.

108. Em. Valvekens, *De inquisitie in de Nederlanden der 16e eeuw* (1949), 181; P. Fredericq, *op. cit.*, IV, 256.

109. R. R. Post, *op. cit.*, 544.

110. Em. Valvekens, *op. cit.*, 176, 186; P. Fredericq, *op. cit.*, IV, 60-76.

111. Em. Valvekens, *op. cit.*, 186, 189-193; P. Fredericq, *op. cit.*, V, 143-147; IV, 272, 284; V, 126, 131, 138, 139.

112. Heinrich Forsthoff, *Rheinische Kirchengeschichte* (Essen: Lichtweg-Verlag, 1929) 65, 68, 77-82, 97, 105-108.

113. Ludwig Keller, *Die Geschichte der Wiedertäufer und ihres Reichs zu Münster*, (Münster, 1880), 81, 54; Heinrich Detmer, *Bilder aus den religiösen und sozialen Unruhen in Münster während des 16. Jahrhunderts. II. Bernhard Rothmann* (Münster, 1904), 58 f., 39.

IV. MELCHIOR HOFMANN: A PROPHETIC LAYMAN

1. Otto Pohrt, *Reformationsgeschichte Livlands* (Leipzig, 1928), 35 f., 46 ff., 64-67. Good as a brief survey. Hofmann's story is presented in a biased manner.

2. Special books on Hofmann are: Friedrich Otto zur Linden, *Melchior Hofmann: ein Prophet der Wiedertäufer* (Haarlem, 1885), 86-103; W. I. Leendertz, *Melchior Hofmann* (Haarlem, 1883); Peter Kawerau, *Melchior Hofmann als religiöser Denker* (Haar-

lem, 1954); B. N. Krohn, *Geschichte der fanatischen und enthusiastischen Wieder-täufer...* (Leipzig, 1785); Abraham Hulshof, *Geschiedenis van de Doopsgezinden te Straatsburg...* (Amsterdam, 1905).

3. F. O. zur Linden, *op. cit.*, 100, 109-113; W. I. Leendertz, *op. cit.*, 102 ff.

4. C. A. Cornelius, *Geschichte des Münsterischen Aufruhrs* II, (Leipzig, 1855), 292; Hermann Barge, *op. cit.*, II, 395 f.

5. W. I. Leendertz, *op. cit.*, 119-123.

6. *Ibid.*, 123-135.

7. H. Barge, *Andreas Bodenstein von Karlstadt*, II, 398 f.; *Elsass* I, 240.

8. E. Kochs, "Anfänge der ostfriesischen Reformation," *JGKAE*, III, (1920), 34 f.

9. W. I. Leendertz, *op. cit.*, 142 f.; *Elsass* I, 240, No. 188.

10. E. Kochs, *op. cit.*, 37.

11. Gerhard Ohling, *Ulrich von Dornum*, 27 f.

12. H. Barge, *op. cit.*, II, 410-415.

13. G. H. Williams, *The Radical Reformation*, 211 ff. General treatments of the Reformation of Strassburg are: Gustav Anrich, "Die Strassburger Reformation" in *Schriften VfR* 36 jrg., Erstes Stück (Leipzig, 1918); T. W. Röhrich, *Geschichte der Reformation im Elsass* I (1832).

14. H. Barge, *Andreas Bodenstein von Karlstadt*, II, 207-216.

15. "Strassburg" in *ME* IV, 639 ff.; G. H. Williams, *op. cit.*, 251 ff.

16. W. I. Leendertz, *op. cit.*, 150 ff.; *Elsass* I, 240, No. 188; H. Barge, *op. cit.*, II, 411. Leendertz thinks that Hofmann contacted Bucer through a letter of recommendation from Karlstadt. It is more likely that the latter sent along a letter to Bucer announcing his plans to come to Srassburg where he would call on Bucer which he had failed to do during his first visit. Hofmann took advantage of this occasion and introduced himself.

17. W. I. Leendertz, *op. cit.*, 153 ff.; *Elsass* I, 240. Title: *Dialogus und grüntliche berichtung gehaltener disputation im land zu Holstein underm künig von Denmarck von hochwirdigen sacrament oder nachtmal des Herren...*

18. W. I. Leendertz, *op. cit.*, 158-191, 373-381; *Elsass* I, 258-361, No. 210; P. Kawerau, *op. cit.*, 134.

19. H. Barge, *op. cit.*, II, 410-420; *Elsass* I, 263, No. 214, 215.

20. *Corpus Schwenckfeldianorum* V (Leipzig, 1916) 522 f.

21. *Elsass* I, 288 f., No. 234; G. H. Williams, *op. cit.*, 262-264.

22. *Elsass* I, 122 f., No. 92, 268, No. 222; 261 f., No. 211; W. I. Leendertz, *op. cit.*, 192-197; T. W. Röhrich, "Zur Geschichte der Strassburger Wiedertäufer," *Niedners Zeitschrift für historische Theologie*, 1860, 2-121; idem, *Geschichte der Reformation im Elsass*, II (1832), 90, 455.

23. H. Barge, *op. cit.*, II, 419 f.

24. E. Kochs, *op. cit.*, III, 10.

25. Eduard Meiners, *Oostvrieschlandts kerkelyke geschiedenisse...* (Groningen, 1738) I, 49 ff., 109 ff.; Kochs, *op. cit.*: *Summa vnde bekenninghe Christliker leer der predicanten in Oostfrieslandt...* (1528), 12-22.

26. C. A. Cornelius, *Der Antheil Ostfrieslands...* 57-59; Kochs, *op. cit.*, III, 25 ff.; Eggerik Beninga, *Volledige chronik van Oostfriesland...* (Emden, 1723), 652.

27. C. A. Cornelius, *Der Antheil...*, 48 (also footnote).

28. E. Beninga, *op. cit.*, 652, 677.

29. Followers of Müntzer were supposed to have fled to East Friesland (*Gründlicher warhafftiger Bericht*, 21). About Hamelmann's unreliable reporting see E. Kochs, *op. cit.*, III, 32, 40 f. (footnotes). However even such a careful reporter as Kochs speaks on p. 70 and other places as if Anabaptism existed in East Friesland before Hofmann's arrival and proceeds describing how he introduced it (p. 72 ff.).

30. Meiners, *op. cit.*, I, 582; Ohling, *op. cit.*, 107.

31. C. A. Cornelius, *op. cit.*, 39 ff., 51 f.; Kochs, *op. cit.*, III, 59-69.

32. The *Ordonnantie* has the following full title: *Die Ordonnantie Godts, De welcke*

hy, door zijnen Soone Christum Jesum, ingestelt ende bevesticht heeft, op die waerach-tighe Discipulen des eeuwigen woort Godts. Door Melchior Hofmann. Ten eersten Ghe-druckt. Anno, 1530. Ende nu door een liefhebber der gerechticheydt, uit het Oostersche, in Nederduytsche ghetrouwelijken overgeset. (Amsterdam, 1611). Reprinted in *BRN* V, 145-170, with an introduction by S. Cramer (127-144); English: *The Ordinance of God,* *LCC,* XXV, 182-203.

33. E. Beninga, *op. cit.,* 652; Carel van Ghendt, *Het beginsel en voortgangck der ge-schillen, scheuringen, en verdeeltheden onder de gene die Doops-gesinden Genoemt wor-den . . ., BRN,* VII, 519.

34. *Bekentenisse Obbe Philipsz. . ., BRN,* VII, 105, 122-124; In English: *A Confession* by Obbe Philips, *LCC,* 208-210; E. Kochs, *op. cit.,* III, 71 ff.

35. "Gespräch mit Karl Barth" in *Stimme,* 15. Dez., 1963, 15. Jhrg. 753 f.

36. E. Kochs, *op. cit.,* III, 7 5f.; Rollin S. Armour, *Anabaptist Baptism* (Scottdale, Pa. 1967) constitutes the first comprehensive study of the subject.

37. E. Kochs, *op. cit.,* I, Vol. 19, chapter "Quellen und ihre Bearbeitung" 109-137; See also E. Meiners, *op. cit.,* I, 31-47.

38. *A Confession* by Obbe Philips in *LCC,* XXV, 206-225; See also preface by S. Cramer, *Bekentenisse Obbe Philipsz, BRN,* VII, 91-108 and K. Vos, "Obbe Philipsz," *DB* (Leiden, 1917), 124-138.

39. See *The Ordinance of God* and the Introduction by G. H. Williams, *LCC,* XXV, 182 f., 184 ff.

40. C. A. Cornelius, *Geschichte . . .,* II, 294 ff., 404 f.; N. van der Zijpp, "Jan Vol-kertsz Trypmaker," *ME,* III, 84.

41. A. F. Mellink, *De Wederdopers . . .,* 144, 163, 241, 348; K. Vos, "Sicke Freerks" in *ME,* IV, 523.

42. Cornelius Krahn, *Menno Simons . . .,* (Karlsruhe, 1926), 22-24.

43. Obbe Philips, *op. cit., BRN,* VII, 123 f.; *LCC,* XXV, 209; E. Kochs, *op. cit.,* III, 76 and footnotes.

44. F. O. zur Linden, *op. cit.,* 257 f. He uses a testimony of Katharina Seid assuming that it took place on Nov. 23, 1534, which according to *Elsass II.* 310 line 24 ff. was not the date. Thus his chief argument for Hofmann's early return is invalidated.

45. C. A. Cornelius, *Geschichte . . .,* II, Beilage X, 295.

46. *Ibid.,* 404.

47. *Honderd jaren uit de geschiedenis der Hervorming en der Hervormde kerk in Friesland* (Leeuwarden, 1876), 41. Was repeated by K. Vos, *Menno Simons,* (Leiden, 1914), 27; A. F. Mellink, *op. cit.,* 241.

48. *Groot Placaat- en Charterboek van Vriesland* II, 650 ff.

49. Obbe Philips, *op. cit., BRN,* VII, 124; *LCC,* XXV, 210.

50. *Elsass* I, 354, Nr. 279 and 355, Nr. 280.

51. *Ibid.* I, 411 f. Nr. 298; *Von der wahren hochprächtlichen einigen maijestat Gottes und der wahrhaftigen menschwerdung des ewigen worts und des sohns des Allerhögsten.* See also W. I. Leendertz, *op. cit.,* 255 ff.

52. *Elsass* I, 411 f. Nr. 298: *Das freudenreiche zeucknus vam worren friderichen ewigen evangelion . . .;* See also: F. O. zur Linden, *op. cit.,* 278-282, 429-432; W. I. Leendertz, *op. cit.,* 252-255.

53. *Elsass* I, 553, Nr. 336.

54. *Ibid.,* II, 120, No. 407.

55. *Ibid.,* II, 14, No. 363.

56. W. I. Leendertz, *op. cit.,* 275 f.; G. H. Williams, *op. cit.,* 277.

57. G. H. Williams, *op. cit.,* 234-298.

58. *A Confession, LCC,* XXV, 209 f.

59. *Elsass* I, 327 ff. No. 244; 575 ff. No. 348; II, 3, No. 357.

60. G. H. Williams, *op. cit.,* 279 ff.; *Elsass* II, ff., No. 358; 25 f., No. 371.

61. *Elsass* II, 14 f., No. 364; 16, No. 266.

62. *Ibid.,* 17-20, No. 368.

63. *Ibid.,* II, 16, No. 356; 70-90, No. 384.

64. *Ibid.,* II, 79, No. 385; 100 f., No. 398.

65. *Ibid.,* II, 111-116, No. 402.

66. *Ibid.,* 117, No. 403.

67. *Ibid.,* 116, W. F. Dankbaar, *Martin Bucers Beziehungen zu den Niederlanden* ('s-Gravenhage, 1961), 16 f.

68. *Elsass* II, 116 f.

69. *Ibid.,* II, 298 ff., No. 533; I, 333, No. 249.

70. *Ibid.,* II, 33, No. 372.

71. *Ibid.,* II, 222, No. 471; 130 f., No. 420. See particularly the letters of Bucer about Hofmann in W. I. Leendertz, *op. cit.,* 354-359.

72. Elsass II, 93, No. 390; 98, No. 395.

73. *Ibid.,* II, 100 f., No. 398; 110 f., No. 400; 233, No. 477, 477a.

74. W. I. Leendertz, *op. cit.,* 354-358.

75. *Ibid.,* 359 f.

76. *Corpus Schwenckfeldianorum* IV, 835; W. I. Leendertz, *op. cit.,* 359 f.; *Elsass* II, 110, No. 400.

77. *Elsass* II, 182-193, No. 444. See also 177-181, No. 441.

78. *Ibid.,* II, 133, No. 424; 203, No. 451; 255-257. Nos. 484, 485; 309, No. 546; 370 f., 594.

79 *Ibid.,* II, 386, No. 607; 393-395, No. 617; 444 f., No. 654; 457, No. 669.

80. *Ibid.,* II, 470, No. 684; 480-484, No. 699, 700.

81. *Ibid.,* II, 134, No. 428.

82. *Ibid.,* II, 204, No. 452; 221, No. 468; 222, No. 471.

83. Obbe Philips, *op. cit., LCC,* XXV, 210; *Elsass* II, 212-215, Nos. 461, 462; 218, No. 466; 221, No. 468; 241, No. 479; Kühler, 66 ff.; E. W. Kohls, "Ein Sendbrief Melchior Hofmanns aus dem Jahre 1534" in *ThZ,* XVII, Heft 5, Sept.-Oct., (1961), 356-465.

84. *Elsass* II, 453, No. 665.

85. G. H. Williams, *op. cit.,* 254-277; J. J. Kiwiet, *Pilgram Marbeck* (Kassel, 1957), 47-51; F. H. Littell, *The Anabaptist View of the Church* (Boston, 1958), 24 ff.

86. See their treatment during and after the synod.

87. *Elsass* II, 198, No. 168; J. J. Kiwiet, *op. cit.,* 42, 49, 84 ff.; K. Vos, "Wat zijn bondgenooten!" in *DB* (vol. 54, 1917), 82-88.

88. *Elsass,* I, 486 f., No. 302.

89. L. Verheus, *Kroniek en kerygma. Een theologische studie over Geschichtbibel van Sebastiaan Franck . . .* (Arnhem, 1958) 41 ff.; Walter Nigg, *Das ewige Reich. Geschichte einer Sehnsucht und einer Enttäuschung* (Zürich: Eugen Rentsch Verlag, 1944), 215 ff.

90. E. Hirsch, *Die Reichgottesbegriffe des neueren europäischen Denkens* (1921), 7; Walter Nigg, *op. cit.,* 221.

91. Walter Nigg, *op. cit.,* 226.

92. *Ibid.,* 232, 267; Franz Lau, *Luthers Lehre von den beiden Reichen* (Berlin, 1953; Friedrich Gogarten, "Die Lehre von den zwei Reichen und das natürliche Gesetz," *Deutsche Theologie* (Stuttgart, 1935); Gustaf Törnvall, *Geistliches und weltliches Regiment bei Luther. Studien zu Luthers Weltbild und Gesellschaftsverständnis* (Munich, 1947); Karl Barth, "Evangelium und Gesetz," *Theol. Existenz heute.* Heft 32 (Munich, 1935); Heinrich Bornkamm, *Luthers Lehre von den zwei Reichen im Zusammenhang seiner Theologie* (Gütersloh: Gerd Mohn, 1960); Harold Diem, *Luthers Lehre von den zwei Reichen, untersucht von seinem Verständnis der Bergpredigt* (1938); P. Althaus, "Luthers Lehre von den zwei Reichen im Feuer der Kritik," *Lutherjahrbuch* 24 (1957); Luther's view of the "two kingdoms" (*zwei Reiche*) has received much attention since World War I. We name only a few studies.

93. C. A. Cornelius, *Geschichte* II, 223 ff. The most detailed and most recent systematic presentation of Hofmann's views in general and his eschatological interpretation was presented by Peter Kawerau, *op. cit.,* in the chapter "Geist und Geschichte," 75-114.
94. *Elsass* II, 118. Bucer's concern in his dealings with the Anabaptists and his relationship to the city council and the attitude of the Anabaptists toward the latter have been treated in the following writings: H. Bornkamm, *Martin Bucers Bedeutung für die europäische Reformationsgeschichte* (Gütersloh, 1914), 33-42; B. Moeller, *Reichstadt und Reformation* Gütersloh, 1962), 43 ff.; R. Kreider, "The Anabaptists and the Civil Authorities of Strassbourg, 1525-1555," in *Church History.* Vol. XXIV, No. 2, (June, 1955), 99-118; H. Hermelink, *Der Toleranzgedanke im Reformationszeitalter VfR* (Leipzig, 1908).

V. ANABAPTISM AT THE CROSSROADS

1. J. G. de Hoop Scheffer, *Geschiedenis der Kerkhervorming in Nederland van haar ontstaan tot 1531* (Amsterdam, 1873) 3; J. Lindeboom, *De confessioneele ontwikkeling der reformatie in de Nederlanden* (The Hague, 1946) 31 f. (See footnote).
2. J. Lindeboom, *op. cit.,* 31 ff.
3. C. A. Cornelius, *Geschichte* . . . II, 404 f., 407, 409; K. Vos, "Kleine bijdragen . . .," *DB* (1917) 159 f.
4. C. A. Cornelius, *op. cit.,* II, 404; G. Grosheide, *Verhooren en vonnissen . . .,* 94-105.
5. K. Vos, *op. cit.,* 98 ff.; A. F. Mellink, *De Wederdopers,* 34.
6. G. Grosheide, *Bijdrage tot de Geschiedenis der Anabaptisten in Amsterdam* (Hilversum, 1938) 94 f.
7. Obbe Philips, *A Confession, LCC,* XXV, 210; *Groot Placaat- en Charterboek van Vriesland* II, 650 ff.; Menno Simons, *CW.* 668 f.; G. Grosheide, *Verhooren en vonnissen . . .,* 95.
8. Joseph Niesert, *Münsterische Urkundensammlung* (Coesfeld, 1826), 297; G. Grosheide, *op. cit.,* 97.
9. *Elsass* II, 204, No. 452; 207, No. 455; 299, No. 533.
10. Jack W. Porter, "Bernhard Rothmann 1495-1535, Royal Orator of the Münster Anabaptist Kingdom" (Ph. D., University of Wisconsin, 1964). See article, "Bernhard Rothmann," *ME,* IV, 367-370.
11. Cornelius Krahn, "Münster Anabaptists," *ME,* III, 777 ff.; Heinrich Detmer, "Das Religionsgespräch zu Münster (Westf.) am 7. and 8. August, 1533. Ein Beitrag zur Geschichte B. Rothmann's . . ." *Monatshefte der Comenius Gesellschaft,* IX (1900) 273-300; Reprint of *Bekentnisse* in H. Detmer and R. Krumbholtz, *Zwei Schriften des Münsterischen Wiedertäufers Bernhard Rothmann* (Dortmund, 1904) 1-85; Lowell H. Zuck, "Anabaptist Revolution Through the Covenant in the Sixteenth Century Continental Protestantism," (Ph. D., Yale University, 1954) 72-85.
12. *Elsass* II, 286-291, No. 519; Pilgram Marbeck, *Vermahnung . . .* in *Gedenkschrift zum 400 jähr. Jubiläum der Mennoniten* (Ludwigshafen, 1925) 178-282; Frank J. Wray, "The 'Vermanung' of 1542 and Rothmann's 'Bekenntnisse'," *ARG,* XLVII, (1956 Heft 2), 243-251; William Klassen, *ME,* IV, 368-370.
13. C. A. Cornelius, *op. cit.,* 386 f.; A. F. Mellink, *op. cit.,* 156 f.
14. Mellink, *op. cit.,* 157.
15 C. A. Cornelius, *op. cit.,* 385 f; 388 f.
16. Mellink, *op. cit.,* 102 ff.; 156 ff.; 164-175.
17. "IJselstein," *ME,* III, f; "Utrecht," *ME,* IV, 792.
18. A. F. Mellink, *op. cit.,* 210 ff.
19. C. A. Cornelius, *Berichte der Augenzeugen über das Münsterische Wiedertäuferreich*

(Münster, 1852) 370; A. F. Mellink, *op. cit.*, 228 f., 222 f.; K. Vos, "Kleine bijdragen,"
DB (1917) 108 f.

20. A. L. E. Verheyden, *Anabaptism in Flanders* (Scottdale, Pa., 1961) 15-17.

21. A. F. Mellink, "Antwerpen als Anabaptistencentrum tot 1550," *NAK*, XLVI, Afl.
3, (1963-64), 155-161; K. Vos, "De Doopsgezinden te Antwerpen in de zestiende eeuw"
(Brussel, 1920) 316 ff.; *Bulletin de la Commission Royale d'Histoire de Belgique,* Vol.
LXXXIV.

22. C. A. Cornelius, *Geschichte* ... II, 229.

23. C. A. Cornelius, *op. cit.,* II, 234 ff., 386; G. Grosheide, *Bijdrage* ..., 95 ff; 235 ff.

24. Menno Simons, *CW,* 81; Opera, 174 f.

25. Gustav Bossert, *Quellen zur Geschichte der Wiedertäufer.* Vol. I, *Herzogtum Würt-
temberg* (Leipzig, 1930) 3-5; Hans H. Th. Stiasny, *Die strafrechtliche Verfolgung der
Täufer* ... 110 ff.

26. Horst W. Schraepler, *Die rechtliche Behandlung der Täufer in der deutschen
Schweiz, Süddeutschland und Hessen* (Weierhof, 1957) 16 ff.

27. "Sicke Freerks," *ME,* IV, 523; Menno Simons, *CW.,* 668 f.; C. A. Cornelius, *op.
cit.,* II, 386 f.

28. Obbe Philips, *A Confession, LCC,* XXV, 211; C. A. Cornelius, *Berichte der Augenzeugen über das Münsterische Wiedertäuferreich* (Münster, 1853) 370, 399; Joseph Niesert,
Münsterische Urkundensammlung (Coesfeld, 1826), 175; C. A. Cornelius, *Geschichte* ...;
B. N. Krohn, *Geschichte der fanatischen und enthusiastischen Wiedertäufer* (Leipzig,
1758).

29. C. A. Cornelius, *Berichte* ..., 370 ff.; J. Niesert, *op. cit.,* I, 175 f.

30. Karl-Heinz Kirchhoff, "Die Täufer im Münsterland," *WZ,* Vol. 113 (1963), 8;
J. de Hullu, *Bescheiden betreffende de Hervorming in Overijssel* (Deventer, 1899) 222
ff.; A. F. Mellink, *op. cit.,* 26 ff.

31. C. A. Cornelius, *op. cit.,* 370 f.; C. A. Cornelius, *Geschichte* ..., II, 345 f.

32. Karl-Heinz Kirchhoff, "Die Belagerung und Eroberung Münsters 1534/35," *WZ,*
Vol. 112 (1962), 78 f.

33. Karl-Heinz Kirchhoff, "Die Täufer im Münsterland," *WZ,* Vol. 113 (1963) 17 f.;
Joseph Niesert, *op. cit.,* I, 6 f.

34. Gerhard de Buhr, "Der Wiedertäufer Heinrich Krechting and seine Sippe"; Karl-
Heinz Kirchhoff, *op. cit.,* 21-25.

35. Joseph Niesert, *op. cit.,* I, 123, 154 ff.; Karl-Heinz Kirchhoff, *op. cit.,* 21 f.

36. Hermann Kerssenbroch, *Anabaptistici furoris Monasterium inclitam Westphaliae
metropolim evertentis historica narratio* (Münster, 1899), II, 509 f., 576, 850; Karl-Heinz
Kirchhoff, *op. cit.,* 23-26.

37. W. J. Kühler, *Geschiedenis der Nederlandsche Doopsgezinden in de zestiende
eeuw* I (Haarlem, 1932) 127 f.; C. A. Cornelius, *Berichte* ..., I, iii, Hermann Kerssenbroch, *op. cit.,* II, 703, 708.

38. *Bekentones des globens* ... is found in reprint in C. A. Cornelius, *Berichte,* I, 445-
464; Philip of Hesse sent three copies of a reprint of the *Bekentones* as well as a copy
of his correspondence with the Münsterites, (*Elsass* II, 433) to the city council of
Strassburg. In A. Corvinus *Acta: Handlungen: Legation und schriffte* ... (1536) a
writing of Philip of Hesse is reprinted which was a response to a letter by the Münsterites dated March 25, 1534, and a booklet entitled *Van der Verborgenheit der schrifft* ...,
which was followed by a refutation of the writing by Philip's *predikanten.* Philip's chief
argument is that all government is from God and that the Münsterites have violated
God's order by driving out of Münster the government established by God and have
established their own. After this follows a refutation of the Anabaptist theological views
(C i). About additional exchanges between the Münsterites and Philip of Hesse see
K. W. Bouterwek, *op. cit.,* 41.

39. Karl-Heinz Kirchhoff, *op. cit.,* 28, 30, 34, 35; Clemens Löffler, *Die Wiedertäufer
zu Münster 1534/35* (Jena, 1923) 86-88, 98-100.

40. *Eyne Restitution/edder Eine wedderstellinge rechter vndde gesunder/Christliker leer, gelouens vnde leuens vth/Gades genaden durch de gemeinte Christi tho Münster an den dach gegeuenn.* Actor. iij. Cap. . . . Reprint in *Flugschriften aus der Reformationszeit* VII, in *Neudrucke deutscher Literaturwerke des XV und XVI Jhr.* 77/78 (Halle, 1888).

41. *Eyn gantz troestlick bericht van der Wrake vnde straffe des Babilonischen gruwels, an alle ware Israeliten und Bundtgenoten Christi, his unde dar vorstroyet, durch die gemeite Christi tho Munster.* Anno 1534 vy Decembre. Reprinted by K. W. Bouterwek, *Zur Literatur und Geschichte der Wiedertäufer* (Bonn, 1864) 66-80; and in *Der linke Flügel der Reformation* (Bremen, 1962) 342-360.

42. C. A. Cornelius, *Berichte* I, 44 ff.; Hermann Kerssenbroch, *op. cit.,* II, 605.

43. Jack W. Porter, "Bernhard Rothmann 1495-1535. Royal Orator of the Münster Anabaptist Kingdom" (Ph. D. dissertation, 1964) IV f.

44. Hermann Kerssenbroch, *op. cit.,* II, 573, 577-586.

45. Hans Ritschl, *Die Kommune der Wiedertäufer in Münster* (Bonn, 1923) 45; Hans Schubert, *Der Kommunismus der Wiedertäufer in Münster und seine Quellen* (Heidelberg, 1919) 5 f.

46. Hans Ritschl, *op. cit.,* 29-32.

47. *Ibid.,* 31 f., 34 ff., 41 f.; B. Rothmann, *Restitution . . .* 71 (Footnote 40).

48. Ludwig Keller, *Geschichte der Wiedertäufer und ihres Reichs zu Münster* (Münster, 1880) 210; Hans Ritschl, *op. cit.,* 43.

49. Genesis 1:28; Bernhard Rothmann, *Restitution . . .* 75, 81, 85; Karl Kautsky, *Vorläufer des neueren Sozialismus* (Berlin, 1947) II, 251 ff.

50. I Corinthians 11:3; Hans Ritschl, *op. cit.,* 48 ff.

51. Hermann Kerssenbroch, *op. cit.,* II, 650 ff.; Clemens Löffler, *op. cit.,* 124 ff; Cornelius Krahn, "Münster," *ME,* IV, 779.

52. W. J. Kühler, *op. cit.,* I, 93 ff.

53. J. de Hullu, *Bescheiden betreffende de Hervorming in Overijssel,* I, Deventer, 1522-1546 (Deventer, 1899) 153 f.

54. A. F. Mellink, *op. cit.,* 31 ff.; J. Wagenaar, *Amsterdam in zijn opkomst . . .* I (Amsterdam, 1760) 237.

55. W. J. Kühler, *op. cit.,* I, 95; C. A. Cornelius, *Augenzeugen . . .* 226.

56. J. de Hullu, *op cit.,* 155 f., 159, 161; Ludwig Keller, *op. cit.,* 311; W. J. Kühler, *op. cit.,* 109 f.

57. K. Vos, *op. cit.,* 151; Obbe Philips, *op. cit.,* 216 f., 219; W. J. Kühler, *op. cit.,* 106 f.

58. Melchior Hofmann, "The Ordinance of God," *LCC,* XXV, 191; C. A. Cornelius, *Historische Arbeiten . . .* 87 f.; W. J. Kühler, I, 176 ff. The Doukhobors of Canada express protests similarly.

59. Bernhard Rothmann, *Eyn gantz troestlick bericht van der Wrake . . .* published by K. W. Bouterwek in *Zur Literatur und Geschichte der Wiedertäufer besonders in den Rheinlanden* (Bonn, 1864). *Ein ganz tröstlicher Bericht von der Rache . . .* edited by H. Fast in *Klassiker des Protestantismus,* IV, *LFR* (Bremen, 1962), 343, 351, 357, 360.

60. J. de Hullu, *op. cit.,* 211 ff.; G. Grosheide, *Verhooren en vonnissen . . .* 96, 102.

61. W. J. Kühler, *op. cit.,* 139 f.; J. de Hullu, *op. cit.,* 180 ff., 211 ff.

62. K. W. Bouterwek, *op. cit.,* 91-109; W. J. Kühler, *op. cit.,* I, 149 ff.

63. G. Grosheide, *Verhooren en vonnissen . . .* 12 ff., 17 f., 94-104.

64. "Jan van Geelen," *ME,* III, 74.

65. Cornelius Krahn, *Menno Simons (1495-1561). Ein Beitrag zur Geschichte und Theologie der Taufgesinnten* (Karlsruhe, 1936) 27-30; Menno Simons, *CW,* 670 f.; Menno Simons, *Fundament* (1538) R iiij.

66. Menno Simons, *CW,* 671; 32-50; Cornelius Krahn, *op. cit.,* 30-32.

67. W. J. Kühler, *op. cit.,* I, 171 ff.; G. Grosheide, *op. cit.,* 104 f.; A. F. Mellink, *op. cit.,* 82 ff.

68. A part of a dissertation at the University of Münster published in *WZ,* Vol. 112

(Münster, 1962) 77-170.

69. Karl-Heinz Kirchhoff, *Die Belagerung . . .*, 166.

70. C. A. Cornelius, *Berichte . . .* II, 233, 239, 260; Karl-Heinz Kirchhof, *op. cit.,* 78, 80-87.

71 *Ibid.,* 88 f.; Friedrich Krapf, "Landgraf Philipp der Grossmütige von Hessen und die Religionskämpfe im Bistum Münster 1532-1536 (Ph. D. dissertation, Marburg, 1951) 95; Ludwig Keller, *op. cit.,* 302 f.

72. Friedrich Krapf, *op. cit.,* 152 ff.; Ludwig Keller, *op. cit.,* 251.

73. C. A. Cornelius, *Berichte der Augenzeugen* I, 56 f., 59; II, 252; Th. Volbehr, *Zur Geschichte der Münsterischen Unruhen* (Nürnberg, 1888) 97-101; Friedrich Krapf, *op. cit.,* 189, 192 ff., 199 f.; Ludwig Keller, *op. cit.,* 280 f; Karl-Heinz Kirchhoff, *op. cit.,* 101 ff.; 119.

74. Karl-Heinz Kirchhoff, *op. cit.,* 129 f., 136; Ludwig Keller, *op. cit.,* 267 ff.

75. Karl-Heinz Kirchhoff, *op. cit.,* 137, 141.

76. Hermann Kerssenbroch, *op. cit.,* II, 805 ff., 812 f.; Joseph Niesert, *op. cit.,* I, 197 ff, 431 ff, 437 ff.; C. A. Cornelius, *op. cit.,* I, 172, 190-197; II, 324, 346, 349 ff.; 357; Karl-Heinz Kirchhoff, *op. cit.,* 135-140.

77. Hermann Kerssenbroch, *op. cit.,* II, 700, 736, 833-856; C. A. Cornelius, *op. cit.,* II, 359 ff, 366 ff., 383 f.; Karl-Heinz Kirchhoff, *op. cit.,* 141-144; Gerhard de Buhr, *op. cit.*

78. Heinrich Detmer, *Bilder aus den religösen und sozialen Unruhen in Münster während des 16. Jahrhunderts.* II. *Bernhard Rothmann.* (Münster, 1904) 144 ff.; Hermann Kerssenbroch, *op. cit.,* II, 842 ff. Some claimed that Rothmann escaped to Oldenburg. Batenburg list in J. de Hulle, *op. cit.,* 256 *(dooper Bernardus).*

79. Hermann Kerssenbroch, *op. cit.,* II, 852 ff.; C. A. Cornelius, *op. cit.,* II, 358 f.; Karl-Heinz Kirchhoff, *op. cit.,* 144 ff.

80. Antonius Corvinus, *Acta: Handlungen: Legation und schriffte: . . . Gespreche und disputation Antonij Coruini und Joannis Kymei mit den Münsterschen König/mit Knipperdölling und Krechting . . .* (1536), c.ff.

81. *Ibid.,* f-f iij; g iij.

82. *Elsass* II, 480 f. Nos. 699, 700; 412, No. 627; 470 f., No. 684-685.

83. *Ibid.,* II, 395, No. 617; "Konrad van Bühel," *ME,* I, 464 f.

84. C. A. Cornelius, *Berichte der Augenzeugen,* II, 398-410.

85. Hermann Kerssenbroch, *op. cit.,* I, 344-346; II, 869-876; Ludwig Keller, *op. cit.,* 287-289.

86. Since the Marxian revolution, this phase of Anabaptism has found great interest among Marxian scholars. An example is Gerhard Brendler *Das Täuferreich zu Münster,* 1534/35 (Berlin 1966) who devotes seventy pages to a critical historiography of the Münsterite Anabaptists and furnishes a helpful and extensive bibliography which includes Russian and other eastern publications on the subject (see review in *Mennonite Life,* July, 1967). For bibliography see also "Münster Anabaptists," *ME,* III, 779 ff. and P. Bahlmann, "Die Wiedertäufer zu Münster" in *Zeitschrift für vaterländische Geschichte und Altertumskunde,* LI (Münster, 1893).

VI. GATHERING A CHRISTIAN FELLOWSHIP

1. Nicolaus Blesdicius, *Historia vitae, doctrinae ac rerum Davidis Georgii* (Deventer, 1642) 13 ff.; B. N. Krohn, *Geschichte der Fanatischen und Enthusiastischen Wiedertäufer . . .* (Leipzig, 1758) 328 ff.; W. J. Kühler, *Geschiedenis der Nederlandsche Doopsgezinden in de zestiende eeuw* I (Haarlem, 1932) 200 ff.

2 Karl-Heinz Kirchhoff, "Die Täufer im Münsterland," *op. cit.,* 60 ff.

3. *Ibid.*, 65 ff.; A. F. Mellink, "Groningse Wederdopers te Münster (1538)" *NAK*, XLIV, Afl. 2, 1960, 87-100.

4. Ludwig Keller, *Die Gegenreformation in Westfalen und am Niederrhein...* (Leipzig, 1887) II, 390 ff.; Cornelius Krahn, "Anabaptism in Westphalia," *MQR* (October, 1961) 282-285.

5. J. de Hullu, *Bescheiden betreffende de Hervorming in Overijssel. I, Deventer (1522-1546)*. (Deventer, 1899), 256.

6. Karl-Heinz Kirchhoff, *op. cit.*, 88 f.

7. Cornelius Krahn, "Hinrich Krechting," *ME*, III, 234 f.; Gerhard de Buhr, "Hinrich Krechting, der 'Kanzler' der Münsterischen Wiedertäufer," *Ostfriesische Familienkunde*, Heft 1, 1960.

8. Karl-Heinz Kirchhoff, *op. cit.*, 64; J. de Hullu, *op. cit.*, 246-252.

9. Menno Simons, *Opera*, 64; *CW*, 215.

10. Menno Simons, *Dat Fundament des Christelycken leers...* (1539) R 7. See also Krahn, *Menno Simons...* (1936) 52-55; K. Vos, *Menno Simons* (1914), 274; John Horsch, *Menno Simons* (1916) 274; Menno Simons, *Opera*, 2, gives reasons for revision.

11. B. Spiegel, *A. R. Hardenberg* (1869) 117; Cornelius Krahn, *Menno Simons*, 16 ff.

12. He could have read Luther's *Von der Menschenlehre zu meiden...* (1521). See *Luther's Werke* (Weimar ed.), Vol. 10, II. Abt. 72-92. Krahn, *op. cit.*, 41 ff.; Kronenberg, "Uitgaven van Luther in de Nederlanden...", 14, No. 56.

13. This account is primarily based on Menno's report, one of the most significant sources of his inner development. It is a part of *A Plain Reply to a Publication by Gellius Faber* (1554). The latter had questioned Menno's calling and this is his reply. Menno Simons, *Opera Omnia*, 256-259, *CW*, 668-671.

14. "Foundation," *ME*, II, 358; Cornelius Krahn, *op. cit.*, 48-55, (Original Dutch titles); Menno Simons, *Dat Fundament des Christelycken leers...* (N. p. 1538); Menno Simons, *CW*, 67-226.

15. Menno Simons, *CW*, 671 f.; *BRN*, VII (ordination 45, 47, 98, 118, 136); (baptism 272, 362, 461); Obbe Philips, *A Confession, LCC*, 223 f.

16. *CW*, 672.

17. Obbe Philips, *op. cit.*, 222 f.; J. ten Doornkaat Koolman, *Dirk Philips*, 10; "David Joris," *ME*, II, 17.

18. K. Vos, *op. cit.*, 256; Menno Simons, *CW*, 761; Obbe Philips, *op. cit.*, 204-235; "Obbe Philips," *ME*, IV, 10; J. C. Burgmann, *Commentatio Historio-ecclesiastica. De Ubbone Philippi et Ubbonitis* (Rostock, 1775). See chapter VII, 4 in this book.

19. Menno Simons, *CW*, 761.

20. *Ibid.*, 524.

21. Cornelius Krahn, "Menno Simons," *ME*, III, 579 f.; A. F. Mellink, *op. cit.*, 393 f.

22. J. S. Theissen, *De regering van Karel V in de noordelijke Nederlanden* (1912) 116, 186; S. Blaupot ten Cate, *Geschiedenis der Doopsgezinden in Groningen, Overijssel en Oost-Friesland* (Leeuwarden and Groningen, 1842) II, 167 ff; J. ten Doornkaat Koolman, *op. cit.*, 17 ff.

23. Gerhard Ohling, *Junker Ulrich von Dornum...* (Aurich, 1965) 16 f., 21 f., 25-28.

24. *Ibid.*, 16, 24, 26 f., 28.

25. Gerhard Ohling, "Aus den Anfängen der Reformation. Ein Brief des Sebastian Franck aus Donauwörth an die Oldersumer Gemeinde," *Ostfriesland* (Norden, 1954).

26. J. ten Doornkaat Koolman, "Joachim Kükenbieter (Nossiophagus), ein lutherischer Eiferer des Reformationszeitalters," *NAK*, XLIV, Afl. 3 (1961) 161 f.

27. J. J. Boer, *Ubbo Emmius en Ost-Friesland* (Groningen, 1936) 5 ff.; C. A. Cornelius, *Der Antheil...* 39-45.

28. Hermann Dalton, *Johannes a Lasco. Beitrag zur Reformationsgeschichte Polens, Deutschlands und Englands* (Gotha, 1881) 208 ff., 217, 223-231.

29. Hermann Dalton, *op. cit.*, 247 ff.; J. a Lasco, *Opera tam edita quam inedita recensuit vitam auctoris*. Ed. by A. Kuiper (Amsterdam, 1866) 574; See also K. A. R. Kruske, *Johannes a Lasco und der Sakramentsstreit* (Leipzig, 1901) 58 f.

30. J. P. Miller, *Die Mennoniten in Ostfriesland vom 16. bis zum 18. Jahrhundert* (Amsterdam, 1887) 19 ff.

31. Heinold Fast, *Heinrich Bullinger und die Täufer* (Weierhof, 1959) 48 ff; J. ten Doornkaat Koolman, "De Anabaptisten in Oostfriesland ten tijde van Hermannus Aquilomontanus (1489-1548)" *NAK*, XLVI, Afl. 2 (1963-64) 88 ff.

32. Eduard Meiners, *Oostvrieschlandts Kerkelijke Geschiedenisse* . . . I, 261-75; Johannis a Lasco, *Opera* . . . II, 566-68; N. M. Blesdijk, *Historia* . . . (1642) 137; Fr. Nippold, "David Joris von Delft," *Zeitschrift für hist. Theologie* (1863) 149-62.

33. Eduard Meiners, *op. cit.*, I, 254-61; Menno Simons, *Opera*, 519; *CW*, 422; Marten Micron, *Een waeraechtigh verhaal der t'zammensprekinghe tusschen Menno Simons en Martinus Mikron* . . . (1556) 53; J. H. Gerretsen, *Micronius* . . . (Nijmegen, 1895) 48 (footnote 1 refers to the Latin edition of Menno's book published by the Emden ministers)

34. Menno Simons, *CW*, 419-54; *Opera*, 517-42; *Een Corte ende clare Belijdinghe ende Schriftlijcke aenwijsinge/Ten eersten van der Menschwerdinge ons liefs Heeren Jesus Christi* . . . (n. p., 1544); J. a Lasco, *Opera*, I, 1-60.

35. *Een klare onwederspreekelyke bekentenisse en aenwysinge* . . . (1554) *Opera* 351-82; *The Incarnation of Our Lord*, *CW*, 783-834.

36. W. J. Kühler, *Geschiedenis* . . . I, 387-94; G. H. Williams, *op. cit.*, 477-82; Fr. Nippold, "Heinrich Niclaes und das Haus der Liebe," *Zeitschr. für hist. Theologie*, XXXII (1862) 321-402.

37. J. P. Müller, *op. cit.*, I, 22 ff.; Eduard Meiners, *op. cit.*, I, 275 f.; J. a Lasco, *op. cit.*, II, 574.

38. J. P. Müller, I., *op. cit.*, 24 f. (footnote 39); Eduard Meiners, *op. cit.* I, 291-93.

39. Hermann Dalton, *op. cit.*, 292 ff., 307 ff.

40. Menno Simons, *Opera*, 234; *CW*, 634.

41. *BRN*, VII, 50 f; K. Vos, *op. cit.*, 256; J. H. Ottius, *Annales Anabaptistici* . . . 99, 109.

42. G. Grosheide, *Bijdrage* . . . 252-56; "Gillis van Aken," *De Tijdspiegel*, Vol. 62, No. 8 (1905) 355-371; "Antonius von Köln," *ME*, I, 133 f.

43. K. Vos, "Bekentenis van Teunis van Hastenrath," *DB* (1909) 120-26; K. Vos, "Martelaars uit Gelderland (1550)" *NAK*, X, (1913) 252-68.

44. K. Vos, "Martelaars . . .", 253, 257, 260 ff.

45. G. Grosheide, *Bijdrage* . . . 252-56; "Gillis van Aken," *ME*, II, 518 f.; K. Vos, *op. cit.*, 95 ff.; K. Vos, "Gillis van Aken," *De Tijdspiegel*, Vol. 62, No. 8 (1905) 355-371; "Antonius von Köln," *ME*, I, 133 f.

46. G. F. G. Goeters, "Die Rolle des Täufertums in der Reformationsgeschichte des Niederrheins," *Rheinische Vierteljahrsblätter*, (Jahrg. 24, Heft 3/4, 1959) 221, 226 f., 229, 235 f.

47. Otto R. Redlich, *Jülich-Bergische Kirchenpolitik* (Bonn, 1907) I, 259.

48. Christiaan Sepp, "Henrick Rol," *Kerkhistorische Studiën* (Leiden, 1885) 1-90; "Henric Rol," *ME*, II, 704 f.; "Gerhard Westerburg," *ME*, IV, 930 f.

49. Hans H. Th. Stiasny, *Die strafrechtliche Verfolgung der Täufer in der Freien Reichsstadt Köln 1529 bis 1618* (Münster, 1962) 4 f., 9 f.

50. G. F. G. Goeters, *op. cit.*, 227.

51. J. a Lasco, *Opera*, II, 476; "Sed scio Mennonem versari nunc potassimum in episcopatu Coloniensi et fucum facere multis"; Karl Rembert, *op. cit.*, 499, footnote 1: ". . . Simone Mennone ne qui ex agrario Pastore factus Episcopus sectarium omnes nobis Ecclesias in his regionibus inquinavit . . ."

52. Cornelius Krahn, *Menno Simons*, (1936), 94 f.; Karl Rembert, *op. cit.*, 476.

53. Cornelius Krahn, *op. cit.*, 64 f.; Menno Simons, *Opera*, 235, *CW*, 635 f.

54. J. F. G. Goeters, "Das älteste rheinische Täuferbekenntnis," *A Legacy of Faith*, ed. by C. J. Dyck (Newton, 1962) 197-212.

55. Günther Franz, *Quellen zur Geschichte des Bauernkrieges* (München, 1963) 193, 195, 523, 532; George H. Williams, *op. cit.*, 161.

56. Ph. D. dissertation (Yale, 1954) "Summary."; John S. Oyer, *Lutheran Reformers against Anabaptists* (The Hague, 1964) 106 ff.

57. "Studien zur Entstehung der sozialen Ideen des Täufertums in den ersten Jahren der Reformation." Ph. D. dissertation (Freiburg, 1932) 21 ff., 35 ff. Manfred Benzing, *Thomas Müntzer und der Thüringer Aufstand, 1525* (Berlin, 1966) 36-62; Hans-Jürgen Goertz, *Innere und äussere Ordnung in der Theologie Thomas Müntzers* (Leiden, 1967).

58. *Elsass* I, 197 ff., No. 168.

59. Balthasar Hubmaier, *Schriften* (Gütersloh, 1962) 219. See also 26 f., 300.

60. Hans Denck, *Schriften* II, 24 f., 62, 82; Regarding Denck's dependence on Müntzer see Walter Fellmann "Theological Views of Hans Denck," *ML* (January, 1963) 44; John S. Oyer, op. cit., 111 f.

61. *LCC*, XXV, 186 f., 190.

62. K. Vos, "Kleine bijdragen," *DB* (1917) 85-87.

63. *Opera*, 621; *CW*, 34.

64. K. Vos, *op. cit.*, 87.

65. Zuck, *op. cit.*, "Summary."

66. Th. J. van Bracht, *Martyrs Mirror* (1950) 21; Cornelius Krahn, "Menno Simons' Concept of the Church," *A Legacy of Faith*, 29 f.; S. Hoekstra, Bz., *Beginselen en leer der oude Doopsgezinden*... (Amsterdam, 1863) 164-190.

67. *Ibid., Opera*, 392a, *CW*, 1055; "Danzig Church Record," Bethel College Historical Library.

68. J. ten Doornkaat Koolman, *Dirk Philips* (Haarlem, 1964) 97 ff., 193 ff.; Cornelius Krahn, "Menno and Discipleship," *Studies in Church Discipline* (Newton, 1958) 63-70.

69. General treatments: R. H. Bainton, *David Joris. Wiedertäufer und Kämpfer für Toleranz im 16. Jahrhundert* (Leipzig, 1937); R. H. Bainton, *The Travail of Religious Liberty* (Philadelphia, 1961) 129 ff.; P. Burckhardt, "David Joris und seine Gemeinde in Basel," *Basler Zeitschr. für Gesch. u. Altertumskunde* XLVIII, 1949, 1-106; J. Kühn, *Toleranz und Offenbarung* (Leipzig, 1923) 271-301; W. J. Kühler, *op. cit.*, I (see index); G. H. Williams, *op. cit.*, (see index); Nicolaus Blesdicius, *Historia vitae, doctrinae ac rerum Davidis Georgi* (Deventer, 1642); R. H. Bainton, *David Joris* has the most complete bibliography.

70. Cornelius Krahn, *Menno Simons* (1936); 65 ff.; K. Vos, *Menno Simons*, (1914) 88-90; 227 ff., 310; Menno Simons, *Opera*, 64, 148, 632 ff.; *CW*, 410, 412, 602, 1021; *BRN*, VII, 302 ff.; *ME*, II, 18.

71. Best known among the writings of Joris is his *Twonder-boeck*... (1542).

72. After the debate at Lübeck, 1546, Menno must have admonished some former followers, who had joined the followers of Joris. This caused Blesdijk to write his *Christelijcke Verantwoordinghe*... (1546) followed by two more writings dealing with the differences between the two groups. See Vos, *op. cit.*, 89 f., and the article "Blesdijk" in *ME*, I, 360 f.

73. Menno Simons, *Opera*, 385 f., 312; *CW*, 489 f., 761. General treatments: Cornelius Krahn, *Menno Simons* (1936) 67-71; K. Vos, *Menno Simons* (1914) 100-105; 331; J. ten Doornkaat Koolman, *Dirk Philips*, 37-54. William Keeney, "Dirk Philips' Life," *MQR*, July, 1958, 171-9; H. W. Meihuizen, *Menno Simons*; ... (Haarlem, 1961).

74. *BRN*, V, 517, 521 ff.

75. *Opera*, 381-91; *CW*, 487-98; Poem by Dirk Philips in S. Blaupot ten Cate, *Geschiedenis der Doopsgezinden in Friesland* (Leeuwarden, 1939) 263 ff.; Adam Pastor, *Underscheit tusschen rechte leer vnde valsche leer*, *BRN*, V, 315-581.

76. V. P., *Successio Anabaptistica*, *BRN*, VII, 51; K. Vos, *op. cit.*, 526.

77. *Geschiedenis der Doopsgezinden in Nederland*, 77.

78. *Het Offer des Heeren*... was first published in 1562 and last in the *BRN*, II, 1910.

The first edition of the Dutch *Martyrs' Mirror* by Thieleman Jansz van Braght, *Het Bloedig Tooneel der Doops-gesinde, En Weereloose Christenen* ... appeared in 1660. See articles "Offer des Heeren" and "Martyrs' Mirror" in *ME*, III, 527 ff., and IV, 22.

79. E. Stauffer, "The Anabaptist Theology of Martyrdom," *MQR*, 1945, 181 f.; See also "A *Martyrs' Mirror* Digest", *ML*, April, 1967.

80. Balthasar Hubmaier, *Schriften* ed. by G. Westin and T. Bergsten in *QFR*, XXIX (Gütersloh, 1962) 79 f.

81. *Offer*, *BRN*, II, 422-29; *Martyrs' Mirror* (Dutch, II, 1660, 11-13); English 422-24

82. "Anneken Jans," *ME*, I, 127.

83. *Offer*, 70-77; *Martyrs' Mirror* (Dutch, II, 1660) 127 ff.; (English, 453 ff.) Or¹ Swartzendruber, "The Piety and Theology of the Anabaptist Martyrs in van Bragt ·· *Martyrs' Mirror*," II, *MQR*, 1954, 129-33.

84. *Offer*, 78 ff.; *Martyrs' Mirror*, (Dutch, II, 1660), 145-49; (English, 468 f.).

85. *Offer*, 509-16; *Martyrs' Mirror*, (Dutch, II, 1660), 144 f.; (English, 467 f.).

86. *Martyrs' Mirror* (Dutch, II, 1660) 503-28; (English, 774-85.).

VII. GROWTH AND MOLDING OF THE BROTHERHOOD

1. P. Genard, *Antwerpsch Archievenblad*, I, 201.

2. A. L. E. Verheyden, *Anabaptism in Flanders*, 1530-1650 (Scottdale, 1961) 26 f.

3. A. L. E. Verheyden, *op. cit.*, 40-43; *Offer*, 98-120; *Martyrs' Mirror*, 486 ff.

4. A. L. E. Verheyden, *op. cit.*, 36.

5. P. Genard, *op. cit.*, II, 355.

6. A. L. E. Verheyden, *op. cit.*, 23-25.

7. N. van der Zijpp, "Jan Mattysz van Middelburg," *ME*, III, 79; A. L. E. Verheyden, *op. cit.*, 26, 37 f.; "Gillis van Aken," *ME*, II, 518 f.

8. A. L. E. Verheyden, *op. cit.*, 45, 49 f., 55.

9. J. C. H. de Pater, *Geschiedenis van Nederland* (Amsterdam, 1936), III, 13 f.

10. A. L. E. Verheyden, *op. cit.*, 21 ff., 39 ff., 49 ff., 60 ff., 114 ff., 138 ff.; Aug. C. J. Commissaris, *Leerboek der Nederlandse geschiedenis*, I, 77 ff., 82 ff., 115 ff.

11. N. van der Zijpp, "Belgium," *ME*, I, 271.

12. A. L. E. Verheyden, *op. cit.*, 23, 30.

13. A. A. van Schelven, *Omgang en invloed der Zuid-Nederlandsche immigratie van het laatste kwart der 16e eeuw* (M. Nijhoff, 1919) 6 ff.

14. *Kort verhael van het leven en de daden van Hans de Ries* (De Rijp, 1644, reprinted 1655); J. S. S. Ballot, "Hans de Ries, zijn leven en werken," *DB*, 1863. 104-24; 1864, 1-74; N. van der Zijpp, "Hans de Ries," *ME*, IV, 330332; C. J. Dyck, "Hans de Ries, Theologian and Church man. A study in Second Generation Dutch Anabaptism" Ph. D. dissertation (University of Chicago, 1962).

15. J. Rogge, *Het Handelshuis van Eeghen* (Amsterdam, 1948); N. van der Zijpp, "Van Eeghen." *ME*, II, 159-161.

16. P. Leendertz Jr., *Het leven van Vondel* (Amsterdam, 1910); A. J. Barnouw, *Vondel* (Haarlem, 1926); G. Brom, *Vondel's bekering* (Amsterdam, 1907); B. H. Molkenboer, "Wanneer werd Vondel Katholiek?" *Vondelkroniek*, III, 1932; N. van der Zijpp, "Joost van den Vondel," *ME*, IV, 851-852.

17. R. Jacobsen, *Carel van Mander* (Rotterdam, 1906); "Carel van Mander," *ME*, III, 453; H. W. Meihuizen, "Dutch Painters in the Time of Vondel and Rembrandt," in *Legacy of Faith*, 119-135; Cornelius Krahn, "Anabaptism and the Culture of the Netherlands," in *The Recovery of the Anabaptist Vision*, 219-236.

18. A. A. Schelven, *op. cit.*, 34; J. A. P. G. Boot, *De Twentsche Katoennijverheid 1830-1873* (Amsterdam, 1935) 2. See also chapter VII, 4 of this book.

19. G. Brandt, *Historie der Reformatie, en andre kerkelyke geschiedenissen...*, (Amsterdam, 1671) I, 406.

20. *Missive van de Societeit der Doopsgezinde Gemeenten in Friesland en Groningen* (Leeuwarden, 1788).

21. A. H. Newman, *A History of Anti-Pedobaptism...* (Philadelphia, 1897) 345 ff.

22. Irvin B. Horst, *Anabaptism and the English Reformation to 1558* (Nieuwkoop: B. de Graaf, 1967) 36, 4 ff.; R. J. Smithson, *The Anabaptists. Their Contribution to Our Protestant Heritage* (London, 1935) 193 ff.; Carl Heath, *Social and Religious Heretics in Five Centuries* (London, 1936) 89 ff.

23. Belfort Bax, *Rise and Fall of the Anabaptists* (London, 1903) 336 f.

24. "England," *ME*, II, 215 ff., (quotation and literature), 220; See also Ernest A. Payne, *The Free Church Tradition in the Life of England* (London, 1951) 33 f.; Johannes Bakker, *John Smyth. De stichter van het Baptisme* (Wageningen, 1964).

25. Walter Kuhn, *Geschichte der deutschen Ostsiedlung in der Neuzeit* (Köln, 1957), II, 60; F. Dekker, *Voortrekkers van Oud Nederland* (The Hague, 1938) 21-25.

26. Horst Penner, *Ansiedlung mennonitischer Niederländer im Weichselmündungsgebiet von der Mitte des 16. Jahrhunderts bis zum Beginn der preussischen Zeit* (Weierhof, 1940) 9f.

27. H. van Alfen, "Documenten betreffende Jan van Sol en zijn voorstel tot vervolging van de Wederdopers," *NAK*, XXIV (1931) 201-360; A. L. E. Verheyden, *op. cit.*, 31-35; K. Vos, "Jan van Sol," *DB*, 1917, 136 f.

28. Felicia Szper, *Nederlandsche nederzettingen in West-Pruisen gedurende den Poolschen tijd* (Enkhuizen, 1913) 22 ff; Walter Kuhn, *op. cit.*, 49, 61 ff.; Horst Penner, *op. cit.*, 69 (document in regard to Philip Edzema (Frese); Karl-Heinz Ludwig, *Zur Besiedlung des Weichseldeltas durch die Mennoniten* (Elbing and Marienburg) (Marburg, 1961) 50 ff.

29. Felicia Szper, *op. cit.*, 61-66.

30. Brunno Schumacher, *Niederländische Ansiedlungen im Herzogtum Preussen zur Zeit Herzog Albrechts* (Leipzig, 1903) 149 ff., 174 f., Anhang, Nr. VII-IX.

31. The letter was published in Menno Simons, *CW*, 1030-35; Cornelius Krahn, *op. cit.*, 71 ff.; K. Vos, *Menno Simons*, 290; J. ten Doornkaat Koolman, *Dirk Philips*, 117 ff. See also Irvin B. Horst, *MSB*, 123.

32. G. Grosheide, *Bijdrage...*, 246 f.

33. Flemish Mennonite Church Record of Danzig *(Gemeynte Godts)*, Bethel College Historical Library; J. ten Doornkaat Koolman, *op. cit.*, 118.

34. A. van Alfen, *op. cit.*, 219 f.; Jan van Sol refers constantly to the *verbont* and *bundgenoeten* (213 f.) and makes the interesting observation in regard to the Danzig Melchiorites who now put all their efforts into church discipline *(bannen ende excommunication)*, even though some had been among the insurrectionists (218).

35. Walter Kuhn, *op. cit.*, II, 64-66; (Kuhn's figure of 3000 must include some Sacramentarians). Horst Penner, *ME*, IV, 922; J. S. Postma, *op. cit.*, 105 f.; Horst Quiring, "Die Danziger Mennoniten...,", *Legacy of Faith*, (Newton, 1962) 192-96.

36. Walter Kuhn, *op. cit.*, 45, 77 ff., 60 ff.; Friedel Vollbehr, *Die Holländer und die deutsche Hansa* (Lübeck, 1930) 16, 21 f., 77.; Herbert Wiebe, *Das Siedlungswerk niederländischer Mennoniten im Weichseltal zwischen Fordon und Weissenburg...*" (Marburg, 1952).

37. Walter Kuhn, *op. cit.*, 64; The Flemish Church Record of the *Gemeynte Godts* at Danzig changed entries from the Dutch to the German in 1784. When later Mennonites left for Russia some still took along Bibles, song books and the *Martyrs' Mirror* in the Dutch language (some of these items are in the Bethel College Historical Library).

38. "Culm," *ME* I, 745.

39. G. Grosheide, *op. cit.*, 225 f.; E. Dekker, *op. cit.*, 25.

40. Ad. Hofmeister, "Zur Geschichte der Wiedertäufer in Rostock," in Wiechmann,

Mecklenburgs alt-niedersächsische Literatur, III, (Schwerin, 1885) (reprint); J. ten Doornkaat Koolman, "Joachim Kükenbieter...", *op. cit.*, 161, 167; J. G. de Hoop Scheffer, "De bevestiger van Menno Simons," *DB* (1884) 15.

41. J. ten Doornkaat Koolman, "Die Täufer in Mecklenburg," *Mennonitische Geschichtsblätter*, 1961, 40 ff. Consult this article for a more complete treatment and bibliography. C. A. Cornelius, *Berichte...*, 410 f.

42. Obbe Philips, *Bekentenisse, BRN*, VII, 96, 114; *A Confession, LCC*, XXV, 204-25. Does not contain the introduction referred to.

43. Dietrich Schroeder, *Kirchenhistorie des Evangelischen Mecklenburg vom Jahre 1518 bis 1568* (Rostock, 1788) II, 518; Johannes Schildhauer, "Reformation und 'Revolution' in den Hansestädten Stralsund, Rostock und Wismar," *Greifswald-Stralsunder Jahrbuch*, I, (Schwerin, 1961) 55, 62 ff.

44. "Never" by Krause, *Allgemeine Deutsche Biographie* (Leipzig, 1886) XXIII, 564 f.; J. ten Doornkaat Koolman, *op. cit.*, 20-32; C. F. Crain, *Die Reformation der Christlichen Kirche in Wismar* (Wismar, 1929) 22-30.

45. J. ten Doornkaat Koolman, *op. cit.*, 32-39; Cornelius Krahn, *Menno Simons...* (1936), 82 ff.

46. L. von Ranke, *Deutsche Geschichte im Zeitalter der Reformation* (Hamburg) III, 328 (Chapter 10, 306-28); W. Jannasch, *Reformationsgeschichte Lübecks...* (1515-1530) (Lübeck, 1958); H. Schreiber, *Die Reformation Lübecks*, 272 f. (Halle, 1902); C. H. Starck, *Lübeckische Kirchen-Historie*, I, (1724); W. Jannasch, "Lübeck," *RGG*, IV, 467 f.

47. Royal Archives, Copenhagen, Hansborg Archives, VII, Nr. 15 f., d.; Reprint in E. F. Goverts, "Das adlige Gut Fresenburg und die Mennoniten," *Zeitschrift der Zentralstelle für Niedersächsische Familiengeschichte* (Hamburg) May, 1925, VII, Nr. 5, 100 ff.

48. E. F. Goverts, *op. cit.*, March, 1925, VII, Nr. 3, 54 ff.; April, Nr. 4, 70 ff, 78 ff. Cornelius Krahn, *op. cit.*, 84 f; B. C. Roosen, *Geschichte der Mennoniten-Gemeinde in Hamburg und Altona* (Hamburg, 1886) 22 ff.; Gerrit Roosen, *Unschuld und Gegen-Bericht der Evangelischen Tauffgesinnten Christen...* (1702) Appendix 97 ff.; "Menno Simons", *ML*, Jan., 1961, 26 ff.

49. Gerrit Roosen, "Godsaelige Oeffeninge tot de Vreeze Gods..." (Hamburg, 1709) 2. (Typewritten copy, Bethel College Historical Library).

50. B. C. Roosen, *op. cit.*, 20 ff.; Robert Dollinger, *Geschichte der Menn. in Schleswig-Holstein, Hamburg u. Lübeck* (Neumünster, 1930) 3 (footnote 1), 192 ff.

51. R. Dollinger, *op. cit.*, 4 f., 10 ff., 72 ff., 124 ff.; E. Crous, "Eiderstedt," *ME*, II, 169 f. Bertram Ahlefeldt was a distant relative of Bartholomäus Ahlefeldt.

52. B. C. Roosen, *op. cit.*, R. Dollinger, *op. cit.*; Richard Ehrenberg, *Altona unter Schauenburgischer Herrschaft* (Altona, 1893) IV, Viertes Kapitel, 22 ff., 45 ff.; VI, Sechstes Kapitel, 90 ff.

53. B. C. Roosen, *Gerrit Roosen* (Hamburg, 1854); B. C. Roosen, *Geschichte unseres Hauses* (Hamburg, 1905).

54. H. Münte, *Das Altonaer Handelshaus van der Smissen 1682-1824* (Altona, 1932). For additional literature see *ME*, IV, 549.

55. "Business Among Mennonites in Germany," *ME*, I, 482 f.; A. Fast, *Die Kulturleistungen der Mennoniten in Ostfriesland und Münsterland* (Emden, 1947); G. von Beckerath, "Die wirtschaftliche Bedeutung der Krefelder Mennoniten im 17. und 18. Jahrhundert" (Krefeld, 1952) Ph. D. dissertation; Cornelius Krahn, "Dutch Mennonites and Urbanism," *Proceedings of the tenth Conference on Mennonite Educational and Cultural Problems* (Chicago, 1955) 65-74.

56. K. Vos, "De *dooplijst*...", 44.

57. K. Vos, *op. cit.*, 64-69, 43; Menno Simons, *CW*, 1038 ff.

58. K. Vos, "Leenaert Bouwens," *ME*, III, 305 (See bibliography).

59. *Successio Anabaptistica, Dat is dat Babel der Wederdopers* (Cologne, 1603) in *BRN*. VII, 52-53; K. Vos, *Menno Simons*, 123-127; Menno Simons, *CW*, 1041 f.

60. Menno Simons, *CW*, 1043 f.; K. Vos, *Menno Simons*, 291.

61. Cornelius Krahn, *Menno Simons*, 90 ff.; Menno Simons, *CW*, 1050 f; *BRN*, VII, 442-50; 53 f. 59.

62. N. van der Zijpp, *Geschiedenis der Doopsgezinden in Nederland* (Arnhem, 1952) 48.

63. Menno Simons, *CW*, 1045, 1051, 1056; *BRN*, VII, 488, 450.

64. *BRN*, VII, 258; W. J. Kühler, *op. cit.*, I, 318; Menno Simons, *Opera*, 486 f., *CW*, 1010; "Waterlander," *ME*, IV, 895 f.

65. Menno Simons, *Opera*, 392; *CW*, 1055.

66. *BRN*, VII, 258 ff.

67. Cornelius Krahn, *Menno Simons*, 94 ff.; Menno Simons, *Opera*, 488b f.; *CW*, 1013.

68. *BRN*, VII, 526; "Eene geschiedenis van de Doopsgezinden ...," ed. by J. G. de Hoop Scheffer, *DB*, 1876, 23; Cornelius Krahn, *op. cit.*, 94 ff.

69. Cornelius Krahn, *op. cit.*, 94 ff.

70. Text of "Agreement": *BRN*, VII, 226 ff.; A. Brons, *Ursprung, Entwicklung, und Schicksale der ... Mennoniten* (Amsterdam, 1912) 97 ff.; Cornelius Krahn, "Incarnation of Christ," *ME*, III, 19 ff.

71. J. G. de Hoop Scheffer, "Eenige opmerkingen en mededeelingen betreffende Menno Simons" VIII, *DB*, vol. 34, 1894, 47-53.

72. Dirk Philips, *Een lieflicke vermaninghe wt des Heeren woort ...* (1558, Den 5. Februari) *BRN*, X, 249-265; J. ten Doornkaat Koolman, *op. cit.*, 96 ff.; Menno Simons, *Een gans grontlijcke onderwijs oft bericht, van de Excommunicatie ... Opera*, 188; *CW*, 959-998; J. G. de Hoop Scheffer (*op. cit.*, 53 ff.) presents the development of Menno Simons' views step by step.

73. *Een verklaringhe: hoe ende wat manieren de Heere Jesus zynen Jongeren inder afzonderinge macht gegeven heeft* (Haarlem, 1618).

74. "Uthtog und affschrifft van einem breef M[ennonis] S[imons] an etlicke brodern geschikt, inholdende und meldende van der affsunderinge twischen eelude, man und frow," *DB*, Vol. 24, 1894, 62-69; Menno Simons, *CW*, 1060-63.

75. *Een Seer Grondelijke Antwoort, Vol met alderley onderwijsinge en goede vermaninge, op Zylis en Lemmeke ... Opera*, 479-490; *CW*, 999-1015.

76. The sources referred to under footnote 70 claiming that there were such meetings in Cologne in 1557 and 1559 are not clear and possibly colored by the later developments when the pendulum had swung to the other extreme.

77. A. A. van Schelven, *Uit den strijd der geesten* (Amsterdam: 1944) 31 ff., 39 f., 88; See also A. A. Schelven, *Willem van Oranje* (Amsterdam, 1948) 99 ff.

78. K. Vos, *Oranje en de Doopsgezinden*, No. 29 *Geschriftjes ...*

79 A. A. van Schelven, *Uit den strijd der geesten*, 35 ff.

80. F. S. Knipscheer, "De Nederlandsche gereformeerde synoden tegenover de Doopsgezinden (1563-1620)" *DB*, 1910, 1-40; 1911, 17-49; J. Reitsma and S. C. van Veen, *Acta der Provinciale en Particuliere Synoden, gehouden in de noordelijke Nederlanden gedurende de Jaren 1572-1620* (Groningen, 1892-1899), 8 vols.

81. H. Klugkist Hesse, *Menso Alting. Eine Gestalt aus der Kampfzeit der Calvinischen Kirche* (Berlin, 1928) 65 ff.; M. F. van Lennep, *Gaspar van der Heyden, 1530-1586* (Amsterdam, 1884) 138-45, 251-53.

82. Joh. H. Ottius, *Annales Anabaptistici ...* (Basel, 1672), 125 ff. (Letters written April 12 and June 5, 1556).

83. Menno Simons, *Opera*, 491-516; *CW*, 541-577 (quotation 558); Irvin B. Horst, *MSB*, 96 f.

84. Menno Simons, *CW*, 560 f., 566 f.

85. *Opera*, 457-473; *CW*, 499-531; Irvin B. Horst, *MSB*, 97 f.

86. *Opera*, 325-330; *CW*, 523-531; Irvin B. Horst, *MSB*, 99.

87. *Opera*, 331-335; *CW*, 533-540; Irvin B. Horst, *MSB*, 99.

88. Martin Micron, *Een waerachtigh verhael der t'zamensprekinghen tusschen Menno Simons en Martinus Micron van der Menschwerdinghe Jesu Christi* ... (1556); Menno wrote *Reply to Martin Micron* etc. (1556) *Opera*, 543-618; For Dutch titles of Menno's writing see Irvin B. Horst, *MSB*, 101. For factual information see: *Opera*, 551 ff.; Micron, *Een waerachtigh verhael* ... 168, 172, 218 f; K. Vos, *op. cit.*, 113-122; Cornelius Krahn, *op. cit.*, 78 ff.; P. H. Muller, *Kerkbouwers* (Amsterdam, 1949) "Martin Micron," 230-238; J. H. Gerretsen, *Micronius. Zijn leven, zijn geschriften, zijn geestesrichting* (Nijmegen, 1895). F. Pijper, *BRN*, I, 421 ff.; Marten Woudstra, *De Hollandsche Vreemdelingen-Gemeente te London* ... (Groningen, 1908) 117 ff. and other places. A. A. van Schelven, *De Nederlandsche Vluchtelingenkerken der XVI eeuw in Engeland en Duitschland* ... (The Hague, 1909) (see index). Martin Micron, *De Christlicke Ordinancien der Nederlandscher Ghemeinten to London* (1554) (The Hague, 1956).

89. K. Vos, *op. cit.*, 108 ff.; Cornelius Krahn, *op. cit.*, 77 ff.

90. *Biographisch Woordenboek* ... (The Hague) I, "Bouma," 542 ff; R. Ritter, "Zur Geschichte des Norder Kirchenstreits vom Jahre 1554. Der Emder Prediger Gellius Faber," *JGKAE*, XXII (Emden, 1927) 329-39.

91. Gellius Faber, *Eine Antwert Gellij Fabri dener des hilligen wordes binnen Emden vp einen bitterhönischen breeff der Wedderdöper, darynne se etlike orsaken menen tho gevuen, worumme se in vnse Kercken vmme Gades wordt tho hören, vnde mit der Gemene de hilligen Sacramente tho bruken nicht kamen willen, vnde de Kercke Gades sampt eren denern schentliken lasteren vnd schelden* (Magdeburg, 1552).

92. Menno's *Plain Reply* is found: *Opera*, 225-324; *CW*, 623-781; Irvin B. Horst, *MSB*, 100; 129-135.

93. J. ten Doornkaat Koolman, "De Anabaptisten ..." *NAK*, XLVI, Afl. 2, (1963-64), 87-96.

94. The title of the first edition was: *Een frundtlyke thosamensprekenge van twee personen, von der Döpe der yungen unmundigen Kynderen* ... (Emden, 1556); Walter Hollweg, "Bernhard Buwo, ein ostfriesischer Theologe aus dem Reformationsjahrhundert," *JGKAE*, XXXIII, (1953) 71 ff.

95. *De Gheschiedenisse ende den doodt der vromen Martelaren* ... Door Adrianum Corn. Haemstedium. an. 1559 den 18. Martii. Numerous editions have appeared since; A. A. van Schelven, "De Moeilijkheden met Adriaen van Haemstede," *Kerkeraads-Protocollen der Nederduitsche Vluchtelingen-Kerk te London*, 1560-63. (Amsterdam, 1921) 445-66; W. G. Goeters, "Haemstede, Adriaen Cornelis van," *ME*, II, 620 f. (See also bibliography).

96. K. Vos, "De Dooplijst van Leenaert Bouwens," *BMHG*, (1915) XXXVI, 65; Eduard Meiners, *op. cit.*, I, 361.

97. K. Vos, *op. cit.*, 65.

98. H. Klugkist Hesse, *op. cit.*, 65 ff.; *Protokoll, das ist alle Handlung des gesprechs zu Franckenthal inn der Churfürstlichen Pfaltz, mit denen so man Widertäuffer nennet* (Heidelberg, 1571).

99. H. Klugkist Hesse, *op. cit.*, 253-259; 225-280.

100. The Emden *Kirchenrats-Protokoll*, 1568-1577 of the Reformed Church (see Jan. 21, 1577); *Protocol. Dath is, alle handelinge des gesprechs tho Emden in Oistfrieszlandt mit den Wedderdöpern, de sick Flaminge nomen, geholden* ... (Emden, 1579); This was the Saxon version which was followed by a Dutch version during the same year. The Anabaptist copy of the minutes written by Carel van Gent has been preserved in the Emden Archives of which the BCHL has a microfilm. See also "Emden Disputation," *ME*, II, 201 f.

101. H. Klugkist Hesse, *op. cit.*, 241 ff., 249 ff., 255 ff., 244 ff.

102. N. van der Zijpp, "Leeuwarden Disputation," *ME*, III, 310 f.

103. Ph. de Marnix van St. Aldegonde, *Ondersoekinge en grondelijcke wederlegginge der Geestdrijuische Leere* ... (Hague, 1595). Reprint in *Godsdienstige en kerklijke geschriften* edited by J. J. van Toorenenbergen (Hague, 1873) II, 1-244; Joseph Lecler, *Toleration and the Reformation* (New York, 1966) II, 286-292.

104. A. Hegler, *Geist und Schrift bei Sebastian Franck* (Freiburg, 1892) 287; Chr. Sepp, *Godgeleerde bijdragen* (Leiden, 1869) 789 ff.; S. L. Verheus, *Kroniek en Kerugma, Een theologische studie over de Geschichtbibel v. Seb. Franck* ...
105. K. Vos, *Menno Simons*, 306, 318; C. Krahn, *Menno Simons*, 40, 106, 111.
106. A. Hegler, *op. cit.*, 57; Bruno Becker, "Nederlandsche vertalingen van Sebastian Franck's geschriften" *NAK*, XXI, 1928, 149-160; Rudolf Kommoss, *Sebastian Franck und Erasmus von Rotterdam* (Berlin, 1934).
107. H. Bongaer, *Dirck Volkertszoon Coornhert* (Lochem, 1941) 65-88; W. J. Kühler, *Geschiedenis* I 359-364; 370-373; Joseph Lecler, *op. cit.*, 271-286.
108. C. Krahn, "The Historiography ..." *CH*, Sept., 1944.
109. H. Fast, *Heinrich Bullinger und die Täufer* (Weierhof, 1959) 77 f.
110. G. Brandt, *Reformatie*, II, 13; Joseph Lecler, *op. cit.*, II, 272, 292 ff; Dutch title of Theodor Beza, *Een schoon Tractaet vande Straffe, welcke de wereltlijke Overicheydt over Ketters behoort te oeffenen* ... (Franeker, 1601).
111. A summary of actions taken against the Anabaptists can be found in the article by Peter de Jong, "Can Political Factors Account for the Fact that Calvinism Rather than Anabaptism came to Dominate the Dutch Reformation." *CH*, Dec. 1964, 392-417; J. H. Wessel, *De leerstellige strijd tusschen Nederlandsche Gereformeerden en Doopsgezinden* ...; See also footnote 80 of this chapter.
112. Philip von Zesen, *Des Weltlichen Standes Handlungen und Urteile wider den Gewissenszwang in Glaubenssachen aus den Geschichten der Keiser, Könige, Fürsten und anderer Weltlichen Obrigkeiten* ... (Amsterdam, 1665); Other writings on this subject besides those already quoted are: Roland H. Bainton, *The Travail of Religious Liberty* (Philadelphia, 1945); H. A. Enno van Gelder, *Vrijheid en onvrijheid in de Republiek*, I, 1572-1619 (Haarlem, 1947); A. A. van Schelven, "De opkomst van de idee der politieke tolerancie in de 16. eeuwsche Nederlanden," *Tijdschrift voor Geschiedenis*, XLVI, 1931, 235-247, 337-388.
113. See "Catechisms" and "Confessions of Faith," *ME*, I, 529 ff., 679 ff.

VIII. CONCLUSION

1. Cornelius Krahn, "Ludwig Keller: A Prophet and a Scholar," *ML*, Vol. XXI (April, 1966) 81 ff.
2. G. H. Williams, *The Radical Reformation* (Philadelphia, Pa., 1962).
3. Franklin H. Littell, *The Anabaptist View of the Church* (Boston, 1958) 79 ff.
4. Alfred Hegler, *Geist und Schrift bei Sebastian Franck* ... (Freiburg, 1892; S. L. Verheus, *Kroniek en kerugma* (Arnhem, 1958) 41-47; H. W. Meihuizen, "Spiritualistic Tendencies and Movements Among Dutch Mennonites of the 16th and 17th Centuries," *MQR*, XXVII (1953) 259-304.
5. Wolfgang Schäufele, *Das missionarische Bewusstsein und Wirken der Täufer* (Neukirchen, 1966) 73 ff., 142 ff., 237 ff., 289 ff.
6. Gottlob Schrenk, *Gottesreich und Bund im älteren Protestantismus* ... (Gütersloh, 1922) 37 ff.
7. See pp. 95-100, 140-143, 190-194, 233-237; H. W. Meihuizen, "Het begrip 'Restitutie' in het Noordwestelijke Doperdom" (Amsterdam, 1966). See also "Ministry" in "Index."
8. Cornelius Krahn, *Menno Simons*, 181 ff; Menno Simons, *Dat Fundament des Christlycken Leers* ed. by H. W. Meihuizen (The Hague, 1967) 109-112.
9. Ibid., 143-149; Cornelius Krahn, "Elder," *ME*, II, 187 ff.
10. Rollin S. Armour, *Anabaptist Baptism: A Representative Study* (Scottdale, Pa., 1966).

11. See chapter III; IV, pp. 44-47; 95 ff.; 112 ff. See "Index" under "Baptism" and "Lord's supper."

12. Cornelius Krahn, *Menno Simons,* 142.

13. N. van der Zijpp, *Geschiedenis der Doopsgezinden in Nederland* (Arnhem, 1952) 80; H. W. Meihuizen, *Galenus Abrahamsz* (Haarlem, 1954).

14. J. A. Oosterbaan, "De theologie van Menno Simons," reprint from *Nederlands Theologisch Tijdschrift* XV, afl. 4, 1961, 6 ff. (Compares Menno's and K. Barth's views); Cornelius Krahn, *Menno Simons* ... 155-161; William Keeney, "The Incarnation ..." in *Legacy of Faith,* 55-68.

15. Roland H. Bainton, "The Anabaptist Contribution to History" and Cornelius Krahn, "Anabaptism and the Culture of the Netherlands" both in *Recovery of the Anabaptist Vision* (Scottdale, Pa., 1962) 317-326; 219-236; Hendrik W. Meihuizen, "Dutch Painters in the Time of Vondel and Rembrandt" in *Legacy of Faith* (Newton, Kansas, 1962) 119-135.

16. Cornelius Krahn, "Crossroads at Amsterdam," *ML,* October, 1967, 153-156.

SELECTED BIBLIOGRAPHY

From several thousand books used only a small number was selected. The "Index" and the "Footnotes" will be helpful in locating additional sources used.

Armour, R. S., *Anabaptist Baptism: A Representative Study* (Scottdale, Pa., 1966).
Bahlmann, P., *Die Wiedertäufer zu Münster*. Eine bibliographische Zusammenstellung (Münster, 1894).
Bainton, R. H., *David Joris. Wiedertäufer und Kämpfer für Toleranz im 16. Jahrhundert* (Leipzig, 1937).
H. Barge, *Andreas Bodenstein von Karlstadt* I, II (Leipzig, 1905).
Bax, W., *Het Protestantisme in het bisdom Luik en vooral te Maastricht, 1505-1557* ('s-Gravenhage, 1937).
Bibliotheca Reformatoria Neerlandica I-X, ed. by S. Cramer and F. Pijper, (The Hague, 1903-1914).
Biographisch Woordenboek van Protestantsche Godgeleerden in Nederland, ed. by J. P. de Bie and J. Loosjes, I-IV ('s-Gravenhage, 1943).
Blesdikius, Nic., *Historia vitae, doctrinae, ac rerum gestarum Davidis Georgi Haeresiarchae* (Daventriae, 1642).
Braght, Thieleman Jansz van, *Het Bloedig Tooneel der Doops-gesinde, en Weereloose Christenen . . .* (Dordrecht, 1660).
Brendler, Gerhard, *Das Täuferreich zu Münster, 1534/35* (Berlin, 1966).
Cornelius, C. A., *Berichte der Augenzeugen über das münsterische Wiedertäuferreich* (Münster, 1853). In *Die Geschichtsquellen d. Bisthums Münster*, II.
Cornelius, C. A., *Geschichte des Münsterischen Aufruhrs* I, II (Leipzig, 1855-1860).
Cornelius, C. A., *Die niederländischen Wiedertäufer während der Belagerung Münsters* (Münster, 1869).
Dalton, J., *Johannes a Lasco* (Gotha, 1881).
Detmer, H., *Bilder aus den religösen und sozialen Unruhen in Münster während des 16. Jahrhunderts* (Münster, 1903-1905).
Dirk Philips, see *BRN*, X.
Dollinger, Robert, *Geschichte der Mennoniten in Schleswig-Holstein, Hamburg und Lübeck* (Neumünster, 1930).
Doopsgezinde Bijdragen (1861-1919), ed. by D. Harting and others.
Doornkaat Koolman, J. ten, *Dirk Philips. Vriend en medewerker van Menno Simons, 1504-1568* (Haarlem, 1964).
Dyck, C. J., editor, *A Legacy of Faith* (The Heritage of Menno Simons) (Newton, Kansas, 1962).
Elsass, I, II. Stadt Strassburg 1522-1535 (Gütersloh, 1959 and 1960), ed. by Johann Adam and others.
Fast, Heinold, *Heinrich Bullinger und die Täufer* (Weierhof, 1959).

Fast, Heinlod, *Der linke Flügel der Reformation* (Bremen, 1962).

Frank, Seb., *Chronica. Zeitbuch vnnd Geschichtbibell von anbegin bisz in diss gegenwertig M. D. xxxvi. jar verlengt*, etc. (Ulm, 1536).

Gerretsen, J. H., *Micronius; zijn leven, zijn geestesrichting* (Nijmegen, 1895).

Grosheide, Greta, *Bijdrage tot de Geschiedenis der Anabaptisten in Amsterdam* (Hilversum, 1938).

Hillerbrand, Hans, *Bibliographie des Täufertums, 1520-1630, in Quellen zur Geschichte der Täufer* X (Gütersloh, 1962).

Hoeckstra, S., *Beginselen en leer der oude Doopsgezinden, vergeleken met die van de overige Protestanten* (Amsterdam, 1863).

Hofmann, Melchior, see *BRN*, V.

Hoop Scheffer, J. G. de, *Geschiedenis der kerkhervorming in Nederland van haar ontstaan tot 1531* (Amsterdam, 1873).

Horst, Irvin B., *Anabaptism and the English Reformation to 1558* (Nieuwkoop, 1966).

Horst, Irvin B., *A Bibliography of Menno Simons* (Nieuwkoop, 1962).

Keller, L., *Die Geschichte der Wiedertäufer und ihres Reiches zu Münster* (Münster, 1880).

Kirchhoff, Karl-Heinz, "Die Belagerung und Eroberung Münsters 1534/35" and "Die Täufer im Münsterland." *Westfälische Zeitschrift* 112, 113 (Münster, 1962, 1963).

Knappert, L., *Het ontstaan en de vestiging van het Protestantisme in Nederland* (Utrecht, 1924).

Köhler, Walther, *Zwingli und Luther. Ihr Streit über das Abendmahl nach seinen politischen und religiösen Beziehungen* I (Leipzig, 1924).

Krahn, Cornelius, *Menno Simons (1496-1561). Ein Beitrag zur Geschichte und Theologie der Taufgesinnten* (Karlsruhe, 1936).

Krahn, Cornelius, "Menno Simons Research (1910-1960)" in *No Other Foundation* by Walter Klaassen and others (North Newton, 1962).

Krohn, B. N., *Geschichte der fanatischen und enthusiastischen Wiedertäufer* . . . (Leipzig, 1758).

Kühler, W. J., *Geschiedenis der Nederlandsche Doopsgezinden in de zestiende eeuw* (Haarlem, 1932-1950) 3 vols.

Kuhn, Walter, *Geschichte der deutschen Ostsiedlung in der Neuzeit*, II (Köln, 1957).

Lasco, J. A., *Opera tam edita quam inedita recensuit vitam auctoris enarravit*, A. Kuyper (1866).

Leendertz, W. I., *Melchior Hofmann* (Haarlem, 1883).

Lindeboom, J., *Het Bijbelsch Humanisme in Nederland* (Leiden, 1913).

Linden, Friedrich Otto zur, *Melchior Hofmann, ein Prophet der Wiedertäufer* (Haarlem, 1958).

Löffler, Klemens, ed., *Die Wiedertäufer zu Münster 1534/35* (Jena, 1923).

Meihuizen, H. W., *Het Begrip Restitutie in het Noordwestelijke Doperdom*. (Algemene Doopsgezinde Societeit, Haarlem, 1966).

Meihuizen, H. W., *Menno Simons. IJveraar voor het herstel van de nieuwtestamentische gemeente (1496-1561)* (Haarlem, 1961).

Meiners, Eduard, *Oostvrieschlandts kerkelyke Geschiedenisse* I, II (Groningen, 1738).

Melink, A. F., *De Wederdopers in de Noordelijke Nederlanden* (Groningen, 1954).

Menno Simons, *Complete Writings*, ed. J. C. Wenger (Scottdale, 1956).

Menno Simons, *Dat Fundament des Christelycken leers op dat alder corste geschreuen* (M. D. XXXIX).

Menno Simons, *Opera omnia theologica, of alle de godtgeleerde wercken* ed. by H. Jz. Herrison (Amsterdam, 1861).

Mennonite Life, ed. by Cornelius Krahn, I-XXII, 1946-1967 (North Newton, Kansas).

Mennonite Quarterly Review, ed. by H. S. Bender, I-XLI, 1927-1966 (Goshen, Indiana).

Micron, M., *Een waerachtigh verhaal der t'zamensprekinghen tusschen Menno Simons ende Martinus Mikron* ... (Embden, 1556).

Miller, Edward W. and Jared W. Scudder, *Wessel Gansfort: Life and Writings* (New York and London, 1917).

Miller, J. P., *Die Mennoniten in Ostfriesland vom 16. bis zum 18. Jahrhundert* (Amsterdam, 1887).

Nederlandsch Archief voor Kerkgeschiedenis, 1829-1966 ('s-Gravenhage), ed. by N. C. Kist and others.

Niesert, Josef, *Beiträge zu einem Münsterischen Urkundenbuche aus den vaterländischen Archiven gesammelt* I (Münster, 1823).

Obbe Philips, see *BRN, VIII*.

Post, R. R., *Kerkelijke verhoudingen in Nederland voor de Reformatie van 1500 tot 1580* (Utrecht, 1954).

Protocol. Dath is, alle handelinge des gesprecks tho Emden in Oistrieszlandt mit den Wedderdöpern, de sick Flaminge nomen, geholden... (Emden, 1579).

Rembert, Karl, *Die "Wiedertäufer" im Herzogtum Jülich. Studien zur Geschichte der Reformation, besonders am Niederrhein* (Berlin, 1899).

Rogier, L. J., *Geschiedenis van het Katholicisme in Noord Nederland in de 16e en 17e eeuw* (Amsterdam, 1945-47) 3 vols.

Romein, Jan, *De lage landen bij de Zee* (Utrecht, 1934).

Rosenfeld, Paul, *The Provincial Governors from the Minority of Charles V to the Revolt* (Louvain, 1959).

Rotmann, Bernh., *Restitution rechter und gesunder christlicher Lehre* (Münster, 1534). *Flugschriften aus der Reformationszeit* VII (Halle, 1888).

Schelven, A. A. van, *Omvang en invloed der Zuid-Nederlandsche immigratie van het laatste kwart der 16e eeuw* (Hague, 1919).

Schoeps, H. J., *Vom Himmlischen Fleisch Christi*. (Tübingen, 1951).

Spitz, Lewis W., *The Religious Renaissance of the German Humanists* (Cambridge, Mass., 1963).

Stiasny, Hans H. Th., *Die strafrechtliche Verfolgung der Täufer in der Freien Reichsstadt Köln 1529 bis 1618* (Münster, 1962).

Theissen, J. S., *Centraal gezag en Friese vrijheid. Friesland onder Karel V* (Groningen, 1907).

Theissen, J. S., *De regering van Karel V in de Noordelijke Nederlanden* (Amsterdam, 1912).

Verheyden, A. L. E., *Anabaptism in Flanders, 1530-1650* (Scottdale, 1961).

Vos, Karel, *Menno Simons, 1496-1561. Zijn leven en werken en zijne reformatorische denkbeelden* (Leiden, 1914).

Williams, George H., ed., *Spiritual and Anabaptist Writers* (Philadelphia, 1957) in *The Library of Christian Classics* XXXV.

Williams, George H., *The Radical Reformation* (Philadelphia, 1962).

Zijpp, N. van der, *Geschiedenis der Doopsgezinden in Nederland* (Arnhem, 1952).

INDEX

PERSONS, PLACES, TOPICS

Many of the Dutch names are found under the bearer's given name, for example: *Menno* Simons not *Simons*, Menno; *Dirk* Philips not *Philips*, Dirk etc.